THE DECLINE OF THE BRITISH ECONOMY

The Decline
of the
British Economy

Bernard Elbaum

and

William Lazonick

CLARENDON PRESS · OXFORD

1986

Oxford University Press. Walton Street, Oxford OX2 6DP

Oxford New York Toronto
Delhi Bombay Calcutta Madras Karachi
Kuala Lumpur Singapore Hong Kong Tokyo
Nairobi Dar es Salaam Cape Town
Melbourne Auckland

and associated companies in
Beirut Berlin Ibadan Nicosia

Oxford is a trade mark of Oxford University Press

Published in the United States

British Library Cataloguing in Publication Data
The Decline of the British economy: an
institutional perspective.
1. Great Britain—Economic conditions—19th
century 2. Great Britain—Economic conditions
—20th century
I. Elbaum, Bernard II. Lazonick, William
330.941'082 HC255
ISBN 0-19-828494-2

Set by Spire Print Services Ltd, Salisbury, Wilts
Printed in Great Britain
at the University Printing House, Oxford
by David Stanford
Printer to the University

Preface

Why should two North American economists put together a volume on British decline? As the world's first industrial nation and a major advanced economy to this day, Britain has long attracted the attention of researchers abroad. Historically, modern economic theory also developed to a very large degree in Britain. Whether they are aware of it or not, economists are still strongly influenced by how they think a competitive British economy functioned in the past.

The study of Britain also has special appeal for North Americans. Cross-national comparison of economies and societies that have so much in common can isolate and illuminate the economic consequences of major institutions and policies. The present volume should be of topical interest on both sides of the Atlantic because, we believe, the lessons of British historical decline are relevant to current debates over laggard economic performance in North America as well as Britain.

While debates over the problem of relative economic decline are fairly recent in North America, they have gone on for over a century in Britain. Like the United States in the 1940s and 1950s, Britain was the world's predominant industrial power in the nineteenth century. If US industry has been outperformed by Japanese industry in recent decades, British industry has been losing its competitive advantage for a much more prolonged period of time.

In the United States, recent discussion of economic performance has already drawn upon the experience of other nations, most notably that of Japan. But if there is much to be learned from the Japanese success, it is our conviction that the United States may have even more to learn from the decline of Britain.

The editors of this volume developed an interest in the British economy while graduate students in economics at Harvard University in the early 1970s. Our research started from the currently unorthodox assumption that relevant economic theory must be based upon a rigorous examination of the historical dynamics of economic development. Lazonick took up the study of the British cotton industry as part of an attempt to assess the strengths and weaknesses of Marx's theory of capitalist development, a theory based mainly on the British experience through the third quarter of the nineteenth century. Elbaum's research on the British iron and steel industry began as an attempt to develop a sound empirical basis for an institutional theory of wage determination.

From the beginning, the historical experience of the US economy provided comparative perspective for our work on Britain. As our research progressed, both of us discovered that, for the US–British comparison at least, the dynamic interaction between structures of industrial organization and industrial relations formed the core of an explanation of the development process.

Around 1980, we realized that a distinctive perspective on British decline
was emerging out of our case studies of two very different but important
British industries. We were encouraged considerably by the reception given
our case-study research by participants in the Harvard Economic History
Workshop. It was Alfred D. Chandler, Jr. who first suggested that our
research could form the basis for a book on British decline. Over the past five
years, Professor Chandler as well as David S. Landes have been extremely
supportive of our project.

During the summer of 1981, we drafted a short prospectus on the institutional determinants of British decline, and sought out case-study contributions from other scholars who were engaged in detailed historical research on
British industries and institutions. Our goal was not a comprehensive coverage of British economy and society, but rather a coherent set of essays based
upon in-depth knowledge. We did not require that contributors agree with us
on all major issues, but only that they be sympathetic to the notion that
institutional arrangements can affect economic development and that
detailed historical research is necessary to fashion an adequate theoretical
perspective.

Over a period of three years of criticizing and redrafting, the eleven essays
that appear in this volume emerged. We would like to think that we helped to
shape the ideas of the contributors with our criticisms just as we know that
they influenced the successive drafts of the introductory chapter of this volume. Obviously, each contributor is ultimately responsible only for his or her
own contribution. Nevertheless, because of the prolonged co-operative effort
that went into each of the contributions, we feel that there is a coherence of
form and matter in this volume that is unusual for a collection of essays.

Drafts of the essays were presented at an Anglo-American Conference on
the Decline of the British Economy held at Boston Unversity on September
30–October 1, 1983. We are indebted to the Sloan Foundation for providing
a grant that was the principal source of funding for the conference. The travel
of conference participants was also facilitated by grants from the German
Marshall Fund of the United States and the Council for European Studies.

The contributors to the volume benefited greatly from discussion and
criticism at the conference. We should express special gratitude to those who
took time from their busy schedules to be active conference participants.
Sessions were chaired by Barry Eichengreen, Sir Arthur Knight, David
Landes, and Peter Temin. Discussants were Bernard Alford, Samuel Beer,
Alfred Chandler, Michael Edelstein, Charles Feinstein, Leslie Hannah, Joel
Krieger, Donald McCloskey, Derek Morris, and Gavin Wright. William
Parker, who at the last minute could not attend the conference, forwarded
very useful comments. The conference concluded with a round-table on
industrial policy in historical and international perspective, with John T.

Dunlop as chair and Alfred Chandler, Sylvia Ostry, and Michael Posner joining the co-editors of this volume as panelists.

Based upon criticisms made at the conference, all the contributions went through a final round of revision. We are also grateful to Lance Davis and Michael Edelstein for perceptive comments on an early version of our introductory essay that was presented at the meetings of the Economic History Association in September 1983 and appeared in the *Journal of Economic History* in June 1984. In addition, some of the essays were presented together in a session on the decline of the British economy at the Social Science History Association meetings in Toronto on October 29, 1985, with Donald Moggridge serving as discussant.

We would also like to thank Dick Cluster for doing a thorough job of copy-editing, and Sue Hughes for ensuring stylistic consistency and correct referencing. Scottie Gibson, Charlene Arzigian, and Emily Gallagher helped with the organization and administration of the conference.

William Lazonick has benefited from many years of intellectual collaboration with his friend and colleague, Stephen Marglin. Bernard Elbaum would like to thank Peter Doeringer for his support and encouragement in the undertaking of the conference on British decline.

Bernard Elbaum
William Lazonick

June 1985

Contents

An Institutional Perspective on British Decline

Bernard Elbaum and William Lazonick
Boston University and Harvard University

The British economy, once the workshop of the world, seems to have fallen victim to some century-long affliction. Ever since the last quarter of the nineteenth century, Britain has lagged behind other advanced nations in productivity growth and has consequently suffered continuing decline in industrial competitiveness and its relative level of per capita income.

For lack of an adequate generic diagnosis, many observers have termed this afflication the 'British disease' (see for example Allen, 1976). There are signs, however, that the disease may be spreading. The United States, in particular, has lagged behind other advanced economies in productivity growth for three decades and has recently suffered competitive challenges in a number of major industries. In the United States as well as in many European countries, there is now widespread concern over relative economic performance, and a renewed interest in explanations of long-term economic growth and decline.

Long-term economic development is, however, a relatively neglected subject for which there is no generally accepted body of theory. It is widely acknowledged that economic development involves complex interactive processes of social, political, and institutional change. But such relationships lie outside the purview of conventional economic analysis.

The research agenda of neoclassical economics abstracts from processes of socioeconomic development under the rationale that these elude the quantification and theoretical tractability that is essential for scientific rigour. By assuming that market conditions approximate those of perfect competition, neoclassical theory also implies that wider institutional arrangements are constrained by competitive compulsion from having significant economic effects.

The lack of an alternative body of theory of comparable rigour and coherence accounts for much of the continuing appeal of the neoclassical approach. None the less, explanations of economic development or decline frequently stray from the neoclassical perspective. Among historians, for example, the most prominent explanation of Britain's relative decline runs in terms ·of cultural conservatism and consequent entrepreneurial failure (Landes, 1969, ch. 5; Wiener, 1981). Other 'institutional' approaches have tended to stray from neoclassical orthodoxy in different directions, but without arriving at a common, compelling, conclusion.

This volume presents an institutional perspective on British relative decline that attempts to synthesize and integrate a wide body of research under a common explanatory theme. We attribute the decline of the British economy in the twentieth century to rigidities in the economic and social institutions that developed during the nineteenth century, a period when Britain was the world's leading economic power and British industry was highly atomistic and competitive in organization. Our conclusions regarding British economic decline run directly counter to the neoclassical presumption that atomistic market competition is the best guarantor of economic well-being.

As neoclassical economic historians have emphasized (McCloskey, 1971; McCloskey and Sandberg, 1973; Floud, 1981; Sandberg, 1981), British businessmen may in general have performed well by the test of cost minimization subject to prevailing constraints. Britain's problem, however, was that economic decision-makers, lacking the individual or collective means to alter existing constraints, in effect took them as 'given'.

In failing to confront institutional constraints innovatively, British businessmen can justifiably be accused of 'entrepreneurial failure'. But this failure cannot be adequately explained by reference to cultural conservatism, despite the frequency of such assertions (Landes, 1969; Wiener, 1981; Caves, 1980). British culture, like its economy, has been subject to historical evolution. It is the product of not only an inherited cultural endowment, but also the deliberate policy choices of current generations. If twentieth-century British society was prevaded by conservative mores, it was in this respect no worse off than Japan or continental European countries that were pre-capitalist, tradition-bound societies when Britain was the workshop of the world. The thesis of entrepreneurial failure, and other culturally based explanations of decline, shed no light on why Britain was less successful than later industrializers in remoulding customary attitudes that encumbered economic performance.

Britain's distinctiveness derived less from the conservatism of its cultural values *per se* than from a matrix of rigid institutional structures that reinforced these values and obstructed individualistic as well as collective efforts at economic renovation. In such countries as the United States, Germany, and Japan, successful economic development in the twentieth century has been based on mass production methods and corporate forms of managerial co-ordination. Britain, however, was impeded from adopting these modern technological and organizational innovations by the institutional legacy associated with atomistic, nineteenth-century economic organization. Entrenched institutional structures—in industrial relations, enterprise and market organization, education, finance, international trade, and state–enterprise relations—constrained the transformation of Britain's productive system. The industry and institutional case studies that are gathered together in this volume document the impact of atomistic economic organization and related institutional structures on Britain's long-term relative economic decline.

The Consequences of Competitive Capitalism

In the third quarter of the nineteenth century, the British economy experienced a long boom that represented the culmination of the world's first industrial revolution. After three centuries of international conflict for the control of world markets, and after seven decades of intense capital investment in productive capacity, Britain emerged unchallenged in the world economy. On the basis of national domination of world markets, there was much in the way of opportunity for aspiring merchants and manufacturers. As they entered into commerce and industry, the structure of British industry became extremely competitive. Much like the characterizations of competitive industries that one finds in today's microeconomic textbooks, Britain's major nineteenth-century staple industries—textiles, iron and steel, coal mining, shipbuilding, and engineering—were composed of numerous firms with small market shares. Their industrial structures were also characterized by a high degree of regional concentration and vertical specialization. Distribution of intermediate and final products relied upon well-developed market mechanisms, often involving specialized merchant firms.

Relying upon market mechanisms to co-ordinate economic activity, nineteenth-century British firms were comparatively simple in their internal organization. Characteristically, firms were run by owner-proprietors or close family associates. Managerial staffs were small, and methods of cost accounting and production control were crude or non-existent. The development of industrial techniques typically relied upon trial and error rather than systematic in-house research. Most enterprises were single-plant firms that specialized in particular lines of manufacture of intermediate or final products. Industries exhibited a high degree of regional concentration based upon geographical advantages as well as external economies provided by local access to skilled labour supplies, transport facilities and distribution networks, capital, and product markets.

Up to the 1870s, the long-term financing for these business ventures came mainly from personal family fortunes, retained earnings, and, to a more limited extent, local banks. The economic crisis of the late 1870s saw the collapse of many local banks that were overcommitted to regionally specialized industries. Subsequently there arose a national branch banking system that had little explicit involvement in the long-term finance of British industry. The national banks provided credit to British industrial firms only in the form of short-term working capital, mainly through overdraft accounts and bills of exchange. Capital that was not extended on a short-term basis to British industry found ample outlets in foreign lending, usually in exchange for fixed-interest bonds, to finance large-scale (typically government-backed) foreign projects such as railways.

Despite the massive export of capital, there is no evidence that British industry was short of funds in the decades before World War I. Under the

conditions of general economic prosperity prevailing up to and through
World War I, short-term loans from banks were routinely rolled over from
year to year. With working capital readily available from external sources,
firms were free to devote retained earnings to long-term finance. In addition,
with the advent of limited liability and the development of provincial stock
markets in the 1860s and 1870s, industrial firms found that they could raise
capital by placing subscriptions with local businessmen, professionals, and
skilled workers who were eager to invest their savings. By facilitating entry
into industry, the ready availability of capital helped to sustain and extend
the highly competitive organization of Britain's staple industries.

One consequence of nineteenth-century competitive capitalism was the
consolidation of job control by many groups of workers in the major British
industries. During the long mid-Victorian boom, Britain's atomistic firms
opted for collective accommodation with unions of skilled and strategically
positioned workers rather than jeopardize their individual fortunes through
industrial conflict while there were profits to be made. The labour movement
also made important political gains that enhanced the ability of workers to
organize unions, build up union treasuries, and stage successful strikes.

A distinguishing feature of British industrial relations was its two-tiered
structure of bargaining. Workplace organizations enjoyed substantial local
autonomy in bargaining, backed by the leverage that national unions could
exert on employers during disputes. From the last quarter of the nineteenth
century, as intermittent but often prolonged recessions occurred and as
foreign competition began to be felt by many industries, firms were unable
to replace the job control of shopfloor union organizations by managerial control. Despite the introduction of many skill-displacing changes in technology,
the power of the union organizations that had developed earlier had simply
become too great. Attempts by Parliament and the judiciary to undermine
the trade union movement—most notably by means of the Taff Vale decision—resulted in the emergence of a distinct political party representing the
interests of labour.

The Challenge of Corporate Capitalism

In Britain, the late nineteenth century was a period of consolidation of the
institutions of competitive capitalism. Meanwhile corporate capitalism was
emerging as the dominant mode of economic organization in other major
national economies, most notably in Japan, Germany, and the United States.
Corporate capitalism was characterized by industrial oligopoly, hierarchical
managerial bureaucracy, vertical integration of production and distribution,
managerial control over job content and production standards, the integration of financial and industrial capital, and systematic research and
development (Chandler, 1977; Chandler and Daems, 1980).

By helping to stabilize prices and market shares, oligopoly facilitated long-run planning, particularly where large-scale capital investments were involved. Managerial co-ordination of product flows within the vertically integrated enterprise permitted the achievement of high-speed throughputs that reduced unit costs. Vertical integration of production and distribution provided the direct access to market outlets that was a precondition for the effective utilization of mass production methods. Managerial control over job content and production standards in turn facilitated the introduction of new, high-throughput technologies. Integration of financial and industrial capital, along with managerial bureaucracy, made possible the geographic mobility of capital and the rapid expansion of capacity to produce for new or growing markets. Systematic research and development provided the mainspring of technological innovation, particularly in such science-based industries as electrical and chemical manufacture.

Successful capitalist development in twentieth-century Germany, Japan, and the United States demonstrates the ubiquitous importance of the visible hand of corporate bureaucratic management. To meet the international challenge, British industries required transformation of their structures of industrial relations, industrial organization, and enterprise management. Vested interests in the old structures, however, proved to be formidable obstacles to the transition from competitive to corporate modes of organization. Lacking corporate management skills and opportunities, British industrialists clung to family control of their firms. Even where horizontal amalgamations did take place, the directors of the participating firms insisted on retaining operational autonomy (Hannah, 1976; Chandler, 1980). In any case, very few of these managers had the broader entrepreneurial perspectives or skills needed to develop modern corporate structures (Lazonick, 1983, 1985).

In contrast to the experience of emerging corporate economies, British bankers lacked direct involvement in industry and had little ability or incentive to use financial leverage to reorganize industrial structures or enterprise management. The concentration of banking in the City of London also gave rise to a relatively cohesive class of finance capitalists with much more concerted and coherent influence over national policy than industrial capitalists, who were divided along enterprise, industry, and regional lines. Problems of industrial competitiveness were aggravated by the policy favoured by bankers of maintaining the value of the pound sterling and protecting the position of the City as the financial centre of the world.

The British educational system in turn hampered industry by failing to provide appropriately trained managerial and technical personnel. On the demand side, there was comparatively little pressure to transform this system as highly competitive businesses could not afford to hire specialized technical personnel and were further reluctant to support industry-wide research institutes that would benefit competitors as much as themselves (Mowery, this volume). On the supply side, the existing system of higher education was designed almost explicitly to remove its 'aristocratic' students as far as possible from the worldly pursuit of business and applied science (Wrigley, this volume). It was the essence of the aristocratic view of the world that innate intellectual superiority rather than hard work was the key to socioeconomic success. Those who owed their success to the application of learned skills could at best become middle-class.

Moreover, when middle-class businessmen sent their sons to the élite public schools or universities, it was to partake in aristocratic culture rather than to challenge it. Beginning in the interwar period, many of the graduates of the élite educational system entered industry in general management positions; but they brought with them little understanding of production technology or the techniques of business administration. Even those technical specialists who came from the civic universities occupied a decidedly second-class status in British firms, with little opportunity of mobility to higher managerial ranks. Social cleavages in British enterprise bureaucracies hampered communication and teamwork between generalists and specialists, impeding managerial co-ordination (Lazonick, 1985).

In the absence of a shift to corporate enterprise structure, British industrialists also were unable to challenge the shopfloor control of trade union organizations. In the United States and Germany, a critical factor in the development of high-throughput production was the ability of management to gain and maintain the right to manage the utilization of technology. In most of Britain's staple industries, by contrast, managers had lost much of this 'right to manage', reducing their incentive to invest in costly mass production technologies on which they might not be able to achieve high enough throughputs to justify the capital outlays. During the first half of the twentieth century, British unionism was able to consolidate its positions of control at both the national and workplace levels, aided by the growing strength of the Labour Party and the emergency conditions of two world wars.

Lacking the requisite degree of control over product and input markets, British managers confronted severe obstacles in adapting their enterprise structures to take advantage of new market opportunities. As a result, in the late nineteenth and early twentieth centuries firms continued for the most part to manufacture traditional products using traditional technologies.

How these firms structured production depended very much on the prospects for selling their output. Contrary to typical textbook theory, Britain's competitive firms did not as a rule assume that the market could absorb all the output they might produce at a given price. Indeed, they produced few manufactures in anticipation of demand. Almost all production was to order, much of it for sale to merchants for distribution to far-flung international markets.

In the heyday of British worldwide economic dominance, these arrangements proved advantageous to British firms. Unlike many of their international competitors, who had access only to much more confining markets, Britain's international marketing structure meant that British firms could get enough orders of similar specifications to reap economies of long production runs, and had a large enough share in expanding markets to justify investment in (what were then) up-to-date and increasingly capital-intensive plant and equipment. But the tables were turned by the spread abroad of tariff barriers and indigenous industrialization. Because Britain had already industrialized, its domestic market for such staple commodities as textiles or steel rails had reached a point of at best moderate growth potential. Under these circumstances, British firms could not find a market at home that could match the dramatic rates of expansion of the foreign markets foreclosed to them. Indeed given its dependence on international markets, British industry was severely constrained to keep its own domestic markets open to the products of foreign firms.

Taking advantage of their more secure and expansive domestic markets, foreign rivals, with more modern, capital-intensive technology, attained longer production runs and higher speeds of throughput than the British. By virtue of their reliance on the corporate form of organization—in particular on vertical integration of production with distribution and more concentrated market power—Britain's rivals were better able to rationalize the structure of orders and ensure themselves the market outlets required for mass production. From secure home bases these rivals also invaded market areas and product lines where the British should have been at no comparative disadvantage.

Forced to retreat from competition with mass production methods, British firms sought refuge in higher quality and more specialized product lines, where traditional craftmanship and organization could still command a competitive edge—in spinning higher counts of yarn and weaving finer cloth, making sheets and plates of open hearth steel, and building unique one-off ships. Unfortunately for the British, in a world of expanding markets, the specialized product of the day all too often turned out to be the mass production item of tomorrow. The arrival of mass production methods and the pace and timing of decline varied among the major staple industries, with British shipbuilding, for example, still holding a commanding competitive position as late as World War II. But all eventually met a similar fate (see the papers in this volume by Lorenz and Wilkinson, Lazonick, Elbaum, and Tolliday).

Institutional Rigidity

From the standpoint of the neoclassical model of competition, these developments would lead one to expect a British response to competitive pressures that would imitate the organizational and technological innovations introduced abroad. In fact, the British only adapted patchwork improvements to their existing organizational and productive structure. Facing increasingly insecure markets, and lacking the market control requisite for modern mass production, the British failed to make the organizational renovations that could have allowed them to escape competitive decline.

With the massive contractions of British market shares that occurred in the 1920s and early 1930s, firms in the troubled staple industries alternated between scrambling for any markets they could get and considering proposals for elimination of excess capacity and concentration of productive structure. In a period of contraction, the market mechanism was anything but an efficient allocation mechanism, in part because existing firms remained in operation as long as they could hope for some positive return over variable costs, their proprietors living, so to speak, off their capital. Co-ordinated attempts to eliminate excess capacity were confounded by numerous conflicts of interest between owner-proprietors, outside stockholders, management groups, customers, banks and other creditors, and local union organizations. In particular, the involvement of the national banks in the attempts to rationalize industry was aimed more at salvaging their individual financial positions than at developing a coherent plan for industry revitalization (see the papers in this volume by Lazonick, Tolliday, and Best and Humphries). In light of the failure to achieve co-ordination, the rationalization programmes that were implemented in the interwar period were half-hearted and of limited effectiveness.

During the interwar period and beyond, the rigid work rules of British unions remained an impediment to structural reorganization. Entrenched systems of piece-rate payment often led to higher wage earnings in more productive establishments, deterring firms from scrapping old capacity and investing in new (see the paper by Elbaum in this volume). Union rules also limited management's freedom to alter manning levels and workloads, which in mechanical, labour-intensive industries such as textiles had particularly adverse effects on the prospective benefits of new technology (see the papers below by Lorenz and Wilkinson, and Lazonick). In general, management could be sure that the unions would attempt to exact a high price for co-operation with any plans for reorganization that would upset established work and pay arrangements. On the other hand, amidst industrial decline the strong union preference for saving jobs even at low wage levels was an additional conservative influence on a generally unenterprising managerial class.

Furthermore, even the new industries were not immune to the wider institutional environment. The slow growth of demand in new product market areas hampered the emergence of large firms and created a need for consolidation of industrial structure. In chemicals, fabricated metals, and electrical machinery, newly amalgamated firms suffered from a dearth of appropriately trained managerial personnel and, initially, experienced serious difficulties in overcoming vested interests and establishing effective co-ordination of their enterprises. In motor car manufacturing, competitive performance was undermined after World War II by a long-established management strategy of using labour-intensive techniques that helped breed control of shopfloor activities by highly sectionalized union organizations (see Lewchuk, this volume).

The Impact on Growth

If difficult to quantify precisely, the overall impact of these institutional rigidities on British economic performance was undoubtedly considerable. Throughout the pre-World War I years, the staple industries remained economically preponderant. According to the 1907 Census of Production, the largest of these industries—coal, iron, and steel (including non-electrical machinery and railway equipment), textiles, and shipbuilding—alone made up roughly 50 per cent of total net domestic industrial production and 70 per cent of British exports. During the long boom of the third quarter of the nineteenth century there was a rapid increase in British output per head, which drew important impetus from growth and technological advance in the staple industries (Matthews, Feinstein, and Odling-Smee, 1982). Subsequently, from 1873 to 1913 a marked slowdown in aggregate productivity growth occurred, with some evidence that growth was particularly sluggish from the late 1890s to World War I.

Detailed industry-level evidence is useful for assessing the accuracy of the aggregate data and the reasons for the pre-war productivity slowdown. British cotton enterprises, for example, did not reorganize the vertical structure of production in order to adopt more advanced technologies. Instead they chose to compete on the basis of traditional organization and techniques by cutting raw material costs and putting the burden of handling inferior cotton on the workers (Lazonick and Mass, 1984). The resultant cost-savings, augmented by the benefits of well-developed external economies, enabled the cotton industry to expand its output and exports despite stagnating labour productivity in the fifteen years or so before World War I. In the British steel industry there was significant ongoing productivity advance in the newer sectors of open-hearth steelmaking. Bessemer practice, however, was comparatively stagnant after 1890 as firms were deterred from investing in new, large-scale facilities by a sluggish domestic market, overseas protection, an increasing threat from foreign imports, and fragmented industrial structure (see paper by Elbaum below).

British growth in output per head not only slowed in the last quarter of the nineteenth century, but also began to lag relative to latter-day industrializing economies that were developing the institutional bases for corporate capitalism. British growth rates first fell behind those of other countries in the 1870s and 1880s. Serious losses in international competition were sustained between 1899 and 1913 and were interlinked with the failure of British industry to match the productivity advances achieved abroad by fully availing itself of the benefits of mass production methods. With the exception of wartime intervals, the gap in relative productivity growth performance between Britain and most of its competitors has remained substantial ever since.

During the interwar period the competitive weaknesses of the staple industries became evident, while the productivity performance of the British economy as a whole remained poor by international standards. There remains, however, considerable controversy over the connection between the performance of the staple industries and that of the aggregate economy. According to one influential perspective, the weak performance of the interwar economy was largely due to the relative lack of mobility of resources from the 'old' to the 'new' industries (Aldcroft and Richardson, 1969, pp. 270–1).

The argument, however, is open to criticism on several grounds. It assumes that the old industries imposed effective supply constraints on the growth of the new—a rather dubious proposition, given the high unemployment levels, ongoing capital export, and housing boom that characterized the interwar period. If there were supply constraints on the growth of the new industries, it was because of the failure of financial institutions to infuse industry with sufficient long-term venture capital and educational institutions to supply the types of personnel required.

A focus on the immobility of resources also implies that the basic problem of the British economy was one of structural adjustment out of industries in which comparative advantage had been lost and possibilities for technical advance had for the most part been exhausted. Yet there is little evidence that shifts in comparative advantage were the root of the competitive problems of Britain's staple industries. Some international competitors in these industries, facing prices for labour and resources greater than or equal to the British, were none the less more successful because they adopted major technical advances.

The staple industries contributed significantly to Britain's relatively poor interwar growth performance, mainly because they still bulked large in the economy and lagged behind seriously in international standards of technological and managerial practice. In 1924 staple manufacturing industries still accounted for 45 per cent of all manufacturing net output. By 1935 this figure had fallen to 35 per cent, but it remained at roughly that proportion into the late 1940s (Von Tunzelmann, 1982). With persistent excess capacity in the staple industries, firms that had long ago written off their plant and equipment always stood ready to 'ruin the market' for firms that might otherwise have invested in the modernization of plant and equipment and enterprise structure.

The Barely Visible Hand

What British industry in general required was the visible hand of co-ordinated control, not the invisible hand of the self-regulating market. Given the absence of leadership from within private industry, increasing pressure fell upon the state to try to fill the gap. Even before World War I, calls were made for greater state intervention. By the interwar period the British state had assumed a distinctly more prominent role in industrial affairs and provision of social and welfare services (Feinstein, 1983).

With further growth of state intervention after World War II—extending to the nationalization of industry and aggregate demand management—critics have pointed accusing fingers at the government for failing to reverse, and even for causing, relative economic decline. At various times and from various quarters the state has been blamed for undermining private sector incentives and the natural regenerative processes of the free market economy, for absorbing resources that would have been employed more productively in manufacturing, or for failing to provide British industry with a needed environment of macroeconomic stability and a competitively valued exchange rate.

In historical perspective, however, state activism must be absolved from bearing primary responsibility for Britain's relatively poor economic performance. In the late nineteenth century, at the outset of relative decline, the most singular features of the British state were its small size and *laissez-faire* policies. Even in the post-World War II period, British levels of government taxes, expenditures, and employment were not particularly high by European standards. Indeed, a distinctive feature of British state policy throughout recent history has been its reluctance to break from *laissez-faire* traditions. It is only in the second instance that state policy is implicated in British decline, by virtue of its failure to intervene in the economy more decisively in order to take corrective measures or to alleviate the social costs of industrial obsolescence and structural change. The consequences of this failure of state policy first became evident during World War I and were dramatized in the interwar period (Hall, this volume).

The Limits of Interwar Intervention

The Underdevelopment of Industrial Research

At the onset of World War I, state concern over the inability of British industry to supply technologically sophisticated materials of strategic military importance led to policy initiatives in the area of research and development. Major initiatives included the establishment of a state-owned corporation (British Dyestuffs) and state-subsidized industrial research associations for the promotion of co-operative research and development by firms in the private sector. British Dyestuffs, however, was handicapped by a lack of trained chemists in top management positions and a reliance on chairs in universities for research efforts.

Government promotion of industrial research associations reflected a concern that few firms in Britain were large enough to undertake their own in-house research and development programmes. As many as twenty-four research associations were established in industries ranging from woollen textiles to laundering. But firms often lacked the in-house technical expertise required to evaluate and employ the results of extra-mural research; as a result, research associations failed to gather the anticipated financial support from the private sector, and their impact on innovative performance was modest. Government-sponsored co-operative research proved an inadequate replacement for the in-house research capabilities of modern corporations (Mowery, this volume).

The Protection of the Pound

During the 1920s, restrictive macroeconomic policies were implemented to set the stage for the 1925 resumption of the gold standard at the prewar parity. Following the lead of Keynes, a long line of economists have argued that these macroeconomic policies had seriously adverse effects on the British economy. A contrast is often drawn between the industrial depression of the 1920s and the relatively strong performance of the economy in the 1930s, when devaluation and protectionism were forced upon the government.

Yet if the deflationary impact of the macroeconomic policies of the 1920s seems beyond dispute, there has been a lively debate about its significance for the trend in growth of output per head. Detailed examination of the staple industries, which were the most seriously affected by the 1920s depression, indicates that slack domestic demand, the strength of the pound sterling, and high interest rates *exacerbated* rather than caused problems of excess capacity, shrinking profit margins, and a heavy debt burden.

The Irrationalities of Rationalization Policy

The difficulties of the staple industries were predominantly structural and long-term in character. Profit margins were squeezed by declining competitiveness, persistent excess capacity, and the imprudent expansion of overdraft borrowing for investment purposes during the short but frenetic boom of 1920–1. The prolonged state of depressed trade that followed in the 1920s placed the banks' loans in serious jeopardy. At that time the Labour government was also considering direct intervention as a means of reorganizing the failing industries and alleviating industrial depression. This combination of circumstances prompted the Bank of England to step in.

For the Bank, rationalization was an economically viable and politically desirable alternative to more far-reaching forms of government intervention that threatened to go as far as nationalization and 'encroaching socialism'. Bank of England Governor Montagu Norman conceived of intervention as limited, temporary, and exceptional. The Bank's approach was highly consensual and 'quasi-corporatist'. Firms were encouraged to form trade associations and develop their own plans for industry rationalization. Within the trade associations, firms were authorized to negotiate common pricing policies, mergers, and production quotas. Even then individual firms were reluctant to let the Bank of England intervene, and it was only the stick of bankruptcy and the carrot of support for tariff protection that enabled it to do so (see the papers below by Best and Humphries, Lazonick, and Tolliday). When the Bank intervened more directly, it was simply to promote mergers rather than to back the modernization of industry. Where the market did not respond, the Bank was unwilling to put up its own funds. With the Bank and Treasury allied in keeping a tight hold on the public purse-strings, the public funds devoted to backing rationalization schemes were negligible. Yet the Bank found that its efforts at voluntary persuasion had little influence over the allocation of market sources of finance (Tolliday, this volume).

As for the government, its interwar industrial policies were confined largely to monitoring industrial affairs through the Import Duties Advisory Committee, established under the 1932 tariff legislation, and to legislative schemes aimed at reducing excess capacity in industries such as textiles. Like the Bank of England, the Advisory Committee pursued influence through conciliation and suasion, seeking no powers of centralized control over industry. Lacking the requisite authority to shape industrial development, the committee found itself overseeing a process of industrial quasi-cartellization that ensured profits for weak and strong firms alike. Government legislation generally responded to the wishes of industry trade associations with similar results.

Public attempts at rationalization left British industry with the worst aspects of both competitive and monopolistic worlds. Productive structure remained highly fragmented and inefficient, while quasi-cartellization and tariff barriers (or imperial preference) protected existing producers from competitive pressure. Rather than achieving its objective of promoting industry rationalization, interwar policy inadvertently reinforced pre-existing institutional rigidities.

The Ruin of the Regions

Industrial decline in the interwar period created severe problems of regional unemployment and decaying infrastructure because of the high degree of local concentration of the staple industries. Interwar regional policies were, however, a limited and *ad hoc* response to diverse political pressures for regional aid, rather than a coherent attempt to deal with the social costs and benefits of relocation of economic activity. The most consistent element in regional policy was the reluctance of the government to become directly involved in industrial development. Instead, the state sought to alleviate regional disparities by policies directed towards improving the operation of labour and capital markets.

The effectiveness of these policies was constrained by macroeconomic conditions, the limited size of the programmes, and the underlying assumption that facilitating the operation of market mechanisms would suffice to combat regional problems. Initially, the government promoted labour transference by providing assistance for individual workers or households to move to more prosperous regions. But the unemployed workers in the depressed regions were mainly adult males, who were heavily unionized, whereas many of the expanding industries sought primarily new entrants to the labour force, particularly women and juveniles.

By 1937 the emphasis had shifted to moving jobs to unemployed workers by providing businesses with special sources of finance and subsidized factory rentals. Provision of capital to firms in the depressed areas, however, could not overcome the limits on investment demand posed by depressed regional markets. Nor could it overcome the inability of the single-industry family firms that predominated in interwar Britain to manage diversified industrial and regional operations. Expanding industries that had already begun to develop in the South prior to the stagnation of the 1920s continued to grow in these more prosperous areas during the interwar period (Heim, this volume).

The Legacy of History

The British economy of the post-World War II period inherited a legacy of major industries too troubled to survive the renewed onslaught of international competition that began in the 1950s. As competitive pressure mounted, the state began to nationalize industries such as coal, steel, and motor vehicles that were deemed of strategic importance to the nation, and (with the exception of steel in 1951) were in imminent danger of collapse. But nationalization, however necessary, was by no means a sufficient response to Britain's long-run economic decline. Public ownership overcame the problem of horizontally fragmented private ownership, but not the inherited problems of productive structure, managerial organization, and union job control. Nationalized enterprises still had to confront these problems while attempting to overcome the technological leads already established by competitors.

Called upon willy-nilly to play an increased role in industrial affairs, the British government has been uncertain in its response. The rise of Keynesianism has led to widespread acceptance of interventionist fiscal and monetary policies. But with respect to industrial policy, successive British governments have veered back and forth between support for greater public planning and a traditional standpoint of *laissez-faire*.

The industrial policy measures that have been implemented reflect the contradictory tensions within British government philosophy. British industrial policies have shifted between a number of conflicting objectives, many of them short-term in character. These include maintaining high levels of employment, reducing regional disparities, fostering exports, improving productivity, and minimizing public expenditures. The greatest pecuniary beneficiaries of government industrial policy have been the long-ailing nationalized industries and unprofitable private sector firms. Public disbursements to British industry have been dominated by a mixture of lemon socialism and support for lame-duck capitalist enterprise.

These inconsistencies of British policy are paralleled and, to some extent, reinforced by contradictory tensions within contemporary economic analysis. Policy-oriented economic analysis in Britain (as in the United States) has been preoccupied chiefly with problems of macroeconomic management. In accordance with the neoclassical paradigm, there is widespread adherence to the presumption that, if only the government pursued the right fiscal and monetary policies, the operation of the free market would suffice to ensure economic prosperity.

Yet there is little evidence that Britain's relatively poor economic performance can be attributed to unusually severe cyclical fluctuations. On the contrary, Britain's relative decline has persisted through enough cyclical ups and downs to indicate that its roots lie deeper than inappropriate macroeconomic management.

Recently, there has been increasingly widespread recognition among economic analysts that relative decline must have complex sources within the British social fabric. A number of institutionally oriented explanations have been offered variously attributing decline to such factors as poor management, a dearth of professional engineers, troubled industrial relations, a rigid class structure, excessively egalitarian tax policies, an over-large public sector, and erratic public intervention. But several of these diverse explanations clash with one another—so much so that a prominent neoclassical observer of the British scene was moved to comment that the various arguments 'lack generality, unity, and hisotrical depth' (Caves, 1980, p. 140). Institutionally oriented analyses have helped provide a basis for British public policy initiatives in the areas of managerial and technical education, industrial relations legislation, tax incidence, and fiscal retrenchment; but they have failed to provide a consistent basis for public policy intervention.

The distinctive conclusions of this volume are that the sources of British decline are multi-faceted, but operate along common lines of historical causation. Britain was impeded from making a successful transition to mass production and corporate organization in the twentieth century by an inflexible nineteenth-century institutional legacy of atomistic economic organization. One element impeding the adoption of mass production methods was market demand conditions. Amidst sluggish domestic growth and free international trade, British firms found it difficult to secure the requisite market outlets to justify mass production. But British firms also faced critical supply-side constraints with respect to industrial organization, managerial and technical personnel, long-term finance, and labour relations. By implication, to break this causal chain and arrest the process of decline requires policy measures that operate on the demand and supply sides in a co-ordinated fashion.

The monetarist policies of the Thatcher government have failed to address the problem of economic development. Invoking free market ideology, Thatcher has attacked the power of the unions and sought economic revival through the severity of market discipline. But the supposition that there are forces latent in Britain's 'free market' economy that will return the nation to prosperity finds little confirmation in historical experience.

The example of late-developing nations suggests that a purposive national programme can enjoy considerable success in adapting institutions to meet growth objectives. The task for political economy is to identify those elements of the prevailing institutional structure that will promote and those that will hinder alternative strategies of economic development. The argument presented in this volume contends that industrial planning by enterprises, financial institutions, and the state has become increasingly important for international competitiveness and economic growth. The task for Britain is to adapt and devise institutions consistent with its democratic traditions, which will afford it the economic benefits of industrial planning.

Bibliography

Aldcroft, Derek H., and H. W. Richardson (1969). *The British Economy, 1870–1939*. London: Macmillan.

Allen, G. C. (1976). *The British Disease*. London: Institute of Economic Affairs.

Caves, Richard E. (1980). 'Productivity Differences among Industries'. In *Britain's Economic Performance*, ed. Richard E. Caves and Lawrence Krause. Washington: Brookings Institution.

Chandler, Alfred D., Jr (1977). *The Visible Hand*. Cambridge, Mass.: Harvard University Press.

Chandler, Alfred D., Jr (1980). 'The Growth of the Transnational Industrial Firm in the United States and the United Kingdom: A Comparative Analysis'. *Economic History Review*, 2nd ser., 33, August.

Chandler, Alfred D., Jr and Herman Daems (eds) (1980). *Managerial Hierarchies*. Cambridge, Mass.: Harvard University Press.

Feinstein, Charles (ed.) (1983). *The Managed Economy*. Oxford University Press.

Floud, R. C. (1981). 'Britain 1860–1914: A Survey'. In *The Economic History of Britain since 1700*, ed. Roderick Floud and Donald McCloskey, Vol. 2. Cambridge University Press.

Hannah, Leslie (1976). *The Rise of the Corporate Economy: The British Experience*. Baltimore: Johns Hopkins University Press.

Landes, David (1969). *The Unbound Prometheus*. Cambridge University Press.

Lazonick, William (1983). 'Industrial Organization and Technological Change: The Decline of the British Cotton Industry'. *Business History Review*, 57, Summer.

Lazonick, William, and William Mass (1984). 'The Performance of the British Cotton Industry 1870–1913'. *Research in Economic History*, 9, Spring.

Matthews, R. C. O., C. H. Feinstein, and J. C. Odling-Smee (1982). *British Economic Growth, 1856–1973*. Stanford University Press.

McCloskey, Donald N. (ed.) (1971). *Essays on a Mature Economy: Britain After 1840*. London: Methuen.

McCloskey, Donald N., and Lars Sandberg (1973). 'From Damnation to Redemption: Judgments on the Late Victorian Entrepreneur'. *Explorations in Economic History*, 9, 89–108.

Reader, William (1972). *Imperial Chemical Industries: A History*, 2 vols. Oxford University Press.

Sandberg, L. G. (1981). 'The Entrepreneur and Technological Change'. In *The Economic History of Britain since 1700*, ed. Roderick Floud and Donald McCloskey, Vol. 2. Cambridge University Press.

Von Tunzelmann, G. N. (1982). 'Structural Change and Leading Sectors in British Manufacturing, 1907–1968'. In *Economics in the Long View*, ed. Charles P. Kindleberger and Guido di Tella, Vol. 3. New York University Press.

Wiener, Martin (1981). *English Culture and The Decline of the Industrial Spirit, 1850–1980*. Cambridge University Press.

Wilson, Charles (1954). *The History of Unilever: A Study of Economic Growth and Social Change*, 2 vols. London: Cassell.

Wilson, Charles (1965). *Unilever 1945–1965: Challenge and Response in the Post-War Industrial Revolution*. London: Cassell.

The Cotton Industry

William Lazonick*
Harvard University

The British Cotton Industry

The cotton industry played a central role in nineteenth-century British economic development. At the core of the world's first industrial revolution in the early nineteenth century, the cotton industry maintained its importance in the last half of the century, employing over 3 per cent of the British labour force in 1900 and contributing over 26 per cent of all the nation's exports (Mitchell, 1962, pp. 60, 188, 284, 305). What is more, the industry experienced a remarkable boom in the decade or so before World War I. In 1914 there were 14 per cent more spinning and weaving firms than there had been a decade earlier, and these firms contained 24 per cent more spindles and 23 per cent more looms (Lazonick and Mass, 1984). With over 600,000 operatives employed just prior to the war, the cotton industry retained its position as Britain's largest manufacturing employer.

The industry was overwhelmingly export-oriented. In 1912, 86 per cent of the linear yards of cotton piece-goods that the industry produced and 70 per cent (by weight) of the raw cotton that the industry consumed were exported (Robson, 1957, pp. 333, 345). The largest markets for all types of British goods were in the less developed areas of the world, particularly India, China, Turkey, Egypt, the Dutch East Indies, Brazil, and Argentina. In the decades before World War I, India (Bombay, Bengal, and Madras) consistently accounted for more than 50 per cent of the value of all British grey cloth exports, about 25 per cent of bleached cloth exports, 20–30 per cent of printed cloth exports, and 10–15 per cent of dyed cloth exports. The combined value of all piece-goods shipments to Bombay, Bengal, Turkey, and China was 45 per cent of the total value of British piece-goods shipments in both 1889 and 1913. Most of the goods exported to these markets were of relatively low quality, although British producers secured a flourishing market in Chinese urban centres for relatively high-quality dyed piece-goods. Other large markets were the white settler 'colonies' of Canada, South Africa, and, especially, Australia—all of which imported more highly finished goods made from much higher-quality cloth than did the markets in the poorer parts of the world. But it was the ability of the British cotton industry to export to mass markets in the less developed areas that accounts

*Substantial parts of this paper are adapted from Lazonick (1983) and Lazonick and Mass (1984). See also Lazonick (1981b, 1981c). Research was funded by a grant from the National Science Foundation (SES 83-09335) and by grants-in-aid from the Merrimack Valley Textile Museum (now the Museum of American Textile History) and Harvard University.

for the large size of the industry in the last half of the nineteenth century, as well as for its burst of expansion in the decade before the war (Lazonick and Mass, 1984).

The British cotton industry managed this early twentieth-century expansion on the basis of machines—the spinning mule and the Lancashire loom—that were rapidly becoming antiquated in most other countries. The mule had been the dominant technology in the British spinning industry from the late eighteenth century, and in the last third of the nineteenth century had been widely introduced in cotton industries throughout the world. But in the 1870s and 1880s, an alternative technology—the ring-frame—was greatly improved, and it began to replace the mule. In the United States the diffusion of the ring-frame was rapid—ring spindles comprised 62 per cent of all spindles by 1890 and 87 per cent by 1913. By way of contrast, in Britain only 19 per cent of all spindles were ring spindles in 1913, despite the fact that British textile machinery firms were manufacturing the ring-frame on a large scale for shipment to producers around the world (Robson, 1957, p. 355).

The British cotton industry was even slower to adopt advanced weaving technology. In 1894 the Northrop automatic loom was invented in the United States, where it immediately began to be introduced. The first Northrops were installed in Britain in 1903, but despite the prewar expansion of the industry, automatic looms made up only 1–2 per cent of all cotton looms in Britain in 1914 (and about half of the Northrops had been installed by one firm, Ashton Brothers). In that year, automatic looms made up 40 per cent of all cotton looms in the United States (Robson, 1957, p. 356; Mass, 1984).

Reliant upon traditional technologies as well as international export markets, the British cotton industry was very vulnerable to import substitution strategies in less developed countries and to the invasion of open markets by 'cheap labour' producers such as Japan. If anything, the prewar boom made the British cotton industry all the more vulnerable; and, indeed, it proved to be a prelude to a postwar collapse from which the industry never recovered. In 1922 the volume of British piece-goods exports was only 61 per cent of the 1913 level, and in 1929, only 53 per cent. Hardest hit was the 'American' section of the industry, which used US-grown cotton to produce coarse to medium goods for markets in the less developed countries (Daniels and Jewkes, 1928; Utley, 1931, pp. 26–7).

Despite the decline in demand for British cotton goods in the 1920s, spinning and weaving capacity failed to contract. In 1929 there were 3 per cent more spindles and only 6 per cent fewer looms in operation than in 1913. As existing firms continued to compete for shrinking markets, there was little incentive for new investment in modern machinery. With firms working short-time on the traditional technologies, labour productivity declined in the 1920s. Rostas (1945) calculated an average annual decline of 0.36 per cent in output per operative between 1924 and 1930. From 1930 to 1937, however, productivity increased by an average of 5 per cent per annum because of the massive elimination of excess capacity from the industry and the strengthening of Britain's access to Commonwealth markets by the trade agreements made at the Ottawa Conference of 1932. But over the long run, the situation of the industry continued to deteriorate as British labour productivity fell further and further behind that of its prime competitors (Lazonick and Mass, 1984).

During the interwar years the British cotton industry lost its lower-quality markets to the Japanese and Indian industries. During the post-World War II period it lost its higher-quality markets to the cotton industries of Western Europe and the United States (Vitkovitch, 1955, pp. 254–7). Antiquated technologies still dominated in British production. In 1954, with 54 per cent of its spindles still on mules, Britain possessed 84 per cent of all mule spindles but less than 10 per cent of all ring spindles in world operation. In 1955 only 12 per cent of British looms were automatic. By this time the mule and power loom had completely vanished from the US industry. In 1960, output per worker in spinning was 30–60 per cent higher in France, Germany, and Holland than in Britain, despite the fact that the average count spun was higher (and therefore, other things equal, the output per spindle-hour lower) in these countries (Pollard, 1969, p. 422; Ormerod, 1963, p. 6).

The post-World War II period thus saw an extension of the long-term decline of the British cotton industry in a world economy extremely favourable to growth. I shall argue that the roots of this decline must be located in the institutional structure that developed in the *laissez-faire* period of the nineteenth century, when serious competitors had not yet arisen and the British industry dominated the markets of the world. In particular, the structures of industrial relations and industrial organization inherited from the heyday of competitive capitalism stood in the way of the transformation of the British cotton industry along modern corporate lines as was being done, for example, in Japan and the United States. The introduction of high-throughput technologies—the ring-frame (and particularly high-draft spinning) and the automatic loom as well as single-process openers and high-speed winding and warping machines—required both the elimination of excess capacity and the creation of vertically integrated organizational structures that would permit co-ordination of new mass production operations.

Given the highly competitive and specialized structure of industrial organization that characterized the British cotton industry, however, Lancashire's cotton businessmen possessed neither the incentive nor the ability to undertake the internal reorganization of the industry. In addition, any plans to re-equip had to take into account the considerable power of the trade unions to control the relation between work conditions and pay—power that, as I have shown elsewhere, derived in large part from the fragmentation of employers in a highly competitive industry (Lazonick, 1979, 1981c). Attempts to raise productivity and cut costs by redivision of labour on the *traditional* technologies were stymied by the desire and power of the unions to protect their positions of job control. At the same time, firms that contemplated the introduction of the new technologies, such as the ring-frame and automatic loom, had to contend with the power of the ring spinners' union or the weavers' union to determine the levels of piece-rates and the number of machines per worker.

In the 1920s, British travellers returned from the United States with glowing reports of the application of 'scientific management' there (Morton and Greg, 1926; Pearse, 1928–9). In Britain, however, cotton managers had long since conceded to their workers far-reaching rights to manage the labour process. Well into the twentieth century, British cotton firms were constrained to abide by well worked-out and deeply entrenched wage lists that had their origins in the last half of the nineteenth century. In the 1920s and beyond, the British cotton industry was afflicted by a severe case of institutional rigidity: it could not adapt organizational structures that had developed during its period of international dominance to the new requirements of international competition.

Institutional Structure and Low-throughput Production

In the two decades before World War I, British cotton firms were able to respond to the growing demand for inexpensive goods and remain competitive on international markets. The industry's organizational structure impeded the pursuit of a cost-cutting strategy based on the adoption of modern, high-throughput technologies, but encouraged an alternative strategy based on the reduction of the quality and quantity of cotton inputs per unit of yarn and cloth.

Minimizing the quantity of cotton inputs per unit of cloth output meant sizing the yarn as heavily as possible prior to weaving, and stretching the cloth as much as possible after weaving, subject to demand constraints. Sizing had two functions, one technical and one commercial. Its technical function was to strengthen the warp yarn to withstand the tension and chafing it underwent during the weaving process. The stronger the unsized yarn (itself a function of cotton grade, staple, and processing), the less sizing was needed for this purpose. In Britain, the amount of sizing that served to strengthen the warp yarn (or 'pure sizing', as it was called) was typically 15 per cent of the weight of the yarn, whereas in the United States it was typically only 6 per cent (Bean and Scarisbrick, 1921, pp. 293–6; Copeland, 1912, p. 78). The commercial function of sizing was simply to substitute a cheap input (typically, China clay mined in Cornwall, which readily absorbed moisture and hence added substantial volume as well as weight to the cloth) for an expensive input—cotton. Prior to World War I, the weight of the yarn in Lancashire 'cotton' cloth was increased by as much as 250 per cent by the addition of size (Nisbet, 1912, pp. 2–4, 46–7; Copeland, 1912, pp. 77–8).

The traditional Lancashire cotton technologies—the mule and the power loom—were well-suited to these cost-cutting strategies. With its intermittent spinning motion, the mule put much less strain on the yarn than did the ring-frame with its continuous motion. For any given yarn count, it was therefore technically possible to use inferior grades and/or shorter staples of cotton on mules than on rings without encountering excessive down-time because of the breakage of the yarn being spun. Softer twisted than ring yarn, mule yarn also held size better and hence was more suitable for heavy sizing (Bean and Scarisbrick, 1921, pp. 297–8, 329–30).

In the weaving process, the greater frequency of yarn breakage—and hence down-time—that occurred when using inferior yarn was less costly on the power loom than on the much more expensive automatic loom which required high throughputs to justify its greater capital cost. As a result, the power loom had a unit cost advantage when inferior yarn inputs were used, and this advantage widened as the quality of the yarn inputs declined. On automatic looms the primary operative task was repairing yarn breakages. Low-quality yarn inputs severely constrained increases in the number of looms per weaver, and hence negated the labour-cost saving potential of the newer technology. By contrast, on the less automated power loom, the most time-consuming task was the changing of shuttles, so that the number of looms per weaver was less affected by yarn quality.

In short, relative to the traditional technologies, the ring-frame and the automatic loom were high-throughput machines that required relatively high-quality cotton inputs to achieve low unit costs. But it was not simply the inherent technical attributes of the *installed* technologies that encouraged the Lancashire cotton industry to pursue its 'cotton-saving' strategy. In the decade prior to World War I there was ample opportunity for investment in the new technologies as the industry underwent its dramatic expansion.

The continued investment in the low-throughput 'cotton-saving' technologies can be understood only with reference to the institutional character of the industry. For it was Lancashire's peculiar structure of industrial organization that favoured the continued use of the traditional technologies, while it was its peculiar systems of industrial relations that made possible, and even encouraged, the use of inferior cotton inputs on these technologies.

Industrial Organization

The foreign demand for British yarn and cloth was serviced by a plethora of exporters and shippers centred in Manchester (Robson, 1950, p. 190; Copeland, 1912, pp. 365–70). Exporters consigned their goods to foreign branch offices or foreign agents, who then sought to find markets for the goods. Such shipments in anticipation of demand, however, made up only a small part of the total volume of cotton goods exports; most of the exports were handled by shippers to fill specific orders from foreign import houses. Shippers would have the grey yarn and cloth that they purchased from spinners and weavers 'finished' (or 'converted') according to the specifications of the order; or, alternatively, they would buy the desired finished goods from other merchant-converters or from finishers.

Spinning and weaving firms produced yarn and cloth almost exclusively to order. To reap the benefits of long runs, each firm sought to attract orders for, and hence to specialize in, narrow ranges of yarn counts or types of cloth. This horizontal specialization was accompanied by a high degree of vertical specialization. In 1884, 60 per cent of the spindles in Lancashire were in firms that only spun, and 43 per cent of the looms were in firms that only wove. By 1911 these figures were 77 and 65 per cent, respectively (Jewkes and Jewkes, 1966, p. 120).

Encouraging the increase in vertical specialization were extensive external economies, available to any prospective entrant to the industry (Lazonick, 1983). Alfred Marshall referred to the Lancashire cotton industry as 'perhaps the best present instance of concentrated organization mainly automatic' (Marshall, 1919, pp. 600–1). A hierarchy of extremely well developed markets linked together the various vertical layers of the industry. On Mondays a spinning manager might take the train to Liverpool to purchase cotton for yarn orders already in hand, and on Tuesdays and Fridays he might visit Manchester to seek out new orders on the floor of the Royal Exchange. In many cases, spinners and weavers would transact their input purchases and output sales through cotton, yarn, and cloth agents, adding more layers to the vertical structure.

The vertically specialized structure of the cotton industry posed factor-cost constraints on the introduction of ring-spinning (Lazonick, 1981a, 1984b). Spinning and weaving were not only highly specialized in different firms, but also highly localized in different areas of Lancashire (Jewkes, 1930, pp. 92–3; Farnie, 1979, ch. 2). As a result, yarn had to be shipped on average about thirty miles from the spinning to the weaving mill. Mule yarn was wound into packages on the bare spindle or on lightweight paper tubes, whereas ring yarn was typically wound into packages on relatively heavy wooden bobbins that were extremely expensive to ship. The alternative of rewinding ring yarn off the bobbins on to paper tubes or into large packages saved on shipping costs but increased processing costs. (For a detailed analysis of these problems and their relation to low-throughput production methods, see Lazonick, 1985).

But the fundamental problem posed by vertical specialization was the absence of co-ordinated decision-making among vertically related firms that was necessary to replace traditional low-throughput methods by modern high-throughput methods (Lazonick, 1985). The vertically specialized structure of production meant that a spinning mill had a short-run incentive to produce inferior yarn, since it could try to save on cotton and processing costs by passing on breakage problems to weaving mills. In turn, specialized weaving mills found it rather risky to invest in high-throughput technologies such as automatic looms because they could not be sure of a steady and adequate supply of the quality-controlled yarn that would make such investments cost-effective (Lazonick, 1981a). Ring yarn, in turn, was more cost-effective when used as part of a high-throughput strategy, but in so far as it was not demanded by weaving firms, spinning firms had no incentive to supply it.

Even the method of buying cotton that prevailed in Britain favoured the retention of the traditional technologies. In the United States, northern and southern cotton textile firms bought the cotton needed for the coming year just after the harvest in order to ensure that, for a given staple length, the yarn would be of the high quality and consistency required for standardized, low yarn-breakage, production. In effect, such advance purchasing and warehousing of cotton was a form of vertical integration—over the course of the year, a regular and consistent supply of a firm's crucial raw material was ensured (Brooks, 1898, pp. 282–4; Copeland, 1912, pp. 180–4).

But in Britain, spinning firms rarely engaged in large-scale buying of cotton, in part because yarn of high and standardized quality was not being demanded by weavers or merchants. Instead, the spinning manager would buy his cotton in Liverpool (or increasingly in Manchester) essentially from week to week, adjusting his cotton purchases to the specifications of current yarn orders, and always keeping his eyes open for feasible mixes of cotton that would enable him to cut costs. The mule, with its intermittent motion, was much more adaptable not only to lower grades of cotton but also to a wider range of cotton quality than was the ring-frame, and hence its use provided the Lancashire spinner with more week-to-week flexibility in the quality of cotton he could feasibly purchase.

Industrial Relations

The industrial relations systems that prevailed in Lancashire also encouraged the use of the traditional technologies. Central to these systems were wage lists that were designed to adjust as far as possible the pay of different workers to differences in the amount and difficulty of the work they performed. Negotiated at the district level, the wage structures inherent in different lists reflected the relative power of businessmen and workers at the time the accords were first reached as well as the types of products that predominated in the districts to which they applied.

In spinning, the Oldham List (established in the 1870s) and the Bolton List (established in the 1880s) were by far the most important district lists, regulating 75 per cent of mule spinners' wages in the Lancashire industry in 1894 and 90 per cent in 1945 (Lazonick, 1979). Any attempts to modify the

lists in favour of employers had to contend with very well-organized workers—prior to World War I virtually all mule spinners in Lancashire were
union members, and the Amalgamated Association of Operative Cotton
Spinners had by far the largest strike fund per voting member of any union in
Britain. Only after World War II were the lists, almost unchanged since the
last quarter of the nineteenth century, superseded in somewhat modified
form by a more general agreement designed to attract young workers into the
industry.

In weaving, there were twenty-two district lists in existence by 1887, of
which the most important was that secured in the plain-cloth Blackburn
district in 1853. From the 1860s, the Burnley district expanded its capacity on
the basis of lower wages, resulting in continual conflict as Burnley weavers
sought to force employers to institute the Blackburn List (Hopwood,
1969, pp. 36, 55; Farnie, 1979, p. 305; Smith, 1954, pp. 294 ff., 545 ff.).
Burnley employers were by no means opposed to the *principle* of wage lists; as
early as 1866 they had called for a uniform list. All they wanted was an
agreement that, compared with other lists, favoured profits more than wages.

But by the late 1880s the weavers' union was gaining in strength. The
membership of the Amalgamated Weavers' Association increased by 143 per
cent between 1889 and 1895, while the number of looms in Lancashire
increased by only 5 per cent (Hopwood, 1969, p. 188; Jones, 1933, p. 277;
Smith, 1954, p. 386). In 1892, at the peak of prosperity in the weaving
industry, a Uniform List covering all the weaving districts was adopted on
terms very favourable to the workers. In late 1932 the Uniform List was
modified to accommodate the 'more-looms' system, but in 1935 it was again
altered, this time to discourage the practice of giving weavers more than four
power looms to tend. To ensure that all employers would adhere to it, the
1935 list was given the force of law by Act of Parliament (Clegg, Fox, and
Thompson, 1964, pp. 117–19; Hopwood, 1969, ch. 17; Fowler and Fowler,
1984).

For operatives, the enforcement of the lists' provisions ensured that higher
levels of output arising from harder work on the traditional technologies
would not result in the cutting of piece-rates. But employers also derived
important benefits from these longstanding agreements. In a highly competitive and labour-intensive industry, widespread adherence to the lists meant
that individual firms would not be forced into wage-cutting competition with
other firms and the continual conflicts with workers over the pace of work
and the rate of pay that would inevitably result. By accepting the wage-lists,
employers gave up the right to lower piece-rates on the traditional technologies, but they were assured that operatives would not engage in the
collective slowdown—what the British called 'ca'canny'—that characterized
many other industries with less stable industrial relations systems. Even
when increases in productivity depended upon more intense or prolonged
work by the operatives, Lancashire spinning or weaving managers knew that

their mule spinners and power loom weavers could be motivated to work harder and longer for higher earnings. (For a theoretical treatment of these issues, see Lazonick, 1984a.)

By means of the wage lists, therefore, a certain harmony between capital and labour was achieved. But the lists did not eliminate all conflict. For one thing, they left room for collective bargaining over the business cycle, employers seeking a reduction (say, 10 per cent) in a downturn and operatives seeking an increase in an upturn. In the 'American' (coarse and medium count) section of the spinning industry, even this aspect of wage bargaining was institutionalized in the form of the Brooklands Agreement of 1893, which limited cyclical increases or decreases to 5 per cent no more than once every 12 months (Porter, 1967; Wiggins, 1939, pp. 230–2).

In 1913 the Brooklands Agreement broke down over the one key aspect of the production process that was never successfully regulated by means of the lists: the use of inferior cotton inputs. Lower-quality cotton meant more yarn breakages per unit of time and, hence, the expenditure of more work effort by workers to produce the same amount of output. Since mule spinners and power loom weavers were paid by the piece, they were by no means indifferent to what they called 'bad spinning' or 'bad material'. If, after a shift to inferior cotton inputs, operatives continued to exert the same amount of work effort as before, they would suffer a decline in output and therefore in earnings. Alternatively, they could attempt to keep earnings up by expending more effort. In either case, they were adversely affected.

From the employer's perspective, however, it was worthwhile using inferior cotton inputs, despite a resultant fall in productivity, if the reduction in unit cotton or yarn costs outweighed the rise in other unit factor costs. A prime skill of a Lancashire spinning manager was the ability to take advantage of cotton price changes on his weekly visits to the Liverpool cotton market in order to spin yarn from a low-cost mix of cotton of various grades and staple lengths. Each spinning manager, therefore, had his own notion of what constituted the 'correct' mix of cotton, which was based on cost as well as technological factors. A weaving manager, on the other hand, could never be certain about the quality of yarn that would be delivered to him. Moreover, fixed piece rates, irregardless of the number of looms tended by each weaver, gave weaving employers an added incentive to cut costs by using inferior cotton, because the extra burden of work would have to be absorbed by the operatives if they wanted to maintain their earnings. In addition, in both spinning and weaving yarn breakages could depend on other variable factors, such as humidity and the carelessness of workers, making the cause of excessive yarn breakages an issue of continual dispute. For these reasons, none of the spinning or weaving lists specified a normal number of yarn breakages per unit of time.

The Oldham spinning list did, however, recognize the problem of bad spinning by specifying a two-step local conciliation procedure in the case of a dispute. Up to the late 1880s, almost all bad spinning disputes were settled without a strike as individual managers agreed to pay compensation to the mule spinners either for harder work involved or for wages lost as the mules were slowed down somewhat in order to reduce yarn breakages.

During a prolonged confrontation in 1891–2, however, employers banded together to form the Federation of Master Cotton Spinners' Associations (FMCSA) for the specific purpose of gaining a freer hand in cutting cotton costs. Their success was mixed. In 1892 they entered into an agreement to pay compensation to mule spinners for bad spinning, as had been the case in the local procedures, and in 1893, as part of the Brooklands Agreement, they joined with union leaders in setting up an elaborate grievance procedure in bad spinning disputes. Neither agreement, however, specified non-compensated standards for numbers of yarn breakages per unit of time (Lazonick, 1981c).

With the formation of the FMCSA and the Brooklands Agreement, individual employers were less constrained in their use of inferior cotton than before because they no longer had to fear the consequences of confronting the union on their own. In bad spinning disputes, they could now count upon support from other firms, since yarn breakage standards set in grievance or strike settlements might be seen as applying to all spinning firms. That the issue of bad spinning was nowhere near resolution immediately prior to World War I was due to the resistance of spinning capitalists as a body to the imposition of constraints on their cotton cost-cutting activities.

Under the Brooklands Agreement, the spinners' union could not support any group of workers in a strike over bad spinning until the remedy of a long, multi-level grievance procedure had been exhausted. Mule spinners voiced discontent with the Agreement throughout its twenty-year history, as they were forced to put up with bad spinning for weeks and even months while each case was adjudicated. Finally in 1913 the spinners withdrew from the Agreement as the number of bad spinning disputes waiting to be resolved reached unprecedented levels (Porter, 1967; Smith, 1954, pp. 21 ff., 394–5, 458–78; White, 1978; Oldham Operative Cotton Spinners' Provincial Association, 1912, 422–3).

The cost-cutting strategy of using inferior cotton inputs is a key to understanding productivity trends in the British cotton industry in the decades prior to World War I. Output per worker increased rapidly in the period 1870–90, and especially in the 1880s, but stagnated thereafter (Lazonick and Mass, 1984). In the decade before World War I, the industry underwent a remarkable expansion. But it did so on the basis of institutional structures that were inappropriate for the competitive environment that was to prevail after the war. With the prewar success of the industry, the old institutional structures became even more entrenched, making them less susceptible to change in the post-World War I era and beyond.

Institutional Rigidities and Industrial Decline

In 1923, an authority on the textile industry wrote in the preface to his book on cotton mill management:

The textile workers of the country are so thoroughly organised in trade unions that the organisation of labour is practically entirely in their hands, and the management must organise almost exactly on the lines laid down in a series of rules recognised by master and man as a basis upon which they must work. These rules have almost the force of laws, and they apply chiefly to the number of people to be employed, their duties, and their remuneration. . . . Here is the place to emphasise the importance of good management, a recognition of a set of fixed conditions established after a long and dreary warfare between master and man, and the clear exhibition to his workmen of his intention to abide by these conditions. (Taggart, 1923, pp. xix–xx.)

'Scientific management' was to find little application in the British cotton industry, where even into the 1960s management was constrained by industrial relations systems that had become entrenched in the late nineteenth century.

The few attempts that were made in the interwar period to alter the 'set of fixed conditions' attest to the power of cotton operatives to control the relation between work conditions and rewards. In 1928, amidst depressed trade conditions, the Federation of Master Cotton Spinners' Associations sought to increase the workweek from 48 to $52\frac{1}{2}$ hours, to remove union restrictions on cleaning and oiling mules outside 'engine hours' (as laid down by the Factory Acts), and to reduce standard piece-rates by 25 per cent (FMCSA, 1927; Labour Research Department, 1928; UTFWA, 1928). The result was, to quote a contemporary, 'the biggest defeat of employers in the history of the trade' (Bowker, 1928, p. 92). Attempts to redivide labour on the mules were similarly unsuccessful until, in the aftermath of World War II, the mule spinners themselves agreed to government intervention to modify the wage-lists in an attempt to deal with a longstanding shortage of auxiliary workers (Great Britain Ministry of Labour and National Service, 1945, 1946; FMCSA, 1951). But even then, the structure of job control exercised by the mule spinning operatives remained essentially unchanged.

In the interwar period, conflicts were much more severe and prolonged in weaving than in spinning, primarily because weaving operatives did not have quite the power of the mule spinners to enforce the status quo. The key issues were the number of looms per weaver and related piece-rate structures. From the last decades of the nineteenth century, attempts had been made to relieve weavers of some auxiliary tasks so that they could each tend six looms. Prior to the 1920s, such systems of work organization—called weaving by American methods—were confined almost entirely to weaving firms that spun their own break-resistant yarn, usually on ring spindles. In 1886 only 2.2 per cent of British weavers were engaged on six looms, and by 1906 only 2.8 per cent (Wood, 1910, pp. 149–53).

By the late 1920s the 'more-looms' system had still made very little progress. But in 1928 the pressure of competition, and particularly the loss of the Indian market to Asian producers, induced some weaving capitalists in Burnley to explore the more-looms system as a means of cutting labour costs. It was claimed that, by the redivision of labour as well as by the use of stronger yarn and larger weft packages for the shuttle, the Japanese had been able to assign ten to sixteen non-automatic looms to each weaver (*CFT*, 2 November 1928, 9 November 1928, 16 November 1928). Lancashire employers also hoped that the utilization of the more-looms system would provide an alternative cost-cutting strategy to the heavy capital investment involved in switching to automatic looms (*CFT*, 26 April 1929, 7 February 1930; see also Fowler and Fowler, 1984, ch. 5). In April 1929 the Burnley weavers' union agreed to a one-year eight-looms-per-weaver experiment on 4 per cent of the looms in twelve local firms. The operatives were to receive an average of 50s. on eight looms as compared with 39s. on four looms, and displaced weavers were promised that employment would be found for them (*CFT*, 26 April 1929, 24 May 1929, 14 June 1929).

When the experimental period ended, the capitalists wanted to extend the more-looms system to all their looms. But the operatives demanded an increase in earnings to 56s.–60s. per week as well as a 'fall-back' or minimum wage to be guaranteed during periods of depressed trade. By December 1930, the bargaining had reached an impasse. The following month, one large Burnley employer instituted the eight-loom system on all his looms without the consent of the union. His mill was struck, and an industry-wide lock-out followed, from which the operatives emerged victorious. Henceforth, there were no concerted attempts to introduce the eight-loom system (*CFT*, various issues from 25 August 1930 to 21 August 1931).

Instead, employers and operatives began to negotiate over a six-loom system, the weavers demanding the fall-back wage as well as effort-saving technical changes on the non-automatic looms. By the end of 1932 agreement was finally reached: the average operative would get 41s. per week and a fall-back wage of 28s.

From January 1933, many firms in Burnley began to move to six looms per weaver, greatly exacerbating an already serious unemployment problem among Lancashire weavers. As a result, the large majority of firms still on the four-loom system went off the Uniform Wage List and began to pay their weavers the much lower six-loom piece-rates. Meanwhile, the six-loom weaving firms pushed competition and intensification of labour even further by gradually moving to inferior warp yarns. By November 1934, the Uniform List and the six-loom agreement were being breached on over one-third of the looms in Lancashire, and on another one-quarter of the looms operatives were making loans to their employers to enable them to stay in business without cutting rates. In order to save the traditional industrial relations system, the weavers' union, in alliance with many of the four-loom employers, turned to Parliament. In July 1935 they successfully secured a Legalized Uniform List that lowered average earnings on four looms but raised average earnings on six and eight looms. This widening of the wage differentials brought the spread of the more-looms system to a halt, with some six-loom firms even switching back to four looms (*CFT*, various issues from 19 June 1931 to 1 February 1935; Fowler and Fowler, 1984, ch. 6).

Thus, the final significant attempt at cost-cutting on the Lancashire power looms ended with the traditional systems of industrial relations and work organization still intact, but with the earnings of the vast majority of Lancashire weavers somewhat reduced. In 1937 only 18 per cent of Lancashire weavers were tending more than four looms (although this proportion was over 60 per cent in Burnley) (Gray, 1937, pp. 10–17). By the 1930s, therefore, Lancashire cotton capitalists had not only neglected to undertake significant investment in new capital-intensive technologies over the previous half-century, but had also failed to overcome deeply institutionalized industrial relations constraints on the traditional labour-intensive machines. Managerial attempts at cost-cutting inevitably resulted in zero-sum conflicts between capitalists and workers over the division of a constant, if not decreasing, social product. With cohesive workers' organizations confronting employers who were themselves divided by competition, the operatives on the traditional machines held the balance of power.

Attempts at Rationalization

From the 1920s many Lancashire businessmen had recognized that they needed 'to put their own house in order' before they could go to the operatives seeking co-operation and concessions. This meant ridding the industry of excess capacity and ruinous competition. In the prewar boom, the spinning and weaving sections of the industry had become more competitive than ever. Besides the formation of two oligopolistic (and multinational) firms in the manufacture and sale of sewing thread (J. P. Coats in 1896 and, in response, the English Sewing Company in 1897), there were only two important amalgamations in the British cotton industry before World War I: Horrockses, Crewdson (1887), a large enterprise that integrated spinning, weaving, and marketing, and the Fine Cotton Spinners' and Doublers' Association (1898), a holding company of some thirty firms spinning very fine yarns, each firm retaining a high degree of operational autonomy (Macrosty, 1907, pp. 124–41; Carter, 1913, pp. 309–15). The number of spinning and weaving firms in the Lancashire cotton industry increased from 1,764 in 1904 to 2,011 a decade later, and the trend was towards greater vertical specialization, and hence horizontal competition, at both the spinning and weaving levels (Jewkes and Jewkes, 1966, p. 120; Jones, 1933, pp. 275–7).

With expanding markets, the development of production in the prewar period came about by the re-equipment of existing firms (albeit typically with the traditional technologies) as well as by the entry into the industry of new, usually larger, firms in booms and the exit of inefficient firms in slumps, thus updating and enlarging the capital stock. But with generally declining markets after World War I, very few firms re-equipped and very few new firms entered the industry. Many inefficient firms that might have been forced to give up had there been technical development and enlargement of the more efficient firms found that they could hang on by living off their invested capital. Throughout the 1920s, spinning and weaving capacity varied little from their prewar levels. Many 'American' spinning and weaving firms remained in business in the early 1920s by shifting some of their capacity, machinery permitting, into the production of finer goods, thereby overcrowding the 'Egyptian' section of the industry by the late 1920s and creating inefficiency through less standardized production within the mills (PEP, 1934, p. 21; Kirby, 1974; Committee on Industry and Trade, 1928, pp. 33–4; Pennington, 1926–7, p. 216).

The problem of excess capacity in the coarser goods section of the industry was exacerbated by what turned out to be an enormous over-capitalization of spinning firms in the brief postwar boom of 1919–20. High profits led to the buying up and recapitalization of existing firms at about three times their prewar value per spindle and with an increase in loan capital of approximately 50 per cent per spindle. Involved in this financial reconstitution were 46 per cent of the spindles in the industry and 14 per cent of the looms, the latter belonging mainly to combined firms. When the slump hit the industry beginning in the mid-1920s, the firms were forced to throw their yarn on the market at any price to meet fixed interest charges. The resultant low yarn prices were probably a prime reason for the survival of many coarse weaving firms in the depressed 1920s.

The financial condition of all the spinning firms was made even more unstable by the fact that shareholders in the Lancashire spinning industry were generally required to have only half of their share capital paid-up with the other half on call for emergencies. When this unpaid share capital was called in during the 1920s, local residents, who were preponderant among the stockholders, often had to withdraw their savings deposits from firms (which also functioned as high-interest savings institutions) in order to retain their equity. The recapitalized firms thus became even more dependent on banks, to which they were already deeply indebted for working capital (Committee on Industry and Trade, 1928, pp. 36–8; Daniels and Jewkes, 1928, pp. 169–77; UTFWA, 1923, p. 15; Jones, 1924, pp. 447–52).

Attempts were made to control competition. In order to keep up yarn prices, the Federation of Master Cotton Spinners' Associations organized short-time work between 1921 and 1926, which, in so far as it was adhered to, created conditions more favourable for the survival of less efficient firms. In 1923 some spinning capitalists (including Charles Macara, who had been President of the FMCSA from 1894 to 1916) advocated a scheme to permit more efficient firms to run while compensating the workers and owners of less efficient firms to cease production. But the FMCSA rejected the plan. In the same year the FMCSA instituted a scheme of minimum prices, and the following year actually sought to have the price list legalized by Parliament in order to enforce it upon 'disloyal' spinners. Unfortunately for the spinners, the weaving industry successfully opposed this attempt to raise the price of one of its basic inputs. In 1927 the FMCSA attempted once again to assert its own authority, setting up a cartel called the American Cotton Yarn Association to set prices and limit production. Within ten months, the cartel had been eroded by competitive forces. Meanwhile the banks, still expecting a recovery—the cotton industry, after all, had always been prone to cyclical fluctuations—continued to extend credit or grant moratoria to the deeply indebted spinning firms, the financial positions of which were being further weakened by the general deflation of the 1920s (Fitzgerald, 1927, pp. 9–10; Committee on Industry and Trade, 1928, pp. 34–6; Daniels and Campion, 1935, pp. 340–1; Macara, 1923, p. 90; Jones, 1924, p. 450; Kirby, 1974, p. 148; Clay, 1929a, pp. 138–9, 1929b, p. 163; Committee on Industry and Trade, 1929, p. 46; Lucas, 1933, pp. 272–3; Keynes, 1981).

By the late 1920s, the banking sector realized that it required some leadership to extract its own members from a difficult situation. Encouraged by the general movement towards 'rationalization' of British industry in the late 1920s, the Bank of England sought to effect a large-scale amalgamation of spinning capacity, which, by providing a highly concentrated entity under centralized control with the financial ability to re-equip, could set the tone for the industry and force inefficient producers out. The plan was to set up a firm—the Lancashire Cotton Corporation—which expected to merge as many as 200 mills and 20 million spindles in the American section of the spinning industry, wiping out all fixed interest charges in the process by issuing preference shares to ordinary creditors and debenture holders, and new common shares to old shareholders (Clay, 1929b, p. 49; Streat, 1958, p. 7; Lucas, 1937, p. 155; Wisselink, 1930, p. 158; Hannah, 1976, ch. 3).

By all accounts, the directors and managers of the Lancashire cotton firms resisted attempts at merger on the grounds—quite rational from the individual point of view—that any such amalgamation would involve their loss of individual control over their enterprises (Keynes, 1981; Streat, 1958, p. 7; Macgregor, Ryan et al., 1930, pp. 360–1; Chandler, 1980; Hannah, 1976, pp. 147–8). As John Maynard Keynes put the problem in 1928,

There [is] probably no hall in Manchester large enough to hold all the directors of cotton companies; they [run] into thousands. One of the first things should be to dismiss the vast majority of these people, but the persons to whom this proposal would have to be made would be precisely those directors. (Keynes, 1981, p. 631.)

Or as John Ryan, Managing Director of the Lancashire Cotton Corporation (and a relative newcomer to the cotton industry brought in by the banks), argued:

I do not think we can leave it to the individuals. Vested interests will always resist a movement which tends to remove them, and vested interests can very easily hold a position which is acceptable to themselves but yet is acting as a parasite on an industry and slowly driving it to death. . . . (In Macgregor, Ryan *et al.*, 1930, p. 361.)

By 1930, the Lancashire Cotton Corporation had coerced 96 firms and 9.3 million spindles (almost one-fifth the Lancashire total) into the fold, as the bankers threatened the reluctant directors of these firms with termination of credit (Hannah, 1976, p. 84; Kirby, 1974, pp. 149–51). Another group of indebted directors sought to create a corporation of 'spinners of American cotton for the benefit of the spinners'. But the individuals who made up the group were (as one observer of the industry put it) 'loath to give up their functions', and the banks refused to lend their support (Wisselink, 1930, p. 159). The Lancashire Cotton Corporation, which did have formal centraliza-tion of control, was unable to develop an effective managerial structure: in 1932 its chief executives resigned when the board of directors decided that the mill managers, who had been displaying a lack of initiative, should be given more autonomy (*The Economist*, 8 October 1932, p. 635; Hannah, 1976, pp. 84–5, Lucas, 1937, pp. 156–9; Kirby, 1974, p. 152).

The problems of the Lancashire Cotton Corporation ultimately benefited the rest of the spinning industry, ridding it of a significant amount of excess capacity. By 1939 it had scrapped about 4.5 million spindles which it had brought under its control (Pollard, 1969, p. 122). As the world-wide depres-sion hit an already stagnant British cotton industry in the early 1930s, it became apparent that a more co-ordinated and explicit scrapping policy was required to eliminate machinery and firms. By 1934 British yarn production had declined by 40 per cent and cloth production by 55 per cent from their 1912 levels, while the number of spindles in the industry had contracted by only about 20 per cent and the number of looms by about 25 per cent (FMCSA, 1935, p. 2).

In approving a scheme for the elimination of spindles in 1934, the FMCSA stated that the problem of surplus capacity had been with the industry for nearly fifteen years, and that the 'ordinary processes of economic law' had not so far solved it. 'The Surplus Spindles Bill', they argued, 'may be regarded as an insurance against a price war between the combines and the smaller independent firms, which, however it ended, could only be a disaster for Lancashire (FMCSA, 1935, pp. 11–13). The scheme, which called for a compulsory per-spindle levy on all operating firms, to be used to buy up and scrap the capacity of those spinning firms willing to go out of business, became law under the Spindles Act of 1936. By World War II, the Spindles Board set up under the Act had acquired and scrapped 6.2 million spindles, reducing capacity to two-thirds the pre-World War I level (Robson, 1957, pp. 229–30, 340).

When the Lancashire Cotton Corporation was in the process of formation in 1929, John Ryan, its first Managing Director, declared to the cotton textile Managers Association: 'The horizontal amalgamation is no use to Lancashire: it must be vertical' (Ryan, 1928–9, p. 24). Vertical co-ordination of spinning and weaving as well as marketing was a necessary condition for the introduction of modern, high-throughput technologies. Yet in the interwar years vertical integration was rarely discussed, let alone attempted. Indeed, despite its initial intention to integrate vertically, the Lancashire Cotton Corporation had enough difficulty managing its horizontal operations, and simply scrapped the 20,000 looms that had been in the mills it had acquired (Robson, 1957, pp. 120–1). The degree of vertical specialization in Lancashire steadily increased from the mid-nineteenth century until after World War II. In 1930 only 26 of the more than 2,000 cotton and yarn producers in Britain had their own marketing facilities, and only 19 of these combined spinning and weaving as well. These 26 firms controlled about 7 per cent of the spindles and 10 per cent of the looms in the industry. They generally had their origins in the nineteenth century, and many in the early phases of the industrial revolution when some form of integration of production and distribution was a requirement for doing business (Jewkes and Jewkes, 1966; Clay, 1931; UTFWA, 1943, p. 156; Robson, 1957, p. 122; Great Britain, Ministry of Labour and National Service, 1946, p. 37; Hopwood, 1969, p. 15; Mills, 1917, p. 50; Muir, 1964; Ellinger and Ellinger, 1930, p. 209).

Nor was significant vertical integration or technical change induced by the more favourable market conditions after World War II. From 1946 to 1951 the British cotton industry experienced a dramatic boom, with yarn production increasing by 50 per cent and cloth production by 56 per cent (Robson, 1957, p. 345)—a recovery that must have confirmed observers such as John Jewkes in the view that vertical specialization was a great *strength* of the British industry, because this more flexible organizational structure gave it a comparative advantage in the production of more specialized products (Jewkes, 1946). Mills that had been closed during the war, and whose plant and equipment had long been written off, were able to enjoy profits on the basis of traditional production methods. In 1951 only 8 per cent of spinning capacity and 6 per cent of weaving capacity was post-World War II vintage. During this period there were no labour productivity gains in spinning and only slight gains in weaving (Miles, 1968, pp. 38–9; Shaw, 1950).

The ossification of the British cotton industry into its horizontal layers, and the attendant problems for technical change, were well summed up in 1950 by the British Productivity Team on Cotton Weaving. Reporting on their recent visit to the US mills, the Productivity Team stressed the multifold advantages of vertical integration—but went on to warn:

To attempt to change the horizontal structure would affect operatives, managements, shareholders, spinners, merchants, merchant-convertors, and many others. New buildings would be needed in addition to new machinery. Clearly such a proposal is out of the question. (Productivity Team Report, 1950b, p. 16.)

Government Intervention

Lancashire cotton managers' complaints of labour shortages during the postwar boom years stemmed from their continued reliance on labour-intensive methods of production, which kept them from matching the wages and work conditions of more modern industries. In 1948 the government intervened to try to solve this problem by recruiting labour for the industry and by passing the Cotton Spinning Industry (Re-Equipment Subsidy) Act. Under the Act, firms with at least three mills and a minimum number of spindles were eligible for a 25 per cent re-equipment subsidy to modernize some of the mills and to close down the remainder. But the Act provided no incentive to integrate spinning and weaving as part of the re-equipment process, let alone to integrate production and distribution. In effect, government intervention took the existing vertical structure of the industry as given. Not surprisingly, the Act of 1948 had only a minimal impact on re-equipment (Miles, 1968, pp. 26–7; Robson, 1957, p. 219; Ormerod, 1963, pp. 8–9).

The postwar boom ended in 1951 with cloth output for the home market somewhat larger than it had been in 1937, but with exports down some 50 per cent and imports up close to 700 per cent (Robson, 1957, p. 345). In 1937 imports had represented only 3.1 per cent of domestic consumption, whereas by 1951 they had grown to 16.1 per cent. Imports came mainly from Hong Kong, Pakistan, and India, all of which enjoyed duty-free access under the 1932 Ottawa agreements, which had been designed to secure Commonwealth markets for British cotton goods. To attribute the stagnation of the British cotton industry that ensued after 1951 to cheap imports, however, would be an oversimplification. In fact, between 1951 and 1958 import penetration was slight (Miles, 1968, p. 26).

The fundamental problem was an industry mired in its own highly competitive and vertically specialized structure, lacking any internal forces to set organizational transformation in motion. In 1958 there were almost 1,500 firms undertaking marketing activities in the Lancashire cotton industry, and over three-quarters had no formal distribution or financial links with any particular weaving firms (Miles, 1968, p. 68). As this mass of marketing firms fed small orders to firms in the vertically specialized production structure, production runs grew shorter while delivery times grew longer, worsening still further Lancashire's competitive position in the world's markets (Lucas, 1937, p. 159; Clay, 1931, p. 68; Vitkovitch, 1955, p. 262; Ormerod, 1963, p. 14; UTFWA, 1957, p. 16; Vibert, 1966).

The weaving sector itself continued to consist of small family firms in the 1950s. Between 1940 and 1959 the average number of looms per firm actually decreased from 470 to 403. Even though the number of firms declined by over 40 per cent during this period, there were still 567 specialized weaving enterprises remaining in the industry in 1959. And despite major governmental intervention in the early 1960s to rid the Lancashire cotton industry of excess and antiquated capacity, 322 specialized weaving firms remained in 1965 (Miles, 1968, pp. 44, 73, 120–1).

On the basis of her first-hand investigations of about one hundred family firms in the industry in the 1960s, Caroline Miles presented the following profile:

... old equipment, largely if not entirely written off; an aging, immobile labour force, possessing skills not readily transferable to modern plant; aging management with no successors in view; and stagnant or declining markets. With low fixed costs and an available labour reserve (since the aging workers were not able to get permanent jobs elsewhere), such a firm was able to disrupt prices, under-cutting firms with relatively high fixed costs when demand was rising and withdrawing again when trade was slack. (Miles, 1976, pp. 203–4.)

Most of the spinning firms were joint-stock companies, although families often owned and controlled these businesses (Bennett, 1933, ch. III). From 1940 to 1959 the spindle capacity of the average spinning firm increased by about 23 per cent, largely because of horizontal amalgamation (some of which was stimulated by the Act of 1948, which applied only to firms with at least three mills). In 1940 there were 280 firms carrying out spinning in the British cotton industry; in 1959, 141 (Miles, 1968, p. 44). The largest of these firms, the Lancashire Cotton Corporation, had never adopted a policy of vertical integration. Other large amalgamations, such as the Fine Spinners and Doublers and the Combined English Mills, were loosely organized federations of largely autonomous units. With persistent over-capacity at the weaving level and their own lack of internal organization, even the largest spinning firms were content to take the horizontal structure of the industry as given during the post-World War II decades. They provided no leadership whatsoever in structural change.

By 1959 the once great British cotton industry was struggling to survive in a highly competitive international environment in which success was based upon tariff protection combined with capital-intensive, high-throughput production. Once again the British government intervened, this time on a much larger scale than ever before, in an effort to improve Lancashire's productive base—a strategy it pursued in lieu of the imposition of strict import controls on goods from Commonwealth countries. The 1959 Cotton Industry Act sought to rid both the spinning and weaving sections (as well as the finishing section) of excess capacity while providing financial assistance for the re-equipment of the plant that remained. Firms were paid for scrapping some or all of their equipment, with a premium being paid to those firms that went out of business. Operatives were also compensated for lost jobs.

Under the Act, 48 per cent of all spinning spindles, 27 per cent of all doubling spindles, and 38 per cent of all looms in the industry were scrapped. Forty-four per cent of specialized spinning firms and 22 per cent of specialized weaving firms left the industry altogether. Integrated firms tended to stay in business, and hence the industry became more verticalized by the process of attrition. By 1963, 80 firms integrating spinning and weaving controlled 70 per cent of spinning capacity and 40 per cent of weaving capacity. But the Act itself had done nothing to promote vertical integration of production in the remaining firms, nor did it deal in any way with the highly fragmented marketing sector (Miles, 1968; pp. 50–7, 60; Fishwick and Cornu, 1975, pp. 27–9; Tippett, 1969, p. 161).

By providing a 25 per cent subsidy for re-equipment, the 1959 Act did result in some modernization of Lancashire's stock of machinery. Of the total machinery in place as of October 1965, 13 per cent of the spindles and 9 per cent of the looms had been purchased with re-equipment grants. Scrapping and re-equipment under the 1959 Act apparently resulted in significant productivity increases in both spinning and weaving compared with the low rates of productivity increase in the decades before (Miles, 1968, pp. 65, 85, 87). But the industry as a whole still retained managerial and marketing structures that impeded the introduction of mass production methods.

Corporate Intervention

From 1964, however, the structure of the British cotton industry underwent a dramatic transformation instigated by a vertically related, but heretofore external force—namely, the producers of so-called 'man-made' (that is, manufactured) fibres. Beginning in the mid-1930s, cellulose fibres, and in particular rayon, had been processed into yarn and cloth using cotton spinning and/or weaving equipment. In 1936 rayon had made up only 1 per cent of total spinning output, but by 1951 it comprised 10 per cent. Although the absolute amount of manufactured fibre used in spinning and weaving remained more or less constant from the early 1950s to the mid-1960s, it became an ever-increasing proportion of the total output of the Lancashire 'cotton' industry as the output of both cotton yarn and cloth steadily declined. In 1966 cotton entered into less than 60 per cent by weight of Lancashire weaving, with manufactured fibres (now both cellulosics and synthetics) making up the rest (Robson, 1957, p. 345; Miles, 1968, pp. 13, 85).

The dominant force in the transformation of the industry was Courtaulds, a corporation that had a virtual monopoly in the supply of rayon to the British market. With the development of synthetic fibres by chemical giants such as ICI in Britain and DuPont in the United States, however, the demand for rayon—Courtaulds' most important product—began to decline. During the 1950s Courtaulds attempted to diversify its products, but was not overly successful. After fighting off a takeover bid by ICI in 1962, the directors of Courtaulds staked the future of their company on the vertical integration and revitalization of their most important single market, the Lancashire 'cotton' industry.

The original Courtaulds plan, drawn up in 1962, was to gain control of five large firms in the spinning industry: the Lancashire Cotton Corporation, Fine Spinners and Doublers, English Sewing Cotton, Tootals, and Combined English Mills. These acquisitions were to serve as a basis for rationalizing the structure of the industry as well as for exerting pressure on the government to protect the home market and thereby provide incentives for the capital-intensive investments that were needed to make the cotton and manufactured fibres industry viable. By 1964 Courtaulds had acquired the Lancashire Cotton Corporation and Fine Spinners and Doublers (one-third of the industry's spinning capacity), and in 1968 it added Ashton Brothers (an old family firm that had long been among the most technologically progressive in the industry). Meanwhile it built completely new facilities to weave its fibres, finding nothing that was worth taking over in the traditional Lancashire weaving industry (Knight, 1974; Coleman, 1977, 1980, pp. 270–81; Miles, 1968, pp. 91–3; Fishwick and Cornu, 1975, pp. 37–9, 76, 78–9).

At the same time, ICI was securing its own manufactured fibres markets by financing acquisitions and plant modernization by other firms with an interest in the Lancashire industry. Viyella International, an outsider to the Lancashire cotton industry which acquired Combined English Mills, was backed by ICI, while the English Sewing Company (which acquired Tootals) was financed by both ICI and Courtaulds.

In 1968 the five-firm concentration ratio in the spinning of cotton and manufactured fibres was 50 per cent, up from 37 per cent in 1963 and 32 per cent in 1958. These firms controlled over one-third of weaving sales in 1968, more than double the market share of the top five firms a decade before. The five largest firms in 1968 were fully integrated concerns, Courtaulds being the most dominant by far, followed by the two other firms that had been financed by the corporate giants of the British chemical industry (Fishwick and Cornu, 1975, pp. 30, 37–9, 179–220; Reader, 1975; Channon, 1973, pp. 173–8; Textile Council, 1969, ch. 2; UK Board of Trade, 1970, p. 131/109; Cowling, 1980). Between 1963 and 1974, employment in the British 'cotton' industry was halved and output remained constant, while productivity rose by 86 per cent, or about 8 per cent per annum (Fishwick and Cornu, 1975, p. 21).

The strategy of forward integration pursued by Courtaulds and supported by ICI overcame the fragmented structure of industrial organization and the technological stagnation that had beset the industry since the nineteenth century. Given the poor performance of the British cotton industry since the 1920s, rationalization of the industrial structure was a necessary condition for successful manufacturing. But it has by no means proved a sufficient condition.

Quite apart from the ever-present danger of bureaucratic ossification, there is evidence that, originating as it did with raw material suppliers, the process of integration has not gone far enough downstream. A recent study of the industry blames its poor international competitiveness over the last decade on the failure to adopt an aggressive marketing strategy (Blackburn, 1982). Since 1974, moreover, the new giants in the textile industry have had to cope with a sagging national economy as well as an unstable international environment. High exchange rates and recessionary policies under Thatcher exacerbated these marketing problems.

Between 1979 and 1981 British output of cotton and manufactured fibre yarn fell by 44 per cent and cloth by 33 per cent, with the absolute decline continuing into 1983 (Blackburn, 1982, p. 42; British Textile Confederation, 1983). With Britain's corporate giants such as Courtaulds the victims of market forces that they could not control, it is ironic that government policy has been based on the simplistic ideology that a highly competitive, free market system is an engine of economic prosperity.

Understanding Organizational Change

Why did it take so long for the British cotton industry to be reorganized in response to the new international environment of the twentieth century? Why, for example, could the British Productivity Team on Cotton Weaving argue in 1950, apparently with good reason, that a strategy of vertical integration was 'out of the question'? In a competitive industry, what prevented the emergence of a number of fully integrated, technologically progressive cotton firms that could force the specialized manufacturing and marketing firms to adapt or get out? Why did the rationalization of the industry have to await the intervention of two giant chemical concerns in the 1960s?

If one reads the 'neoclassical' account of the performance of the British cotton industry, such issues are not even raised. Drawing explicitly on neoclassical methodology, Sandberg (1974) defines the successful enterprise as one that engages in the adaptive activity of optimizing subject to given constraints, not as one that engages in innovative activity to alter constraints. (For a general summary of the neoclassical position, see McCloskey and Sandberg, 1971.) Far from searching for the causes and exploring the consequences of institutional rigidities that inhibit innovative activity, Sandberg is content to demonstrate that British cotton managers of the early twentieth century continued to optimize subject to constraints imposed by industrial development of the nineteenth century (Sandberg, 1974, 1984; for an extended critique, see Lazonick, 1981a, 1983, 1984b).

From the perspective of the individual firm, managerial choices of technique and organizational form may have been optimal in the context of the rapid expansion of the British cotton industry prior to World War I. But the long-run impact of such choices was to render the industry incapable of competing on world markets. That is, the very nature of the prewar expansion of the British cotton industry contributed to its postwar decline. On the demand side, the industry became more reliant on markets in poorer areas of the world in which consumers wanted low-quality cotton goods, making the industry more vulnerable to cheap-labour competition and import substitution strategies during World War I and its aftermath. On the supply side, the continued reliance of the British industry on traditional technologies in conjunction with effort-augmenting strategies to cut costs represented the antithesis of modern, high-throughput production methods. The structures of industrial organization and industrial relations that characterized the industry not only encouraged this type of supply-side response but also became more entrenched in the prewar period, posing severe obstacles to reorganization of the industry after the war (Lazonick and Mass, 1984).

When applied to choice of technique in the British cotton industry, therefore, the predictive power of neoclassical theory may well be apt (although for empirical problems with Sandberg's analysis, see Lazonick, 1981a, 1984b; Lazonick and Mass, 1984). But the historical relevance of the theory is limited by the scope of its intellectual enterprise. With its analytical focus on managerial choices subject to *given* market and technical constraints, orthodox economic theory does not take us very far in understanding issues of institutional change. In his influential article on 'The Nature of the Firm' (published, significantly enough, in Britain in the late 1930s), Ronald Coase portrays the decision of whether or not to integrate as a matter of 'substitution at the margin', thus bringing the theory of vertical integration within the theoretical scope of neoclassical economics (Coase, 1937). Operating within factor-price constraints as set by market forces, the manager of the firm will decide to use the market to supply an input or to sell an output when the cost of doing so is less than the cost of superseding the market by organizing the particular vertically related process under his own management, and vice versa when the cost of doing so is more. As a proposition subordinating the choice of enterprise form to the decision to maximize profits subject to given constraints, Coase's theorem is a perfectly logical extension of neoclassical economic analysis. But as a fundamental proposition for analysing the nature and development of the modern capitalist enterprise, Coase's approach is highly misleading, for three basic reasons.

First, if it is to reap the benefits of mass production, the modern enterprise cannot shift its mode of operation with every change in relative factor prices.

Rather, it must engage in long-term investment planning which includes a firm commitment of capital to producing certain products by certain inter-related technical processes. Indeed, in the post-World War II Lancashire cotton industry, we find spinning and weaving, or weaving and marketing, firms combining and then separating for the sake of short-term supply and demand advantages without in the least altering their organizational or technical methods of production. Such actions constituted precisely Coasian managerial decision-making. But, ironically, these actions *exemplified the failure to develop the modern corporate enterprise*. In 1962 the Managing Director of Ashton Brothers explained the essence of such 'opportunistic' activity:

In 1946, 22.5% of installed looms were owned by combined operations—I have avoided the term 'verticals'. By 1959 this figure had risen to 33%. . . . Most of the 'combined operations' were not vertical in the strictest sense. The vertical operation converts fibre into the final fabric, merchandising the goods through appropriate trade channels. The three horizontal tiers—spinning, weaving and finishing—are, of course, included, as are yarn processing and stitching operations if appropriate. The mere ownership of facilities in all sections does not necessarily satisfy this definition. Financial control is not integration. Unless fused commercially, adminstratively and technically such units can be mutually inhibiting, and the combined activities weaker than the horizontal constituents. The history of post-war organizational changes confirms this. In the late 1940s, weavers frequently acquired converting facilities to obtain a more secure marketing basis; convertors acquired weaving facilities to obtain assured supplies. These associations were frequently short-lived. Of 264 weaving units closed down in the four years before the 1959 Act, 109 were also convertors. A further 62 were members of groups which covered converting.

Under the Yarn Spinners' Association, and with fixed prices, spinners tended to integrate forward to secure weaving facilities and so obtain indirect yarn business, being content to weave at cost and obtain the constituent yarn profit. Today, the reverse is occurring, and we have supposedly-vertical organizations closing spinning units because it is claimed either that yarn can be imported cheaper than it can be spun in the UK or that capital can be conserved. One essential requirement for vertical integration is stability. This is incompatible with such an opportunist approach to organization. (Ormerod, 1963, pp. 10–11; See also US Productivity Team, 1952, p. 6; Miles, 1968, p. 56; Furness, 1958, pp. 214–17.)

In short, the manager who integrates and disintegrates operations according to the ebb and flow of the market situation does so in lieu of the long-term planning of the organizationally interconnected and technically interrelated production and distribution processes that characterize the modern corporation.

Second, the Coasian approach ignores the role of concentrated product market power in the development of the modern enterprise. No firm will produce a product unless it has a reasonable chance of selling it. And no firm will *mass*-produce a product unless it has reasonable prospects of mass sales. Moreover, since mass production requires long-term planning, reasonable sales prospects must be long-term as well. It is for this reason that the development of the firm's ability to mass-distribute is a necessary condition for the development of its incentive to mass-produce. Hence the firm's control over markets must precede, or at least emerge simultaneously with, the development of large-scale, standardized production (Chandler, 1977, Parts II–IV).

In this sense, the development of the British textile industries in the sixteenth to eighteenth centuries was in large measure induced by the development of national supremacy over world markets. In the eighteenth and nineteenth centuries, national market power created the opportunities for numerous merchants to enter the cotton industry, thus creating for the British industry as a whole a structure of mass distribution characterized by numerous competitors and specialization along product lines. The fragmented structure of marketing worked admirably in the decades prior to World War I, during which world trade was expanding, the Japanese economy was still in the process of commercial development, and British control over India—by far its largest cotton goods market—remained supreme.

But when challenged during and after World War I, Lancashire merchants proved incapable of unified and concerted response. Burnett-Hurst describes how, when World War I broke out, disrupting Lancashire production and distribution facilities,

[the two largest] Japanese mercantile houses . . . opened branches in Bombay and a large number of agencies and subagencies throughout India. These firms also acquired and operated ginneries and presses. The Yokahama Specie Bank and other Japanese banks extended the fullest facilities for financing the trade with India, while Japanese shipping lines established regular and direct services between India and Japan. There is no doubt that the immediate success achieved by Japan in the Indian market was due largely to the rapidity with which she secured her position by the effective co-operation of her various commercial interests. (Burnett-Hurst, 1932, pp. 399–400.)

Between 1914 and 1932 Britain's share of Indian piece-good imports declined from 97 to 50 per cent while Japan's share rose from 0.1 to 45 per cent. In the latter year the British Trade Commissioner in India warned:

It should be realized that unless steps are taken very quickly to re-establish the competitive power of United Kingdom goods we shall lose the valuable cooperation of many efficient distributing organizations upon which we have relied for more than half a century. Meanwhile Manchester merchants appear to be losing that close touch with the Indian situation which has been so valuable in the past. Travellers no longer visit India, correspondence falls off in these difficult times, and, to an observer on the spot, it sometimes appears as if the greatest single export trade in the world is gradually being allowed to 'peter out', no active measures being taken to deal with the situation. (Quoted in Burnett-Hurst, 1932, p. 422.)

In 1929 one united attempt—the Eastern Textile Association Ltd.—actually had been made to mass-distribute in China, but its quick failure was 'the death-knell of all attempts to unite in promoting new developments from the selling angle' (Streat, 1958, p. 14; also Robson, 1957, pp. 215–16; Daniels and Campion, 1935, p. 342). Instead there remained over a thousand merchants in the Lancashire export trade and many hundreds more in the home trade from the 1920s to the 1950s (Miles, 1968, p. 68; Alfred, 1965–6, p. 9). A precondition for any significant structural and technical reorganization of production was a concentrated marketing sector, which would create the incentive for producers to mass-produce and perhaps integrate forwards, and could itself integrate backwards. Such a reorganization of the cotton industry along corporate lines had taken place in the United States by the 1950s, bringing to dominance a small number of giant, fully integrated cotton corporations (Barkin, 1949; Markham, 1950; Kessler, 1951; Crook, 1951; US House of Representatives, 1955; Simpson, 1966, ch. 6; Alfred, 1965–6, p. 21; Knight, 1974, p. 46). Neither the development of American enterprises such as Burlington Industries and J. P. Stevens nor the massive forward integration by Courtaulds in Britain in the 1960s can be understood as 'substitution at the margin' by optimizing managers taking market forces as given. Rather, such structural change was the result of entrepreneurial strategies to attain or maintain concentrated market power. Up to the 1960s at least, such power was lacking in Lancashire precisely because 'perfect' competition, and the dominance of marginal decision-making by spinning, weaving, and marketing managers to which it gave rise, made the necessary co-ordination impossible.

Third, Coase's approach ignores the problem of *managerial structure*, the implicit assumption being that it does not change qualitatively with changes in vertical or horizontal organization but only perhaps quantitatively in terms of the number of managers who are incorporated into the existing mode of management. As Chandler has shown, the key to the successful development and stability of the large corporation in the United States has been the development of new hierarchical structures of managerial control (Chandler, 1962, 1977, Part V). The development of hierarchical managerial structures in the transformation of a number of smaller firms into a large corporate entity entails the coming to power of some managers and the loss of power of others as the structure of decision-making and authority is qualitatively altered.

Horizontal amalgamation in itself does not necessarily mean, however, an end to managerial autonomy for the heads of the participating firms. The case of the Lancashire Cotton Corporation, in which local mill managers refused to abide by, and eventually overturned, centralized control, is a case in point. The pattern is also true of British industry in general. The development of hierarchical managerial structures did not follow large-scale amalgamations, primarily because the directors of the constituent firms insisted on maintaining family control and substantial decision-making autonomy even within the new amalgamated setting (Chandler, 1980; Hannah, 1974, pp. 252–70; Mathias, 1975).

The implications of the failure to develop co-ordinated control of an amalgamation are well illustrated by the case of Combined English Mills (CEM), a combination of fourteen largely autonomous spinning mills that had been formed in the late 1920s in an attempt to support yarn prices, and that produced 5 per cent of the total yarn output of the British cotton industry in the early 1960s. CEM had taken advantage of re-equipment subsidies under the 1959 Act, and by the end of 1963 was producing all its output on modern machinery. Even though output per spindle rose by 38 per cent and labour productivity by 25 per cent between 1960 and 1964, CEM was experiencing losses.

In 1964 the amalgamation was taken over by Viyella International, which then proceeded to rationalize CEM's spinning operations and integrate them with other textile activities. Within two years under corporate management, half the mills had been closed, and the remaining mills were producing for 120 relatively large customers rather than for the 735 relatively small customers that had previously been serviced. As a result, inventories were dramatically reduced, output per customer was increased by about 550 per cent, output per spindle rose by 60 per cent, while labour productivity rose by 50 per cent. The profitability of CEM was restored (Miles, 1968, pp. 22–3, 91).

As a general rule, the directors of family firms in the British cotton industry insisted on retaining managerial control over their enterprises, even though handing over the reins of power to a centralized source might have proved to be in their long-term interests as shareholders. Raymond Streat, a prominent figure in Lancashire cotton affairs in the interwar years, recalled that '[e]ven some spinners who joined passionately in the debates [on amalgamation in the 1920s and 1930s] never really contemplated that their own mill should be amalgamated though they may scarcely have realized themselves that they were so built that their sole and personal authority was something they would never part with voluntarily' (Streat, 1958, p. 7). The prolonged persistence of excess capacity in the industry, which absorbed all the attention of government programmes from the 1930s into the 1960s, was due in part at least to the persistence of family firms. Very much in the tradition of the handloom weavers a century before, the owners of these firms hung on to their businesses despite extremely low profits in order to maintain their relatively independent status (Fabian Research Group, 1945, p. 13n.). As Miles argues, higher prices for scrapped machinery under the 1959 Cotton Industry Act would not have enticed more firms to leave the industry: 'the main barrier to movement has been and still is the lack of "mobile" management skills. For the owners of most small firms the choice lay between retirement and continuing in the same business, however small its return' (Miles, 1968, p. 74).

By the same token, owner–managers who did remain in business had little interest or ability to participate in vertical integration. The Lancashire spinner, for example, typically knew nothing about weaving, let alone marketing (Helm, 1900–1, p. 57; Whittam, 1907, p. 13; *Journal of the British Association of Managers of Textile Works*, 1911–12, pp. 127–36; Bolton, 1920, p. 39; *Journal of the National Association of Textile Works Managers' Associations*, 1925–6, pp. 94–6; Streat, 1958, p. 3). He was a specialist in his trade with particular expertise in the buying of cotton. As one spinning manager opposed to combination argued in the early 1930s, 'every practical cotton spinner, who understands spinning thoroughly, but has only a slight working knowledge of weaving, is anti-vertical combine' (*Journal of the National Association of Textile Works Managers' Associations*, 1932–3, p. 9).

The vast majority of businessmen in the British cotton industry had neither the incentive to participate nor the ability to lead in the internal restructuring of their industry. The competitive and specialized organization of the industry had bred managers with specialized skills and individualistic attitudes who were ill-suited for involvement in a transition from competitive to corporate capitalism. Indeed, by their very presence in the industry they obstructed such a transition.

Unable to reorganize within their own ranks, employers in the British cotton industry were hardly in a position to confront the well-organized unions over issues of work organization and pay. As we have seen, the wage lists and modes of work organization that remained prevalent well into the post-World War II period were themselves the products of the highly competitive conditions of the last half of the nineteenth century, when the fragmented employers had been willing to grant workers substantial shopfloor control and earnings stability in exchange for labour peace and uninterrupted production. In the twentieth century, the power of worker organization and the underdevelopment of managerial structure went hand in hand. As workers won the right to co-ordinate production activities, British cotton employers lost the incentive to develop modern managerial skills. To be sure, British cotton managers developed considerable skill in adapting traditional technologies to impenetrable industrial relations constraints. But lacking the power to reorganize themselves and confront the workers, they gained little experience in the co-ordination and utilization of new mass production methods.

The historical evolution of the British cotton industry demonstrates, therefore, that the modern capitalist corporation does not automatically or even logically evolve out of competitive market conditions. In the British cotton industry, corporate organization failed to emerge on any significant scale until the 1960s precisely because competitive market forces had been so deeply entrenched. In the labour market, moreover, where the operation of supply and demand was largely superseded, it was workers rather than managers who held the balance of power. The result of this institutional legacy was a prolonged technological backwardness and industrial decline.

Bibliography

Alfred, A. M. (1965–6). 'U. K. Textiles—A Growth Industry'. *Transactions of the Manchester Statistical Society*.

Barkin, Solomon (1949). 'The Regional Significance of the Integration Movement in the Southern Textile Industry'. *Southern Economic Journal*, 15(4), April.

Bean, Percy, and S. Scarisbrick (1921). *The Chemistry and Practice of Sizing* (10th edn). Manchester: Hutton, Hartley.

Bennett, G. (1933). 'The Present Position of the Cotton Industry in Great Britain'. MA thesis, University of Manchester.

Blackburn, R. (1982). 'The Vanishing UK Cotton Industry'. *National Westminster Bank Review*, November.

Bolton and District Managers and Over-lookers Association (1920). *Report of the Delegates on American Tour*. Bolton.

Bowker, B. (1928). *Lancashire under the Hammer*. London: Hogarth.

British Textile Confederation (1983). *Review of 1982–83 and Annual Report for 1982*. London.

Brooks, C. (1898). *Cotton*. New York: Spon & Chamberlain.

Burnett-Hurst, A. (1932). 'Lancashire and the Indian Market'. *Journal of the Royal Statistical Society*, 95, Part III.

Carter, G. (1913). *The Tendency Towards Industrial Combination*. London: Constable.

Chandler, Alfred D. Jr. (1962). *Strategy and Structure*. Cambridge, Mass.: MIT Press.

Chandler, Alfred D. Jr. (1977). *The Visible Hand*. Cambridge, Mass.: Harvard University Press.

Chandler, Alfred D. Jr. (1980). 'The Growth of the Transnational Industrial Firm in the United States and the United Kingdom: A Comparative Analysis'. *Economic History Review*, 2nd ser., 33, August.

Channon, D. (1973). *The Strategy and Structure of British Enterprise*. Boston: Harvard Graduate School of Business Administration.

Clay, Henry (1929a). *The Problem of Industrial Relations*. London: Macmillan.

Clay, Henry (1929b). *The Post-War Unemployment Problem*. London: Macmillan.

Clay, Henry (1931). *Report on the Position of the English Cotton Industry*. Confidential report for Securities Management Trust, Ltd, 20 October.

Clegg, H., A. Fox, and A. Thompson (1964). *A History of British Trade Unions Since 1889*. Oxford: Clarendon Press.

Coase, Ronald (1937). 'The Nature of the Firm'. *Economica*, n. s., 4, November.

Coleman, D. C. (1977). 'Courtaulds and the Beginning of Rayon'. In B. Supple (ed.), *Essays in British Business History*. Oxford: Clarendon Press.

Coleman, D. C. (1980). *Courtaulds: An Economic and Social History*, Volume III. Oxford: Clarendon Press.

Committee on Industry and Trade (1928). *Survey of the Textile Industries*. London: HMSO.

Committee on Industry and Trade (1929). *Final Report*. London: HMSO.

Copeland, M. T. (1912). *The Cotton Manufacturing Industry of the United States*. Cambridge, Mass.: Harvard University Press.

Cotton Factory Times (CFT), various issues.

Cowling, K. (1980). *Mergers and Economic Performance*. Cambridge University Press.

Crook, W. (1951). 'Corporate Concentration in the Textile Industry'. In *Textiles—A Dynamic Industry*, Colgate University Textile Study Project.

Daniels, G. W., and H. Campion (1935). 'The Cotton Industry and Trade'. In British Association, *Britain in Depression*. London: Pitman.

Daniels, G. W., and John Jewkes (1928). 'The Post-War Depression in the Cotton Industry'. *Journal of the Royal Statistical Society*, 91.

Ellinger, B., and H. Ellinger (1930). 'Japanese Competition in the Cotton Trade'. *Journal of the Royal Statistical Society*, 93, Part II.

Fabian Research Group (1945). *Cotton—A Working Policy*. London: Gollancz.

Farnie, D. A. (1979). *The English Cotton Industry and the World Market, 1815–1896*. Oxford: Clarendon Press.

Federation of Master Cotton Spinners' Associations (FMCSA) (1927). *State of Trade: Sub-Committee's Report and Recommendations*. Manchester: Royal Exchange, 2 December.

Federation of Master Cotton Spinners' Associations (FMCSA) (1935). *Cotton Spinning Industry Bill (1935): The Industry's Case for the Bill*. Manchester: Royal Exchange.

Federation of Master Cotton Spinners' Associations (FMCSA) (1951). *Handbook of Agreements on Wages and Conditions*. Manchester: Royal Exchange, November.

Fishwick, F., and R. Cornu (1975). *A Study of the Evolution of Concentration in the United Kingdom Textile Industry*. Luxemburg: Commission of European Communities.

Fitzgerald, P. (1927). *Industrial Combination in England*. London: Pitman.

Fowler, Alan, and Lesley Fowler (1984). *The History of the Nelson Weavers Association*. Nelson: Burnley, Nelson, Rossendale & District Textile Workers' Union.

Frankel, M. (1957). *British and American Manufacturing Productivity*. University of Illinois Bulletin Series no. 81.

Furness, G. W. (1958). 'The Cotton and Rayon Textile Industry'. In D. Burn (ed.), *The Structure of British Industry*. Cambridge University Press.

Gray, E. M. (1937). *The Weaver's Wage*. Manchester University Press.

Great Britain, Ministry of Labour and National Service (1945). *The Cotton Spinning Industry*. London: HMSO.

Great Britain, Ministry of Labour and National Service (1946). *The Cotton Spinning Industry*. London: HMSO.

Great Britain, Ministry of Production (1944). *Report of the Cotton Textile Mission to the USA*. London: HMSO.

Hannah, Leslie (1974). 'Managerial Innovation and the Rise of the Large-scale Company in Interwar Britain'. *Economic History Review*, 27(2), May.

Hannah, Leslie (1976). *The Rise of the Corporate Economy: The British Experience*. Baltimore: Johns Hopkins University Press.

Helm, E. (1900–1). 'The Middleman in Commerce'. *Transactions of the Manchester Statistical Society*.

Hopwood, E. (1969). *The Lancashire Weavers' Story*. Manchester: Amalgamated Weavers' Association.

Jewkes, John (1930). 'The Localisation of the Cotton Industry'. *Economic History*, 2(5), January.

Jewkes, John (1946). 'Is British Industry Inefficient?' *Manchester School*, 14, January.

Jewkes, John, and Sylvia Jewkes (1966). 'A Hundred Years of Change in the Structure of the Cotton Industry'. *Journal of Law and Economics*, 9, October.

Jones, G. T. (1933). *Increasing Return*. Cambridge University Press.

Jones, O. (1924). 'The Agitation for the Control of the Lancashire Cotton Industry'. *Harvard Business Review*, 2, July.

Journal of the British Association of Managers of Textile Works (1911–12). 'Problems between spinners and manufacturers' (Lancashire Section), IV.

Journal of the National Association of Textile Works Managers' Associations (1925–6). 'The most essential improvement required in the cotton trade', V.

Journal of the National Association of Textile Works Managers' Associations (1932–3). 'Combinations in the cotton trade', XII.

Kessler, W. (1951). 'Chapters in Business History'. In *Textiles—A Dynamic Industry*, Colgate University Textile Study Project.

Keynes, J. M. (1981). 'Industrial Reorganisation: Cotton'. In D. Moggridge (ed.), *The Collected Writings of John Maynard Keynes*, Volume 19, Part II, 578–637. Cambridge University Press.

Kirby, M. W. (1974). 'The Lancashire Cotton Industry in the Inter-War Years: A Study in Organizational Change'. *Business History*, 26, July.

Knight, Arthur (1974). *Private Enterprise and Public Intervention: The Courtaulds Experience*. London: Allen & Unwin.

Labour Research Department (1928). *The Attack on the Cotton Workers*. Labour White Paper no. 39, April.

Lazonick, William (1979). 'Industrial Relations and Technical Change: The Case of the Self-Acting Mule'. *Cambridge Journal of Economics*, 3(3), September.

Lazonick, William (1981a). 'Factor Costs and the Diffusion of Ring Spinning in Britain prior to World War I'. *Quarterly Journal of Economics*, 96(1), February.

Lazonick, William (1981b). 'Competition, Specialization, and Industrial Decline'. *Journal of Economic History*, 41(1), March.

Lazonick, William (1981c). 'Production Relations, Labor Productivity, and Choice of Technique: British and US Cotton Spinning'. *Journal of Economic History*, 41(3), September.

Lazonick, William (1983). 'Industrial Organization and Technological Change: The Decline of the British Cotton Industry'. *Business History Review*, 57(2), Summer.

Lazonick, William (1984a). 'Work Effort, Pay, and Productivity: Theoretical Implications of Some Historical Research'. Photocopy, Harvard University.

Lazonick, William (1984b). 'Rings and Mules in Britain: Reply'. *Quarterly Journal of Economics*, 99(2), May.

Lazonick, William (1985). 'Organization, Throughput, and Competitive Advantage'. Photocopy, Harvard University.

Lazonick, William, and William Mass (1984). 'The Performance of the British Cotton Industry, 1870–1913'. *Research in Economic History*, 9, Spring.

Lucas, A. (1933). 'The Bankers' Industrial Development Company'. *Harvard Business Review*, 11, April.

Lucas, A. (1937). *Industrial Reconstruction and the Control of Competition: The British Experiments*, London: Longmans, Green.

Macara, Charles (1923). *The New Industrial Era* (2nd edn). Manchester: Sherratt & Hughes.

Macgregor, D., J. Ryan, *et al.* (1930). 'Problems of Rationalisation: A Discussion'. *Economic Journal*, 40, September.

Macrosty, H. W. (1907). *The Trust Movement in British Industry*. London: Longmans, Green.

Markham, Jesse (1950). 'Integration in the Textile Industry'. *Harvard Business Review*, 28(1).

Marshall, Alfred (1919). *Industry and Trade*. London: Macmillan.

Mass, William (1984). 'Technological Change and Industrial Relations: the Diffusion of Automatic Weaving in Britain and the United States'. PhD thesis, Boston College.

Mathias, Peter (1975). 'Conflicts of Function in the Rise of Big Business: The British Experience'. In H. Williamson (ed.), *Evolution of International Management Structures*. Newark: University of Delaware Press.

McCloskey, Donald, and Lars Sandberg (1971). 'From Damnation to Redemption: Judgments on the Late Victorian Entrepreneur'. *Explorations in Economic History*, 2nd ser., 9, Fall.

Miles, Caroline (1968). *Lancashire Textiles: A Case Study of Industrial Change*. Cambridge University Press.

Miles, Caroline (1976). 'Protection of the British Cotton Industry'. In W. Corden and G. Fels (eds.), *Public Assistance to Industry*. Boulder, Colo.: Westview.

Mills, W. (1917). *Sir Charles W. Macara, Bart*. Manchester: Sherratt & Hughes.

Mitchell, B. R. (1962). *Abstract of British Historical Statistics*. Cambridge University Press.

Morton, W., and H. Greg (1926). 'The Cotton Textile Industry in the USA'. *Journal of the Textile Institute*, 17, October.

Muir, A. (1964). *The Kenyon Tradition*. Cambridge: Heffer.

Nisbet, H. (1912). *Theory of Sizing*. Manchester: Emmot.

Oldham Operative Cotton Spinners' Provincial Association (1912). *Monthly Report*. Oldham, September.

Ormerod, A. (1963). 'The Prospects of the British Cotton Industry'. *Yorkshire Bulletin of Economic and Social Research*, 15, May.

Pearse, A. (1928–9). 'Efforts to Rationalize the Cotton Industry of the USA'. *Transactions of the Manchester Statistical Society*.

Pennington, J. (1926–7). 'Competition and Specialisation in the Cotton Trade'. *Journal of the National Federation of Textile Works Managers' Associations*, 6.

Political and Economic Planning (PEP), Industries Group (1934). *Report on the British Cotton Industry*. London: PEP.

Pollard, Sidney (1969). *The Development of the British Economy 1914–1967* (2nd edn). London: Edward Arnold.

Porter, J. (1967). 'Industrial Peace in the Cotton Trade, 1875–1913'. *Yorkshire Bulletin of Economic and Social Research*, 19(1), May.

Productivity Team Report (1950a). *Cotton Spinning*. London: Anglo-American Council on Productivity.

Productivity Team Report (1950b). *Cotton Weaving*. London: Anglo-American Council on Productivity.

Reader, W. (1975). *Imperial Chemical Industries*, Volume II. London: Oxford University Press.

Robson, R. (1950). 'Structure of the Cotton Industry: A Study in Specialization and Integration'. PhD thesis, University of London.

Robson, R. (1957). *The Cotton Industry in Britain*. London: Macmillan.

Rostas, L. (1945). 'Productivity of Labour in the Cotton Industry'. *Economic Journal*, 55, June–September.

Ryan, John (1928–9). 'Combination in the Cotton Trade'. *Journal of the National Federation of Textile Works Managers' Associations*, 8.

Sandberg, Lars (1974). *Lancashire in Decline*. Columbus: Ohio State University Press.

Sandberg, Lars (1984). 'The Remembrance of Things Past: Rings and Mules Revisited'. *Quarterly Journal of Economics*, 99(2), May.

Shaw, D. (1950). 'Productivity in the Cotton Spinning Industry'. *Manchester School*, 18(1), January.

Simpson, W. (1966). *Some Aspects of America's Textile Industry*. Columbia: University of South Carolina Press.

Smith, Roland (1954). 'A History of the Lancashire Cotton Industry between the Years 1873 and 1896. PhD thesis, University of Birmingham.

Streat, R. (1958). 'The Cotton Industry in Contraction: Problems and Policies in the Inter-War Years'. *District Bank Review*, 127, September.

Taggart, W. (1923). *Cotton Mill Management*. London: Macmillan.

Textile Council (1969). *Cotton and Allied Textiles*, Volume I. Manchester: Textile Council.

Tippett, L. (1969). *A Portrait of the Lancashire Textile Industry*. London: Oxford University Press.

United Kingdom Board of Trade (1970). *Census of Production*, Summary Tables. London: HMSO.

United States House of Representatives, Committee of the Judiciary (1955). *The Merger Movement in the Textile Industry*. Washington: GPO.

United States Productivity Team (1950). *The British Cotton Industry*. London: Anglo-American Council on Productivity.

United Textile Factory Workers Association (UTFWA) (1923). *Inquiry into the Cotton Industry*. Blackburn: UTFWA.

United Textile Factory Workers Association (UTFWA) (1928). 'Memorandum on the Cotton Industry'. Prepared by the Labour Research Department, January.

United Textile Factory Workers Association (UTFWA) (1943). *Report of the Legislative Council on Ways and Means of Improving the Economic Stability of the Cotton Textile Industry*. Ashton: Cotton Factory Times.

United Textile Factory Workers Association (UTFWA) (1957). *Plan for Cotton*, Ashton: Cotton Factory Times.

Utley, Freda (1931). *Lancashire and the Far East*. London: Allen & Unwin.

Vibert, F. (1966). 'Problems in the Cotton Industry'. *Oxford Economic Papers*, n.s., 18.

Vitkovich, B. (1955). 'The UK Cotton Industry'. *Journal of Industrial Economics*, 3, July.

White, Joseph (1978). *The Limits of Trade Union Militancy: The Lancashire Textile Workers, 1910–1914*. Westport, Conn.: Greenwood.

Whittam, William (1907). *Report on England's Cotton Industry*. Washington: GPO.

Wiggins, M. (1939). 'The Cotton Industry'. In F. Gannett and B. Catherwood (eds), *Industrial and Labour Relations in Great Britain*. London: King.

Wisselink, J. (1930). 'The Present Condition of the English Cotton Industry'. *Harvard Business Review*, 8, January.

Wood, G. H. (1910). *The History of Wages in the Cotton Trade during the Past Hundred Years*. Manchester: Sherratt and Hughes.

The Steel Industry before World War I

Bernard Elbaum*
Boston University

When mass production of steel began, Britain assumed a commanding technological and competitive lead. In 1870 Britain's share of world tonnage output was 50 per cent for pig iron, 37 per cent for wrought iron, and 43 per cent for steel. Britain imported just 8 per cent of home consumption of wrought iron and steel, and so dominated international markets that exports took 70 per cent of national output and constituted over three-quarters of total world exports (Burnham and Hoskins, 1943, pp. 272–8).

By 1913 Britain had suffered major competitive reverses. The United States now produced 40 per cent, and Britain just 10 per cent, of world output of pig iron and steel. More tellingly, British imports comprised 29 per cent of home consumption of wrought iron and steel, and exports were down to 44 per cent of national output and less than one-third of world exports. Germany, Britain's chief competitor, was the world's largest steel exporter, and after the United States the world's largest steel producer (Burnham and Hoskins, 1943, pp. 272–8). The British steel industry had surrendered world leadership and entered a spiral of competitive decline from which it has never fully recovered. The US and German industries, on the other hand, had grown from infancy to an international prominence that they maintained, to lesser degree, a half-century later.

The Historiography of Steel Industry Decline

A long line of economic historians has blamed the failings of the British steel industry on numerous and diverse factors (or sets of factors acting in combination). These factors include an alleged British inferiority in entrepreneurship, management, or education and technical training; or alleged handicaps posed by comparatively slow market demand expansion, natural resource endowments, imperfections of competition, foreign dumping, the interrelatedness of required redevelopment investments, trade union impact, capital market institutions, and government trade and industrial policies. The performance of the British steel industry before World War I has also been defended.

No other industry has figured so prominently within wider debate over British economic performance, or served as the case in point of so many competing perspectives. Despite this diversity of viewpoints, historiographic

I would like to acknowledge my debts to Frank Wilkinson and Peter Temin, who generously lent me their time to discuss the material covered by this paper. Donald McCloskey was also kind enough to furnish me with the notes and materials compiled during his own research.

debate had, until recently, come to a common agreement that the steel industry's problems were closely related to its structure. At present, however, debate has reached an impasse in which there is little or no collective clarity of judgement concerning the causes of British competitive decline in iron and steel manufacture.

The Route to Interpretative Impasse

Debate arrived at its present impasse by a circular route. In Britain at the turn of the century, competitive reverses in steel helped provoke national economic controversy over tariff reform. The Tariff Commission Report of 1904 concluded that steel industry setbacks were due to Britain's free trade policy and the anti-competitive organization and dumping practices of foreign industries, which destabilized prices and market shares and discouraged British investment in large-scale plant and equipment embodying up-to-date technology. Backed by much of steel industry opinion, the Tariff Commission advocated protectionism.

Free trade was defended by such notable turn-of-the-century economists as Alfred Marshall and A. C. Pigou, who contended that the steel industry's relative competitive decline was an inevitable result of industrialization abroad and the loss of Britain's comparative advantage in natural resource endowments. In the eyes of the leading defenders of economic orthodoxy, British markets were more than adequate to afford scope for plant-level economies of scale, even amidst sporadic dumping (Marshall, 1903; Pigou, 1906; Burn, 1961a, p. 311).

By the 1920s a consensus was established among observers that the British steel industry suffered from basic problems of productive structure. Before a government committee that convened in 1916 to consider prospects and appropriate public policies for the postwar industry, iron and steel manufacturers testified that British firms had failed to avail themselves of the full benefits of mass production, a failure evidenced by relatively low output per plant. Attainment of productive economies was hampered by Britain's fragmented industrial organization, which contrasted unfavourably with the much more concentrated organization of the United States or Germany (Great Britain Board of Trade, 1918).

Persuaded by the testimony of the steel manufacturers, Alfred Marshall forsook his own earlier analysis, and attributed the decline of the British industry to its excessive fragmentation and short and variegated production runs (Marshall, 1923, pp. 557–8). Further confirmation of these conclusions came from interwar reports of various consultants and commissions concerned with industry rationalization, and from the production and cost data which they gathered (see pp. 59–60 below).

The same basic conclusions were in turn adopted from the 1930s through the 1960s by such traditional historical treatments as those of Burn (1961a),

Burnham and Hoskins (1943), Landes (1970), and Aldcroft (1964). Structural fragmentation was seen by these historians not as the root cause of industry decline, but as its most debilitating symptom, one that retarded technological progress and relocation near low-cost ore fields, perpetuated itself by fostering a patchwork pattern of investment, and had to be alleviated if competitiveness were to be regained. With this much agreed, debate was joined chiefly over whether structural rigidity and the resulting decline in competitiveness were at bottom due to entrepreneurial failure or other factors.

In recent-day debate, however, economic historians have scarcely mentioned industrial structure. It has been denied that the British iron and steel industry suffered before World War I from any deficiencies in productivity performance, entrepreneurship, or ore supply costs. The degree of consensus that previously prevailed has come undone, as new economic historians have analysed the steel industry under much the same orthodox theoretical assumptions as Marshall and Pigou employed at the turn of the century.

Steel Industry Structure and Performance

Though by now worthy of study in its own right, the historiography of the British iron and steel industry is beyond the scope of this paper. The argument presented below, however, suggests that the new economic historians, like Marshall and Pigou before them, have been misled by their adherence to a theoretical framework that is static in conception and views free competition as a guarantor of economic well-being. Within this theoretical framework, it has proved difficult to comprehend the developmental problems of an industry like iron and steel, where economies of scale and vertical integration were of major and increasing importance, and where Britain, with the most atomistic structure of the chief competing nations, ended up with the weakest competitive position.

The argument which follows is that British competitive decline in iron and steel derived from interactive lines of causation perceived but inadequately comprehended from traditional viewpoints of the industry. In particular, traditional historians lacked—and the following account seeks to provide—a firm grasp of the origins, efficiency ramifications, and inertial momentum of steel industry structural fragmentation, and of the relative weight of the various factors affecting industry structure and performance. These issues are taken up in turn below. The conclusion considers, in addition, what corrective policy measures might have stemmed Britain's decline in iron and steel manufacture.

I shall argue, in brief, that the British steel industry declined in competitiveness because its firms lagged behind foreign rivals in adoption of new mass production methods. In general, individual firms find it profitable to introduce mass production methods only when their prospective market outlets are sufficiently great and secure. British iron and steel firms were more constrained than their foreign rivals from making large-scale investments by virtue of Britain's fragmented and rigid industrial structure, and a relatively slow aggregate rate of market demand expansion, amidst domestic market maturity and foreign tariff barriers. As a consequence, the British iron and steel industry experienced adverse international competitive dynamics. Reinforcing these competitive dynamics were a number of additional, related factors, among which the most significant were the wage structure established in Britain under collective bargaining and differential costs of iron ore acquisition.

As is evidenced by their testimony before government commissions, many British industrialists were aware of the new mass production methods and of the advantages they afforded. That British firms none the less lagged behind their competitors was less the result of entrepreneurial failure—as the term is conventionally understood—than of the constraints on individual entrepreneurial action posed by market conditions and a rigid institutional environment.

The Origins of Structural Divergence

At the middle of the nineteenth century the British iron industry was similar in structure to that of the United States. Numerous firms were engaged in the making and shaping of wrought iron. Only the largest of these firms, the rail manufacturers, were integrated backwards with pig iron produciton, a process that required a comparatively large investment in capital equipment. The chief difference between the British and US industries was in product composition. Britain had the world's predominant shipbuilding industry, and a major product of British wrought iron manufacture was ship-plate. Britain also dominated world markets for the high-quality products of galvanized sheet and tinplate.

In the United States, industry structure was radically transformed by the introduction of Bessemer steel-making, used chiefly, at first, in the production of rails. Adoption of the Bessemer process suddenly imposed requirements of large-scale plant, high temperatures, and strict chemical controls. Compared with wrought iron manufacture, output per Bessemer converter was enormous, and operative Bessemer plants were correspondingly few in number. At a critical stage of US industry development, the Bessemer revolution led to integration with pig iron manufacture and provided an impetus towards industrial concentration (Temin, 1964).

Previous literature has generally neglected the impact of the Bessemer revolution on the structure of the British industry, which initially was affected similarly. Although scales of converter operations were from the first much greater in the United States than in Britain, this was of little consequence for industrial concentration as it was offset by the British having roughly twice as many converters per plant. At proximate years in the 1880s the British and US steel industries had roughly comparable structures of loose oligopoly (American Iron and Steel Association, 1887; Great Britain, 1881).

The two industries diverged sharply in structure only as a result of subsequent developments. In the United States, the initial impetus towards concentration provided by the Bessemer process was carried along much further by forces of oligopolistic competition. By contrast, the British industry was flooded by numerous new entrants employing the open-hearth steel-making process in small-scale plants. While Bessemer steel-making remained loosely oligopolistic, the overall British concentration rate declined sharply and only gradually regained its former level over the next half-century (Elbaum, 1982, p. 272; Tolliday, 1978, p. 37a).

This divergence in British and US structure reflected differences in the development of market demand. These differences—in both the rate of growth of demand and the product composition—grew out of Britain's relative economic maturity as well as changes in the international trading environment. In brief, industrial organization became decentralized in Britain because the demand for British Bessemer steel peaked in the 1880s, while demand for open-hearth steel expanded most rapidly between 1880 and 1900. The shift in emphasis from Bessemer to open-hearth production, therefore, took place in Britain *before* technological innovations increased the benefits of integrated, large-scale open-hearth operations.

Initially the minimum efficient scale of open-hearth plant was a fraction of that for Bessemer facilities. In the United States in 1880 the average capacity of open-hearth steelworks was about 10,000 tons, as against 114,000 tons for Bessemer steelworks and 12,000 tons for iron rolling mills (Grosse, 1948, pp. 281–2). In Britain comparable figures are unavailable, but would be less dramatic only by degree. The first open-hearth furnaces were also charged by hand with cold pig iron and scrap, which had to be reheated.

Open-hearth steelworks gradually increased in scale with the introduction of capital-intensive methods that afforded the means for achieving higher throughput as well as the incentive for spreading capital costs over greater output. A number of these innovations involved improved casting and handling methods. Key innovations that directly affected the main constraint on scales of output—the process of open-hearth steel-making—were mechanical charging, hot metal practice, and the Talbot tilting furnace. All the latter innovations were introduced after 1890, and were employed only in exceptional British works in 1900 (Temin, 1964, pp. 140–5, 164; Carr and Taplin, 1962, pp. 215–18; Burn, 1961a, pp. 202–3; Andrews and Brunner, 1951, pp. 44–7).

Under the technical conditions prevailing between 1880 and 1900, the most likely entrants into open-hearth steel-making in Britain were the wrought iron manufacturers, which had already been supplying iron plate and bar to the shipbuilding and sheet industries. Britain's Bessemer producers were beset by problems of slack demand and low profitability, and had little incentive to enter open-hearth steel-making, where they would have little or no competitive edge by virtue of their large plant and financial resources, and would face unfamiliar product markets and, in many cases, a necessity for relocation. In Britain, open-hearth steel-making was first undertaken by numerous small-scale family firms which became established within markets segmented along product and regional lines before Bessemer firms were able to consolidate oligopolistic control over heavy steel-making.

In the United States, on the other hand, the industry turned to open-hearth steel-making some ten to fifteen years later than in Britain. By then, large-scale Bessemer steel-makers were the predominant oligopolistic producers within the US industry, and these firms proceeded to set best practice standards for open-hearth operations. The high and growing volumes of steel output produced by US Bessemer plants had instigated a transformation of blast furnace and rolling mill methods so that these too required integrated, large-scale facilities for efficiency. Average output per blast furnace increased severalfold with the introduction of hard driving, which employed hotter blasts under greater pressure in larger furnaces. US rail producers introduced a series of elaborate mechanical devices for transferring and manipulating hot metal that increased throughput dramatically and were generally adopted in heavy steel rolling.

The quest for high rates of throughput within vertically integrated facilities also led US Bessemer producers to be among the first to develop modern methods of factory management. Mass production of Bessemer steel required systematic means of scheduling, co-ordinating, and controlling the flow of work between different processes. Borrowing from previous experience on the railroads, Andrew Carnegie introduced to the US industry an administrative structure that employed accountants for the maintainance of detailed statistical cost controls, as well as engineers, chemists, and production and general managers. When the United States finally turned to open-hearth production, large steel-makers such as Carnegie continued to apply the mass production methods and organization that had earlier been developed in Bessemer steel. Bessemer converters were replaced with open-hearth furnaces in existing integrated, large-scale plants; new facilities were built to match; and new and old operations were directed by a modern system of management (Temin, 1964, pp. 157–65; Chandler, 1977, pp. 258–69).

Market demand can be isolated as the critical force behind these differences between Britain and the United States with respect to the timing of the change-over in steel-making processes and consequent structural development. Open-hearth production costs were initially greater than Bessemer (Temin, 1964, pp. 140–5; Burn, 1961a, pp. 170–1; Burnham and Hoskins,

1943, pp. 183–5). Offsetting the greater production costs were two advantages: the open-hearth process could refine pig iron made from a wider range of ores, and it could produce steel of higher quality. Ore costs can be excluded as a factor in Britain's earlier recourse to open-hearth methods because, at first, open-hearth steel was adopted solely for higher-quality products (British Iron Trade Association, 1877–1906). Moreover, until the turn of the century virtually all British open-hearth production utilized the acid process and drew upon the same ore supplies as Bessemer steel-making.

The technological basis for the quality advantages of open-hearth products should be underlined. The rapidity of combustion in the Bessemer process made chemical sampling and quality control difficult. More importantly, Bessemer steel contained nitrogen impurities that made it prone to fracture. 'It was not the average performance of the two steels that worried people, it was the chance of an extreme movement, a failure, on the part of the Bessemer steel' (Temin, 1964, p. 150). The risk of fracture was especially costly when steel was to be used as the basic construction material in large structures. Bessemer steel was accordingly quite adequate for railways, but was anathema to British shipbuilders and was the less preferred material in US as well as British sheet and tinplate manufacture (Clark, 1949, p. 69). Since it has been argued that British Bessemer producers were negligent in failing to overcome problems of product quality, it should be pointed out that only during World War II did German scientific analysis pinpoint nitrogen impurities as the chief source of Bessemer steel's problems, and the addition of mill scale, iron ore, or scrap to the converter charge as an appropriate remedy (Burn, 1961b, p. 99).

The effects of market demand on the steel-making processes utilized can be observed from examination of output data. As can be seen from Table 1, the

TABLE 1

Output of steel by process in Britain and the United States, 1880–1914

	Total steel output, 5-year averages (in '000 tons)		Open-hearth steel output, 5-year averages (in '000 tons)		Output of open-hearth steel as % of total output	
	Britain	USA	Britain	USA	Britain	USA
1880–4	1,790	1,485	391	122	22	8
1885–9	2,814	2,706	996	273	35	10
1890–4	3,143	4,235	1,506	657	48	16
1895–9	4,260	7,544	2,496	1,644	59	24
1900–4	4,995	13,294	3,181	5,096	64	38
1905–9	5,995	20,833	4,205	10,767	70	52
1910–14	7,026	27,023	5,497	18,332	78	68

British steel industry shifted rapidly from the Bessemer to the open-hearth steel process throughout the last quarter of the nineteenth century. Between 1880–4 and 1900–4, British open-hearth steel production grew at the annual rate of 11 per cent, then slowed to about half this pace between 1900–4 and 1910–14. By comparison US open-hearth steel output was small in volume until the latter 1890s, and then grew 3.6 times between 1900–4 and 1910–14, or at an annual rate of 13.8 per cent. The share of open-hearth steel in total output remained much greater in Britain than in the United States until 1910–14, when rising costs for Bessemer ores were decisive in leading the US industry to abandon Bessemer for open-hearth steel-making (Temin, 1964, pp. 224–30, 278–9).

The principal difference in the pattern of demand facing Britain and the United States from the early 1880s until after the turn of the century was in the relative importance and dynamism of markets for rails, constructional steel, ship-plate, and tinplate and sheets. In both the United States and Britain, rails were the principal source of demand for Bessemer steel during the steel industry's infancy, but by the 1880s they were a much smaller part of *total* demand for British steel. Much of Britain's railway system had already been lain with iron rails, and with the system's essential completion in the 1870s, domestic rail demand was limited to replacement needs. In addition, important export markets for British rails evaporated with the development of foreign steel industries behind tariff barriers.

By the 1880s additional outlets were found for Bessemer steel, most notably in constructional demand. But industrial Britain could not match the constructional demand of such newly industrializing countries as the United States any more than it could match their rail demand. Bessemer output peaked in Britain in 1889, while it increased fourfold in the United States between 1889 and the peak production year of 1906 (Temin, 1964, pp. 270–1, 278–9; Warren, 1973, pp. 117–19).

After the early 1880s, the most dynamic sector of British steel-making was ship-plate production. By 1910–12 shipbuilding absorbed 30 per cent of Britain's total steel output and 42 per cent of its open-hearth output (Pollard, 1957, p. 439). Sheet and tinplate were the other principal products of the British steel industry, as, in these highly finished, specialty product lines, nineteenth-century Britain alone had access to workers with the requisite production skills and a far-flung international merchant network. By contrast, in the United States output of such higher-quality goods as ship-plate, tinplate, and sheets was small in volume until the latter 1890s.

Only a minor part of the difference in British and US demand patterns, it should be stressed, can be attributed to declining British competitiveness. In aggregate, between 1890 and 1913 British steel output grew at an annual rate of 3.4 per cent as against a US rate of 9.0 per cent. Britain's growth performance could have been significantly better had it outpaced the competition in 'neutral' markets, where it was at no disadvantage by virtue of tariffs, location, or colonial ties. But the largest and most expansive markets in the world were foreclosed to Britain by US and continental tariff barriers and by the greater proximity of the United States to Canada and of Germany and Belgium to major continental markets. Even had Britain turned in a strong enough competitive performance to have imported at only one-third its 1913 level, exchanged its 1913 share of neutral markets for Germany's, and made comparable gains in market share elsewhere, aggregate British output in 1913 would have increased by just 2.4 million tons, or 31 per cent, and the British average annual growth rate between 1890 and 1913 would have only increased from 3.4 to 4.6 per cent (Temin, 1966, pp. 140–55).

Nor, on a disaggregated level, would improved British competitiveness have narrowed more than a minor portion of the gap in rates of expansion of Bessemer steel output. The British Bessemer industry came nearest to matching its 1889 peak output of 2.1 million tons in 1905, when output was 2.0 million tons. Even on generous assumptions about possible improvements in British trade performance in Bessemer steel in 1905, Britain would be left with less than half the US expansion rate between 1889 and 1905–6 and less than one-third the US level of output. Britain similarly could not hope to match German levels or rates of expansion of aggregate or Bessemer output (Elbaum, 1982, pp. 294–5).

By the turn of the century, the contrast between British and US industrial structure was dramatic. In the United States oligopolistic competition and a subsequent merger movement among Bessemer producers led to the formation of a single giant firm—US Steel Corporation—which supplied half the industry's steel ingots and the bulk of the semi-products for the finishing trades. In Britain, on the other hand, over a dozen steelmakers produced ship-plate, a dozen or so supplied the sheet and tinplate industries with sheet-bar, and a declining group of Bessemer firms still supplied rails and various sections.

The Efficiency Ramifications of Structural Fragmentation

The best evidence of the efficiency ramifications of British structural fragmentation comes from the industrialists themselves. Their testimony before a World War I government committee has already been mentioned. The 1917 committee report, which reflected predominant industry opinion, complained of the inability of remodelled British facilities to compete against entirely new foreign installations employing improved mass production methods. It also recommended protection and the formation of combinations of steel companies, if necessary with government assistance, to build new large-scale works (Great Britain Board of Trade, 1918).

Although these policy conclusions were temporarily shelved during the heady optimism of the post-World War I boom, the analysis essentially coincided with that of consultant reports of the latter 1920s and 1930s recommending rationalization (Brassert & Co., 1929, 1930; Gardner, 1930; Great Britain Economic Advisory Council, 1930). These consultant reports drew on information regarding costs of production in existing plants as well as engineering estimates of costs in plants to be built, information similar in kind to that frequently relied upon by students of industrial organization today. Among existing plants, the data indicated, there was a large dispersion in efficiency, and the most efficient were those with newer facilities that were integrated, capital-intensive, and large in scale. These were the plants that came closest to the technological practice employed in the United States or Germany.

Although this information refers to a period subsequent to the one with which we are presently concerned, its basic findings may reasonably be extrapolated back to the pre-World War I industry. The structure of the industry was roughly the same before the war as in 1917 or the interwar period. A pattern of British inferiority in productivity, scales of operation, vertical integration, and competitiveness, analogous to that observed in the interwar period, can also be documented from prewar data.

There have been a number of attempts to measure the comparative pre-World War I productivity performance of the major competing iron and steel industries. McCloskey (1973) paints British performance in favourable light, but his figures are based upon the difference between product prices and the weighted sum of input prices, and so muddle together the effects of productivity growth and shrinking profit margins (Allen, 1979). Allen measures total factor productivity from data on output per unit input, which show the British to be well behind the German and US industries, but his figures are also open to criticism (Allen, 1979; Elbaum, 1982, pp. 258–63).[1] What available data indicate most strikingly is that British labour productivity was substantially less than that of the United States or Germany. On the other hand, British wage levels, though less than those of the United States, were substantially greater than German levels. This suggests that before World War I, as today (Crandall, 1981), best-practice steel industry technology displayed limited variation in response to relative wage levels, and that labour productivity was comparatively low in the British industry because Britain lagged behind in adopting new, best-practice methods.

Progressive deterioration in Britain's relative productivity performance is further suggested by data on scales of steel-making output. In 1878 the average annual output of Bessemer converters in operation was about 13,000 tons in Britain and 37,000 tons in the United States; for 1890 the corresponding figures were 25,000 and 49,000 tons (Carr and Taplin, 1962, pp. 154–5). Subsequently, British Bessemer practice was virtually stagnant, and by the turn of the century rates of Bessemer productivity in the United States were more than four time those in Britain (British Iron Trade Association, 1890, 1901; Hogan, 1971, p. 218; American Iron and Steel Association, 1890).

At an early stage of development, open-hearth furnace outputs were of similar scale in Britain and the United States. In 1887 Britain averaged 4,420 tons of steel output per furnace in operation; the United States, with open-hearth production still in its infancy, averaged 3,830 tons. But by 1901 the British industry had fallen substantially behind as output per furnace averaged just some 8,660 tons, compared with 11,600 tons in the United States. Subsequently the British industry fell still further behind US production standards. Average output per furnace in Britain was 10,900 tons in 1906 and 11,250 tons in 1910, while the United States reached an average tonnage of 20,500 by 1909.[2]

Britain and the United States also differed in their distributions of open-hearth furnaces by nominal capacity per heat. Having had a head start in open-hearth production, Britain led the United States in the introduction of furnaces of capacity of 100 tons or more, most of which were Talbot tilting furnaces, but this lead was eliminated by 1914. A more lasting difference was that, compared with the United States, Britain had a dearth of furnaces of intermediate size, and a long tail of small furnaces. In 1909–10 only 26 per cent of total British capacity, as opposed to 68 per cent of US, was in furnaces of 50–99 ton capacity. Conversely, over 60 per cent of British capacity, as opposed to 32 per cent of US, was in furnaces of less than 50 ton capacity (US Census of Manufacturers, 1914; *Ryland's Directory*, 1910).

The significance of this difference in furnace size distributions lies in the correlation of furnace capacity with the employment of new mass production methods. In particular, modern facilities for mechanical charging, or for vertical integration and hot metal practice, offered significant economies in handling and/or heat conservation, but involved high capital costs. Firms that employed these technologically modern facilities had an evident preference for larger furnaces in order to help spread their capital costs over a large output. Data on British open-hearth heavy steel production in 1919 indicate that output was substantially greater for plants with mechanical charging or hot metal practice, and that these technologies were seldom used with furnaces of less than 50 tons capacity (Iron and Steel Trades Employers Association, 1926).

With some backwards extrapolation, we can infer from the available data that in 1910 roughly 50 per cent of British output was made with hand-charged, cold metal practice, and 25 per cent with hot metal practice. By contrast, in the United States only a handful of old plants employed hand charging, and vertically integrated practice dominated heavy steel-making.

Britain also fell behind in scales of tinplate manufacture between the 1890s and World War I. US firms modified basic British technology by building larger, more capital-intensive mills which were operated by larger crews and yielded higher throughput. The rationalization policies of the tinplate trust also increased US productivity, as, upon amalgamation in 1899, one-third of the operative plants were closed to eliminate excess capacity, and output per plant increased by 90 per cent in the next five years (Dunbar, 1915, pp. 15,

19). In Britain, industry journals commented on the prospective benefits of similar rationalization, but none occurred. Instead, excess capacity remained a recurrent British problem, with family firms continuing in business as long as there was hope of earning a surplus over variable costs (Minchinton, 1957).

Sheet industry development paralleled that of tinplate. Only the two larger British firms, Lysaghts' and Summers, approached US levels of throughput. In Lysaghts' new plant in Newport, 'The productivity of the old mills was much, and that of the newer mills, slightly below that of US mills' (Warren, 1970, p. 116). According to a retrospective article later published in an industry trade journal,

One of the most astonishing features of this area is that, as late as 1908–12, mills were being built in Wales to virtually the same design as those laid down 40 years earlier despite the fact that the strides being made by the Americans, and how they were made, were perfectly well known to most people closely interested. These new mills were obsolete before they were placed in commission. . . . Mills of the 1860 design were still in commission in 1939. (Warren 1970, p. 117.)

The Persistence of Structural Disparity

The central question regarding the decline of the British iron and steel industry is why structural fragmentation should have persisted, despite its adverse effects on efficiency and competitiveness, when sizeable ongoing investments were made in new capacity between the turn of the century and World War I. What particularly requires explanation is why British firms in general failed to adopt best-practice technology even though many firms apparently were well aware of its superiority.

The best explanation for British investment behaviour lies in the constraints on enterprise action. The fundamental problem confronting British iron and steel firms was that their market demand was limited by prevailing structural fragmentation, the maturity of the home market, and an institutional context of international trade which at once protected the more expansive domestic markets of foreign rivals and exposed the British to adverse competitive dynamics.[3] This made it more difficult for the British to adopt new technology embodied in plant and equipment of large and increasing capital intensity and scale.

Problems of this sort are common among competitive industries and are by no means a uniquely 'British disease'. Recent empirical evidence suggests that similar difficulties are found within a wide variety of industries in contemporary advanced economies, even in as large an economy as that of the United States (Scherer et al., 1975; Weiss, 1976; Deutsch, 1973; Gupta, 1979; Cory, 1981).[4] The disabilities of the British iron and steel industry, however, were particularly severe as a result of the coincidence of rapid industrialization, protectionism, and market consolidation abroad with British legacies of economic maturity, free trade, and a relatively atomistic competitive structure at home.

Steel Industry Decline: The Main Lines of Causation

The essence of the problem was that an individual steel firm, like any sizeable enterprise, found it profitable to introduce new capacity employing improved mass production methods only when there were sufficiently good prospects of securing market outlets for the increased output. These prospects tended to be better when the firm had a large share of a big and growing market, and to be more secure when the relevant market was protected and either cartellized or organized along stable oligopolistic lines.

In mass production industries, unlike the idealized world of pure competition, firms do not in general assume they can sell all the output they wish to at the going price. On the contrary, where the prospective output from new capacity constitutes a substantial fraction of market supply, firms contemplating investment normally anticipate the supply repercussions. Firms in mass production industries have also characteristically endeavoured to secure their market outlets through such devices as forward vertical integration and the establishment of exclusive dealerships (Chandler, 1977).

For such large manufacturing firms, investment in new vintage, large-scale plant pays only when the firms can attain a high level of capacity utilization without incurring prohibitive costs of interim idle capacity or competitive struggle. In general, a waiting period is required after the benefits of a new technology are established for demand to expand sufficiently to warrant an expansion of capacity. The length of the required waiting period for profitable investment depends upon technological conditions, the size and growth of market demand, and the competitive behaviour of firms in the industry. The waiting period will be longer the smaller the prospective efficiency gains, the greater the minimum efficient scale and capital intensity of new vintage plant, the steeper the slope of the new vintage average variable cost curve at points of less than full capacity utilization, and the smaller the size and absolute growth of market demand.

The greater the prospective efficiency gains, the greater will be the amount of capacity scrapped upon the introduction of new vintage plant. If new vintage technology is profitable at prices that warrant the scrapping of much of existing capacity, it may pay to introduce it immediately, without any waiting period whatsoever.

On the other hand, when technological progress is gradual and evolutionary rather than sudden and radical, new vintage plant may offer a better return on investment but yield unit total costs in excess of the unit variable costs of the bulk of old vintage capacity. Under these circumstances firms may end up making suboptimal investment decisions which result in a relatively slow rate of technological progress, or even in technological stagnation.

Two cases of firm competitive behaviour should be distinguished: (1) the case in which each firm assumes it can capture total industry demand accretion if it is the first to expand capacity, and (2) the more realistic case in which firms have fairly stable market shares and each firm views encroachment upon the potential or actual markets of another as likely to be costly. The first case most naturally corresponds to initially atomistic competitive conditions, although in logic it might correspond to other conditions as well.

In the first case suboptimal investment is possible if the waiting period required for profitable investment in new vintage plant is sufficiently long. A long waiting period could result, for example, from a minimum efficient scale of new vintage plant which is large relative to the absolute growth of demand in a relatively stagnant market. During a long waiting period, the risk each firm faces is that in the interval another firm may invest in plant employing smaller-scale and less progressive technology and thereby forestall its markets. Markets can be forestalled in this way because, once in place, suboptimal plant can withstand price competition. Although such defensive investment yields a comparatively low rate of return, it may be attractive in light of the risk of forgoing all opportunity for profitable investment by waiting.

In formal terminology, the firms are in a non-zero-sum game situation. The ideal solution would be for firms to co-ordinate their investment in planned fashion, so that each could take turns installing a new vintage plant, with investments spaced out over an appropriate period of years. But this outcome is readily attainable only within a tightly organized cartel or a single firm monopoly, or perhaps through a process of quasi-merger in which other firms are bribed not to expand capacity.

If firms remain within atomistic competitive arrangements, suboptimal investment is a likely outcome because it constitutes a self-fulfilling equilibrium. As long as each firm suspects others of planning to invest in suboptimal plant before the new vintage waiting period is up, it is rational for each firm itself to adopt the same investment plan.

In the more realistic case in which firms are reluctant to encroach upon each others' market shares, how likely firms are to wait in order to invest in new vintage plant depends, in addition, upon firm size and the degree of competition. The larger firm, the shorter will be the waiting period before the firm's normal share of demand accretion is enough to warrant investment.

The degree of competition in turn determines the cost of invading other firms' markets. If markets are so competitive that firms' market shares are highly insecure and unstable, suboptimal investment may result much according to the logic of the previous case. Each firm's waiting period will be comparatively short because it will feel able to capture a large portion of the market. But since other firms feel the same, the risks will be comparatively great that its markets will be forestalled.

On the other hand, if market shares are highly secure and stable, the firm may wait with comparatively little risk to invest in new vintage plant. But the firm is then under comparatively little compulsion to choose the most efficient investment.

Just how much competition is most conducive to technological progress, therefore, cannot be determined *a priori*. When only a short waiting period is required before investment in new vintage plant is profitable, competition may lead to an efficient outcome. In other circumstances, however, the advantages of co-ordinated investment planning argue for a high degree of industrial concentration, as long as the negative effects of monopoly can be warded off by oligopolistic competition or regulatory control.

When competition is international in scope, the danger is that an industry which lags behind in the introduction of best-practice technique may wind up with a declining share of the world market. Two effects must be considered: that of international trade on productive efficiency, and of productive efficiency on international competitiveness.

Economists have traditionally argued that trade promotes productive efficiency. They generally reason that the larger markets available through exports will facilitate the introduction of large-scale new plant, and that competition from imports will compel the adoption of best-practice technique. At the extreme, the capacity of each new vintage plant may be miniscule compared with the size of world markets, and the applicable case for analysis will be that of perfect competition (e.g. Caves, 1974).

Yet international trade may also have important implications for competitive dynamics. These implications arise whenever international markets are less than perfectly unified in that firms have differential access to national markets. Differential access to national markets may reflect tariff barriers, transportation costs, marketing advantages, product differentiation, formal or informal restrictions on imports, or simply prior market entrenchment. When international markets are segmented in this fashion, firms will face downward-sloping demand curves. This is the empirically relevant case for the pre-World War I steel industry, in which the geographical locus of exports was limited by tariffs and transport costs, and individual market areas, including that of Britain—the largest distinct open market in the world—were dominated by an international assemblage of firms that was far from numerous.

In this trading environment, as long as the introduction of new vintage plant requires a substantial waiting period for virtually all firms, the firms with the strongest competitive positions will be those that are largest and have access to the biggest markets in terms of size and growth. These firms will be able to introduce large-scale, new vintage plant more rapidly than their competitors. They may also attempt to have their cake and eat it too by invading competitors' markets, relying upon their superior productive efficiency to give them a competitive edge. The logic of these competitive dynamics is that the strongest firms should be able, over time, to obtain increasing shares of the world market, until a stable situation of world-wide oligopoly is reached. This logic will be compounded if dynamic 'learning effects' add over time to the cost advantages of adopting best-practice technique. An evident implication is that infant industry arguments have more to them than usually meets the eye.

Steel Industry Competitive Dynamics, 1890–1913

How this theoretical logic applies to the British pre-World War I iron and steel industry should by now, at least in rough outline, be apparent. After 1890, compared with its competitors, the British industry was comprised of numerous and small firms situated in small and slowly growing markets. It found itself in these straits, despite its earlier domination of world trade, as a result of the limits placed on demand by domestic market maturity and the growth of foreign industries behind tariff barriers.

From behind the tariff barriers that protected the world's largest and most expansive markets, Britain's rivals could better afford to invest in modern large-scale plant. By virtue of their edge in productive efficiency, they could also invade and demoralize Britain's traditional markets. The rivals' initial entry into Britain's markets was gained through dumping. Their success at increasing their market share through cyclical booms as well as busts, however, indicates that in time they found it profitable to undercut British prices. Penetration of British markets was facilitated by the willingness of British merchant firms to provide the modest marketing and distribution network that was necessary.

Losses in competitiveness were greater in British sectors where the market constraints on enterprise investment behaviour were more severe and productivity performance relatively poor. British Bessemer firms were the most vulnerable. In the 1890s their markets were seriously depressed. By the time demand turned up, their markets were being invaded and demoralized by exports that came principally from a larger German industry, which had expanded throughout the 1890s.

Between 1900 and 1913, while British Bessemer output fell, German output increased by an average of 500,000 tons per year. As already indicated, even if generous allowance is made for possible British improvement in competitive performance at the principal expense of Germany, Britain's absolute growth potential would remain far behind. German Bessemer firms also had considerably larger market shares than their British counterparts.

For an individual British Bessemer firm, investment in a modern large-scale plant would pay only if a substantially greater market share could be wrenched within a sluggish market in which there was already excess capacity. Some space was cleared in Bessemer markets by the elimination of weaker British firms, but the scourge came less from domestic than from foreign competition. Most British Bessemer firms withstood the first wave of foreign competition, while following conservative investment policies and suffering reduced profit margins and market shares. Subsequently, as demand continued to shift towards higher-quality products, and hematite ores grew more costly, British firms progressively withdrew from competition in Bessemer steel-making.

Britain fared better in open-hearth steel-making, where its markets were relatively larger and more expansive and scale economies initially were slight. But even in open-hearth steel-making, the British were in a difficult situation after 1900, when their markets became relatively less expansive, best-practice technology was embodied in plant of increasing minimum efficient scale, the pace of technological change was gradual rather than radical, and British industrial structure was encumbered by a heritage of small, unintegrated producing units.

Between 1900 and 1913, when the British industry fell far behind that of the United States in the average scale of open-hearth operations, British open-hearth output increased from 3,156 to 6,003 million tons. The average annual increase in British output was some 224,0000 tons. There is no precise information on the minimum efficient scale of an integrated open-hearth steel works during this period, but the aggregate rate of British demand expansion was certainly sufficient to support new efficient plants after a modest waiting period. On the eve of World War I, one of the largest open-hearth works in Britain was Colville's at Dalzell, with an output of the order of 300,000 tons (Payne, 1979, p. 129). The new Normanby Park works incorporating the most advanced technique in Britain had a capacity of 100,000 tons (Warren, 1970, p. 111).

The growth of British market demand, however, was divided along regional and product lines, and within these perimeters among several firms. As a result, even firms that were expanding their market share faced a long waiting period before their market outlets would sustain a large new plant. For example, the firm of Colville's, which grew between 1900 and World War I to be the leading firm in Scotland and one of the six largest steel firms in Britain, had an average annual increase in output of the order of 11,000–12,000 tons. This absolute growth in output much more easily supported the series of incremental improvements and additions to existing plant that Colville's implemented than a major new, integrated installation. Dorman Long's, the British industry's largest firm, had in its three works an output more than twice as large as Colville's. But with its output divided between distinct product markets for Bessemer and open-hearth steel, and its management structure resembling a federation of distinct family firms, Dorman Long's market share was still too small to make its situation qualitatively different (Warren, 1970, p. 111).

Some new open-hearth works were established in Britain, and some old facilities were adapted to integrated working. But most new or remodelled works remained small in scale, built to fit into the interstices of demand. An example was the Skinningrove works on the north-east coast, remodelled for integrated working as late as 1907–10, yet only a fraction the scale of the older plants of its nearby rivals.

By contrast, between 1900 and 1913, when the United States was switching from Bessemer to open-hearth steel production, US open-hearth steel output increased from 3,398 to 21,600 million tons. The average absolute growth of open-hearth steel output in the United States in these years, at 1.4 million tons, was more than six times the British figure. US firms also had much greater market shares than their British counterparts. The absolute growth of open-hearth steel output of US Steel Corporation alone was sufficient to allow the installation of two good-sized steel-making facilities per year. Although in 1900 the German industry only had two-thirds the British level of open-hearth output, the average absolute growth of German output between 1900 and 1913, at 420,000 tons per year, was nearly twice the British figure.

Britain's competitive performance in open-hearth product lines was mixed. The higher transport and input costs of the US industry kept the competitive threat from this quarter largely at bay. In the making of quality open-hearth products, the British also benefited from their accumulated skills and experience. For such products as sheetbar, however, with a smaller premium on quality, British inferiority in productive efficiency set the stage for competitive losses, chiefly to continental basic Bessemer producers, which began before World War I.

The greatest concentration of modern facilities in Britain were the large-scale open-hearth steel-making works of the North-East and Scotland, whose markets for shipbuilding steel proved largely impervious to foreign competition. Both before the war and in the depressed 1920s, British ship-plate producers met brief foreign competitive incursions with an association scheme that successfully drove out imports by providing rebates to shipbuilders who bought steel only from domestic suppliers (Carr and Taplin, 1962, pp. 258–9, 435–6). By 1913, however, Britain was importing significant volumes of steel plate for purposes other than shipbuilding (Burnham and Hoskins, 1943, pp. 326–7).

Even in tinplate and sheet manufacture, where the minimum efficient scale of plant was comparatively small, the constraints on the investment behaviour of British firms seriously affected competitive performance. For the British, adoption of US tinplate and sheet manufacturing methods was difficult because they were more capital-intensive than existing methods and required substantially greater output per mill and establishment.

In the case of tinplate manufacture, by 1907 output per mill was 65 per cent greater, and output per establishment 50 per cent greater, in the United States than in South Wales. Since aggregate British tinplate output increased by less than 50 per cent between the peak production years of 1891 and 1912, an increase in market outlets commensurate with a fixed share of industry output was insufficient for the average British tinplate works to grow to US scale (Dunbar, 1915, p. 27; Minchinton, 1957, pp. 80, 92).

Furthermore, for the adoption of the more capital-intensive US technology to be profitable, finishing firms would require long runs of a standardized product. The prevailing system of producing to merchant order made this condition hard to fulfil, and gave producers cause for complaint regarding merchant practices (Minchinton, 1957, pp. 81–2, 148–52). The problems that smaller British tinplate and sheet firms had in securing market outlets of sufficient size and standardization appear to explain why those that obtained the levels of throughput most comparable to that reached in the United States were the largest firms, which generally had integrated forwards in order to control their own marketing (Minchinton, 1957, pp. 81–2, 148–52; Warren, 1970, p. 116).

By 1910 US firms were successfully out-competing Welsh tinplate manufacturers in the Canadian market, and they had earlier captured from the Welsh the US re-export trade (for which there were no tariff barriers on imported inputs of Welsh blackplate). European and US sheet exports were also cutting into traditional British markets in the immediate prewar years (Minchinton, 1957, pp. 69, 82–3; Warren, 1970, pp. 89–90).

Steel Industry Decline: Reinforcing Lines of Causation

A number of additional influences contributed to the competitive decline of the British iron and steel industry, by adding either to the difficulties that British firms faced in adopting large-scale, capital-intensive methods, or to the cost advantages that foreign rivals gained by employing such methods. Particularly significant in this regard were the wage structure established under collective bargaining and the costs of iron ore acquisition. Various other influences to which steel industry decline has been attributed—imperfections of competition, dumping, and technical interrelatedness—can safely be characterized as being of only secondary import. The main aspect of British decline that requires separate explanation is the steel industry's failure to reorganize by consolidation, or to alter in other ways the institutional constraints that hampered its ability to compete.

Collective Bargaining, Wage Structure, and Industry Development

The wage structure established under collective bargaining adversely affected technological development in the British steel industry by relating wage earnings to plant productivity. This deterred both enterprise investment in new, more productive plants in which higher wages had to be paid, and enterprise scrapping of old plants that survived by paying low wages. Most strikingly, the prevailing industry wage structure helps account for the persistence in Britain, despite competitive pressures, of a long tail of small-scale, unmechanized open-hearth facilities. By affording such facilities relatively low labour costs, British collective bargaining arrangements protected them from competitive elimination, and added to the obstacles confronting large-scale new investment.

The pattern of collective bargaining settlements for the bulk of the British steel industry was established in open-hearth steel-making. In 1905 a basic, national agreement was reached between the Steel Smelters Amalgamated Association, then the dominant union in the industry, and the Steel Ingot Manufacturers' Association. At that time union organization was confined to operatives who held strategic positions of responsibility at bottlenecks in the production process. These strategically positioned operatives were paid on tonnage rates which related individual worker earnings to crew tonnage output, a system of wage payment that had evolved out of earlier subcontracting arrangements.

The 1905 agreement set out a national sliding-scale formula stipulating that tonnage rates would vary up or down from a base level with variations in product price. The level of base rates was left for determination at the workplace, and was subject to national regulation only through disputes procedures.

Through this two-tiered structure of bargaining, which combined the leverage of a national union with a highly decentralized structure of bargaining authority, the Smelters approximated the behaviour of a discriminating monopolist. During the 1890s they successfully employed strike threats against individual firms in order to resist reductions in tonnage rates when the capacity of hand-charged cold-metal furnaces was increased. The Smelters also maintained a rigid floor under tonnage rates in mechanically charged furnaces, but conceded reductions when more radical changes in methods were introduced, such as hot metal charging, Talbot-tilting furnaces, or larger ingot moulds.

As a result, within hand or machine-charged cold-metal furnaces, melting crew earnings varied by more than 2 to 1 across plants. Virtually all of the earnings variation can be explained by variation in furnace output as tonnage rates remained fixed. On furnaces with hot-metal practice, despite tonnage rate concessions, the range of inter-plant earnings was only slightly less, and for furnaces of similar output the level of earnings was roughly the same. On Talbot-tilting furnaces, however, the earnings distribution was much narrower, and despite much greater scales of output, earnings were only average compared with other furnace operations (Iron and Steel Trades Employers Association, 1926).

Available data allow only a rough calculation of the magnitude of the union wage impact on industry cost structure. As much as half the iron and steel industry wage bill was paid to workers in the form of incentive wages (Great Britain Board of Trade, 1911, pp. 23, 34), and on average, in British steel-making and rolling, labour costs were approximately 21 per cent of total costs (Allen, 1979, p. 916). This suggests, as a maximum figure, that the prevailing wage-setting arrangements saved the least productive British firms some 5 per cent on total costs.[5] The actual figure, in general, would have been smaller, because tonnage wage bargaining, while fairly pervasive in the industry, had an impact which varied with the specific production process and alteration in methods. Even a considerably smaller figure, however, would remain significant relative to industry profit margins.

Two qualitative considerations help to put an upper limit on the independent impact of union wage structure on industry development. The most technologically progressive sectors of British steel-making were in the union strongholds of the North-East and Scotland. Apparently, where rates of market expansion were greater, British firms proved better able to adopt new mass production methods even though they thereby incurred higher wages.

Union wage structure in Britain was also, to a considerable extent, an outgrowth of the influences on industry development already discussed. Divided by atomistic competition, British employers were individually no match for a national union and were unable to resist discriminatory wage bargaining. Shortly after the turn of the century, when the Steel Ingots Manufacturers Association repeatedly discussed staging a nationwide collective lockout of the Smelters, it failed to get the unanimous agreement among member firms that was considered essential to success. By contrast, in the United States, analogous union practices of wage discrimination were eliminated, along with union organization, in successive conflicts with Carnegie Corporation and US Steel Corporation—large, multi-plant firms that deployed their oligopolistic power in the product market to advantage in the labour market.

The Costs of Ore Acquisition

In the pre-World War I period, the British industry was increasingly dependent on imported iron ore which it obtained chiefly from Spain. As the Spanish ore fields were progressively played out, British ore import costs rose (Burnham and Hoskins, 1943, p. 110; Flinn, 1955, pp. 84–90; Roepke, 1956, p. 98). Traditional historical treatments by Burn (1961a, pp. 167–8) and Burnham and Hoskins (1943, pp. 102–35) fault British industry for its failure to avail itself, through relocation, of domestic supplies of low-grade, basic ores in the East Midlands which were as cheap as any ores in Europe or the United States. In their eyes, recourse to the East Midland ores would have conferred production as well as resource economies by allowing a change-over to the basic Bessemer process. According to Burn (1961a, p. 167), 'the comparative neglect of the cheap native ores was, indeed, the most amazing feature of British steel-making.'

These traditional historians, however, do not adequately explain why the British industry should have suffered from any disadvantage in ore acquisition costs by virtue of its reliance on imports. By 1900 Germany's chief steel-making centre in the Ruhr relied for more than 50 per cent of its ore supplies on imports from Sweden, a source no further from British ports than from German (Pounds, 1968, p. 112). An adequate account of Britain's ore cost situation therefore involves two questions: (1) Did British firms neglect the East Midlands ores, and if so, why? (2) Why should dependence on imported ores have been any more costly for the British than the German industry?

On the first question, Donald McCloskey (1973) and Robert Allen (1979, pp. 911–39) have each maintained that the British industry should be absolved of charges of neglecting the East Midland ores. McCloskey, in particular, argues from scattered data for 1904 that it was no cheaper to assemble raw materials in the East Midlands than in the Cleveland district, the largest and most dynamic region of pig iron production in Britain between 1870 and World War I. McCloskey also finds that between the 1890s and 1920s the increase in iron got from East Midlands ores was only 36 per cent of the increase in British basic steel production, from which he infers that the growth of basic steel-making was disconnected from industry expansion in the East Midlands. Allen in turn cites geological sources on the vastness of Cleveland's ore deposits, and suggests that a trend was apparent in the pre-World War I industry for British investment to reap high returns by availing itself of Cleveland's ore resources (Allen, 1979, pp. 936–7).

McCloskey and Allen, however, overlook the developmental problems that were the main concern of the traditional historians. Although plentiful, Cleveland ironstone was of diminishing iron content and increasingly uneconomical to mine. Documentation of diminishing returns to Cleveland ore mining is extensive. By 1917, in testimony to the Scoby-Smith Committee, the Cleveland Ironmasters Association could say, 'The native Cleveland ironstone is in a commercial sense within measurable distance of exhaustion' (Great Britain Board of Trade, 1918). While Cleveland pig iron capacity expanded throughout the pre-World War I years, it increasingly relied upon imported ores. Local ore output peaked in 1880, and the production of Cleveland pig iron made from local ore declined from 90 to 47 per cent between 1875 and 1913 (Roepke, 1956, p. 78). Properly interpreted, McCloskey's own data indicate that, between the 1890s and 1920s, over 75 per cent of the increased British output of basic steel may well have been based upon increased use of the East Midlands ores for steel-making.[6] After 1890, the East Midlands became the British industry's main source of basic ores, and no viable competitive alternative was to be found in the Cleveland district.

The problems with expansion of steel production in the East Midlands were twofold, and were referred to by Burn himself. Unless the industry were to be radically reorganized, large-scale expansion in the East Midlands would have to cater to the growth areas of market demand. As already argued these growth areas were for open-hearth rather than Bessemer steel. This put serious obstacles in the way of expansion of basic Bessemer capacity favoured by Burn and by Burnham and Hoskins.

The alternative to Bessemer production was to use the ores of the East Midlands for basic open-hearth steel-making. But the principal open-hearth products in demand were ship-plate, tinplate, and sheet. Orientation towards shipbuilding and export markets gave manufacturers of these products a firm attachment to coastal locations distant from the East Midlands. This attachment was reinforced, particularly for the finishing firms, by dependence on local supplies of skilled labour. Although the East Midlands districts had the cheapest available ores, they were too distant from relevant product and factor markets to prompt a large-scale migration of steel-making. The major investments that were made in East Midlands capacity by Lysaght's before World War I, and by Stewart and Lloyd's in the inter-war period, came from large finishing firms that could guarantee captive markets for steel semi-products. Stewart and Lloyd's also brought much of its workforce with it from Scotland.[7]

As an ore importer, Britain was at a competitive disadvantage compared with Germany because resource as well as production costs favoured ore imports from Sweden and employment of the basic Bessemer process. Spanish ore was a high-grade hematite, low in phosphorus content, and well suited for the acid Bessemer and open-hearth steel-making processes on which the British industry relied primarily before World War I. The principal Swedish ores, on the other hand, were so highly phosphoric that they could be economically refined only by the basic Bessemer process, in which the phosphorus serves as a source of fuel and is burned off rapidly. Refining of such highly phosphoric ore in the open-hearth process incurs prohibitively reduced efficiency, as more basic material must be added to the charge (Fritz, 1974; US Steel Corporation, 1971; Wiberg, 1955).

With the progressive exhaustion of Spanish ore, the price of hematite gradually increased. The German industry accordingly imported hematite from Sweden and Spain only in small amounts for its more specialized acid steel-making sector. Lacking a basic Bessemer industry of any size, the British steel industry was forced to turn to hematite and to its domestic supplies of less phosphoric basic ores.

Without better data than are presently available on the grades of purity and costs of purchase, transport, and refining of various ores, the differential cost burden borne by the British cannot be estimated with precision.[8] Even a small percentage difference in ore costs, however, would have been of competitive significance, as metallic inputs were the most important cost item in iron and steel manufacture. By virtue of the market demand structure and competitive dynamics that deterred the British from large-scale investments in Bessemer capacity, the German industry gained an edge in ore costs that added to its ability to penetrate British markets.

Influences of Secondary Import for British Steel Industry Development

According to Burn (1961a, p. 263), a prime cause of British steel industry decline lay in imperfections of competition that fostered structural rigidity by sheltering British firms from elimination. There is, however, little support for the contention that imperfections of competition were peculiarly significant in Britain. In general, the degree of competition prevailing in different industries is not amenable to exact assessment. But in the US as well as the British steel industry, encroaching upon a competitor's market was considered hazardous and costly. The risk of a costly oligopolistic struggle was in fact one factor that helped precipitate the formation of US Steel Corporation. Nor were market shares so very secure in Britain, as firms suffered major competitive losses, most notably from imports.

As Burn himself recognized (1961a, pp. 219–33), the British industry suffered from a pattern of defensive, suboptimal investment primarily because it was too atomistic in structure. In this light, the efforts of British steel-makers to integrate forward and form quasi-cartellized associations seem less an effective means of restricting competition than a means of salvaging a temporary, modest, and inadequate degree of refuge in an increasingly insecure environment.

Frankel (1955) emphasized that technical interrelatedness made it more difficult for the firms operating many of the British industry's older plants to introduce certain kinds of technological change. For example, unless a steel-making site was spacious enough to permit the production of pig iron and steel in appropriate balance, the site would have to be extended or the plant relocated in order for blast furnaces to be introduced. Analogous difficulties could confront the introduction of mechanical charging or other large-scale mechanized methods.

Aggregate demand expansion for British steel, however, was more than sufficient to permit the establishment of entirely new, integrated facilities at greenfield sites. Technical interrelatedness was a significant factor in British industry development mainly because investment so often took the form of patchwork modification of existing plant, rather than installation of new facilities.

Finally, by exacerbating British price and output fluctuations, dumping by foreign competitors during cyclical downturns added to the forces deterring large-scale, capital-intensive investment. The case for the prime importance of dumping for British performance that was made by contemporaries, and more recently by Steven Webb (1980), rests primarily on a comparison with the relative price and output stability achieved by the German industry through tariff barriers and cartel regulation. Cartel enforcement of monopolistic pricing in the home market reduced the risk that prices would fall during recessions to levels that would fail to cover operating costs and force firms to shut down their plants and absorb their fixed costs as losses. By barring foreign competition from the German market, protection also reduced fluctuations in domestic output and capacity utilization.

US experience, however, suggests that price and output fluctuations had only a secondary impact on industry choice of technique (Elbaum, 1982, pp. 330–3). Between the 1890s and World War I, fluctuations in prices and output were much greater in the United States than in Britain. Despite tariff barriers, US billet prices, for example, fell by fully one-half amidst cut-throat oligopolistic warfare and a cyclical downturn in the 1890s. After the turn of the century, US cyclical fluctuations were less marked and industry consolidation introduced greater price rigidity. But by then the US industry was already the world leader in employment of large-scale, capital-intensive methods, and between 1900 and 1913 the level of prices and output remained substantially more unstable in the United States than in Britain. For the large firms that dominated the US industry, decisions regarding investment in new, large-scale facilities were shaped less by the severity of cyclical fluctuations than by the anticipated size and growth of their markets.

Conclusions

Contrary to the classical economic analysis offered during Britain's turn-of-the-century debate over tariff reform, the British iron and steel industry experienced competitive decline even though it need have been at no comparative disadvantage. While wages in Britain were higher than on the Continent, in the United States wages were higher yet and US goods none the less made increasing competitive inroads into world markets, including the British market (Temin, 1966, p. 148). As an ore importer, Britain was in the same boat as its German competition, and its East Midlands ores were as cheap as any in Europe or the United States (Temin, 1966).

Britain's free trade and *laissez-faire* policies left the iron and steel industry exposed to adverse competitive dynamics. Unless these policies were modified, there was little that the British government could do to aid steel industry competitiveness. Devaluation, for example, would have given Britain's steel manufacturers slight comfort. By increasing the internationally competitive price of steel in pounds sterling, devaluation could theoretically boost industry profit margins and market shares. But in practice, ore and coal, like steel, were internationally traded commodities, and devaluation would also increase their prices in pounds sterling. With the wages of unionized workers pegged to domestic price levels by a sliding scale, any increase in domestic steel prices would automatically be partially offset by an ensuing wage increase. Since mineral resources and labour were the industry's main inputs, the only firms that would benefit substantially from devaluation would be the relatively small number that owned ample domestic mineral supplies from which they could reap increased implicit rents.

The main policy options that could have improved British steel industry performance were protection and industrial reorganization. Even with protection, the British would have been at a disadvantage compared with firms in Germany and the United States, which faced markets that were more expansive as well as protected, and would still be able to introduce new, mass production technology more rapidly. In this sense, industrialization abroad made a certain degree of relative contraction of the British industry inevitable, with repercussions for its share of world exports, as well as world production.

But by introducing protection, Britain in one stroke could have deprived its chief competitors of their most important export market and secured the home market for domestic producers. With the respite gained from competitive pressure, British producers would have been better placed to meet home market demand through investment in new, large-scale capacity embodying best-practice methods, and to export from an efficient productive base.

Protectionism, however, was opposed by a formidable array of economic interests as well as by longstanding free trade ideology. Although most iron and steel industrialists favoured protection by 1917, some remained among the free trade bloc, including British steel re-rollers, who imported continental semi-products for finishing, often through British merchant organizations.

By itself, protectionism was also insufficient. Long-run competitive vitality could be assured only by industrial reorganization. Protectionism could facilitate reorganization by affording British firms breathing space from competitive pressure while they modernized. But it could also remove the incentive to modernize and allow firms to practise monopolistic pricing and output restriction in the home market.

By reorganizing, the British industry could have stemmed, if not entirely avoided, its competitive decline. On the strength of larger market shares, consolidated enterprises could have rationalized Britain's manufacturing facilities and undertaken an investment programme yielding superior productive efficiency. Yet only limited steps towards reorganization were taken.

Historically, the most influential interpretation of the British industry's inability to rise to the occasion is that of entrepreneurial failure. This interpretation puts primary emphasis on the distinctiveness of British culture, and in particular on pervasive social values which inhibited entrepreneurs from making the necessary institutional innovations. As support for this thesis, reference is commonly made to short time horizons exemplified by British investment behaviour; neglect of managerial and technical education, and a consequent unfamiliarity with new organizational and production methods; a bifurcation between banks and industry; and a preference of families with established business fortunes for an aristocratic style of life.

The difficulty with this interpretation is that it explains too much and too little. British competitive performance, like that of other nations, was far from uniform across time or sectors. If, on the whole, British industry proved overly conservative, a number of more progressive enterprises, notably in open-hearth steel-making, adopted technology that approximated best practice. Stronger British firms also sought and won larger market shares from competitors. By virtue of its focus on the behaviour of individual entrepreneurs, the hypothesis of enterpreneurial failure is unable to explain the systematic sources of variation in enterprise performance. Nor can it explain why those British firms that were more dynamic were unable either to enforce high standards of efficiency on their competitors or to rise to positions of industry predominance.

The analysis presented in this paper suggests that emphasis is more aptly placed upon the constraints on individual entrepreneurial action. This also was the view of the industrialists themselves, who by 1917 and again in the interwar period favoured co-ordinated intervention.

By and large, British iron and steel manufacturers were well aware of the advantages and principles of the methods employed in competing industries, even as they were falling further behind. But the options open to British firms were limited. The market constraints they faced suffice to explain a pattern of investment exemplifying short time horizons. The comparatively small size of British family firms also limited their incentive and capacity to develop sophisticated managerial systems or more extensive means of training and employing technical personnel. Given the impetus towards industrial decentralization provided by the initial growth of open-hearth steel-making, it is not surprising that a countervailing process of concentration should still have left the British industry before World War I with a more fragmented structure than that of foreign competitors.

The obstacles to effective co-ordinated intervention in iron and steel are best illustrated from a longer-term vantage point, which spans interwar attempts at rationalization. These attempts came to little despite a broad-ranging agreement that some form of major structural reorganization was required. As Tolliday demonstrates in the following paper, individual firms quarrelled with the specifics of the various rationalization plans and went along only when the plans favoured their own expansion or when they were too beholden to their bankers to do otherwise. Although in principle firms could have obtained mutual benefits from consolidation, in practice individual firms found themselves buffeted between the rival interests of family owners, management, unions, private shareholders, and banks, who were out to protect their respective stakes in the firm's family identity, managerial positions, jobs, and financial liabilities. Despite attempts by the Bank of England to enlist the major private banks behind a co-ordinated policy, the banks too chose to differ in order to protect their separate interests, and, after finally reaching unity on a plan among themselves, let it founder for lack of venture capital. Efforts to reorganize were hampered by a fragmentation of interests that was difficult to overcome either through the market or through available institutional mechanisms for planned adjustment.

Notes

[1] For example, Allen's data on labour productivity fail to correct for hours worked. Making this correction reduces the ratio of US to British labour productivity from 1.8 to 1.4. Allen's data on the productivity of metallic inputs also conflict with that cited in Elbaum (1982).

[2] It should be noted that wildly incorrect figures on average output per furnace are given in Burnham and Hoskins (1943, p. 181), and that incorrect British figures are also given in Clark (1949, vol. 3, p. 66) and in Burn (1961a, p. 238). Our figures are calculated from aggregate output data and data on the number of operative furnaces published in British Iron Trade Association (1887, 1901); American Iron and Steel Association (1890); Hogan (1971); *Ryland's Directory* (1906, 1910); and US Census of Manufactures (1914).

[3] This model resembles that of Temin (1966) in its emphasis on the market demand constraints facing the British industry. Temin's model, however, assumes implicitly that British steel firms introduced best-practice technology just as soon as their market opportunities warranted, and therefore cannot explain the industry's decline in competitive performance. Temin's discussion of relative decline refers only to the relative growth rate and average productivity of the British industry, not to its relative competitiveness or to the productivity of plants on the margin of obsolescence or best practice.

[4] Statistical estimates by recent authors who have attempted to explain the share of shipments across modern-day US industries supplied by plants of suboptimal scale suggest that British firms would have been severely handicapped by the market conditions prevailing before World War I. See Cory (1981) and Weiss (1976).

[5] This rough calculation is based on the assumptions that rigid tonnage wage rates cause the wage bill for workers on incentive pay to constitute approximately 10 per cent of total costs for firms paying low as well as high wages, and that payment of a standard competitive wage would cause an increase of some 50 per cent in wages within less productive plants.

[6] The computation is straightforward. McCloskey (1973, pp. 68–9) reports that, between the 1890s and 1920s, British basic steel output went from 0.56 to 4.7 million tons while East Midlands ore output went from 3.4 to 5.9 million tons. He computes that the latter incease in ore output can explain only 36 per cent of the former increase in steel output on the assumptions that the iron content of East Midlands ore was 30 per cent and that pig iron and scrap each made up 50 per cent of metallic inputs for steel-making in the 1920s. But on these same assumptions, the volume of East Midlands ore output in the 1920s was enough to account for some 75 per cent of British basic steel output, as $5.9 \times 0.3 \times 2/4.7 = 0.75$. In the 1890s East Midlands ore output was several times greater than basic steel output, and so must have been used primarily for other purposes. Roepke (1956, p. 86) indicates that the Cleveland district was the major supplier of ore for basic steel-making in 1890, but of declining significance thereafter. This suggests that East Midlands ore was increasingly diverted for use in basic steel-making after 1890, when it substituted for Cleveland ore.

[7] Ironically, in longer-term perspective, the British industry's failure to relocate on the East Midlands ores turned out to be fortunate, for the balance of locational advantage was shifting decisively towards the coast, whence raw material imports

and manufactured exports could flow to and fro with relative ease (Langley, 1951).

[8]Burn (1961a, p. 157) reports that, at the Rhine ports of Germany's Westphalian steel industry, 'Swedish ore always cost less than Spanish in relation to iron content.'

Bibliography

Aldcroft, Derek H. (1964). 'The Entrepeneur and the British Economy, 1870–1914'. *Economic History Review*, 2nd ser., 17.

Allen, Robert (1979).'International Competition in Iron and Steel, 1850–1913'. *Journal of Economic History*, 39, December.

American Iron and Steel Association (various years, 1876–1900). *Directory to the Iron and Steelworks of the United States*. Philadelphia.

American Iron and Steel Association (1912). *Statistics of the American and Foreign Iron Trades*. Philadelphia.

Andrews, P. W. S., and Elizabeth Brunner (1951). *Capital Development in Steel*. New York: Augustus M. Kelley.

Brassert, H. A., & Co. (1929). 'Report to Lord Weir of Eastwood on the Manufacture of Iron and Steel'. Unpublished paper.

Brassert, H. A., & Co. (1930). 'Memorandum on the Rationalization of the British Iron and Steel Industry'. Unpublished paper.

British Iron Trade Association (various years, 1877–1906). *Annual Report*. London.

Brittania Melting Iron Rates and Manning Agreement between Steel Ingot Manufacturers' Association and British Steel Smelters Amalgamated Association, 14 January 1909.

Burn, Duncan (1961a). *Economic History of Steel Making, 1867–1939*. Cambridge University Press.

Burn, Duncan (1961b). *The Steel Industry, 1939–59*. Cambridge University Press.

Burnham, T. H., and G. O. Hoskins (1943). *Iron and Steel in Britain, 1870–1930*. London: George Allen and Unwin.

Carr, J. C. and Taplin, W. (1962). *History of the British Steel Industry*. Cambridge, Mass.: Harvard University Press.

Caves, Richard (1974). *International Trade, International Investment, and Imperfect Markets*, Special Paper in International Economics, no. 10. Princeton University Press.

Chandler, Alfred D. Jr. (1977). *The Visible Hand*. Cambridge, Mass.: Harvard University Press.

Clark, Victor S. (1949). *History of Manufacturers in the United States*. Volume 3, *1893–1928*. New York: Peter Smith.

Cory, Peter (1981). 'A Technique for Obtaining Improved Proxy Estimates of Minimal Optimal Scale'. *Review of Economics and Statistics*, 63, February.

Crandall, Robert W. (1981). *The US Steel Industry in Recurrent Crisis*. Washington, DC: Brookings Institution.

Deutsch, Larry L. (1973). 'Elements of Market Structure and the Extent of Suboptimal Capacity'. *Southern Economic Journal*, 40, October.

Dunbar, D. E. (1915). *The Tinplate Industry*. Boston: Houghton Mifflin.

Elbaum, Bernard (1982) 'Industrial Relations and Uneven Development: Wage Structure and Industrial Organization in the British and US Iron and Steel Industries 1870–1970'. PhD dissertation, Harvard University.

Flinn, M. W. (1955). 'British Steel and Spanish Ore'. *Economic History Review*, 2nd ser. 11.

Frankel, Marvin (1955). 'Obsolescence and Technical Change in a Maturing Economy'. *American Economic Review*, 45, June.

Fritz, Martin (1974). *German Steel and Swedish Ore*. Gothenberg: Gothenberg University.

Gardner, C. Bruce (1930). 'Report on the Structure of the Iron and Steel Industry Incorporating Plans for Rationalization'. Unpublished paper.

Great Britain (1881). *Mineral Statistics of the United Kingdom*. Lonon: HMSO.

Great Britain Board of Trade (1911). *Report of an Enquiry Into Earnings and Hours of Labour in the UK in 1906*, Cd. 5814. London: HMSO.

Great Britain Board of Trade (1918). *Report of Departmental Committee on the Position of the Iron and Steel Trades After the War*, Cd. 9071. London: HMSO.

Great Britain Economic Advisory Council, Iron and Steel Committee (1930). *Report on Continental Steel Industries*. London.

Grosse, R. N. (1948). 'Determinants of the Size of Iron and Steel Firms in the United States. 1820–1880'. PhD dissertation, Harvard University.

Gupta, Vinod K. (1979). 'Subopotimal Capacity and its Determinants in Canadian Manufacturing Industries'. *Review of Economics and Statistics*, 61, November.

Hogan, William T. (1917). *Economic History of the Iron and Steel Industry in the United States*, Volumes 1–4. Lexington, Mass.: D. C. Heath and Co.

Iron and Coal Trades Review (various issues, 1907–14).

Iron and Steel Trades Employers Association (1926). 'Survey of Melters' Earnings'.

Landes, David (1970). *The Unbound Prometheus*. Cambridge University Press.

Langley, S. J. (1951). 'The Location Problem in the British Steel Industry'. *Oxford Economic Papers*, 3, June.

Marshall, Alfred (1903). 'Memorandum on the Fiscal Policy of International Trade'. In *Official Papers of Alfred Marshall*. London: Macmillan, 1926.

Marshall, Alfred (1923). *Industry and Trade*. London: Macmillan.

McCloskey, Donald (1973). *Economic Maturity and Entrepreneurial Decline*. Cambridge, Mass.: Harvard University Press.

Minchinton, W. E. (1957). *The British Tinplate Industry*. Oxford: Clarendon Press.

National Federation of Iron and Steel Manufacturers (1921). *Statistical Report on the Iron and Steel Industries*.

Payne, Peter L. (1979). *Colvilles and the Scottish Steel Industry*. Oxford: Clarendon Press.

Pigou, A. C. (1906). 'Protective and Preferential Duties'.

Pollard, Sidney (1957). 'British and World Shipbuilding 1890–1914'. *Journal of Economic History*, 17, September.

Pounds, Norman G. (1968). *The Ruhr*. New York: Greenwood Press.

Pugh, Sir Arthur (1951). *Men of Steel*. London: Iron and Steel Trades.

Roepke, Howard G. (1956). *Movements of the British Iron and Steel Industry— 1720–1951*. Illinois Studies in the Social Sciences, Volume 36. Urbana: University of Illinois Press.

Ryland's Directory (various years).

Scherer, Frederick M. (1980). *Industrial Market Structure and Economic Performance*. Chicago: Rand McNally.

Scherer, Frederick M. *et al.* (1975). *The Economics of Multi-Plant Operation*. Cambridge, Mass.: Harvard University Press.

Temin, Peter (1964). *Iron and Steel in Nineteenth Century America*. Cambridge, Mass.: Harvard University Press.

Temin, Peter (1966). 'The Relative Decline of the British Steel Industry, 1880–1913'. In *Industrialization in Two Systems*, ed. Henry Rosovsky. New York: John Wiley.

Tolliday, Steve (1978). 'Industry, Finance and the State'. PhD dissertation. Cambridge University.

US Bureau of the Census (1914). *Census of Manufacturers*. Washington, DC: US Government Printing Office.

US Commissioner of Corporations (1913). *Report on the Steel Industry*, Volumes 1–3. Washington, DC.

US Steel Corporation (1971). *The Making, Shaping, and Treating of Steel*, 9th edn. Pittsburgh: Herbick and Held.

Warren, Kenneth (1964). 'The Sheffield Rail Trades, 1861–1930: An Episode in the Locational History of the British Steel Industry'. *Transactions and Papers of the Institute of British Geographers*, no. 34.

Warren, Kenneth (1970). *The British Iron and Sheet Steel Industry Since 1840*. London: G. Bell & Sons.

Warren, Kenneth (1973). *The American Steel Industry 1850–1870: A Geographical Interpretation*. Oxford: Clarendon Press.

Webb, Steven B. (1980). 'Tariffs, Cartels, Technology, and Growth in the German Steel Industry, 1879 to 1914'. *Journal of Economic History*, 40, June.

Weiss, Leonard W. (1976). 'Optimal Plant Size and the Extent of Suboptimal Capacity'. In *Essays On Industrial Organization in Honour of Joe S. Bain*, ed. Robert Mason and P. D. Qualls. Cambridge: Ballinger.

Wiberg, Martin (1955). 'Relation of Type of Ore to Smelting Process'. In *Survey of World Iron Ore Resources*. New York: United Nations Department of Social and Economic Affairs.

Steel and Rationalization Policies, 1918–1950

Steven Tolliday
King's College, Cambridge

This essay examines the interrelation between the development of the British steel industry and the institutional structures affecting the industry between 1918 and 1950. It looks at such structures on three levels: the enterprise, the banks, and the state.

In the literature on the twentieth-century British economy, these relationships have been much neglected. As far as firms are concerned, there has been a bifurcation of historical work between the detailed description of individual companies (Payne, 1979) and studies of aggregate industry performance (Warren, 1979; Payne, 1968). The impacts of enterprise structures have implicitly been assumed to average out over an industry, so that industry development can be understood in the narrow terms of market analysis. The focus here is instead on how structures of decision-making and power within the firm shaped responses to market opportunities, and on how the structure of competition between firms hampered either reorganization or the emergence within the industry of a few predominant firms.

Similarly, while considerable attention has been paid to the relationship between the City and British industry in aggregate (Pollard, 1970; Longstreth, 1979; Edelstein, 1982), much less has been said about the involvement of financial institutions with particular industries. I argue that this involvement has been consistently underestimated, and that the historical record of the 1918–50 period reveals important lessons about outside intervention in industrial reorganization.

Finally, studies of the economic impact of the state have focused on the impact of macroeconomic fiscal and monetary policies. With the exception of the politicized conflicts surrounding the coal industry, little attention has been paid to the state's interaction with business enterprises (Kirby, 1977; for other exceptions see Hannah, 1977, 1979a; Reader, 1977). Yet between 1918 and 1950, the British state was in many cases a determinant force and was so particularly for the iron and steel industries.

Throughout the interwar years, leading industrialists, bankers, and governments regularly argued that the success and competitive efficiency of the iron and steel industry could best be secured by 'rationalization'. The term was often used imprecisely, but it generally implied reorganizing the industry through amalgamations which would eliminate excess capacity, concentrate production, and realize economies of scale and best-practice methods. The potential of such solutions to achieve their goals will be touched on later. What is not in doubt, however, was that 'rationalization' invariably headed the agenda in discussions on the reform of the industry, and that, in practice, little was achieved. The argument here is that to understand why this was so, we need to look beyond the simple economics of the industry to wider factors of economic organization and business institutions. The institutional structures of firms, banks, and the state were rooted in their nineteenth-century histories. Each had evolved erratically in response to certain historical problems and requirements. These institutional structures were not necessarily appropriate to the tasks of a period of crisis and adjustment, and though they were not unchanging entities, their legacy was inescapable.

Market Environment and Company Decision-making

The preceding paper by Bernard Elbaum has described the roots of the structural problems of the British steel industry. It is necessary here only to call attention to some of the principal features of the industry in the interwar years.

Steel was not yet in the grip of terminal decline. It fed into both rising and declining industries, and its interwar record on output compared favourably with that of its European competitors. Between 1913 and 1936–7, total European output increased by only 36.5 per cent (from 39.1 to 53.4 million tons), and that of Germany by 36.4 per cent (from 14.3 to 19.5 million tons): British output increased by 61.5 per cent, from 7.8 to 12.6 million tons.

The output figures, however, mask a serious problem of overcapacity. At a time when the fragmentation of the world market and the intensification of economic nationalisms marginalized world trade, the arena in which the overcapacity problem had to be tackled became, for the first time, home markets rather than export ones. The most acute crisis of overcapacity lasted from 1921 to 1933, during which time British steel capacity utilization fell as low as 30 per cent in 1921 and 1927 and rarely topped 60 per cent. The heavy steel sector reached 50 per cent utilization in only one year, 1929.

After 1933, the position was eased by the rapidly increasing demands of rearmament and the rather more moderate upswing of demand for thin flat products for consumer goods. The essential points to note here are, first, that the biggest traditional markets (shipbuilding and heavy steel) revived very vigorously after their dramatic slump, and, second, that before the war no other leading sector emerged to take their place. Shipbuilding, railways, and constructional and mechanical engineering accounted for 61 per cent of sales in 1924, and this had fallen only to 54.4 per cent in 1937. There was nothing comparable to the automobile 'leading sector' in the USA, and the take-off of demand for tubes, tinplate, and sheet steel was prolonged and difficult. In 1937 motors, cycles, and aircraft accounted for only 7 per cent of steel consumption, still less than the 9.5 per cent accounted for by hardware and hollow-ware. The continuities in the pattern of demand were highly significant.

TABLE 1
Concentration in steel, 1920–1937

	1920	1929	1937
Share of top 3 firms in total output	25.9%	28.5%	36.4%
Share of top 5 firms in total output	36.4%	38.2%	47.0%
Share of top 10 firms in total output	51.5%	57.2%	67.9%
No. of firms producing 80% total output	34	27	17

Source: Tolliday (1980).

Industry structure was highly fragmented. The interwar period displayed only a very weak trend towards concentration. As Table 1 shows, the top ten firms accounted for only 51.5 per cent of total output in 1920, 57.2 per cent in 1929, and 67.9 per cent in 1937. Yet competition was always restrained by the industry's division into several loose oligopolies along product lines, with a high degree of regional specialization. Within the regions, customer linkages based on product specialization and ownership were of great importance. Competition for major customers tended to be spasmodic, though when it came it could be cut-throat. In newer products such as tubes, tinplate, and sheet, oligopolies were established on the basis of quality and specialization. For example, Lysaghts, until the early 1930s, produced some 90 per cent of high-quality autobody sheet (Warren, 1970).

The major cyclical swings in demand and profitability that dominated the period underscored the inertia of the industrial structure. The profits of the heavy steelmakers collapsed and then recovered dramatically, while in the relatively new, lighter products profits fell less in the slump but accelerated less spectacularly in the late 1930s. The key to survival for most firms was moderating the impact of the troughs so as to make it through to the next upswing. Often the relationship of financial structure to profit swings was vital. Heavily geared firms were vulnerable to collapse, but those with more flexible capital structures and less debt encumbrances could sit out depressions with a degree of comfort. For either type of firm, however, it was hard to see the way ahead clearly. In such a segmented and fluctuating market, no size-class of firms enjoyed a clearly better level of performance than any other. Middle-size or small firms could find market niches and prosper while larger firms were often brought low by their high overheads. In general, exit from the industry usually resulted only from a long and painful process of attrition (Tolliday, 1980, Part One).

The static industry-wide structure was mirrored *within* firms. Many firms owned best-practice units, but few were low-cost producers taken as a whole. The character of competition, along with the intensely cyclical chronology of plant construction, led to a spectrum of vintages and costs within the units of a given firm. (For a detailed analysis based on company records, see Tolliday, 1980, Tables I.vii and I.viii.) In a depressed market, diseconomies of scale were prevalent (Burn, 1940; Warren, 1970). For most of the interwar period, the main force for cost reduction was a continuous stream of piecemeal modifications. Investment in new capacity, when it came, occurred in sudden increments. The overheads of best-practice new plants operating below capacity could be crippling, while old fully amortized plants could attain remarkable longevity.

What determined the ways in which firms in the various sectors of the market responded to the constraints and opportunities that faced them? In what follows I argue that, in each of three of the most important sectors of the industry (heavy steelmaking on the north-east coast and in Scotland, and the tinplate industry in South Wales) the firms' patterns of ownership, control, and decision-making structures played a determinant role in the varying outcomes. Power relations within the firms interacted with the technical and market environment to close certain options or promote others, with a variety of consequences for the 'rationalization' of the industry.[1]

Heavy Steel-making on the North-East Coast

On the north-east coast, four major firms had built up an overlapping, oligopolistic industrial structure since the 1880s. By and large, the firms produced the same range of heavy steel products and shared and periodically fought over the same classes of customers. Often they duplicated each other's plants on adjacent sites. All had organizations that were strong at certain points in the chain of production and weak at others. In the conditions of long-term overcapacity in the 1920s, this structure might appear to be conducive to reorganization by merger. Merged firms could have contracted in size and re-equipped internally. But this did not happen. The fragmented structure of the industry in the region survived intact through the interwar years, even though its weaknesses and the desirability of structural changes were widely acknowleged.

This inertia was based on the interaction between product market conditions and internal conflicts involving creditors, shareholders, families, managers, and customers of each enterprise. From the 1890s, a slow growth of demand had led to relatively low rates of return from scrapping and new building and had made incremental returns from improvements generally more attractive (Allen, 1981). Expansion had to come largely at the expense of competitors who had considerable defensive strengths. Piecemeal expansion during World War I was superimposed on this, and by the 1920s the region had come to possess a motley collection of new and old plant.

When traditional markets contracted in the 1920s, the lack of metal fabricating outlets made diversification difficult. South Durham, for example, tried but failed to break into the pipe trade. But there remained a certain resilience in the traditional products and firms like Dorman Long pursued the option of searching ever wider for markets for their existing products. Even in the over-supplied ship-plate market, firms depended on their tight linkages to existing customers.

Shipbuilders put a premium on the reliability of product quality, on-the-spot specifications, speed of delivery, and detailed consultation. A period of cut-throat competition occurred between 1925 and 1927 as firms with new plant attempted violently to rearrange these customer networks. Once that was past, the makers were able to restrict competition among themselves, hold on to their principal customers, and maintain prices relatively effectively in a period of falling costs. Generally speaking, the crisis of the traditional markets was not severe enough to compel firms into a stark choice between bankruptcy or merger.

Still, proposals for rationalization by merger loomed large in the region from the early 1920s until the mid-1930s. They were publically endorsed by industry leaders, government inquiries, and expert consultants, but little came of them. The mergers under discussion usually had desirable features; but they depended on assessments of trends and perceptions of long-term advantages that rarely made them seem *overwhelmingly* desirable. And they were argued out in the context of historical rivalries and channelled through internal decision-making processes that made the taking of calculated risks very unlikely.

Mergers were made difficult, to begin with, by the irritable gerontocracies that headed the firms. Dorman Long was led into the 1930s by two octogenarian managing directors; the board meetings of Bolckow Vaughan in the 1920s had to be conducted in slow loud voices for the benefit of the chairman's ear-trumpet. Old animosities constantly polluted the atmosphere of the discussions. But, even when these management figures had been committed to re-organization, this commitment was not decisive, for these directors no longer exerted the sort of unitary control over the businesses that they once had. Expansion and financial crises had brought a host of new centres of power on to the scene.

Within the major firms there were congeries of rival interests, each of which benefited differentially from alternative strategies, and each of which had varying powers within the firm to influence merger discussions. These powers were more frequently the power to block or forbid an option than to compel a particular outcome, and they generally rested on a mix of financial and legal rights. In the critical period of merger discussions between 1929 and 1934, the size and complexity of firms precluded the direct personal bargaining between owners that had characterized the last wave of mergers around World War I. There was no way to avoid long, drawn-out processes of careful conciliation and recomposition of rival interests.

Any major reorganization of the region through merger necessarily centred on bringing together the operations of the two biggest firms: Dorman Long and its neighbouring rival, South Durham & Cargo Fleet. In both firms control was diffuse. On the South Durham side of the equation, the senior management was divided into two factions. The older figures behind Ben Talbot wanted nothing to do with the 'old deadheads' at Dorman Long. The directors favouring a merger, however, counted on the support of the Furness family who had overall control of the company as a part of their widespread shipping and shipbuilding empire. For a while, Dorman Long engaged in conspiratorial machinations with Ethelbert Furness to engineer the ousting of Talbot and the transfer of boardroom control into sympathetic hands. But the scheme was of doubtful probity and had to be dropped. Talbot had an effective base of support among the ordinary shareholders who had enjoyed a much better earnings record than those of Dorman Long in the 1920s. The shareholders took the view that in a future expansion they would do just as well as an independent concern as they would do in a cumbersome agglomerated combine with heavy debt burdens and inherited over-capitalisation. Likewise, it was hard for them to see how a merger could eliminate the enormous short-term overcapacity of the depression.

Managers and shareholders, however, proved ultimately persuadable about the value of a merger. The group that could not be persuaded was the strategically crucial customers and local interests who dominated the relatively small class of preference shareholders and whose consent was vital for an amalgamation. They were effectively marshalled by Hartlepool shipbuilding interests, who feared that a merger would result in the closure of South Durham's Hartlepool steelworks and thus jeopardize their on-the-spot relationship with local steel-making. They were able to conduct a prolonged delaying action.

On the Dorman Long side of the picture there were similar internal complications. There, the crucial obstacle was the debenture holders. It was hard for the company to argue that an assured earning power in a merger could compensate them for surrendering their current security in the event of a liquidation. The directors browbeat the debenture holders into accepting the scheme with the aid of a misleading prospectus issued to them by their trustees, Barclays Bank. A minority of debenture holders, however, contested the prospectus in the chancery courts and forced the company to set the scheme aside and re-submit another. This combined with the rearguard action at South Durham to finally terminate the scheme.

One further set of vested interests served to complicate matters still further: the banks who held the various companies' massive overdrafts. In theory, they could use a firm's financial weakness as a lever to push forward the sort of reorganization by merger that they deemed desirable. Unlike any of the other interests involved, with the possible exception of the Furness family, they could potentially back their power within a firm with access to cash for reconstruction, and they could threaten to force a recalcitrant company into liquidation. In practice, the banks were reluctant to take on an active role in reorganization. The local clearing banks, particularly Barclays and National Provincial, had interests that spanned rival firms, and, rather than throwing their weight behind particular concerns, they often got bogged down in trying to preserve their 'neutrality'. They treated their loans primarily on an actuarial basis, and most often sought to remain as outsiders with their liquidity unimpaired. Only at Bolckow Vaughan, where a financially top-heavy company was foundering, did the banks take steps to force a merger.

The Bank of England, through the Bankers' Industrial Development company (see below, p. 96), took a strong interest in the schemes for amalgamation on the north-east coast. As we shall see, the Bank was committed to an industrial strategy of regional amalgamations, but without a powerful group of entrepreneurs to push forward such a scheme on the ground, the BID confined itself to external exhortation. It opposed 'buying out' awkward interests on principle and refused to use its financial muscle to induce activity. The BID also wanted to see the local bankers doing more. In the end, both Barclays and the BID looked to the other to take on a role of risk-bearing merger promoter that they were not willing to take on themselves.

The failure of the merger proposals meant that development in the 1930s was a ramshackle affair. By 1937, for instance, Dorman Long produced 1.5 million tons of ingots from twenty blast furnaces and thirty-three steel furnaces at five works, four of which were almost within a stone's throw of each other. Expansion, when it came in the mid-1930s, was based on pressing every existing unit into service. New construction was rare, and bottlenecks were a constant headache. Although merger and rationalization would not have been a panacea, it is probable that a major shake-out, concentration, and centralization of control and investment would have brought higher profits and efficiency in the 1930s (Heal, 1974; Warren, 1979). Yet the revival also showed that the more conservative managers, shareholders and creditors had been no fools in believing that they could do very nicely within the existing structures of production when the revival came. They pursued, in effect, a reasonably low-risk strategy of battening down the hatches, and their cramped decision-making structures were capable of no broader horizon of decisions.

Heavy Steel-making in Scotland

In contrast to this multi-firm fragmentation, a near-monopoly emerged by 1939 in the Scottish region under Colvilles Ltd. Yet this process was too slow to position Colvilles to make production changes at the opportune time. Really, the amalgamation occurred after the idea of a radical solution to structural problems had been abandoned.

The growth of the near-monopoly in Scotland did not result from a pursuit of economies of scale, relocation or the introduction of new processes of production. Nor, contrary to Payne's (1979) argument, did it result from a strategic campaign by the biggest firm's leading entrepreneur, John Craig of Colvilles. In fact, the Scottish firms were every bit as incapable of restructuring themselves by their own efforts and every bit as crippled by the antagonisms of rival interests within and between firms as on the north-east coast. The difference between the regions was the strategic influence of the giant shipbuilders and the bankers.

In the 1920s, the Scottish steel industry was fragmented, small-scale, lacking in integration between iron and steelmaking, based in anachronistic locations, and heavily dependent on scrap as a raw material. Moreover, it was utterly dependent on shipbuilding customers—a dependence that had been reinforced in the postwar boom when *all* the major Scottish steelmakers were taken over by their shipbuilding customers in a scramble to secure their suppliers. This scramble had little effect on the future pattern of sales, though it did often have dire consequences for the parties involved in these overcapitalized mergers. The most important result, however, was that it brought the formidable financial power and resources of the Lithgow family into close touch with the industry. The Lithgows had enormous financial reserves, and their tramp shipping business was one of the few shipbuilding enterprises that consistently made profits all through the depression. Sir James Lithgow was one of the rare entrepreneurs of the period with the power of the purse and financial resources to back his entrepreneurial judgements.

The crucial agenda in the rationalization of the Scottish industry was the creation of a fully integrated new steelworks on a new site through either co-operative action or amalgamation by the major steelmakers. During the 1920s a variety of alternatives were explored, based on various Scottish or Anglo-Scotish amalgamation schemes to make better use of existing production facilities. All of these foundered on the problems arising from different perceptions of relative advantages or barriers posed by certain interests. At Lanarkshire Steel Co., bank control ensured the survival of a firm that might otherwise have left the industry to the advantage of its competitors. At the Steel Company of Scotland, the controlling consortium of shipbuilders was unwilling to undertake any merger moves that might strengthen the hand of their shipbuilding rivals either inside or outside the consortium. Nevertheless, other shipbuilders like Lithgow were becoming more and more afraid of the implications of dependence on an ailing industry. For a while they could be tempted by cheap imports, but these were never an adequate substitute for a healthy local steel industry.

In the late 1920s, the basis for a comprehensive solution seemed to be offered by the report of the American consulting engineers H. A. Brassert & Co. drawn up for the steelmakers at the initiative of outside financial and City interests. The Brassert plan called for centralizing best-practice operations on a tidewater site, and it stands up remarkably well to the test of hindsight (Warren, 1965). For a while it seemed possible that the scheme might go ahead, but in the event it was undermined by the impact of falling import prices, rising costs of construction, and the threat of high financial burdens of overcapacity and narrow profit margins. It was a high-risk strategy, and again rivalries, vested interests, and limited decision-making horizons blocked it.

Once the Brassert scheme was abandoned, any real opportunity to link amalgamation directly to a fundamental reorganization of production was past. The development of a regional monopoly that followed occured *despite* this. It probably would not have occurred if it had been left to the steel firms alone. Colvilles continued to seek a more powerful position through mergers, but time and again they stopped short because, as the lowest-cost producer in the region, they found that the advantages of mergers were slim and the possible cash-flow problems perilous. They decided on the price they were prepared to pay and stuck to it, even if a few percentage points might result in the failure of a merger. They held endless discussions but baulked at the requisite flexibility. Meanwhile, in the trough of the depression, high-cost firms in the region benefited from their superior adaptability to low levels of output.

Revival brought faster amalgamation because of a new, strong line taken by shipbuilders and bankers. In contrast to Craig's grudging assessment of the specific costs and benefits of mergers, they took a 'view from above'. Unlike the north-east coast situation, the Bank of England found in Scotland Sir James Lithgow, a powerful entrepreneur whom they could ally with to push their ideas forward. From 1930 Lithgow held a powerful financial stake and partial control in Colvilles, and in the mid-1930s he forced through a series of mergers on the basis of his own direct initiatives and personal coups, aided and abetted by the Bankers' Industrial Development Company (BID). The only thing that came close to stopping him was the complex problem of preventing the reorganization of Scottish steel from bailing out or assisting his shipbuilding arch-rivals, Harland and Wolff, who also held massive steel interests.

But rationalization of production did not follow. After the failure of the Brassert scheme, there was no re-exploration of *how* the unification of owner-ship would lead to a reorganization of production. While merger diplomacy filled the centre of the stage, long-term planning was neglected. Patching, improvisation, and second-best solutions were carried through to remarkable effect and greatly reduced the relative inefficiency of the Scottish industry. But these developments took place at the frontiers of their limited pos-sibilities from the moment of their inception. When unified control came in the late 1930s, it was too late. Costs of construction were soaring, and speed of expansion was the main priority to meet soaring demand. Radical remedies were off the agenda, and the developments of the 1930s fatally compromised the future of the Scottish industry (Warren, 1979). External forces re-shaped the structure of firms, competition, and decision-making, but they could not remodel production.

Steel and Tinplate in South Wales

In marked contrast to the North-East and Scotland, the tinplate sector, based in South Wales, experienced a major change in markets, technology, and industrial structure. New demands for consumer goods produced new opportunities for higher-quality and larger-scale production; the new technology of the continuous strip mill provided the means. Alongside this came a shift from the nineteenth-century world of teeming small producers to a world in which one giant, Richard Thomas and Co., appeared for a time to have the possibility of taking a comprehensive grip on the industry.

Such changes would appear to offer an opportunity for a radical break from the old forms of industrial organization and for the emergence of what Alfred Chandler has called the 'modern' business enterprise, with greater control and co-ordination at all levels of production and a strategy of market control and vertical integration. In fact, however, the way in which mass production emerged from the world of small producers stamped it indelibly with the institutional legacy of the industry's past.

By the 1920s, there was world overcapacity in tinplate as successive countries cornered their home markets. Empire markets provided some stability, but from World War I onwards home demand was catching up on exports. Through the 1920s the industry served scattered and diverse consumer markets. Production was fragmented, entry to the industry was easy with little capital involved, and family partnerships predominated. Tinplate technology had changed little since the seventeenth century. Techniques were labour-intensive, and firms coped with cyclical fluctuations by laying off labour and closing mills (Minchinton, 1957). There was no technical imperative to quantity production or integration with steel; indeed, the availability of cheap continental semi-finished steel encouraged re-rollers to manoeuvre between British and continental suppliers. As a result, merger activity in the 1920s was confined to the elimination of some of the weakest of the family firms. A tail of small firms persisted, sustained by numerous speculative merchants who linked small producers to heterogeneous consumers.

During the 1930s a significant diversity of demand remained. In the United States the technology of the continuous strip mill had developed on the basis of demand for high-quality volume production of sheet steel, notably for the motor vehicle industry. In Britain, however, demand for sheet and tinplate never exhibited the uniformity, the technical rigorousness, or the market power of giant hegemonic consumers that characterized America. The result was a lively debate about the applicability of such mass production techniques in Britain. The economic space for a strip mill in Britain was very narrow. The new technology would press against the limits of the market. The demand for either sheet or tinplate *alone* was generally not thought to be enough for a strip mill, and any push for dominance through innovation would entail major risks.

William Firth, the managing director of Richard Thomas and Co., nevertheless opted for such a strategy in the mid-1930s. He was able to act decisively within the firm because the Thomas family had transferred their personal grip on the business intact into the hands of this rising entrepreneurial autocrat in the late 1920s. But he faced considerable problems with his competitors. After the tariff had killed off imported semi-finished steel and paved the way for effective price maintenance and quota agreements, cartellization had frozen the fragmented structure of the industry. In order to innovate, therefore, Richard Thomas had to undertake a tangled process of marshalling both supply and demand to establish a tinplate monopoly and invade strip production. Firth had to buy up competitors, close them down, and retain their quotas.

Many competitors resisted, often with the encouragement of Richard Thomas's larger rivals, and the take-over process proved to be slow and costly. Their rivals (Baldwins, Lysaghts, and GKN) seized the opportunity of the weak financial underbelly of the scheme and campaigned to frighten off the City. Faced by these difficulties, Firth enlisted government approval to ease his path by the expedient of building the new mill at Ebbw Vale, in the heart of depressed South Wales, rather than at the preferred site of Redbourn in Lincolnshire. He expected that the strip mill would produce steel so much more cheaply than the rival mills that this would offset the disadvantages of a poor site and location. He also hoped that the government would exert pressure to give the new works a clear run by discouraging future rival developments.

In practice, wooing the government was double-edged, pushing the firm into a second-best location for their otherwise best-practice plant, and not yielding as much protection as Firth hoped. When the scheme ran into financial difficulties in the slump of 1938, the rivals had a second opportunity to attempt to stifle it. They used their position in the British Iron and Steel Federation (BISF) to capture partial control of the Richard Thomas board as the price of financial support by the Bank of England. Once established, they attempted to use their position to restrict the new development. After a period of boardroom trench warfare they were eventually ousted, but soon after Firth was also removed by the Bank and the BISF for refusing to run Ebbw Vale in co-operation with his rivals. The centralized firm of the early 1930s, which had proved uniquely capable of strategic decision-making, was thereby transformed into a federal parlour of BISF representatives, rival firms, bankers, and figurehead personalities. The firm's drive to transform the industry was undermined.

The Influence of Structure on Enterprise Strategy

Despite the constraints of the market for steel, certain opportunities had existed for significant progress in the varying sectors: consolidation and the avoidance of overlapping development in the North-East, relocation and new building in Scotland, and new technology and volume production in tinplate. All of these options were, however, limited by the historical structures of firms and institutions of management and by the frozen, fragmented industry structure in which they operated. In a situation of loose oligopoly, interests within firms could bicker and hesitate endlessly over the terms of reorganization. Strategic failure resulted from the interaction of competitive constraints and intra-firm institutions. At the same time, this log-jam was often abetted by external forces. Existing industrial structures were reinforced by powerful regional consumers like the shipbuilders, by the bankers, and by government policies. For British steel firms, structure persistently determined strategy.

Numerous parallels to the experience of steel can be found in other industries. Internal conflicts of interest shaped the strategies of many of the big defensive federations such as Associated Portland Cement, English Sewing Cotton or Imperial Tobacco. Consumer interests imposed themselves on producer industries and constrained their lines of development as in the striking examples of the 'builder's friend' system in shipbuilding, the newspaper proprietors' control of papermaking, and government restraints on the evolution of the Anglo-Persian Oil Co. (APOC) (Alford, 1979; Slaven, 1982; Reader, 1982; Ferrier, 1982).

In a world of ambiguous markets and arguable options, diffuse entrepreneurship and power rivalries had a pivotal role in preventing rationalization. Yet new forms of co-ordination and planning were needed, not as ways of tackling new expansionary economic needs, but in order to curb the excessive and rapidly rising costs of the existing industrial structure. The possibility therefore arose of a different sort of 'visible hand' in industry based on an active role by banks or the state to correct a perceived failure of the market. Most interpretations have argued that banks and government remained fairly marginal in the interwar years (e.g. Aldcroft, 1970; Phillips and Maddock, 1973). In fact, as we shall see, they were more extensively involved in promoting and shaping industrial reorganization than is often recognized. Though they were not always successful in achieving their aims, they were crucial not only in steel, but also in cotton textiles, shipping, electricity supply, coal, agriculture, aircraft, oil, armaments, and railways, and were of considerable significance in a number of other industries.[2]

Britain's traditional industries depended on a market that was breaking down. Yet the institutions that might have had the potential to intervene had been formed by the same historical developments that shaped the crisis in which they were intervening. Britain's early start, and the long span and relatively slow pace of its industrial and commercial development, had resulted in the development of political and financial, as well as managerial, institutions that were as resistant to change as the structure of production itself. The 'visible hands' of banks and state themselves needed to be remodelled and to develop new functions and capabilities before they could operate effectively to reorganize the economy.

Banking and Rationalization

Early British industrialization required relatively limited amounts of capital and was uniquely self-financing compared with economies whose late take-off required more systematic mobilization of funds. The main requirement of the British financial system was a regime of sound money, and the financial sector looked mainly to the lucrative, liquid and marketable British and foreign government stocks, railway holdings, and gilt-edged bonds for their profits. Until 1900, industrial capital formation remained predominantly in the hands of friends, family, or business contacts. There is little evidence that British industry had any large unsatisfied demand for capital from the London money market. In contrast to German and Japanese banks, British banks developed neither ownership roles nor skills and expertise to evaluate or intervene in managerial performance (Kennedy, 1976).

The decline of British world power and the gold standard and the onset of economic crisis in the aftermath of World War I were bound to place under stress the notion that banking and industry were separate but happily complementary spheres. What was not so predictable was that, as the stresses began to emerge, a number of banking concerns should find themselves caught with a higher level of industrial commitments than at any time in the past.

Bankers shared in the euphoria of the industrialists in the 1919–20 boom. This last spasm of Britain's old primacy in the world economy saw a violent deflection of banking capital towards domestic industry that had no parallel, except perhaps in the brief domestic boom of the 1890s. It mainly took the form of overdrafts, freely given and with slack provisions for repayment. The lure of high profits overcame traditional caution, and the banks' overdraft business (traditionally centred on a speedy turnover) became tied up in frozen loans in the downturn of the 1920s. The position was then exacerbated by further lending to support the original loans.

By 1929, 14 per cent of non-government overdrafts were in heavy industry. Several banks had 4–10 per cent of their overdrafts in steel alone, and these were dominated by giant frozen overdrafts to a few large companies. Some dozen companies held around 40 per cent of the steel overdrafts in 1929. The size of the overdrafts to steel were neither as big nor as concentrated as in cotton (where the lending position threatened to bring down major banks

like William Deacons), but it seriously narrowed their cash ratios and introduced rigidity into their lending (Tolliday, 1980; Balogh, 1947; Thomas,
1978).

For the steel companies, this 'overdraft crisis' had important ramifications.
By the second half of the decade, overdraft finance amounted to a sum almost
equal to that from all other forms of loans. Consequently, many firms were
dependent on the goodwill of their bankers to avoid a receivership or liquidation. But bank power was limited. The bankers lacked expert knowledge, and
in a competitive banking environment they feared to interfere lest their more
profitable industrial customers should move their accounts elsewhere. Nor
did they want to place themselves in a position of liability to their clients by
pushing certain courses of action. Mostly they acted defensively, as just one
creditor interest among many, seeking greater security, nursing their loans,
or maximizing the nuisance value of their clients' businesses. No structural
or institutional changes resulted from the experience, and revival in the
1930s sent banks scrambling to get out of their industrial loans so quickly
that later in that decade they were bemoaning the lack of lucrative industrial
advances.

Central banking faced distinct but related problems.[3] The 1920s saw the
Bank of England struggling to retain its world role. One corollary of its
global view was a greater willingness than the clearing banks to take a broad
overall perspective and to contemplate a role in restructuring British industry. However, the Bank of England lacked any institutional mechanisms to
influence the policy of the clearing banks. For most of the 1920s it did little
more than exert moral pressure on them to 'face facts' and not to relieve
market pressures on lame ducks to reorganize or go bankrupt. Where it was
itself involved as a banker to industrial clients, the central bank did not act so
very differently from the clearers. The crisis of 1929–32, however, brought
about a major re-evaluation.

The Bank of England's developing concern for the basic industries grew
out of several simultaneous developments. During the 1920s it had been
drawn into the crises of several industrial firms as a result of its prewar
practice of combining a commercial banking business with its role as a
central banker. At the same time, the crisis of the traditional industries
spilled over into the banking sector itself. The cotton crisis, for instance,
precipitated a banking crisis in Lancashire. It also undermined Montagu
Norman's cherished plan to create a 'Big Sixth' bank to counterbalance the
growing power of the 'Big Five', and Norman feared that similar problems
might lead to a need for further expensive rescue operations.

Against this background, a milieu of rationalizing ideas was highly
influential within the bank. 'Rationalization' centred on the idea of eliminating excess capacity by creating big amalgamations which would use the best
available units from the preceding enterprises in a co-ordinated fashion at
much higher levels of capacity utilization. The new combines could then use

the advantages of an improved cash-flow, increased market power, and centralized management to introduce best-practice investment. Norman was sympathetic to these elegant, efficient, and logical solutions emanating from figures like Weir, Mond, MacGowan, and McKenna. The personnel of the Securities Management Trust (SMT), the organization that the Bank created in 1929 to deal with its industrial affairs, were recruited from these circles. Here and in the Bankers' Industrial Development Company (BID), which was formed a year later, the Bank for the first time began to equip itself with an apparatus for knowledgeable intervention in industry. By the late 1920s, the threat of increased government intervention was pushing Norman to make industrial reorganization a high priority. With the coming of the second Labour government he saw the Bank as the front line of a 'bulwark to keep the Socialist Government from tampering with industry', as Nigel Campbell, a senior member of the BID, described it.

The hub of this project was the BID, formed by Norman in alliance with the main merchant banks in the City to provide finance for approved schemes of industrial rationalization in 1929. Norman's idea was to use the BID for a strategic intervention ('a brief and particular object which could be accomplished within five years or never') to reorganize key basic industries. As far as steel was concerned, such a reorganization was to be based on a blueprint drawn up within the BID by Charles Bruce Gardner in consultation with Brassert. The plan was radical and cursory, but it was sound enough in outline (Warren, 1965; Payne, 1979). However, it ignored the problems of history and the means by which such a transition could be carried out.

To carry the plan through required a major break with banking traditions which the BID was not prepared to undertake. It was not prepared to act as an investment bank, viewing itself instead as a merger promoter. Where the market would not respond, it was not willing to put up its own funds. Later, when the market became more willing to invest, the BID found that it no longer had significant influence over where funds should go. As far as its own capital was concerned, the BID oscillated between a desire for an 'exceptional' role and an insistence that, unless it applied the same tests of soundness as other bankers, competitive deformations would result. Even where some of the BID staff were prepared to step beyond this framework, they were not able to persuade the issuing houses to support them.

The only alternative that remained was to draw in government finance, but this contradicted the Bank's *political* aims. According to Norman,

To invoke government aid now would be tantamount to an admission that it was indispensable to rationalization and [would] offer a dangerous weapon to that section of the Government and its supporters who were only too anxious to seize an opportunity to bring industry in some degree or other under state control.

The Bank was prepared to block government moves towards intervention with brutal directness. Most notably, when Ramsay MacDonald and the President of the Board of Trade raised the possibility of a Public Utility Company for steel in 1931, they were at once threatened with non-co-operation by the City and browbeaten into withdrawing the proposal. Norman and the BID aspired to a role of strategic direction in industry, but they recoiled from its implications.

This imbalance between the Bank's aspirations and the means employed to realize them also dominated its involvement in particular reorganization schemes. Starting in the late 1920s, the Bank played a major role in nearly all of the big steel restructuring projects. Armstrong Whitworth was one of the Bank's biggest commercial clients. Their troubles in the 1920s placed the SMT in a crucial position in the reorganization of their extensive iron and steel interests. These were hived off into two separate companies: the English Steel Corporation and the Lancashire Steel Corporation (LSC). In both of these companies the Bank not only failed to achieve its wider aims, but also jeoparized the more restricted goals which the company managements themselves wished to pursue.

At LSC there was constant conflict between SMT and the managerial agents whom they put in to run the firm. The latter wanted to pursue limited policies of growth and modernization; Norman, however, constantly pressed them to pursue the shadow of wider amalgamations. Norman's broad aim was to merge LSC with United Steel, the dominant company in the region. But in the end, his own caution vitiated the larger scheme. In 1930 he refused to take up an option on the control of United Steel, then in a receivership, which would have placed him in the driving seat of a regional merger. Instead of the verve of a company promoter or entrepreneur, he applied the traditional caution of a banker, and the scheme lost its way.

The Bank's broad rationalizing aspirations also made them an interested party in Stewarts and Lloyds' scheme to build a new Basic Bessemer plant at Corby in the East Midlands ore-fields. Although the Bank's own technical advisers argued in favour of this large-scale plant on the basis of maximum efficiency, Norman forced them to curtail the scheme. His aim was to prevent the emergence of a powerful new force in the area which might cut across his blueprint for reorganization. Once demand began to revive, however, Stewarts and Lloyds were quickly able to escape from dependence on the BID and to scale up their scheme as it proceeded.

Far from acting as a coherent force for rationalization, the Bank became more and more embroiled with the conflicting interests in the Midlands and the North-West and were implicated in several developments that were partially conflicting and overlapping. At LSC they exercised control over a firm that they were not wholly sure should be in existence. At Corby they sought to confine one of the most dynamic schemes of the interwar years to suboptimal levels. When a trade war between United Steel and Stewarts and Lloyds loomed in the mid-1930s, the Bank was caught between the two camps. They dared not even sell up their interests for fear of the effect this might have on the balance of forces between the rival companies. Their power to influence events became an embarrassment, and their original grand plans declined into a harassed and prolonged campaign for extrication. A sense of helplessness and frustration permeated the BID. It became clear that they needed the assistance of big and powerful firms like United Steel more than United Steel needed them. Yet they feared the consequences of throwing their weight into the scales in favour of one firm against its rivals. In the end, they were left on the sidelines.

The Bank encountered similar problems of translating financial control into managerial control in their involvement with the steel and armaments firm of Beardmores on Clydeside. When Beardmores was on the brink of collapse the Bank put up the necessary cash to keep the firm alive and to forestall intervention by the new Labour government in 1929. The stated aim of Bank control was the orderly liquidation of the company. Beardmores's management, however, wanted to save the business and build it up, and splits developed within the SMT on this issue. Norman lacked a new management team that he could put in to implement his policy decisively, and it was some eighteen months before the management was fully purged and brought into line with bank policy. Furthermore, the Bank then created further difficulties for its own goal of orderly liquidation by its unwillingness to use its funds strategically.

Norman tried to run the Beardmores business within a tight actuarial framework which came close to precipitating a rushed and expensive closure. The SMT was actually less flexible than the clearing banks in extending facilities to nurse their client through a trough. Norman tended to swing between rigid short-term financial controls which made the business hard to run, and exceptional semi-political policies in the long term. Once again disengagement proved difficult. The obvious course of selling the assets to Lithgow was long delayed by the Bank's fear of appearing to show him favour. When the Bank did finally sell to him, Lithgow's strategy was one that they strongly disapproved of.

At Beardmores, English Steel, LSC, and Corby, the Bank's wider schemes all came to nothing. Norman was almost obsessed with grand schemes, but where they proved not to be feasible, he and the BID lacked the sort of managerial capabilities and industrial expertise to devise and pursue more flexible strategies. Once the industrial strategist was scratched, the orthodox banker lurked not very far below the surface.

By the late 1930s the clearing banks, with some ease, and the Bank of England, rather more slowly, had largely got themselves out of their involvements arising from the collapse of the old industrial giants. But the problems of high-risk large-scale investment in new technology drew the Bank back into the industry in the late 1930s on a larger scale than ever before—to rescue the strip mill schemes of Richard Thomas and John Summers when their over-extended financial base threatened to cave in.

When the Bank rescued Richard Thomas in 1938, it demanded control. This time it hoped to use the national steelmakers' association, the British Iron and Steel Federation (BISF), to exercise control in an ordered way in the 'national interest'. Instead, the Bank ran into the problems of the internal rivalries that existed within the BISF. Richard Thomas's new board became engaged in prolonged and vicious boardroom infighting with the old management.

The alliance with the BISF proved no more successful in running a controlled firm than the attempts to run LSC and Beardmores with the Bank's own agents. This time the Bank did not seek to impose a blueprint for amalgamations: but it became apparent that it lacked ideas for non-merger solutions as well. There was no attempt to use the opportunity of a major technical change to back the most efficient single producer against its rivals. The Bank simply devolved its managerial responsibility to the BISF.

The Bank's commitment to support projects blessed by the BISF also drew it into the problems of Summers's new sheet strip mill. Here, though Norman persistently sought to tie the project into wider reorganization schemes, control of a weak and vulnerable firm was no springboard for rationalization. The real question at issue was the survival of the strip mill. The Bank was in no position to do more than arbitrate between alternative tactical amalgamations that might help achieve this.

Though formally in control, in practice the Bank depended entirely on the attitude taken by Summers's rivals. Behind the scenes, United Steel called the tune. United Steel had previously been apprehensive about leaping into a new product market and a new technology through the outright takeover of Summers's sheet business. Bank control, however, enabled United Steel to ease itself into the driving seat at Summers step by step. The bigger firm broke down the resistance of the Summers family through the creation of interlocking directorates and a progressively increasing shareholding stake, while the Bank was unable to force any advance commitments to rationalize the business in line with Bank policy. The always somewhat abstract theme of 'rationalization' had now become vacuous. It recurred as a theme and aspiration but no longer had any purchase on the industrialists in charge on the ground. The Bank was no more than a pressure group—and one that could be manipulated by skillful industrialists to their own ends.

Thus the interwar years saw the weakening of the old pattern of mutual autonomy between finance and industry. Many banks became vitally interested in industrial decision-making and restructuring. The Bank of England in particular saw the need for planned reorganization, both to prevent state intervention and in the interests of efficiency. Invariably it viewed the appropriate path as achieving economies of scale via merger, and aimed to act as a sort of neutral national interest grouping that could play an important intermediate technocratic role. The Bank was most deeply involved in steel and cotton, but its industrial interests were far more widespread. In all of these fields Norman tended to see big amalgamations as a universal solution.

In locomotives and cotton textiles, Norman's vision of big amalgamations may not have been appropriate, but many of the steel schemes stand up well to detailed examination. In practice, however, the Bank was not willing to shoulder the burdens of entrepreneurial leadership. Above all, the weight of banking traditions made this unlikely to happen. Norman, the SMT, and the BID were all ultimately committed to profoundly orthodox economics which left no space for the idea of absorbing short-term losses for long-term advantages. They lacked any extensive range of managerial capabilities, and time and again got bogged down in conflict-ridden relationships *within* the enterprise.

Beyond this, they were reluctant to change their relationship to the state. Large-scale industrial responsibility pointed towards political accountability; the sheer size of schemes implied the need for government consent or even guarantees. Yet this contradicted Norman's long-term determination to preserve the independence of the Bank, his virulent anti-Labourism, and his opposition to government intervention. Hence the peak of Bank involvement came in 1929–31 to prevent involvement by the Labour government. Though Norman toyed for a time with the development of interventionist financial institutions, he and the BID finally backed away from the task in the light of disappointing experiences. The revitalization of the traditional modes of industrial finance out of retained profits in the 1930s took much of the pressure off them, but their experience with large-scale new technology at Richard Thomas and Summers in the late 1930s showed that the problems arising from industrial intervention remained unresolved.

The State and Rationalization

Did the state prove any more capable than the banks of developing a role of economic management to compensate for market failure?

While in many European economies the state was deeply involved in the early period of capitalist production, this was not so in Britain. In terms of state involvement in industry, Britain was at the low end of the international spectrum before World War I. Nevertheless, as we noted above, state intervention in the interwar years became more extensive than the textbooks might lead one to think.

Britain, therefore, is a rare example of a transition from a little to a great deal of state intervention. Generally speaking, British state institutions developed at one remove from business around fiscal, legal, imperial military, and labour matters. The state that emerged was not the product of periods of deliberate state-building but an accumulation of structures and institutions that did not bear any clear relation to overt changes in government ideology or policy.

In the first quarter of the twentieth century the government was slowly forced into economic management by the demands of national efficiency and military supremacy (optical glass, cellulose, dyestuffs, fuel oil, etc.), the impact of industrial crises on labour (coal and railways), and the regulation of monopoly power to protect consumers (railways and electricity supply).[4] Fears that either labour or rival capitalists would turn state intervention to their own advantage were widespread in government and business circles. It was clear that government risked embroilment in complex, conflicting demands if it once began to involve itself with established industries. Politicians and civil servants themselves believed that government was not equipped with the administrative and managerial skills to take an active part in the reorganization of industry.

The government's regulatory experiences in railways and electricity supply, before and immediately after World War I, were not very satisfactory. In both cases, the government had identified the problem as excessive competition, but had been unable to promote technocratic solutions. Instead, regulation had politicized the clash between rival interests and created grave problems for the government in mediating the disputes. Controversy was resolved only when the economic dangers arising from private control meant that the government could no longer allow itself to bend to the claims of the private interests (Cain, 1972; Hannah, 1979b).

In the early 1920s, complicated inter-capitalist divisions paralysed the government in its dealings with the oil industry. Divided industrial interests posed similar problems in coal and steel. But while labour problems sucked the government into coal, the state was able to avoid intervention in the case of steel. A steel industry united behind a programme for reorganization and protection might have succeeded in winning a measure of government support as a 'special case'. But internal divisions made steel manufacturers an ineffective lobby. Within the government, partisans of active reorganization like Steel-Maitland and Cunliffe-Lister lost the day to the orthodox Treasury people, who argued that market forces should hold sway and that government intervention could only do harm. Successive governments in the 1920s preferred to leave the task of encouraging reorganization to the banks.

Ideologically and organizationally, the government was unprepared for the power and responsibility over the steel industry that the establishment of a tariff thrust upon them after 1932. The government knew that protection was likely to hinder reorganization: that had been one of their main reasons for refusing it. Yet the tariff had finally arrived, a belated recognition that the old world economic order was defunct and that Britain had willy-nilly to come into line with the new economic nationalism.

The core of the new policy towards industry in the period after the tariff was 'industrial self-government' and the fostering of business collectivism. At the same time, the strategy of reorganization favoured in such industries as steel was one of rationalization through regional or product amalgamations. This strategy ultimately depended on resolving conflicts of interest between firms in favour of the most efficient producers. Yet dealing with the industry collectively made a solution conciliating all interests more likely.

Through the creation of central representational machinery in the form of the BISF, the government opted to rely on the 'good sense' of the industry as a whole. But in the absence of a workable consensus about reorganization among the steel-makers, this meant government responsibility for the industry without power over it. That was exactly what the Bank of England had predicted, and leading Cabinet figures like Runciman and Snowden were soon lamenting that they were being 'bamboozled' by the steel industry. *Actual* rationalization would probably have torn the BISF apart. The only consensus within the industry was around the need to maintain the tariff, keep up prices, and develop a more effective national voice to lobby for those aims.

The Import Duties Advisory Committee (IDAC), the supervisory body that monitored the affairs of the industry, accepted these developments somewhat unhappily.[5] The civil servants involved never wanted real control over the industry. They rejected central planning and believed that effective reorganization could only come from within the industry. Their aim was a strong and institutionalized persuasive influence, and a sort of industrial autonomy under a state umbrella. Yet an autonomous industry might act contrary to the wishes of government. IDAC set themselves to minimize this possibility by what they saw as a long-term task of breaking down the 'individualism' of the industry. They legitimized the new industry-wide structures and sought to make the best of a bad job by pursuing conciliation and suasion. The appointment of Andrew Duncan as Chairman of BISF in 1934 signified the acceptance by the government that they could not in the short term push the steel-makers where they did not want to go. Duncan's task was to build up an effective central organization through which the government could eventually hope to bring its influence to bear on the overall policy of the industry. In the meantime, however, the result was a state-sponsored cartel.

Until 1939, Duncan concentrated on overcoming the steel-makers' traditions of individualistic and sectional action, a tradition characterized by a leading IDAC official as 'one of the last examples of the baronial system in British industry, but without an overlord to hold it together'. Duncan aimed to convince the steel-makers of the need to develop a working relationship with government within a framework of compromise, rather than taking up a suspicious or antagonistic stance. Duncan developed this policy around the issues of cartel, price, and planning policies before World War II.

Government support for the industry in their bargaining with the International Steel Cartel was a great boost to the steel-makers' confidence in IDAC, and to their belief in the value of talking to government. At the same time, Duncan developed a highly flexible price policy centred on compromise around politically sensitive indicators, a policy that promoted consensus among the steel-makers at the expense of any impetus to structural change. Price competition was outlawed. The price 'umbrella' allowed the least efficient to stay in business and the more efficient to earn inflated profits. These restrictions on competition created effective barriers to entry against potential new enterprises such as the Jarrow scheme, where a consortium of financiers wanted to take advantage of the rearmament boom by reviving a derelict steelworks on the north-east coast. It was impossible for such a new venture to succeed commercially when the other producers did not co-operate. More and more, BISF became an organization effectively geared to defending the interests of its existing membership rather than promoting change in the industry (Burn, 1940).

Thus the BISF, the body that the government had established in the 1930s to promote restructuring, became the guarantor of long-term organizational inertia. World War II stimulated closer co-operation between BISF and the government, and by the late 1940s the continuing active relationship with government had transformed the weak, fragmented, and obstinately individualistic steel-makers into a coherent and effective lobby. This lobby, ironically, proved capable of co-ordinating resistance to government policies in the run up to nationalization and afterwards. Regulation was increasingly aimed at freezing the industrial structure. The price 'umbrella' was replaced by cost-spreading policies which tended to equalize profits between the most and least efficient producers, and the overriding priority of price restraint subdued the relative advantages of particular firms.

In the expansionist environment of the late 1940s and early 1950s, these arrangements allowed increasing investment and high profits (though not the highest attainable), and they were accepted by both the wartime coalition and the Labour government. Inter-party conflict was confined largely to the issue of public ownership itself, rather than to the content of industrial policy. Indeed, many inside the leadership of the Labour Party, such as Morrison and Greenwood, were lukewarm about nationalization because they did not think that the state could run the industry any better than the steel-makers. Despite Labour government arguments of the need for public ownership to facilitate radical change, they had no policies for achieving such radical change. The Labour government prioritized first the minimization of social disruption, and second the quantity of output rather than the cost structure. Therefore it leaned as strongly as the steel companies towards piecemeal adaptations.

When denationalization came, it restored the old form of regulated competition with something akin to the old IDAC system of governmental supervision, thus perpetuating a remarkable institutional continuity from the

1930s to the 1950s. Despite government goals of reorganization, government policies had reinforced the old industry structure with a new layer of powerful institutions that embodied the old structural problems. During the 1950s, while international competition remained slight, the weaknesses of the regulatory system and of the industry did not penalize British steel. The industry could remain strong internationally through piecemeal adaptation. In the 1960s, though, the weaknesses of the 'fair-weather edifice' were painfully revealed (Burn, 1961; MacEachern, 1980; Heal, 1974).

The 'visible hand' of the state reinforced the structural deadlock of the industry. The traditions, organizational forms, and political ideologies of both the National and the Labour governments made them inadequate to the task of reorganizing a major declining industry. In the event, maximizing efficiency was not the state's primary goal. It demonstrated a stronger commitment, instead, to other goals: to preventing the collapse of the industry and preserving national self-sufficiency; to mitigating the social effects of crises; and to preserving a balance among the steel-makers, their customers, and other manufacturers. The only positive policies were concerned with prices and locations, and here, by and large, the policies worked against rationalization.

What was true for steel was also true for coal and agriculture. Institutions stimulated by the government provided a defensive umbrella and not a framework for change. In the 1920s governments had hoped to stand behind the banks; in the 1930s they hoped to stand behind producers' associations. In order to do that, they had to establish the preconditions, if need be by legislation, for effective associations to exist. The aim was to set industries on a self-governing basis and then exert a pervasive advisory influence. In practice, the more effective the self-government was, the less effective the persuasion. The National government ended up sponsoring autonomous groups in steel, coal, and agriculture whose conduct it regarded as dubious, and reluctantly propping up industrial structures that its experts regarded as anachronistic.

Conclusion

In the steel industry, as in many other British industries in the early twentieth century, control of the firm was neither unitary nor coherent. The background to this fragmentation lay in the relatively slow and fluctuating pace of expansion in the late nineteenth century and the prevalence of segmented and specialized markets. This contributed to the characteristic pattern of enterprise structure marked by a history of piecemeal changes in management and financial structures, problems of absorbing competing enterprises through merger, and the continuing dominance of powerful founding families. This sort of diffuse control posed problems in normal times, but the problem was greatly magnified by the industry's interwar crisis.

A long-term strategy for the industry was undercut by those with shorter-term interests of salvaging investments, employment, local steel supplies, or managerial or ownership positions. Stock holders, debenture holders, and bankers exerted influence through the financial leverage they had over debt-ridden firms. Local steel consumers had financial as well as political lever-age. Pressures for rationalization and merger heightened tensions between firm managers and family owners. Once regulatory policies were introduced, labour too exerted a certain amount of political leverage. The loosely oligopolistic structure of competition within the industry exacerbated the problem by heightening the defensive strengths of many enterprises.

Thus, even though the need for rationalization was widely accepted as being in the long-term interest of the industry as a whole, specific proposals invariably became bogged down in a welter of conflicting interests. External forces, such as the banks and government, that shared these rationalizing aspirations might have played a critical role in breaking such log-jams. But neither the clearing banks nor the Bank of England had the requisite capac-ity or inclination to achieve reorganization through employing financial leverage. The government similarly lacked the capacity or political inclina-tion to intervene effectively. Government regulatory policy was captured by enterprise interests within the industry, and eventually by a quasi-cartel.

This should not be taken to imply that 'rationalization' was an ideal solution or a high road to economic success. Its merits were focused narrowly on matters of industry efficiency and competitive advantage, and its social costs would have been high. Even within a narrow framework, its success was bound to be contingent on the unfolding of subsequent decisions. Prob-lems of monopoly control would have succeeded problems of industrial frag-mentation. Large-scale amalgamations and best-practice investment depended for their success on major swings in the world economy; if rearm-ament and war had not occurred and the sluggish economic climate of the depression had persisted, big new combines would probably have collapsed under their own weight. It is not at all clear what historical criteria are best suited for assessing the success or failure of business performance. In many respects, the interwar steel industry did not do too badly. With hindsight certain opportunities for greater success may have existed; yet, even by muddling along, the industry equalled or bettered the performance of its European rivals and survived to serve the war economy and prosper in the postwar boom.

The question at issue in this essay has not been the economic assessment of industry performance which should take all of these issues into considera-tion, but what the history of the industry shows us about how economic choices were actually made. The play of market forces and economic calcula-tion presented a variety of options and possibilities. The actual outcomes were the results of power relations within and between institutions and the historical structures of competition in the industry. The strategy of rationalization enjoyed a wide consensus within industry, banking, and government; and, whatever its limitations, it provided viable solutions to certain of the perceived problems of the industry. Yet the existing institutions were unable to carry the strategy through. Only major changes at the level of state industrial policy or banking organization could have provided the basis for large-scale strategic reorganization, and this did not prove to be a real political possibility.

Notes

[1] What follows draws heavily on detailed research presented in Tolliday (1980, Part One).

[2] The most important texts on these relationships are: for cotton textiles, Kirby (1974) and Sayers (1976); for shipping, Green and Moss (1982); for electricity supply, Hannah (1979a); for coal, Kirby (1977); for agriculture, Lucas (1937) and Whetham (1978); for oil, Ferrier (1982); for armaments, Trebilcock (1966); for railways, Cain (1972) and Channon (1981).

[3] A detailed analysis of Bank of England policy is contained in Tolliday (1980, Part Two). See also Sayers (1976).

[4] For optical glass see MacLeod and MacLeod (1975); for cellulose, Coleman (1975); for dyestuffs, Reader (1977); for fuel oil, Jones (1981); for coal, Kirby (1977).

[5] A full analysis of government policy and the operation of the Import Duties Advisory Committee is contained in Tolliday (1980, Part Three).

Bibliography

Aldcroft, D. H. (1970). *The Inter-War Economy: Britain 1919–39*. London: Batsford.

Alford, B. W. E. (1979). 'The Chandler Thesis—Some General Observations'. In *Management Strategy and Business Development. An Historical and Comparative Study*, ed. L. Hannah. London: Macmillan.

Allen, R. C. (1981). 'Entrepreneurship and Technical Progress in the North-East Coast Pig-iron Industry, 1850–1913'. *Research in Economic History*, 6.

Balogh, T. (1947). *Studies in Financial Organisation*. Cambridge University Press.

Burn, D. L. (1940). *Economic History of Steelmaking, 1867–1939*. Cambridge University Press.

Burn, D. L. (1961). *The Steel Industry, 1939–59: A Study in Competition and Planning*. Cambridge University Press.

Cain, P. J. (1972). 'Railway Combination and Government, 1900–1914'. *Economic History Review*, 25(4), November.

Channon, G. (1981). 'The Great Western Railway Under the British Railways Act of 1921'. *Business History Review*, 55(2), Summer.

Coleman, D. C. (1975). 'War Demand and Supply: The "Dope Scandal", 1915–19'. In *War and Economic Development*, ed. J. M. Winter. Cambridge University Press.

Edelstein, M. (1982). 'Foreign Investment and Empire, 1860–1914'. In *The Economic History of Britain Since 1700*, ed. R. Floud and D. McCloskey. Cambridge University Press.

Ferrier, R. W. (1982). *The History of the British Petroleum Company*. Volume 1, *The Developing Years, 1901–32*. Cambridge University Press.

Green, E., and M. Moss (1982). *A Business of National Importance: The Royal Mail Shipping Group, 1902–32*. Cambridge University Press.

Hannah, L. (1977). 'A Pioneer of Public Enterprise: The Central Electricity Board and the National Grid, 1927–40'. In *Essays in British Business History*, ed. B. Supple. Oxford University Press.

Hannah, L. (1979a). *Electricity Before Nationalisation*. London: Macmillan.

Hannah, L. (1979b). 'Public Policy and the Advent of Large-scale Technology: The Case of Electricity Supply in the USA, Britain and Germany'. In *Law and the Formation of Big Enterprises in the 19th and Early 20th Centuries*, ed. N. Horn and J. Kocka. Göttingen: University Press.

Heal, D. W. (1974). *The Steel Industry in Post-War Britain*. Newton Abbot: David and Charles.

Jones, G. (1981). *The State and the Emergence of the British Oil Industry*. London: Macmillan.

Kennedy, W. P. (1976). 'Institutional Response to Economic Growth: Capital Markets in Britain to 1914'. In *Management Strategy and Business Development*, ed. L. Hannah. London: Macmillan.

Kirby, M. W. (1974). 'The Lancashire Cotton Industry in the Interwar Years: A Study in Organisational Change'. *Business History*, 16(2), July.

Kirby, M. W. (1977). *The British Coalmining Industry, 1870–1946: A Political and Economic History*. London: Macmillan.

Longstreth, F. (1979). 'The City, Industry, and the State'. In *State and Economy in Contemporary Capitalism*, ed. C. Crouch. London: Croom Helm.

Lucas, A. (1937). *Industrial Reconstruction and the Control of Competition: The British Experience*. London: Hart-Davis.

MacEachern, D. (1980). *A Class Against Itself: Power in the Nationalisation of the British Steel Industry*. Cambridge University Press.

MacLeod, R., and K. MacLeod (1975). 'War and Economic Development: Government and the Optical Industry in Britain, 1914–1918'. In *War and Economic Development*, ed. J. M. Winter. Cambridge University Press.

Minchinton, W. E. (1957). *The British Tinplate Industry. A History*. Oxford University Press.

Payne, P. L. (1968). 'Iron and Steel Manufacturers'. In *The Development of British Industry and Foreign Competition, 1875–1914. Studies in Industrial Enterprise*, ed. D. H. Aldcroft. London: Macmillan.

Payne, P. L. (1979). *Colvilles and the Scottish Steel Industry*. Oxford University Press.

Phillips, G. A., and R. T. Maddock (1973). *The Growth of the British Economy 1918–68*. London: Heinemann.

Pollard, S. (1970). *The Gold Standard and Employment Policies Between the Wars*. London: Methuen.

Reader, W. J. (1977). 'ICI and the State'. In *Essays in British Business History*, ed. B. Supple. Oxford University Press.

Reader, W. J. (1982). *Bowater, A History*. Cambridge University Press.

Sayers, R. S. (1976). *The Bank of England, 1891–1944*, 3 vols. Cambridge University Press.

Slaven, A. (1982). 'British Shipbuilders: Market Trends and Order-book Patterns Between the Wars'. *Journal of Transport History*, 9, November.

Thomas, W. A. (1978). *The Finance of British Industry, 1918–76*. London: Methuen.

Tolliday, S. W. (1980). 'Industry, Finance and the State: An Analysis of the British Steel Industry, 1918–39. PhD thesis, Cambridge University.

Trebilcock, C. (1966). ' "A Special Relationship"—Government, Rearmament and the Cordite Firms'. *Economic History Review*, 19, November.

Warren, K. (1965). 'Locational Problems of the Scottish Iron and Steel Industry Since 1760'. *Scottish Geographical Magazine*, Part 1, 81(1), April; Part 2, 81(2), September.

Warren, K. (1970). *The British Iron and Steel Sheet Industry Since 1840: An Economic Geography*. London: Bell.

Warren, K. (1979). 'Iron and Steel'. In *British Industry Between the Wars: Instability and Industrial Development, 1918–39*, ed. N. K. Buxton and D. H. Aldcroft. London: Scolar Press.

Whetham, E. H. (1978). *The Agrarian History of England and Wales*. Volume 8, *1914–39*. Cambridge University Press.

The Shipbuilding Industry 1880–1965

Edward Lorenz and Frank Wilkinson*
University of Cambridge

In 1890 Britain held a position of undisputed pre-eminence in international shipbuilding, controlling over 80 per cent of the world market. By the turn of the century, the build-up of German, US, French and Dutch capacity behind protective barriers had reduced this share to 60 per cent.[1] Nevertheless, as late as 1913, Britain still retained 80 per cent of the unprotected export market (British and Foreign Trade and Industry, 1909; Parkinson, 1956, pp. 242–3).

During World War I, Scandinavian countries entered the market while British exports were shut off. The postwar reconstruction boom, by stretching British capacity to the limit, allowed a further build-up on the Continent, primarily in Germany, Holland, and Belgium (Jones, 1957, ch. 3). In the interwar years of recession in world shipbuilding, Britain sustained a further loss in market share, but still controlled 35 per cent of the world market.

In contrast to the slow decline of the depressed interwar period, Britain's market share fell sharply during the postwar boom. The more-than-twofold increase in world output of the 1950s saw the proportion of ships built in Britain cut to 15 per cent, and by the mid-1960s the industry faced total collapse. Paradoxically, British competitive failure had taken place during the most rapid and sustained expansion in the history of world shipbuilding.

The aim of this study is to explain that failure by an analysis of the economic and institutional forces that shaped the British shipbuilding industry's structure and determined its distinctive pattern of development. More specifically, we aim to show that the organizational and industrial relations structures that evolved with nineteenth-century success contributed to competitive failure in the twentieth century. The study is divided into two main sections, the first exploring the factors that determined the industry's pre-1914 success, and the second assessing the causes of its relative decline from the interwar period

Competitive Success: 1880–1914

Product Markets and Industrial Structure

Most historical studies of the British shipbuilding industry have placed considerable emphasis on the strong world position of British ship owners and

*We would like to thank Bernard Elbaum for his helpful comments on earlier drafts of this paper. We also benefited from suggestions made by participants of the Anglo-American Conference on the Decline of the British Economy, Boston University, 1983.

operators. With British shipping interests controlling some 35 per cent of the world fleet between 1880 and 1914, British builders had the advantage of a comparatively large and secure domestic market. The continuity in demand for different classes of vessels allowed British firms to achieve a degree of specialization among yards that proved impossible in competing maritime nations (Basso, 1910, pp. 88–93; Hardy, 1951, p. 39; Pollard, 1957, pp. 433–6; Pollard and Robertson, 1979, pp. 84–7; Roux-Freissineng, 1929, p. 31).

While there is undoubtedly merit in this analysis, it is important to consider the forces that limited the tendency to product specialization. The demand for seaborne trade fluctuated widely around a rising trend during the nineteenth and early twentieth centuries. Ease of entry into shipping and intensive competition during periods of recession militated against a high degree of concentration. Although well-known lines operating a large number of ships did develop, in general ownership and operation of ships remained widely dispersed (Gripaois, 1959, p. 24; Kirkaldy, 1914, pp. 174–200).

The chronic swings between overcapacity and shortage of ship space were reflected in marked fluctuations in demand for new construction. This made ship production very risky and ensured that most builders built only to order. In turn, the bespoke nature of demand, coupled with the large number of owners and their idiosyncracies in ship design, limited the scope for standardizing ship production. Yards tended to specialize by general class of vessel (i.e. liner, cargo tramp, or warship), but variations in the specifications for particular vessels remained wide (Kendall, 1894–5, p. 224; Le Maistre, 1926–7; Pollard and Robertson, 1979, pp. 28–9).

These features of the shipbuilding product market profoundly affected the industry's structure. Most firms retained small-scale, labour-intensive production techniques in order to avoid high overhead costs during recessionary periods (Pollard and Robertson, 1979, pp. 28–9, 231). Lack of standardization in ship design meant that even large yards were not in a position to benefit from the scale economies associated with series production.

Tables 1 and 2 provide evidence on the continued vitality of small-scale production during this period. During the boom that preceded and followed World War I, industry output increased primarily through the creation of new firms, the large majority of which were single-yard establishments. The degree of concentration in the industry remained roughly constant.

There were offsetting influences in specialized segments of the market. The larger size and technical sophistication of liners and warships required the small group of firms specializing in their production to install larger berths, greater crane capacity, and a variety of specialized equipment for outfitting or ordnance work.

Liner specialists, in addition, were able to secure a degree of market protection through establishing close ties with owners. Large shipping lines such

TABLE 1

Output per yard and per firm in British shipbuilding, 1910–1920 (thousands of mercantile tons launched)

	No. of yards	No. of firms	Average Output		Total industry output
			Per Yard	Per Firm	
1910	91	85	12.5	13.3	1,134
1920	126	109	16.3	18.9	2,056

Source: The Shipbuilder and Marine Engine Builder, January number of each year for output per yard in British shipbuilding. These figures exclude boat, barge and yacht builders. Industry output figures from Lloyd's Register of Shipping.

as the Cunard Line, the P and O Line, and the Furness Line had sufficient resources to build during recessions. This promised a stabilization of demand and encouraged a strategy of vertical integration between builders and own- ers, which, by lessening the risk of capital investment, encouraged these firms to expand the scale of their yards (Burns, 1940, pp. 272–4; Pollard and Robertson, 1979, pp. 92–6; Robertson, 1975; Shield, 1949, p. 55).

Warship builders acquired a similar degree of market protection from their established connections with the Admiralty, which restricted its contracts to a small and select 'list' of yards whose equipment and methods of construc- tion met strict standards. As the Admiralty tended to put greater emphasis on quality than on economy of construction, the few favoured firms did not face market constraints comparable to most commercial yards (Pollard and Robertson, 1979, pp. 211–14).

The large integrated firm, however, was the exception in Britain. The majority of shipyard enterprises remained small and independent. Fre- quently under family ownership or control, they tended to a jealous guarding of independent action. Below we show how their character as small pro-

TABLE 2

Concentration in British mercantile shipbuilding

	Percentage of industry output accounted for by:			
	Top 2 firms	Top 3 firms	Top 5 firms	Top 10 firms
1910	17.0	23.1	33.2	49.5
1920	19.1	27.4	34.4	45.5

Source: The Shipbuilder and Marine Engine Builder, January number of each year. Figures are in terms of tons launched.

ducers affected the technology and organization of work employed, assuring a premium on maintaining a highly skilled workforce.

Production and Skills

Late nineteenth-century ship production involved a long gestation period with distinct phases of production requiring a wide range of skills. The main stages were design and preparation, hull construction, and fitting-out. The first stage involved the design and planning of the ship, the transformation of the general plans into detailed blueprints, and finally the preparation of full-scale templates and moulds to serve as guides in shaping the metal framework and plates of the ship. Hull construction involved the fashioning of the various metal sections of the ship and their assembly at the berth. At the fitting-out stage, the ship was provided with its motive power, services, facilities for carrying passengers and freight, paint, and decoration (Abell, 1948; Holms, 1918; Pollock, 1905; Reid, 1980, ch. 6).

Initially production techniques were very labour-intensive, based largely on hand tools adapted from British tinsmithy and boilershop practice of the 1850s and 1860s. From these simple beginnings, there evolved during the late nineteenth century an increasingly specialized and heavy class of machine tool designed to manipulate large and extremely heavy metal sections (*The Engineer*, 5 May 1889; Hume, 1976). One factor was the shift from iron to steel hull construction during the 1880s. Wrought iron plates and sections were shaped by heating in furnaces and hammering. Steel is easier to shape in a cold state, and its use encouraged producers to employ powerful hydraulic bending machines (Reid, 1980, pp. 113–18).

The new machine tools, however, were not single-purpose instruments designed for mass production of identical components. The lack of standardization in ship production assured that shipyard machine tools remained sufficiently versatile to produce a variety of components of differing dimensions. Correspondingly, many of the operations required a skilled hand, as precision was needed in marking and positioning the components for processing. Indeed, in most cases the aim of mechanization was not to deskill craft workers, but rather to enhance productivity on jobs requiring considerable expertise. This is reflected in the fact that, as late as the turn of the century, over 60 per cent of the workforce was classified as skilled (Reid, 1980, p. 442).

The tasks of riveting and caulking, requiring considerable physical exertion but little variation in motion, were exceptions to this general rule. These tasks were eminently susceptible to mechanization and consequently deskilling, but even here the process was slow. The bulk of riveting and caulking took place at the assembly stage, in the berths, and the machines had to be small and portable. Not until the early twentieth century, with the development of pneumatic power, were really useful machines introduced (Holms, 1918, p. 309; Hume, 1976, p. 165; Southwest of Scotland Board of Trade, 1932, pp. 39–40).

More progress was made with the mechanization of the handling of plates and other ship's components, both in the shops and on the berth, by the development of mobile and overhead cranes. But such machines substituted for unskilled and semi-skilled workers rather than skilled. Moreover, mechanized handling equipment was introduced extensively only in the larger British yards that specialized in liner or warship production, such as Harland and Wolff of Belfast and Swan Hunter and Wigham Richardson of Wallsend. The majority of shipbuilders retained their fixed cranes, manually operated derricks, and push carts on rails. Rather than increase fixed costs by using more capital-intensive methods, they retained the practice of shifting the burden of market uncertainty on to labour through periodic layoffs (Fairburn, 1902, p. 226; Hume, 1976, pp. 167–8; John, 1914; Pinczon, 1930, pp. 89–90).

Product innovation was rapid after 1880, with the development of new types of specialized ships such as refrigerated vessels, oil tankers, and bulk carriers; increases in the average size and speed of ocean-going vessels; and the use of new materials. The main effect of these changes on the labour force, however, was to proliferate the number of skilled trades with little or no impact on the general level of skill (Pollard and Robertson, 1979, pp. 18–23, 152).

The most significant twentieth-century technical development in ship construction was the replacement of riveting by welding, a process which began during the interwar years and was completed during the 1940s and 1950s. This allowed for the prefabrication of ships' sections, increased the importance of work in the plating shops relative to that on the berths, and increased the possibility of applying mass production techniques. This latter tendency was reinforced by a growing acceptance of standardized vessels in the world market. The combined effect of the new methods of construction and the new types of ships was progressively to increase the competitive advantages of heavily capitalized and large-scale shipyards and to further the scope for substituting semi-skilled for skilled labour.

Labour Supply and the Division of Labour

Throughout the pre-World War I period, shipbuilding technology placed a premium on a highly skilled and versatile workforce. Consequently British builders were able to benefit from their favoured labour supply position. Ample supplies of skilled labour in Britain resulted in part from a distinctive pattern of nineteenth-century industrial development. By the turn of the century, over 75 per cent of the British workforce engaged in commodity production were in industry (O'Brien and Keyder, 1978, p. 94). British industrialists drew on stable concentrations of wage labour, for the most part permanently attached to industrial employment and habituated to its conditions.

The British shipbuilding workforce in particular combined the advantages of a high degree of skill and specialization, permitting a fine division of labour, with employment relations that minimized the fixity of labour costs. In Adam Smith's famous example, the pin moved from one pair of specialized hands to another, each undertaking a separate task. By contrast, in British shipbuilding the ships lay at different stages of construction in different small, separately owned shipyards. The specialized workers moved from yard to yard, as demand for their particular skills ebbed and flowed, making their particular contributions to each ship's construction (Price, 1981, pp. 6–12).

What made this arrangement possible was the heavy concentration of shipyards in certain regions. By contrast, in other maritime nations the comparatively few yards located in any one region precluded builders as a *group* from achieving the same degree of continuity in demand for workers with specialized skills. Facing greater difficulty in recruitment of skilled labour, these firms in turn offered greater employment security, making use of the workers in a more flexible manner which sacrificed the benefits of a fine division of labour (Bohlin, 1980, p. 13; Lorenz, 1984; Svensson, 1980, pp. 12–13).

The Costs and Benefits of Trade Union Organization

The evolution of union organization mirrored the technical and organizational development of iron and steel shipbuilding. During the era of wooden shipbuilding, trade union organization had developed around the principal craft, that of the shipwright. However, with the introduction of metal ships the shipwrights initially refused to work with the new material, and later they were supplanted by the various boilermaker trades as the principal occupational group[2] (Dougan, 1975, p. 3; Reid, 1980, p. 84).

Metal ships gave rise to a large number of highly specialized trades: angle ironsmiths, platers, riveters, iron moulders, sheet metal workers, etc. In the early days, possibilities existed for workers to be upgraded between trades of different levels of skill. However, as the main shipbuilding trades became organized by separate unions of Boilermakers, Shipwrights, and Blacksmiths, the tendency was for all occupational groups to be classified as skilled with the means of entry confined to apprenticeship (Pollard and Robertson, 1979, pp. 152–3).

As ships became more sophisticated, new trades—engineering, electrical, plumbing, painting and decorating—were introduced. These latter groups were generally already organized by craft unions whose main organizational base was outside shipbuilding. Therefore, the influx of new skills was accompanied by a growing complication of the trade union structure (Pollard and Robertson, 1979, pp. 152, 164; Wilkinson, 1973, Pt 2, pp. 4–8). Unskilled and semi-skilled workers were excluded from the craft unions, which often suppressed their attempts at independent organization until the very end of the nineteenth century. After 1890, however, the labourers' unions made progress in organizing less skilled shipbuilding workers (Clegg, 1964, pp. 38–47).

The unions placed an important restriction on management by reducing flexibility in the allocation of work, especially as changing production methods and the introduction of new materials continuously blurred the edges between trades. Within unions, craft lines were defined by strict limits on the tools and materials each trade could use; but between unions jurisdiction over areas of work were bitterly disputed. The problem was exacerbated by the growing overlap between, for example, platers and shipwrights, joiners and woodworking shipwrights, and plumbers and pipe-fitters. Efforts were made to handle such disputes by the creation of demarcation lists and the provision of systems of arbitration. None the less, periods of rapid change were accompanied by a rush of demarcation disputes until the main lines of the division of the new work were agreed (Eldridge, 1968, pp. 91–125; Roberts, 1967; Robertson, 1975; Wilkinson, 1973, Pt 4).

Management was also restricted in its ability to introduce non-craft workers into craft areas. This took two forms: one was a restriction on the number of apprentices and the other was a restriction on dilution (i.e. the use of semi-skilled labour in craft areas). The craft unions in shipbuilding were successful in both controlling entry into the trade and capturing and establishing manning levels for the machines that replaced manual skills (e.g. riveting and caulking) (Lorenz, 1983, pp. 57–69; Reid, 1980, pp. 242–68, 397–401).

It would be misleading to conclude, however, that the effects of unionization were solely negative as far as employers were concerned. Unionization conferred important benefits in three areas: the organization of production; the orderly transmission of skills; and cyclical flexibility in hiring and firing. Labour historians have too often ignored or discounted these benefits.

The squad system—whereby groups of skilled workers contracted for tasks (say a row of plates)—provided the basis for further specialization within the framework of general skills. Particular members of the squad, although sufficiently skilled to undertake all aspects, took responsibility for specialized parts of general tasks and thus provided the basis for specialization within a framework of self-imposed general supervision which reduced the need for specialized management (Holms, 1918, pp. 473, 527). Second, the protection afforded to recognized apprentices by craft unions provided the basis for the orderly acquisition of skills that individual firms, subject to wide swings in demand, would have found difficult to provide. Further, the geographically based union branches functioned as a labour exchange and facilitated the movement of labour between yards and between districts. Craft unions provided social welfare services to their members such as unemployment and health benefits which helped maintain the labour force and its attachment to the industry.

In important respects, the experience of British shipbuilders prior to 1914 was typical of other British industries, in the retention of craft-based production methods and small-scale production techniques despite the trend to large-scale production and capital intensity in other industrializing nations. However, British shipbuilding, unlike other staple industries, retained its competitive advantage and remained overwhelmingly superior until World War I.

British competitive success can be explained partly by the greater size of the British market which allowed greater inter-yard specialization. Another factor was the skill and organization of the labour force. The existence of a well organized labour force whose continuity was ensured at least partly by trade union organization helps to explain how small-scale production captured the economies of scale of trade specialization. The access of British producers to a labour force that was, to an important extent, self-trained and self-supported gave it a competitive edge over countries lacking such a trained labour force. Other countries' attempts to compensate by introducing capital equipment had the liability of increasing fixed costs; their more flexible use of skilled workers sacrificed economies of trade specialization.

Competitive Failure: 1920–1965

During the interwar period Britain remained the world's foremost producer of ships, accounting on average for 40 per cent of world output. After World War II Britain's share fell rapidly, even by the standards of other major nineteenth-century staple industries. By the mid-1960s British yards produced less than 10 per cent of world output. The industry was suffering a severe profitability crisis and was increasingly dependent on government subsidization for its survival.

British decline in the export market was if anything more precipitous. As late as 1927–30, Britain's share of export markets that were not protected fluctuated between 40 and 50 per cent. As shown by Table 3, Britain's share fell rapidly with the recovery in world demand for ships after 1935, increased

TABLE 3

Percentage shares of the world export market (in terms of tons launched)

	Britain	Japan	Germany	Sweden	France	Holland
1936–38	21.0	1.3	33.0	16.8	0.3	4.7
1948–50	35.0	2.2	0.3	18.3	0.1	6.0
1951–55	22.0	10.6	14.9	12.9	2.1	8.6
1956–60	6.9	31.6	20.7	12.0	5.8	5.8
1961–65	4.5	38.8	13.0	15.7	5.5	4.4

Source: Lloyd's Register of Shipping, Annual Shipbuilding Returns.

TABLE 4

Ships delivered to the UK registered fleet (in terms of tons launched)

	Percentage from UK yards	Percentage from foreign yards
1948–50	100.0	0.0
1951–55	96.8	3.2
1956–60	81.1	19.9
1961–65	61.7	38.3
1966–70	26.0	74.0

Source: Lloyd's Register of Shipping, Annual Shipbuilding Returns

somewhat during 1948–50, and then plummeted to 22 per cent in 1951–4 and 6.9 per cent in 1956–60.

As Table 4 shows, import penetration followed closely on the heels of the loss of the export market. Import penetration began at a slow pace, but accelerated from the late 1950s as British owners were swayed by the lower prices and quicker delivery dates offered abroad (Ministry of Transport, 1963).

The decline of British shipbuilding took place in a period of technical change and sharply changing demand conditions. In short order, the composition of the world fleet was transformed towards larger and more standardized vessels, and welding and prefabrication techniques were substituted for traditional shipbuilding technology. These changes undermined the basis of Britain's traditional comparative advantage in world shipbuilding.

The Changing Environment

The benefits of large-scale production are well known. When there are significant divisibilities in capital equipment, overhead costs can be spread over a larger volume of output. Producing long runs of particular components shortens the machine set-up time and potentially allows for a shift from job-shop to straight-line work organization. In industries involving complex machining and assembling tasks, producing standard products in series may also confer important 'dynamic scale economies'.[3]

Prior to 1914, as already indicated, the scope for benefiting from these scale economies was very limited in shipbuilding. During the interwar years, however, important trends emerged which favoured larger-scale and more capital-intensive yards.

As world energy use shifted from coal to oil, demand for tankers grew. Tankers were relatively simple craft with long flat surfaces that could easily be built up from a large number of standard components or panels.[4] The development and perfection of welding during the 1930s increased the possibilities of preassembly and of adopting a straight-line organization of work.

These nascent tendencies proved overwhelming during the 1950s with further economic and technical change. The expansion in world demand for ships during this period was rapid and stable by historical standards. By lessening the problem of high overhead costs during cyclical downswings, stable growth in demand favoured the adoption of larger-scale and more capital-intensive methods of shipbuilding. The average size of vessels also increased, and there was a growing acceptance in the market for standard designs for tankers, bulk carriers, and general-purpose cargo ships. Product standardization potentially allowed firms to benefit from economies of the learning process, generally estimated to confer a 20 to 30 per cent improvement in labour productivity over the first four to five standard vessels built (Ollson, 1981, p. 13; Rapping, 1965, pp. 81–6; Stopford, 1979).[5]

The generalization of welding and prefabrication techniques during the 1940s and 1950s also encouraged larger-scale production. Prefabrication led to an abandonment of the traditional 'keel-up' system of hull construction in which sections (plates and beams) were constructed on a job-shop basis and then fitted piece by piece at the berth. With prefabrication, large three-dimensional block sections of the vessel were built up indoors from a large number of standard panels and then were transported by rail or crane to the berth, which led to a flow or straight-line organization of production.

By the late 1950s, a version of Ford's assembly line was being applied to the initial stages of hull construction in which standard panels, the basic building blocks in shipbuilding, were being automatically produced in mass. While the use of this capital-intensive technology offered potentially important gains in productivity, it was both expensive and required long runs to secure maximum benefit (Cuthbert, 1969, pp. 123–4, 127–9; Forbes and Varney, 1976, p. 39; Wolfenden, 1976, pp. 67–8).

The rise of large-scale and capital-intensive shipbuilding diminished the importance of flexible access to a highly skilled, mobile workforce. The larger volume of production of individual yards and the greater standardization of output provided a firmer basis for continuously employing workers with specialized skills, while greater mechanization increased the amount of semi-skilled machine-tending work. The shift to prefabrication led to a division of labour more industrial in character, based on location in the flow of production as opposed to type of activity or craft, which increased the possibilities of imparting skills through simple systems of on-the-job training associated with upgrading or internal promotion (BETURE, 1978, pp. 84–7; Oury, 1973, pp. 122–5; Patton Report, 1962, p. 85).

In general, competitive performance in shipbuilding now depended less on having a skilled workforce sufficiently versatile to produce complex vessels to customer specifications, and more on producers' ability to expand the scale of their yards, standardize their production, and provide for effective managerial co-ordination of production from above. In all these latter critical respects, however, British firms proved far *inferior* to their major competitors abroad. British yards were on average smaller, and their product mix generally was more diversified. Management showed a comparative lack of talent and interest in applying systematic planning methods. Below we argue that Britain's competitive failures can be explained by rigidities in the institutional structures that had led to nineteenth-century success, in conjunction with the particular labour market and product market conditions that producers faced during the 1950s and 1960s.

The Anatomy of Competitive Failure

Product Markets and Industrial Structure

Prior to the interwar period, small scale constituted no competitive disadvantage in shipbuilding. Shipyards producing in the range of 15,000 to 20,000 tons annually could capture the scale economies inherent in the technology of the era. Larger-scale production began in the 1930s, and after World War II the average size of yards in the more competitive maritime nations increased rapidly. By the mid-1950s, specialized yards such as Gotaverken in Sweden and Nederlandsche in Amsterdam would produce annually in the range of 70,000–100,000 tons. By 1960 it was not unusual for large yards producing series of standard vessels to complete over 150,000 tons annually.

During the 1950s the absolute size of the British market was sufficient to allow British firms to capture all scale economies implicit in the changing technology and products of the period. Prior to 1956, the British industry was still the world's largest, and its annual output remained well over a million gross tons throughout the decade. If British yards remained small in comparison to foreign competitors, one can only conclude that a structural problem was at fault. That is, the British shipbuilding industry failed to allocate the existing demand in a way that allowed the full realization of potential scale economies.

During this time, British shipbuilders did face some serious market constraints in comparison with their principal international competitors, notably Japan and Sweden. These competitors benefited from faster-growing domestic markets in which they enjoyed protected positions stemming from such factors as established ties between owners and builders, geography, and government subsidization (Drewry, 1972–3; Jones, 1957, pp. 224–5).[6] Table 5 shows a particularly striking advantage in the rate of growth of home market demand for Japan, which emerged as the most competitive producer by the late 1950s. In addition, Swedish shipbuilders were in a privileged position not only at home, but also in the second-fastest market shown in the table, that of Norway (Ollson, 1980, pp. 7–10).[7]

With its relatively slow-growing home market, the only way for Britain to

TABLE 5

Registration of ships launched

('000 of gross tons)

	Average for 1950–2	Average for 1964–6	Percentage Increase
UK	844	1,204	43
Germany	222	446	101
Japan	362	2,194	506
Holland	135	221	64
Norway	536	2,076	287
Sweden	186	404	117
France	284	332	17

Source: Lloyd's Register of Shipping.

have maintained its share of world production would have been progressively to boost its share of the unprotected parts of the export market. However, there is little reason to believe that British firms were in a position to do this in the 1950s. Britain enjoyed no significant resource cost advantages or any monopoly over technology that might have conferred a competitive edge (Parkinson, 1960, pp. 198–206).

Given these constraints on market expansion, constraints that were not faced by foreign competitors, British firms had only one way in which they could increase the scale of their yards as much as firms abroad: namely, by undergoing a process of structural change. They would have had to close certain yards, and concentrate demand and output in the ones that remained.

The point is clearly illustrated in Table 6, which shows the average output per yard and per firm in the British, Swedish, and French shipbuilding industries between 1938 and 1970. As the table shows, though the Swedish industry was small in absolute terms in 1938 compared with the British, the average size of its yards was about the same. Facing rapidly expanding demand, Swedish firms were subsequently able to expand the scale of their yards without the need for structural transformation. In the case of the comparatively stagnant British industry, such marginal increases in yard scale as took place after 1950 were made possible only by the closure of a number of yards and firms.

Nevertheless, the size of the British market as a whole was sufficient to support a number of yards of best-practice size, and so the difficult question remains: Why didn't some British firms take the initiative in 1950 and, by adopting the methods being applied abroad, progressively capture the market share from their domestic competitors with a view to benefiting from scale economies?

TABLE 6

*Average output per yard and per firm in British, French and Swedish
mercantile shipbuilding
('000 of tons launched)*

| | No. of yards | No. of firms | Average output | | Total Industry output |
			Per yard	Per firm	
Britain					
1938	54	47	19.1	21.9	1030.0
1950	58	46	24.1	28.8	1324.6
1960	52	43	25.6	30.9	1331.5
1970	40	27	30.7	45.8	1237.1
France					
1938	17	14	2.8	3.4	47.0
1950	17	14	10.6	12.9	180.8
1960	15	12	39.6	49.5	594.4
1970	8	6	120.0	160.0	960.2
Sweden					
1938	9	9	18.4	18.4	166.0
1950	10	10	34.8	34.8	348.0
1960	10	10	71.1	71.1	711.0
1970	11	7	155.6	244.5	1711.2

Sources: Industry output figures from *Lloyd's Register of Shipping* British figures from the January number of *The Shipbuilder and Marine Engine Builder*: French figures derived from Puech (1969) and Chardonnet (1971). Swedish figures from Projekt Svensk Varindustri, Gothenberg. The figures exclude boat, barge, and yacht builders.

Part of the answer has to do with the imperfectly competitive structure of the industry, which made it very difficult to capture market share from competitors. Ships are expensive products and have a long life (averaging some twenty years). Product quality is a major consideration in the decision to purchase, and owners place a high premium on the established reputation of shipbuilders. For these reasons, strong, though frequently informal, ties tended to develop between owners and builders, ties that competitors found difficult to undermine unless they could offer substantial improvements in terms of price and delivery dates.

This latter form of competition was restricted by its large initial investment requirements and the risk of competitive retaliation. Yards built only a few vessels simultaneously. Capturing competitors' market share, then, could not be accomplished on the basis of piecemeal investments in technical modernization. Rather, a firm would have to commit substantial resources to expanding its capacity so that competitive delivery dates could be guaranteed. Such investments would be contemplated only if aggressive tendering were reasonably certain to secure a larger share of the market. With one British firm's success implying a large reduction in the sales of domestic competitors, however, the pricing policies of firms could not be regarded as independent. Each firm would have to retaliate if it were to remain in business. The risk to all of such a competitive scramble engendered a live-and-let-live attitude in British shipbuilding which gave customers little to choose from between yards.[8]

It is also probable that the increasing cost disadvantages of traditional methods were not obvious to British producers until they found foreign competitors penetrating the home market towards the end of the 1950s. Only at this time, with British owners abandoning British builders, did the firms in the industry generally seek to modernize their facilities (Department of Scientific Research, 1960).

In short, with slow growth in demand and a sizeable overhang of outmoded but serviceable capacity, no firm was prepared to take the risk of embarking on a major programme of investment and modernization. Here the distinctive position of British producers should be kept in mind. Swedish or Japanese firms, simply because they faced rapidly expanding demand, were in a position to expand the scale of their yards without bearing the risks of a competitive struggle for market share.

Related considerations help explain the distinctive lack of product specialization and standardization in British yards during the 1950s and 1960s. Even with British yards remaining small on average, there was scope to benefit from product-specific scale economies of specialization by reallocating the industry's fragmented market demand between firms. Yet this form of restructuring also involved considerable risk-taking by individual firms. Shipbuilding is an industry where production is rarely speculative and a firm's survival depends on obtaining orders. Given the fragmented market demand faced by British firms, any strategy of specialization implied having to *give up* some orders, while attempting to obtain orders that normally would have gone to competitors. Much the same point about market impediments to product specialization was made in a previous book on British shipbuilding by industrial economist J. R. Parkinson:[9]

In the present circumstances it is difficult to see how the distribution of orders can be improved without some changes in the organisation of shipbuilding and shipowning. It is the character of the market more than any other single factor which weights the scales against further specialisation in shipbuilding. There is no question that it is more economical to build similar ships today than it was half a century ago when skilled labour was abundant and ships were largely hand-assembled at the stocks. The prospects of getting a sufficiency of orders are at least as good. Yet it appears that further specialisation and standardisation will not result unless ship owners and shipbuilders concert their efforts to concentrate demand and production on as limited a range of types and sizes of vessels as is consistent with the real requirements of various trades. . . . This could not, however, occur without some interference with normal marketing arrangements either by the establishment of some central agency governing the placing of orders amongst shipyards or by outright amalgamation. (Parkinson, 1960, pp. 150–1.)

The alternative to a struggle for market share would have been a consolidation of ownership in the industry followed by the closure of certain yards and concentration of capacity in others. The transformation of the industry's structure into a comparatively few large multi-yard firms would also have created the basis for specialization between yards. Owing to its control over a large volume of orders, a large multi-yard firm would have been in a position to co-ordinate the flow of orders between its yards and so achieve a high degree of inter-yard specialization without affecting the level of risk born by individual yards.

But the fragmentation of the industry and the history of competitive relations led each firm to view its interests as separate. Independence of action was arguably reinforced by the retention of the industry's traditional pattern of ownership. Family-controlled private limited status continued to be the most common form of ownership during the 1950s (Slaven, 1980, p. 13). The few mergers that took place at this time were between adjoining yards and were instigated to meet the technical requirements of building larger vessels, rather than any broader vision of the industry's needs.

The technical modernization of the British shipbuilding industry depended on the reform of its structure, and the record suggests that market adjustment was a slow and ineffective agent for restructuring compared with outside intervention. The case of French shipbuilding is illustrative here. Comparatively small in absolute size, the industry similarly faced slow-growing or stagnant home market demand and a fragmented structure of production (see Tables 5 and 6). Yet, owing in part to the impact of government policy, the scale of the yards in the industry was increased to almost the same extent as yards in Sweden.

There were two distinct stages to government intervention into French shipbuilding. During the 1950s, the government pursued a policy of subsidization which allowed firms progressively to capture the home market and establish a strong position in the export market[10] (see Table 3).This was followed, starting in 1960, by a policy of forced amalgamation and yard closures accompanied by substantial reductions in the level of government assistance. By 1968, the industry had been reduced from sixteen to eight comparatively specialized yards; and, despite the lower levels of assistance, French producers maintained their share of the export market and marginally improved their position in the home market (Chardonnet, 1971; Prêcheur, 1968).

State intervention in British shipbuilding was, by comparison, hesitant and ineffectual. It was only after 1966 that a serious effort was made to reform the industry's structure. The government's 1966 Shipbuilding Inquiry Committee Report (Geddes Report) recommended a regrouping of firms to form larger regional shipbuilding consortia with an annual capacity of 400,000–600,000 tons and comprising four to six specialized yards. The 1967 Shipbuilding Industry Act provided financial backing for the scheme by authorizing direct grants to yards participating in the restructuring.[11] A considerable regrouping took place during the next three years, though below the expectations of the Committee.[12] The possible benefits of the reform were never assessed, however, owing to the collapse of the tanker market in 1973–4 and the general depression that ensued.

The failure to reform the structure of the British shipbuilding industry during the 1950s precluded builders from realizing the plant-specific and product-specific scale economies that gave a competitive edge to foreign producers. Below we argue that industrial fragmentation in Britain had further negative effects by hindering the adoption of more systematic forms of labour management.

Taylorism versus Craft Control

It has frequently been noted that British shipbuilders were less receptive than competitors to the introduction of systematic forms of management after World War II. The following quote by the technical director of W. Doxford and Sons is representative of management attitudes immediately following the war:

My mind goes back a year or two ago when I was directly connected with a similar planning scheme which was tried out, but it was found that what could be applied in an engineering shop was not suitable in a shipyard. The scheme did not work very successfully at that time. . . . I think shipbuilding is an industry which is distinct from any other, and to get improved production in shops the detailed production planning system as applied to engineering is in my humble opinion, rather out of the question (Orenstein, 1944–5, p. D62).

As producers in such countries as Sweden, France, and Germany showed success in applying Taylorist forms of work organization during the 1950s, however, British management became more interested in the approach. The report prepared by the Patton Committee's 1960–1 investigatory mission to continental and Scandinavian yards, in particular, showed a keen awareness of British failures in this respect:

The British shipbuilding industry has a long tradition of working with a minimum managerial and technical staff and requires to learn how to effectively integrate and use specialist functions in its management structure, so that real advantage commensurate with the increase in overhead costs is obtained. (Patton Report, 1962, p. 75.)

Despite this heightened concern, British firms made little progress in improving production planning outside of yards specializing in warship production, where Admiralty construction contracts required certain standards of planning for which cost allowances were made. The Booz-Allen and Hamilton report on shipbuilding commissioned by the Department of Trade and Industry in 1972 noted:

Except in yards building warships, control of quality and dimensional accuracy is provided by the *workforce*. . . . informal scheduling and planning, depending on the skill and experience at foreman level, is often the only detailed planning available once original plans have been bypassed and due dates have been missed. (Department of Trade and Industry, 1973, pp. 143–4; our emphasis.)

The initial tendency of British producers to discount 'scientific management' can best be explained by the legacy of skilled labour-intensive forms of production. As discussed in the first section of this paper, the complexities of bespoke production had precluded the easy replacement of skilled craftsmen by machines. These technical constraints had led builders in such countries as Holland, France, and the United States, where the supply of skilled labour was less assured, to organize the division of labour in a way that placed greater reliance on supervisory and technical personnel.

This point can be illustrated by contrasting the templating systems used in British and foreign yards. Templates were wooden models or replicas used to mark the dimensions of the steel plates that formed the shell of the vessel's hull, and their construction required design and technical competencies. In Britain, the usual practice was for squads of manual workers to prepare templates after frame erection had begun by pressing flexible wooden battens against the surface of the partially erected hull. Abroad, on the other hand, the tendency from quite early on was for all templates to be produced in advance by a specialized technical staff on the basis of specifications provided by the design offices. In effect, the connection between conceptual or technical tasks and manual tasks was managed in quite different ways, the two being more clearly distinguished and separate abroad (Benoist, 1905, pp. 830–43; Holms, 1918, ch. 36; Lorenz, 1983; Montgomery, 1937–8, pp. 156–8 and D80–5; Pinczon, 1930, pp. 92–4).

The pretemplating system, unlike the British system, required that the dimensions and positioning of all component parts of the vessel be determined in advance, and this concentration of technical knowledge in a specialized staff laid the ground for the application of more systematic methods of planning at a later stage. In a few well-documented cases it is clear that firms also sought to apply in a formal manner Taylor's system of 'scientific management', primarily with a view to making fuller use of semi-skilled workers (Lavalée, 1919; Lorenz, 1983; Ollson, 1980).

As long as ships remained bespoke products, there were comparative advantages to using the British pattern of labour organization based on 'craft control' of production. Scientific management proved too bureaucratic and clumsy for an industry that lacked product standardization and was subject to severe cyclical instability, as the necessary increase in managerial personnel weighed heavily on unit overheads. When simpler, more standardized vessels began to dominate international demand from the 1930s, however, the scope for systematic planning increased. Ironically, lack of skilled labour in the longer run proved an advantage for foreign producers, leaving them better predisposed towards, and more experienced with, systematic planning methods.

The retention of traditional forms of work organization, then, further narrowed the limits imposed on British shipbuilding by the industry's fragmented structure and diversified output. All told, worker specialization in British yards continued to be on a fairly broad occupational base, rather than the narrow base of detailed tasks at particular points in the flow of production. The continued emphasis on skill in the workforce discouraged builders from attempting a rationalization of the division of labour away from 'craft control', towards a sharper division between the tasks of conception and execution which could have improved the industry's ability to compete in the world market. Below, we assess the extent to which the structure of industrial relations that developed with nineteenth-century success also contributed to economic decline.

Industrial Relations

Trade union organization helped to perpetuate traditional forms of work organization in Britain. Union defence of craft demarcations created particular difficulties as the extension of welding, burning, and prefabrication techniques eliminated riveting, caulking, and much plating work, and created the basis for a new division of labour cutting across traditional craft boundaries.

As new techniques were 'captured' by the skilled trades, their flexible use across occupational boundaries was precluded. Welding provides a notable example. In the 1930s the employers failed to prevent the Boilermakers Society from establishing jurisdictional control over welding. Consequently they found it extremely difficult to extend the operation of welding equipment to other engineer and metal trades or to create a class of semi-skilled welders. The introduction and extension of welding and related techniques of burning and prefabrication were the occasion for a new wave of demarcation disputes (McGoldrick, 1982, pp. 168–80; SRNA Archives, Federation Circulars, 1931–4, passim).

To a considerable extent, these problems were peculiar to Britain. The industrial structure of unionism in other major maritime nations meant that unions did not have the same vested interest in establishing control over particular tasks, tools, or materials. For an industrial union, unlike a craft union, such jurisdictional control did not serve the union's long-term interest of preserving its employment base.

Britain was also distinguished by its tradition of militant shop-level control over job content by work groups seeking to defend their own interests. In British shipbuilding, the strength of controls over the content of jobs and access to them reflected a symbiotic relationship between the action of occupational work groups at the yard level, concerned with preserving their job opportunities and relative earnings levels, and union action on a wider regional and national level, concerned with the institutional goal of protecting the occupational base of craft union organization.

Yet trade unionism played no more than a secondary role in British decline. Any attempt to cut costs through a combined strategy of intensifying the work pace and substituting lower paid semi-skilled for skilled labour, even if successful in the short term, would not have provided an adequate basis for longer-term productivity growth. The technical and economic conditions for the adoption of a true rationalizing approach based on scientific management methods simply did not exist. As long as British producers remained small and continued to produce a bespoke product, a premium would continue to be placed on skill. It is difficult to see how a dilution of labour could have gone much beyond marginal shifts in the balance between skilled and unskilled work, regardless of how effective or ineffective labour resistance might be.

Furthermore, the industrial relations problems of British shipbuilding were themselves in large part a reflection of the industry's structural features. The small scale and lack of specialization of firms in the industry continued to dictate high rates of labour turnover for workers with specialized skills (Robertson, 1954). By heightening workers' concern over employment security, casual employment prompted demarcation conflict.

Conclusion

Students of the British shipbuilding industry have offered a wide range of often mutually exclusive explanations for the industry's relative decline. At one extreme, neoclassical historians see through the veil of relative decline to argue that no competitive failure took place. Different experiences were a matter of rational responses to different factor endowments.

At the other end of the spectrum are the proponents of the 'English disease' explanation for relative decline. While not denying competitive failure, they explain it exclusively in terms of pervasive social values which result in bad management and bad industrial relations. The evidence cited for entrepreneurial failure is that firms failed to adopt more up-to-date technologies and forms of work organization.

That argument faces the immediate difficulty of explaining the uneven timing of competitive failure. For example, why did shipbuilding continue to lead the world for decades after cotton and steel had begun their long decline? It seems unreasonable to argue on the one hand that the explanation lies in general cultural values and at the same time to hold that such values strike in different places at different times. The real weakness of this school, however, is that it lifts these phenomena from the economic and institutional context specific to each industry and period of time. Without such a context, it is impossible to evaluate the quality of entrepreneurial decision-making.

We have argued that the failure of the British response in shipbuilding can be understood only by considering the particular technical and market conditions in which firms operated, and the ways these conditions interacted with the system of industrial relations. The fragmentation of output in small-scale yards and the system of craft specialization it spawned, hallmarks of nineteenth-century success, led to competitive failure in the twentieth century. The slow rate of growth of demand and its distribution among many yards meant that individual firms could not achieve the minimum efficient scale of production without eliminating competitors; however, the risk of mutual damage implied in such a market solution precluded concentration by this route.

This fundamental weakness was exacerbated by worsening industrial relations. A high degree of trade specialization reinforced by craft unionism meant a narrow basis for employment opportunities. Industrial decline further reinforced the job protectiveness underlying demarcation rules and skilled worker resistance to dilution. Thus worker organization interacted with industrial organization to generate competitive failure.

Once the interrelationship between the dynamics of supply and demand fundamental to the growth process are taken into account, the weaknesses of both the neoclassical and entrepreneurial failure explanations become apparent. Central here is the notion of 'dynamic economies of scale' secured when successful productive systems[13] increase their share of expanding markets. As supply responds to demand, the pace of technical progress accelerates with the greater benefits of learning by doing more. Bottlenecks to increasing output are overcome and raised expectations reduce perceived risk. For these reasons success tends to breed success, and by the same token firms caught in the process of progressive failure may find it difficult to extricate themselves. How they respond in these circumstances depends on the broader economic and institutional context.

In the particular case of shipbuilding, no single firm had sufficient market power to impose a solution. Consequently a strong case can be made that co-ordinated action was required early in the 1950s to reform the industry's structure. To account fully for the lack of such a collective response would require a different study, one exploring in detail the motives and actions of individual entrepreneurs. But it does seem clear that the industry's fragmented structure was an obstacle to overcoming the intense individualism that hindered effective action. Consequently, structural reform required the intervention of an outside agency: the state.

The British government progressively intervened in shipbuidling from the early 1960s until the industry was finally nationalized in 1977. During the late 1960s the government pressed for the merger of yards into compact regional groupings. At the same time, employers and unions concluded a series of agreements relaxing restrictive practices—an industrial relations reform eased by changes in industry structure that facilitated enterprise offers of guaranteed employment (Shipbuilding and Shiprepairing CIR Report no. 22, 1970–1; Wilkinson, 1973, Pt 4, pp. 16–18).

These actions of the government were too little and too late. Their impact was just being felt when world market conditions dramatically changed, with the collapse of the tanker market in 1973–4 and the general depression that ensued. British shipbuilders, like producers elsewhere, have since then suffered from sluggish world demand, excess capacity, and intensified competition, as levels of subsidization by governments have risen. In these conditions the industry was taken into public ownership.

Ironically, as control of British shipbuilding became unified, increasing uncertainty in world markets has made it more difficult generally for firms to consolidate 'mass' markets. The most striking evidence has been the collapse and nationalization of the highly specialized Swedish industry during the late 1970s. European firms are now showing a distinct preference for less capital-intensive and more flexible methods than those characteristic of the 1960s, and under these conditions it is unclear whether large-scale specialized facilities will prove an advantage or a handicap.

It may well be argued that these conditions are temporary, and that some future recovery will again place the competitive advantage with large specialized yards producing standard vessels in series. But the rapid rise of shipbuilding in Brazil and Korea speaks poorly for the long-run ability of builders in the UK, or any other comparatively high-wage country, successfully to pursue a strategy of standardization, given the ease with which a workforce can be trained to produce these comparatively simple vessels. In a manner parallel to the pre-1914 period, it may well be the case that the future success of European yards will depend on the ability of firms to diversify their product range, seek specialty markets, and develop the processes to do this efficiently.

If this proves a reasonably accurate assessment, what are the British industry's likely prospects? The industry's comparatively diversified structure may provide the basis for a more flexible response to changing product market conditions. But regardless of any such advantages, the continued inflexibility in work assignments and the comparatively poor development of technical and design services will hinder competitive performances. The crucial question in this respect is whether the necessary flexibility in response can be effected by the industry's centralized structure of control.

Notes

[1]Figures on output and shares of world production here and elsewhere in the paper are taken from *Lloyd's Register of Shipping*.

[2]'Boilermaker' encompasses the following specialized trades: plater, angle iron-smith, riveter, caulker, and holder-up. Shipwrights' responsibilities were reduced to mould loft work, erecting and fairing the vessel's frames, certain woodwork (mainly decking), and the ship's launch.

[3]Dynamic scale economies refer to the reduction in unit costs that come with cumulative volume of output as both management and labour accumulate experience and skill. See Arrow (1962) and Kaldor (1978).

[4]A panel consists of a series of three or four steel plates—cut rectangular and welded together—to which steel beams are welded to stiffen the structure.

[5]Rapping's study of productivity gains in mass-producing Liberty vessels in the United States during World War II shows a remarkable gain of 122 per cent between December 1941 and December 1944, or an average annual gain of some 40 per cent. The regression analysis carried out by Rapping suggests that over half of this can be attributed to the learning process *per se*. The conditions, as he notes, were exceptional. Labour without prior experience in shipbuilding was placed under management similarly inexperienced.

[6]Established ties carry such weight in shipbuilding because of the expense and long life of the product. Confidence, once gained, is not easy to lose. Having been lost, it is difficult to regain (Cairncross and Parkinson, 1958, p. 104).

[7]The figures provide an imperfect measure of domestic market expansion because nationals of shipbuilding nations may register their ships with flags of convenience such as the Panamanian or Liberian flags. As J. R. Parkinson has observed, 'Much of the tonnage registered [under flags of convenience] is owned by international shipping operators to whom it is a matter of indifference where ships are produced provided that they represent good value for money, and in consequence the markets of Liberia and Panama provide a better opportunity of assessing the competitive position of main shipbuilding countries than their performance in home markets' (Parkinson, 1960, p. 91).

[8]For a general discussion of how limited market horizons may interact with imperfectly competitive market structures to encourage firms to adopt less than minimum efficient scale plants, see Scherer (1975). For a development of these ideas applied to the case of British steel, see Elbaum (this volume).

[9]For a related argument, see Thomas (1983). Thomas attributes the post-World War II decline of British shipbuilding to the nature of demand linkages between owners and builders. On his account, yards were perfectly adapted to building the types of ships British owners traditionally demanded. When owners' preferences suddenly shifted during the mid-1960s for types of ships being built abroad, which British yards were poorly suited to construct, a crisis ensued. The problem with this explanation is that it does not account for the British failure to respond to increasing import penetration which was already well advanced by the early 1960s.

[10]French producers increased their share of the domestic market from 36 per cent in 1948–50 to 83 per cent in 1956–60.

[11]This restrictive clause was removed in 1968 and the cash limit of grants was increased (Hogwood, 1979, pp. 87–93).

[12]The Committee proposed the formation of one as opposed to two groups on the Wear and recommended that Vickers, which remained independent, be attached to the Tyne and Tees group (Shipbuilding Inquiry Committee Report, 1966, p. 91).

[13]Productive system in this context includes not only technical and economic factors, but also the social and political structure in which these factors are enmeshed. (For a discussion see Wilkinson, 1983.)

Bibliography

Books, Articles, and Theses

Abell, W. A. (1948). *The Shipwright's Trade*. Cambridge University Press.

Arrow, K. (1962). 'The Economic Implications of Learning by Doing'. *Review of Economic Studies*, 29, pp. 155–73.

Basso, L. (1910). 'Les Enterprises françaises de construction navales'. Thesis, University of Paris.

Benoist, C. (1905). *L'Organisation du travail: la crise de l'état moderne*, Volume I. Paris: Librarie Plon.

Bohlin, J. (1980). 'Employment Fluctuations and Labour Turnover in the Gothenburg Shipbuilding Industry 1920–1944'. In *Proceedings of the SSRC Conference on Scottish and Scandanavian Shipbuilding*, ed. J. Kusse and A. Slaven. University of Gothenburg.

Burns, D. (1940). *Economic History of Steel Making, 1867—1939*. Cambridge University Press.

Cairncross, A. K., and J. R. Parkinson (1958). 'The Shipbuilding Industry'. In *The Structure of British Industry: A Symposium*, Volume II, ed. D. Burns. Cambridge University Press, pp. 93–129.

Chardonnet, J. (1971). *L'Economie française: les grandes industries*, Volume II. Paris: Dalloz.

Clegg, H. A. (1964). *General Union in a Changing Society*. Oxford: Basil Blackwell.

Cuthbert, D. (1969). 'Welding in Modern Ship Construction'. *Welding and Metal Fabrication*, Exhibition Number, April, 122–32.

Dougan, D. (1975). *The Shipwrights*. Newcastle-upon-Tyne: F. Graham.

Drewry, H. P. (1972–3). 'Shipbuilding Credits and Government Aid'. London: H. P. Drewry (Shipping Consultants).

Eldridge, J. E. T. (1968). *Industrial Disputes*. London: Routledge and Kegan Paul.

Fairburn, W. A. (1902). 'Methods of Handling Material over Shipbuilding Berths in American Shipyards'. *Transactions of the Institution of Naval Architects*, 44, 229–70.

Forbes, S., and J. B. Varney (1976). 'Ship Assembly Technology'. In *Structural Design and Fabrication in Shipbuilding*, International Conference, London, 18–20 November.

Gripaois, H. (1959). *Tramp Shipping*. New York: Thomas Nelson and Sons.

Hardy, J. (1951). 'L'Industrie des constructions navales en France'. Thesis, University of Rennes.

Hogwood, B. (1979). *Government and Shipbuilding: The Politics of Industrial Change*. Farnborough, Hants: Saxon House.

Holms, C. A. (1918). *Practical Shipbuilding*. London: Longmans, Green.

Hume, J. R. (1976). 'Shipbuilding Machine Tools'. In *Scottish Themes: Essays in Honour of Professor S. G. E. Lythe*, ed. J. Butt and J. T. Ward. Edinburgh: Scottish Academic Press, pp. 158–80.

John, T. G. (1914). 'Shipbuilding Practice of the Present and Future'. *Transactions of the Institution of Naval Architects*, 56, 291–312.

Jones, L. (1957). *Shipbuilding in Britain: Mainly Between the Two World Wars*. Cardiff: University of Wales Press.

Kaldor, N. (1978). 'Causes of the Slow Rate of Economic Growth in the United Kingdom'. In his *Further Essays on Economic Theory*. London: Duckworth.

Kendall, S. O. (1894–5). 'Turret-Decker Cargo Steamers'. *Transactions of the North-East Coast Institution of Engineers and Shipbuilders*, 11, 209–24.

Kirkaldy, A. W. (1914). *British Shipping*. London: Kegan Paul, Trench, Trubner and Co.

Lavalée, L. (1919). 'Resultats obtenus par l'application des nouvelles méthodes de travail dans un chantier de 3000 ouvriers'. *Bulletin de la Société d'Encouragement pour l'Industrie Nationale*, 118(1), 429–94.

Le Maistre, C. L. (1926–7). 'The Trade Value of Simplification and Standardization in the of Ships and their Machinery'. *'Transactions of the North-East Coast Institution of Engineers and Shipbuilders*, 43, 269–90.

Lorenz, E. H. (1983). 'The Labour Process and Industrial Relations in the British and French Shipbuilding Industries from 1880 to 1970: Two Patterns of Development'. Unpublished PhD thesis, University of Cambridge.

Lorenz, E. H. (1984). 'The Labour Process in British and French Shipbuilding from 1880 to 1930'. *Journal of European Economic History*, 13(3), 599–634.

McGoldrick, J. (1982). 'Crisis and the Division of Labour: Clydeside Shipbuilding in the Inter-War Period'. In *Capital and Class in Scotland*, ed. A. Dickson. Edinburgh: John Donald and Co.

Montgomery, J. (1937–8). 'Shipbuilding Practice Abroad'. *Transactions of the North-East Coast Institute of Engineers and Shipbuilders*, 54, 153–76.

O'Brien, P., and C. Keyder (1978). *Economic Growth in Britain and France, 1780–1914: Two Paths to the Twentieth Century*. London: George Allen and Unwin.

Ollson, K. (1980). 'Tankers and Technical Development in the Swedish Shipbuilding Industry'. In *Proceedings of the SSRC Conference on Scottish and Scandanavian Shipbuilding, University of Gothenberg*, ed. J. Kusse and A. Slaven.

Ollson, K. (1981). 'Markets and Production in Swedish Shipbuilding'. Discussion Paper for Gothenberg Conference on Shipbuilding History, 27–9 November, University of Gothenberg.

Orenstein, H. (1944–5). 'Method and Motion Study Allied to the Shipbuilding Industry'. *Transactions of the North-East Coast Institution of Engineers and Shipbuilders*, 61, 75–110.

Oury, L. (1973). *Les Prolos*. Paris: Editions Denoël.

Parkinson, J. R. (1956). 'Trends in the Output and Export of Merchant Ships'. *Scottish Journal of Political Economy*, 3, 235–45.

Parkinson, J. R. (1960). *The Economics of Shipbuilding in the United Kingdom*. Cambridge University Press.

Pinczon, M. (1930). 'Mission en Angleterre et en Ecosse avec la délégation du Conseil National Economique'. Inquiry of the Conseil National Economique, 1929–30. *Situation de l'industrie de la construction navale*. Chambre Syndical des Constructeurs de Navires, Circulaire 11B, Paris.

Pollard, S. (1957). 'British and World Shipbuilding, 1890–1914: A Study in Comparative Costs'. *Journal of Economic History*, 17(3), 426–44.

Pollard, S., and P. L. Robertson (1979). *The British Shipbuilding Industry, 1890–1914*. Cambridge, Mass.: Harvard University Press.

Pollock, D. (1905). *The Shipbuilding Industry*. London: Methuen.

Prêcheur, C. (1968). *Les Industries françaises à l'era du Marché Commun*. Paris: Société d'Enseignement Supérieure.

Price, S. (1981). 'Labour Mobility in Clyde Shipbuilding 1889–1913'. Discussion Paper for Gothenberg Conference on Shipbuilding History, University of Gothenberg, 27–9 November.

Puech, R. (1969). 'Evolution de la construction navale française depuis 1913'. *Journal de la Marine Marchande*, April, 147–82.

Rapping, L. (1965). 'Learning and World War II Production Functions'. *Review of Economics and Statistics*, 47, 81–6.

Reid, A. (1980). 'The Division of Labour in The Shipbuilding Industry, 1880–1920, With special reference to Clydeside'. PhD thesis, University of Cambridge.

Roberts, G. (1967). 'Demarcation Rules in Shipbuilding'. Cambridge University Department of Applied Economics Occasional Paper no. 14.

Robertson, D. J. (1954). 'Labour Turnover in the Clyde Shipbuilding Industry'. *Scottish Journal of Political Economy*, 1, 9–32.

Robertson, P. L. (1974). 'Shipping and Shipbuilding: The Case of William Denny and Brothers'. *Business History*, 16(1), 36–47.

Robertson, P. L. (1975). 'Demarcation Disputes in British Shipbuilding Before 1914'. *International Review of Social History*, 10(2), 220–35.

Roux-Freissineng, M. (1929). 'L'Industrie des constructions navales en France'. Thesis, University of Aix.

Scherer, F. M. (1975). *The Economics of Multi-plant Operation: An International Comparisons Study*. Cambridge, Mass.: Harvard University Studies.

Shield, J. (1949). *Clyde Built: A History of Shipbuilding on the River Clyde*. Glasgow: W. MacMillan.

Slaven, A. (1980). 'Growth and Stagnation in British/Scottish Shipbuilding, 1913–1977'. In *Proceedings of the SSRC Conference on Scottish and Scandinavian Shipbuilding*, ed. J. Kusse and A. Slaven. University of Gothenberg.

Slaven, A. (1981). 'Shipbuilding Industry Organizations and Policies 1920–1977'. Discussion Paper for Gothenberg Conference on Shipbuilding History, 27–9 November, University of Gothenberg.

Stopford, M. (1979). 'UK Cost Competitiveness'. Mimeo, British Shipbuilders, Newcastle-upon-Tyne.

Svensson, T. (1980). 'From Patriarchalians to Proletarians: Gothenberg Shipyard Workers 1875–1960'. In *Proceedings of the SSRC Conference on Scottish and Scandanavian Shipbuilding*, ed. J. Kusse and A. Slaven. University of Gothenberg.

Thomas, D. (1983). 'Shipbuilding–Demand Linkage and Industrial Decline'. In K. Williams *et al.*, *Why are the British Bad at Manufacturing?* London: Routledge and Kegan Paul.

Wilkinson, F. (1973). 'Demarcation in Shipbuilding'. Department of Applied Economics Working Paper, University of Cambridge.

Wilkinson, F. (1983). 'Productive Systems'. *Cambridge Journal of Economics*, 7(3/4), 413–29.

Wolfenden, F. T. (1976). 'The Submerged Arc Process in Shipbuilding'. In *Structural Design and Fabrication in Shipbuilding*, International Conference, London, 18–20 November. London: Welding Institute.

Official Publications

BETURE (Bureau d'Etudes Techniques pour l'Urbanisme) (1978). *Les Ouvriers de la sidérurgie et de la métallurgie* Secrétariat d'Etat aux Transport, Trappes.
British and Foreign Trade and Industry (1909), Volume 47. Cd. 4954. London: HMSO.
Conseil National Economique (1930). *Situation de l'industrie de la construction navale, 1929–30*. Paris.
Department of Trade and Industry (1973). *British Shipbuilding 1972*, Booz-Allen and Hamilton Report.
Department of Science and Industrial Research (1960). *Research and Development Requirements of the Shipbuilding and Marine Engineering Industries*.
Ministry of Transport (1963). Peat, Marwick, and Mitchell Report.
Shipbuilding Industry Training Board (1966–67). *Report and Statement of Accounts*, Volume 38.
Shipbuilding Inquiry Committee Report 1965–6 (1966). Cmnd. 2937. London: HMSO.
Shipbuilding and Shiprepairing, Commission on Industrial Relations (1970–1). *Report no. 22*, Volume 25, Cmnd. 4756. London: HMSO.
Southwest of Scotland Board of Trade (1932). Industrial Survey.

Periodical Publications

The Engineer.
Lloyd's Register of Shipping.
The Shipbuilder and Marine Engine Builder.

Other

Patton Report (1962). *Productivity and Research in Shipbuilding*. Report prepared under the Chairmanship of Mr J. Patton to the Joint Committee of the Shipbuilding Conference, the Shipbuilding Employers Association and the British Shipbuilding Research Association.
SRNA (Shipbuilders and Shiprepairers National Association) Archives, Federation Circulars, Greenwich, London.

The Motor Vehicle Industry

W. Lewchuk
McMaster University

The decline of the British motor vehicle industry came suddenly and swiftly during the first half of the 1970s. The collapse of the industry and the subsequent government salvage operation have stimulated a number of investigations by the state and by academic researchers. The reports have differed in the importance they allocate to the various aspects of the industry's experience, but a general consensus has emerged on the industry's basic characteristics. It is agreed that the period since the mid-1950s saw the transition from a relatively strike-free industry to one with a high incidence of strikes. It is also agreed that by the 1970s the level of labour productivity in the industry was well below that in the United States and on the Continent. It has been suggested that this was the result of both low levels of investment in fixed plant and the ability of labour to exercise some control over effort levels. There is also general agreement that various aspects of managerial performance, including labour control and co-ordination, cost accounting, marketing policies, investment policies, and profit distributions, have not been consistent with long-run growth.[1]

Despite this general agreement concerning basic characteristics, there has been disagreement over the chain of causation and the factors that were ultimately responsible for the industry's bankruptcy. One line of approach argues that managerial failure and shifts in government macroeconomic policy destabilized the security of employment in the industry. This in turn led to heightened labour unrest, disruptions through strikes, low productivity, and low profits. An alternative interpretation focuses on the union structure and the regularity of labour disputes, which, it is argued, caused low levels of labour productivity which reduced profits and cash flows. This in turn constrained management from investing in new plant and new models and from improving the quality of managerial co-ordination and control functions.

In trying to identify the direction of causation, most studies of the industry have tried to blame labour or management or both for failing to adapt to modern factory production. They have suggested either that labour failed to accommodate itself to the realities of factory production and the demand for regular productivity, or that management failed to adjust its methods of operation in a way which was consistent with large integrated factories. This paper will argue that it is misleading to suggest that either labour or management failed to adopt an optimal strategy. The study will take a long-run view of the industry's history. I shall suggest that the behaviour of management was consistent with its search for higher profits and that the behaviour of labour was consistent with its search for higher wages and better working conditions. The failure, if there was one, was not on the part of either labour or management, but rather in the competitive market system within which both operated.

My interest in the history of the industry was stimulated by the parallels between the types of criticism made of the industry in the 1970s and those made of the industry during the first fifty years of its existence. The quality of management, its ability to co-ordinate and control labour, and its receptivity to new methods have been questioned on numerous occasions. There has also been concern about the level of investment in fixed capital and the commercial and sales strategies. Labour's willingness to co-operate with management has long been an issue. The industry has been plagued since the early years of the century with comparatively low levels of productivity (Maxcy and Silberston, 1959, p. 211; Saul, 1962).

Given these basic weaknesses over such a long period, it is rather remarkable that profit rates and yields on shares remained as high as they did for so long. Profit levels remained high until well into the 1960s, and it was not until the early 1970s that financial analysts began to warn investors that motor vehicle shares had become a risky investment. As time went on, even *The Economist* had to wonder out loud that 'It is remarkable that with such low productivity BL is still one of the more profitable European car companies' (*The Economist*, 13 January 1973, p. 67).

I shall argue that, between 1905 and 1920, British producers adopted a strategy markedly different from the Fordist one. The Fordist strategy ensured high levels of productivity by combining rigid managerial control, flow production technology, and relatively high wages paid on fixed day rates. In contrast, the British strategy can be characterized as one with weak managerial control over labour, low wages, low capital–labour ratios, low levels of machine integration along flow principles, and piecework payment systems. This strategy allowed a relatively unproductive technology to generate relatively high levels of profits on invested capital. The adoption of the British system in this early period had many implications for the future evolution of British techniques of production.

In the process of maximizing profits under the new British system, a well defined institutional framework emerged—a unique relationship between labour and shopfloor management, a managerial class with specific strengths and weaknesses, and particular patterns of financing and distribution. These British institutions differed from parallel developments in the United States, and in many cases were inconsistent with US methods (Lazonick, 1981, 1983).

These institutional differences became critical in the late 1950s when it was growing obvious that the British managerial strategy was no longer consistent with the more capital-intensive technology being used. Management required more direct control of the production process along Fordist lines. The collapse of the industry in the 1970s is evidence of the difficulty of making such a transition. Our analysis of the industry's collapse raises serious questions about the appropriateness of the industry's belated attempt under Michael Edwardes to move towards a Fordist managerial system.

Early Experiments in Production and Management: 1896–1914

In this section we will focus on the patterns evolving in the motor vehicle industry prior to 1914. Two factors stand out as being of critical importance. The first, and most important, was the need to resolve a serious labour relations problem in the early factories. The second factor was the inability of any firm to achieve a dominant position in the industry and to achieve a significant degree of market power.

The motor vehicle industry began production during two of the most turbulent decades in British economic history. Between 1896 and 1914, Britain lost its dominance of world markets, while at home tensions between labour and capital had reached crisis proportions. In the older industries such as textiles, steel, and shipbuilding, structural constraints appear to have prevented any major movement towards American-style mass production techniques (Lazonick, 1983; Elbaum and Wilkinson, 1979; Pollard and Robertson, 1979). The motor vehicle industry was free from many of these structural constraints and was able to adopt modern production techniques and repetition methods well before 1914. However, the industry was not free from the social tensions being generated by Britain's relative decline. These tensions emerged as a conflict between labour and capital, forcing British firms to organize their factories along lines distinctly different from the Americans.

The commercial production of motor vehicles in Britain began in 1896 at the Daimler Motor Company as part of H. Lawson's attempt to monopolize the British industry. Lawson's strategy was to gain control of all of the patents pertaining to vehicle production. Daimler, Humber, New Beeston Cycle, and the Great Horseless Carriage Company were to produce vehicles, each company being allocated a specific segment of the market. Lawson succeeded in using the public capital markets to float the British Motor Syndicate with a face value of £1 million but his scheme failed within a few years as technological advances rendered his patents worthless.

The attempt to monopolize the British motor industry bears a striking resemblance to a number of the US initiatives to achieve market power, including Standard Oil and US Steel. Had Lawson been successful, he might have created the conditions necessary for the transition to corporate capitalist organization in Britain.[2] Even in failure, Lawson's venture had two major lasting effects. First, Daimler and Humber survived as independent producers. Second, Lawson opened the door for other firms to use the public capital markets, even though Lawson's failure made future investors wary. Access to public capital markets eased entry into the industry and prevented the type of market power Lawson envisioned from becoming a reality.[3]

The early motor vehicle producers drew heavily on the production experience of the British cycle industry. They learned to organize work so that it flowed progressively through the shops, and they also learned the potential value of modern repetition machinery and unskilled operatives. The cycle trade had begun as a craft industry, but by the late 1890s a wholesale conversion to repetition methods was under way (*Cycle Referee*, 1899). These new methods spread rapidly to vehicle production. By 1897 Daimler was reported to have spent £20,000 on US machinery, and by 1899 specialized and automatic machinery could be found, employed on long-runs of identical tasks.[4] Other firms followed and soon surpassed the lead given by Daimler. Belsize was reported to be a large user of US methods, while the following description of the Humber works in 1902 was given:

Advantage has been taken of the long experience which Humber have had in the employment of labour saving tools for the production of bicycle parts, and it would be difficult to find a better regulated machine tool shop, or one with a greater output capacity, high speed steel being employed throughout . . . limit gauges and micrometer working are universal. (*The Engineer*, 1903, p. 232.)

Indicative of the speed of change, the question of boy labour on production machines became an issue at the Daimler works in 1899 (Amalgamated Society of Engineers, Coventry Branch Minute Books (hereafter ASE(COV)), 12 July–15 August 1899). By 1914 contemporary reports suggested that large segments of production work were done entirely by unskilled operatives, with the skilled worker limited mainly to the tool room (Linley, 1914; Legros, 1911).

Another important feature of the early vehicle firms was their preference for manufacturing virtually the entire motor vehicle. US producers, in contrast, almost all began as assemblers, and depended on outside suppliers for finished components. Two critical factors help to explain this difference. The first was the greater experience of British workers on metal working machines. This made the British worker more versatile and better suited to manufacturing operations in which they might be called upon to do a large number of diverse, if unskilled, tasks. Second, British firms found it easier to raise capital than did US firms. Ford, for instance, had to use outside component suppliers for the majority of manufacturing operations because he was unable to raise sufficient capital to buy his own machines.

As manufacturers, British firms had to employ many more workers for a given level of output than did the US assemblers. The level of output of even the largest British factories was small compared with US output levels. Yet the British firms had almost as many workers as the US firms. By 1905, Argyll was employing over 1,200; by 1908 Humber employed over 5,000 and by 1910 Daimler employed 4,500. In comparison, Ford in the United States did not begin to employ more workers than Daimler until just before World War I; in 1913, when he produced over two hundred times as many cars as the largest British producer, his company was employing only three times as many workers (Nixon, 1946, p. 112; Saul, 1962, p. 25; Nevin and Hill, 1954, p. 644; Daimler Minute Books, March 1910).

The decision to manufacture a large portion of the vehicle was important for two reasons. British management was forced to co-ordinate production units which were much more complex than US assembly shops; and they had to co-ordinate and control bodies of workers that were comparable in size with US firms. It will be shown below that British management was unable to fulfil either of these functions in the pre-World War I period. Management's resolution of these problems led to a degree of 'labour independence' on the shopfloor and a managerial class with only partial control over the shopfloor and labour effort (Walker, 1981).

It should not be assumed that 'labour independence' was necessarily advantageous to labour. Management had lost some control of one aspect of the firm, but it was still firmly in control of the firm overall. It appears that, prior to 1950, management was able to take advantage of existing social and economic factors to maintain profits despite their looser control over labour. I would suggest that this paradox of an 'independent' but unorganized workforce in the interwar period helps to reconcile different views concerning the sources and extent of labour's postwar bargaining strength (Lyddon, 1983; Zeitlin, 1983).

The earliest motor vehicle factories employed mainly craft workers from either the Amalgamated Society of Engineers or the United Kingdom Society of Coachmakers. These workers brought with them their experience of unionism, and by 1899 shop stewards were being appointed in the factories to protect labour's interests (ASE(COV), 6 June 1898 and 12–26 July 1899). Managers found it relatively easy to introduce new machine methods into the industry, but when they attempted to use these new machines to speed up the pace of work and reduce wages by employing less skilled workers they met with resistance. At Humber, attempts to reduce piece-rates paid on a new model that was being produced in batches of 100 met with severe resistance. Management hoped to pay just one-third of the piece-rate the existing gang expected for the work. Management concluded, 'The inference to be drawn from the above was that the men had agreed amongst themselves not to do the work at a reasonable rate.'[5] The firm initially responded by trying to hire only non-union men, but this strategy seems to have been unsuccessful, and two years later the shop was transferred from Nottingham to Coventry.[6]

At Daimler, despite glowing reports in the trade journals, management had difficulty in co-ordinating the works and in controlling the relatively highly unionized workforce. Company accounts suggest that production was sporadic, disorganized, and excessively expensive. A committee of investigation appointed by the board of directors found that all orders prior to 1898 had been put through the shops at a trading loss.[7] As a result, significant changes were made in the system of supervision, the payment system employed, and the administration of the works. The number of foremen was reduced, and the Premium Bonus wage payment system was adopted for most work.

P. Martin, the Daimler works manager, saw this as a move from 'driving supervision' to 'induction'.[8] For Martin, the Premium Bonus system was the heart of a clearly worked out strategy to cope with production in large factory units. His intention was to overcome both management's inability to co-ordinate the complex operations of a vehicle factory and the associated problem of its inability to control labour effort. Martin declared that, with his new managerial strategy:

Instead of the staff driving the workers for output, the workers drive the staff to supply them with material, and jobs are finished off by virtue of fresh ones pushing them out. . . . The usual driving system is absolutely reversed. The staff and everybody connected with the company is kept on the jump all the time to keep the man supplied with material, so that he can earn more wages; and I think the greatest advantage of the bonus system is to be found in that very fact.[9]

Faced with an organized workforce and managers who were unable to co-ordinate factory production, Martin attempted to create a factory system in which the workforce, paid by the piece, would itself fulfil a number of managerial tasks such as parts delivery, machine maintenance, and quality control. Notwithstanding the rhetoric surrounding the defence of managerial rights by the Engineering Employers Federation (EEF), the reality of factory life in the British environment allowed labour to maintain a good part of its control over the pace of work. In the British context, piece-work systems helped to generate a tradition of labour independence on the shopfloor, in the sense that management had only partial control over labour effort. With the favourable conditions facing labour during World War I and World War II, this independence was formalized in the rise of shop stewards and shop stewards' committees.

However, as long as management retained control over the setting of piece-rates it was able to maintain control over the wage effort bargain. This appears to have been the case until at least the early 1950s (ASE(COV), 7 February 1927, and Shop Stewards Reports, Misc. Firms, 1925 and 1930, ASE Archives, Coventry). Labour retained the ability to reduce throughput in the factories, but only at the cost of reduced wages. The low levels of productivity in the industry suggest that this is precisely what happened. As long as capital–labour ratios were sufficiently low, the low throughput on capital equipment could be balanced by paying low wages. This left management with acceptable profits despite the low productivity. Under these conditions, 'labour independence' on the shopfloor could be tolerated. It was not until the 1970s that changes in technology forced management to reassess its lack of control over labour effort.

It has already been stated that British motor vehicle firms were able to raise significant amounts of capital on the public capital markets. In contrast, US motor vehicle firms were virtually excluded from the public equity markets until after World War I (Seltzer, 1928). The ability of British firms to raise capital publicly was the result of the more mature financial institutions in Britain and the relative capital abundance of the economy (Kennedy, 1976). Prior to 1908, Humber and Argyll were able to raise £500,000. By 1914 there were twenty-three publicly quoted firms, and over £6 million had been raised in fifty-one separate equity issues (Michie, 1981, pp. 167–71).

In fact, if one looks at the entire prewar period, the public firms in the industry used new share and debt issues as their main sources of capital. In 1905 the major firms in the industry had raised 72 per cent of their capital publicly, while retained earnings represented only 4 per cent of capital. What is even more surprising is that, by 1914, the twenty-three publicly quoted firms had found 65 per cent of their capital on the public financial markets, while retained earnings represented only 10 per cent of capital. In contrast, the leading US firms relied overwhelmingly on retained earnings for new capital. Seltzer estimated that the eight leading US firms had raised just under 80 per cent of their capital from internal sources prior to 1926 (Seltzer, 1928, p. 266). It is unlikely that British firms could have resorted to internal financing to the same degree as US firms because profit levels were not as spectacular in Britain. None the less, perhaps with an eye to raising capital publicly in the future, British firms were more willing to distribute the profits they earned as dividends. Eleven of the leading British firms distributed over 60 per cent of their profits, while the comparable figure for US vehicle firms was 50 per cent (see Appendix Tables 1 and 2 below).

The combination of high payout ratios and relatively sophisticated public equity markets significantly eased entry into the industry. New entrants were able to use the institutional structure and cash in on the good will generated by existing firms to finance their own entry. By 1914, at least twenty major firms had joined the original four vehicle firms in raising capital on the public financial markets (Lewchuk, 1985). Between 1897 and 1913, there were no fewer than eighty-one entrants into the industry. No one firm came even close to establishing the type of market power that Lawson had envisioned and Ford had achieved (Maxcy, 1958, p. 365). This legacy of a competitive industrial structure proved exceedingly difficult to shed. Too many firms with too much capacity played a significant role in the collapse of the industry in the 1970s (Expenditure Committee, 1975).

How successful was this British managerial strategy which depended upon external financing, relatively rapid movement into advanced repetition machinery, Premium Bonus payment systems, concessions to labour over the control of the shopfloor, and weak managerial direction? In terms of productivity, the British producers seem to have been unable to match the US producers, but in terms of profits, relative performance is less clear.

Franklin, a US producer of quality output, required 2,000 labour hours to complete a vehicle, whereas Ford required 200 labour hours; the best British producers required between 1,000 and 3,000 labour hours in 1913 (Saul, 1962; Babcock, 1917, Ford Archives Acc 125; Model T Cost Books; and miscellaneous contemporary journals). Yet between 1905 and 1914 the average yield on ordinary shares issued by British motor vehicle firms was 17.5 per cent per annum. In comparison with non-British shares held in British portfolios, this was very good. This latter group of shares yielded just under 10 per cent between 1897 and 1909 and under 2 per cent between 1910 and 1913 (Lewchuk, 1985; Edelstein, 1976; Merrett and Sykes, 1973). Interpretation of share yields is a hazardous exercise, but the available evidence is sufficiently strong to justify rejecting a profit failure thesis.

In the short run, then, the strategy adopted by the industry was relatively profitable. But the pattern established by 1914 persisted through the period that followed, and left the industry unable to respond to the changed conditions of the late 1960s.

Period of Dominance by British Vehicle Producers, 1914–1960

Between 1914 and 1960, British producers dominated the home market and at times played a leading role in world markets. Imports represented a negligible share of the British market, and it was not until the 1960s that foreign producers broke into the British market to any meaningful extent. British-based US producers also had their problems, particularly during the first half of this period. Ford's share of the market was kept to under 10 per cent until after the opening of its new works in Dagenham in the 1930s, and General Motors' subsidiary, Vauxhall, remained a small producer until after World War II (Church and Miller, 1977; Dunnett, 1980).

Not only did the British firms remain dominant, they also remained profitable. Between 1922 and 1939 Austin's average gross profits were 19 per cent on net tangible assets. The average per annum yield on ordinary shares issued by British motor vehicle firms was 8.4 per cent between 1921 and 1932, while the yield on US shares held in British portfolios over the same period was only 5 per cent. After World War II, a strong sellers' market insured relatively healthy levels of profits which continued until the late 1960s (Church, 1979, p. 143; Edelstein, 1976; Expenditure Committee, 1975, no. 30). Between 1947 and 1956, Austin, Morris, and BMC earned between 12 and 48 per cent net profit on net tangible assets with the average rate being in excess of 20 per cent (Maxcy and Silberston, 1959, p. 175).

At the same time, British levels of productivity continued to lag behind those being achieved in the US motor vehicle industry. In 1935 US labour productivity was 3.1 times that of the British, in 1950 it was 2.9 times greater, and in 1955 it was 2.5 times greater (Maxcy and Silberston, 1959, p. 211; Rostas, 1948, pp. 167–77). Evidence suggests that for some time British firms outproduced their continental competitors, but that by the early 1960s this advantage had been reversed (Pratten and Silberston, 1967). The obvious question is, how did an industry with markedly lower levels of labour productivity over such a long period maintain its level of profits? In the following section, we will trace the British industry's response to their productivity problem and particularly their response to the Ford system introduced in the Ford factories during 1913 and 1914.[10]

World War I did not witness any drastic change in either the amount or the type of machinery employed in the production of motor vehicles. We have already indicated that by 1914 the industry had made significant progress in introducing unskilled operatives. The limited data we have strongly supports the thesis that there was no major change in the amount of capital employed per worker during the war. In the prewar period fixed capital employed per worker ranged between £70 and £120 in the major factories. Austin employed £76 of fixed capital per employee in 1914. The immediate impact of wartime expansion was a fall in capital employed per worker. In 1918 Austin used £54 per employee while Sunbeam reported £51 of fixed assets per employee. This fall may be, in part, a reflection of new accounting procedures made attractive by the new tax systems introduced during the war. It is also probable that the fall can be explained in part by the extension of multiple-shift operations and the more intensive use of land and buildings, which represented a significant component of fixed capital employed in motor vehicle factories (see Appendix Table 4).

The war was important from another perspective. The years before 1914 had witnessed a dramatic fall in union density as the unorganized unskilled workers entered the vehicle factories. The war allowed the unskilled to establish new labour unions and allowed the skilled workers to extend their organization. It was only a matter of time until these unions tried to exploit the looseness of management's shopfloor control. Shop stewards and shop stewards' committees allowed the wartime workers temporarily to transcend the limitations of 'labour independence' and resulted in a major challenge to management's overall control of the firm.

The vehicle producers, who before the war had played only a minor role in the EEF, responded by joining the Federation and exerting a major influence on its policy. In particular, the Coventry and Birmingham employers were concerned about the spread of labour radicalism and workers' control (EEF S(4)6, CDEEA to EEF, 14 April 1917, and Works Committee Agreement, 20 May 1919). After the war, the employers moved to weaken union strength and the strength of the shop stewards. This is well documented in the drastic drop in union membership in cities such as Coventry. These changes were occurring at the same time that Henry Ford was introducing and perfecting the new production system known as Fordism at his Detroit and Manchester factories. As will be shown below, the rise in the demand for workers' control in Britain had an important impact on how British management viewed the new Fordist strategy.

It has already been suggested that piece-work was seen by some vehicle producers as the solution to their managerial and labour relations problems before the war. The rise of the shop stewards as an effective labour voice, and the radical nature of the more aggressive elements within the workforce, made piece-work even more attractive to management (Holton, 1976). It was argued that direct control of labour was not practical in Britain, and that only monetary incentives that were directly linked to productivity could keep output levels up. The implication of this managerial philosophy towards labour was that British management took a very dim view of the widely acclaimed Ford system and its policy of direct labour control. Management was sceptical that the Ford production system, with its high capital–labour ratios, its dependency on direct managerial supervision, the machine pacing of labour, and the linking of tasks into a flow process, could be effective in the post-World War I British context. One of the most surprising aspects of the motor industry's interwar history was that it was labour that called the most loudly for Fordism, managerial reorganization, and high wages, while management adopted the more critical attitude.[11]

Fordism was first introduced into Britain by the Ford Motor Company at its Manchester works before World War I. The factory began production in late 1911 as an assembly shop, and began the actual manufacture of vehicle components in 1912. At first, a managerial strategy similar to that found in Detroit was adopted. Management retained the right to allocate labour to tasks irrespective of existing custom or practice. Machinery and unskilled labour were widely used, and the local going rate for factory work was paid. Resistance to this system by the established unions was evident throughout 1912, and in 1913 erupted into a twenty-two-week strike. At the end of the strike, labour capitulated on all its work process demands, but was granted a general increase in wages. For the first time at any Ford shop, wages were allowed to rise dramatically relative to that paid by other employers in the area. During the period of labour agitation, wages rose from a minimum of 5*d*. per hour in 1911, to 6*d*. in 1912, to 10*d*. by September 1913, and to 15*d*. by April 1914. These relatively high wages effectively silenced organized labour's attempt to protect established customs for the time being. It was not until the Ford wage differential disappeared in the late 1930s that trade unionism became a factor at Fords in Britain.

The relatively high day wages being paid in the Ford Manchester factory, plus the news of the pay revolution that Ford had introduced in Detroit with the $5 day, made British labour somewhat sympathetic to Fordist ideas, though it is likely that few really understood the radical changes in the organization of the factories that Fordism represented.[12] In the post-World War I negotiations over the return to private work, the unions were consistently more sympathic to aspects of Fordism than were the employers' associations. The unions showed a willingness to surrender partial shopfloor control for higher wages. As Coventry shifted from war work to private work, the unions called for a total switch to day work (Lewchuk, 1983, pp. 89–91).

British management in the vehicle industry argued that day work was an obsolete strategy and that only incentive systems should be considered by progressive employers. For a brief period the Coventry unions unilaterally placed their members on day work, but in early 1919 an agreement, which became known as the Humber agreement, was negotiated. The essence of this agreement was that payment by results became the accepted payment system, and that recognized bonus rates would be allowed to increase from their prewar level of one-third to a new rate of one-half of a worker's base rate. This agreement tied wages even more closely to productivity than in the prewar period and also increased the penalty paid by labour for managerial weaknesses in planning and co-ordination. There is little doubt that this agreement was consistent with the system of 'induction' proposed by Martin in 1905.[13]

At Austin, the strategy of 'induction' as a substitute for managerial control and machine pacing reached an advanced state. The Austin managers, suffering from severe cash-flow problems and an uncooperative work force after World War I, rejected the Ford strategy of heavy investment in labour-pacing machinery. They opted for a strategy whose main component was a unique payment system under which labour earned time credits for production. The payment system was supplemented by a managerial campaign to convince labour that it was in their own interest to co-operate with management and raise productivity (Lewchuk, 1983, pp. 99–101).

Statements by leading Austin managers indicate that motivation of the workers through the cash nexus was seen to be critical to the success of the strategy. C. R. F. Engelbach, the works director, was of the opinion that 'Good organization and an indifferent plant achieve better results than a good plant and indifferent organization.' Perry Keene, the head of the cost department, suggested that 'The obvious difficulty at the moment is lack of confidence as between employer and employed.' He went on to suggest that the key to the Austin strategy and its ability to overcome the distrust between labour and capital was the Austin payment system:

[On] such a basis, many economic problems become common to both employers and employed, and interests flow in one direction. ... The reason why the system of control became really efficient was that they inculcated into the whole staff a maximum idea of personal responsibility to the firm itself whereby they and the firm were likely to prosper.[14]

Well into the 1930s, even after Austin had made significant progress towards flow production, the Austin managers continued to reject complete managerial control of the pace of work and driving supervision:

There are still a few employers who object to piecework on principle. Their stand-point is that an efficient management ought to be able to get the same results at an agreed rate of wage without having to pay more money to encourage the men to work harder. . . . Some form of extra wage must be paid to a man if he is expected to work harder. The only alternative is to pay a high wage similar to the Ford system, and insist upon task achievement. The obtaining of results by this system could not be regarded with favour by an Employers' Federation, as the advantage would be to one particular firm only. When every other concern came into line, the status quo would be again obtained, and a circle of rising wage competition would begin. . . . The daily task system at fixed wages may perhaps, be workable in America, or even Continental factories, but the necessary . . . driving works policy would not be acceptable either to English Labour or Management.[15]

Management was able to use the new payment systems and their loose control over labour effort to advantage as long as trade unions remained weak. Management promoted an individualistic relationship between the workers and the firm. Union officials complained that management had convinced labour that it was the company that looked after their interests and not the unions (ASE Quarterly Report, April 1921). At Austin, the shop stewards' committee was suppressed after 1922, and by 1928 the managing director claimed that the shop was completely free of shop stewards and shop stewards' committees (Keene, 1928, p. 28). Even the EEF had recognized that Austin was able to work its payment system only because labour organization was relatively weak in the shops (EEF Archives, A(1)51, G. E. Nines, Austin Payment on Time System). The seasonality of production in the industry prior to 1950 made it relatively easy for any firm to weed out unwanted workers.

As well as rejecting Fordism, the British industry continued to operate within a highly competitive framework. By the interwar period in the United States, Ford and General Motors had grown to dominate the domestic market. In Britain, the number of firms fell from eighty-eight to thirty-one during the 1920s, but no single firm was able to dominate the British market as Ford dominated the US market. Many of the firms that disappeared were simply absorbed into existing firms without any attempt to rationalize production. By the mid-1950s there were still five major firms competing in the British mass production market, while a US market ten times larger supported only three major firms.[16] Since British output levels were relatively low, there was little need to integrate sales and production operations. The large US firms had been successful in forcing their dealers to sell only one firm's product. This helped to establish brand loyalty and also gave the producers a signific-ant amount of control over the dealers. In Britain, the agency system dominated. Most dealers sold the products of a number of firms and were less vulnerable to the dictates of the producers (Church, 1981, p. 69).

In the absence of either monopoly market power or superior levels of productivity, high levels of profits were earned by keeping both capital–labour ratios low compared with US producers and by keeping wages in the British factories below those in the US plants. By World War II, the assembly line and a version of flow production had been adopted by most of the major producers. Capital–labour ratios did begin to edge up, but remained significantly below the levels found in the Ford factories. Throughout the 1930s, Austin employed between £175 and £200 of fixed capital per employee. At Ford's in Detroit, the amount of fixed capital employed per worker rose from $1,210 in 1908 to $3,194 in 1919 and to $5,544 in 1921.[17]

The use of less capital and more labour cannot be viewed as simply a shift along a given production isoquant. British firms exhibited not only a lower output–labour ratio but a lower output–capital ratio. At Rover, prior to World War I labour productivity was about one-eighth of the Ford level and capital productivity about one-third.[18] Furthermore, the assembly line and the Ford managerial system spread to European factories much earlier, despite the fact that wages on the Continent were lower (Friedenson, 1978). I would argue that the decision to use less capital per worker was taken by management to insulate themselves from the economic penalties that incomplete control over labour effort implied. The economics of the British system was made even more attractive by the significantly lower wages paid to British workers relative to US workers (see Appendix Table 3). There was also a differential between the wages paid to production workers in British vehicle factories and those paid to workers in British-based US factories. In 1928 Ford was paying its Manchester workers between £6.50 and £7.50 per week while British piece-workers in the industry earned £3.90 per week (Ford Motor Company; EEF). The combined effect of the lower capital–labour ratios and the lower British wage allowed British firms to earn relatively high levels of profit. When the wage differential between British and British-based US factories disappeared after World War II, the change created problems for British firms (Turner, Clack, and Roberts, 1967; Brown, 1971).

In the interwar period, profitable British firms continued to distribute a significant portion of their profits as dividends rather than re-investing in new capacity. Again, it appears that the short-run demands of investors for dividend income took precedence over long-run growth. The successful British firms were unable to consolidate their short-term economic advantage and allowed less successful firms to grow, contributing to the continued absence of market power in the industry. Between 1922 and 1939, Austin paid out nearly 70 per cent of profits on ordinary and preferred dividends and on interest on long-term bonds (Church, 1979, pp. 214–15). Between 1927 and 1951, Morris earned nearly £55 million in pre-tax profit, but retained only 26 per cent in the firm (Overy, 1976, p. 129). Between 1929 and

1938 the two most successful firms, Austin and Morris, accounted for only 36 per cent of the net increase in assets of the six biggest producers. Between 1947 and 1956 this same figure fell to 26 per cent. Between 1938 and 1956 Austin and Morris's share of total net assets reported by the six biggest producers fell from 46 to 30 per cent (Maxcy and Silberston, 1959, p. 178).

In hindsight, the strategies of Austin and Morris were certainly not consistent with long-run profit maximization. Had they invested a larger percentage of their interwar profits in their own firms, or called on the capital markets for new funds, their supposedly defensive merger of the 1950s might not have been necessary. We do not yet have sufficient information to understand fully why such a short-run strategy was adopted, but it appears to have been a function of the degree of perceived risk in the British economy and the dependence on external financing.

With the ending of World War II, the British motor vehicle industry moved into its final stage of prosperity. For a time the industry's long-run problems could be ignored, for the postwar years witnessed a sellers' market during which Britain became the largest exporter of vehicles in the world. The war-induced shortages prevented the most efficient firms from expanding, because the government allotted scarce materials on the basis of export performance rather than on the basis of improvements in profits or productivity. Between 1948 and 1956, despite signs that with the new postwar technology there were too many firms for the British market, only three firms exited, bringing the total number of firms down to twenty (Dunnett, 1980, pp. 32–3; Maxcy, 1958, p. 365).

While the British producers had not pushed the technological frontier forward in the interwar period, preferring to rely on low capital–labour ratios and low wages for high profits, they could not avoid the advances being made after the war. In particular, the automatic transfer machine, which Morris had pioneered but had abandoned in the early 1920s, was successfully reintroduced by Ford at its Cleveland engine plant in 1946. Between the late 1940s and 1960 this new technology spread to most of the British factories (Turner, Clack, and Roberts, 1967, p. 78). Capital–labour ratios rose during this period, and British producers faced even further increases if they were to keep up with Ford. By the mid-1950s, Standard was employing £600 of fixed capital per employee and was faced with the prospect of increasing this investment to £3,000 per employee, a level that Ford reached by 1970. As capital–labour ratios rose, unit capital costs rose because of the persistance of low productivity. Under the prevailing piece-work payment systems, unit labour costs did not fall sufficiently to offset the cost increases associated with more capital-intensive production methods.

It was becoming increasingly obvious to many in the industry that the interwar strategy of granting labour a degree of control over the pace of work through the piece-work system could severely backfire. Under conditions of full employment, labour was able to exploit weak managerial control through the establishment of formal trade unions (see Tolliday, 1982). Labour found itself in a position to use its shop stewards' committees both to control the pace of work and to raise wages. In fact, by the 1960s the differential between the Ford-UK worker and the British motor vehicle worker had disappeared, and had even been reversed in some cases.

As long as the sellers' market continued, the British producers were able to avoid reconciling their deteriorating cost position. When their market position collapsed in the mid-1960s, they were forced to consider switching to a Ford-style direct control strategy. In attempting the transition, the British producers found not only that labour had developed an effective set of defences, but also that the long years of dependence on 'induction', and on the performance by labour of the co-ordination details that make a complex factory run, had made management singularly unprepared for the new role.

The Switch to Fordism and the Collapse of the British Motor Vehicle Industry, 1960–1982

One of the first firms to change its strategy drastically in the postwar period was the Standard Company. Their experience is extremely interesting because, rather than moving towards the Ford system, they pushed the interwar strategy to its extreme limit. After the war, the firm made extensive changes introducing new automatic and semi-automatic machinery. In 1956 they converted their tractor factory and portions of their vehicle operation to automatic transfer machines. Standard had been paying slightly more than the going wage rate. Along with the new automatic machines, they introduced two important organizational changes. They allowed average wages to rise even higher, to a level about 65 per cent above the industry level. And, in order to encourage high productivity on the new machines, they drastically remodelled their payment system in a way that one author has interpreted as a challenge to the traditional hierarchical system found in modern factories (Melman, 1958).

The workforce was divided into fifteen gangs in the vehicle plant and a single gang in the tractor works. The gangs were paid as a unit and were allowed to determine how many workers were necessary in the gang, how the work was to be divided, and even the types of machinery that might be best employed. The control that labour had over shopfloor operations was greatly extended. Standard attempted to combine the machine methods that the Ford system had perfected with a managerial strategy built firmly on the British experience that allowed labour greater control over the pace of work. For a short time the strategy worked, providing both higher wages and higher profits than the industry average. The experiment broke down when the system was unable to accommodate itself to a depressed market situation and the need for lay-offs. In effect, labour refused to impose upon itself the logic of the economic cycle, and in so doing was forced to abandon much of the control over shopfloor conditions that it had been granted (Melman, 1958, pp. 12–13; Friedman, 1977, pp. 213–15).

Most of the other firms in the industry delayed major organizational changes while the sellers' market continued. As market conditions became less favourable, there is some evidence to suggest that high profit rates were maintained by reducing the rate of investment and by rather questionable depreciation charges. By the late 1960s the gap between British levels of fixed capital per employee and those of continental and US producers had widened further: in 1969 British Leyland (BL) companies employed an average of £1000 of fixed capital per employee, while Ford in the UK and most continental producers averaged over £3000 per employee.

With the deterioration in the market situation during the 1960s, there was downward pressure on profits in the industry. BL continued to pay dividends though, distributing over 94 per cent of reported profits to shareholders (Expenditure Committee, 1975, nos 31, 37; Ryder, 1975, p. 19, Fig. 4.2). One justification for this strategy was the need to preserve future sources of external financing. We see again the tendency of British producers to maximize short-run payments to shareholders at the expense of long-run growth. In the highly profitable years before World War I, during the profitable years of the 1930s, and during the lean years of the late 1960s and early 1970s, distributions from profits seem to have exceeded the level consistent with long-run growth.

By the late 1960s, serious attempts were being made to change the managerial system employed by the industry since the early 1920s. Events in the industry beginning in the late 1960s represent a rather belated transition to Fordism and direct control. Attempts were made to remove the incentive payment systems and move to day work. In the process, the organization and co-ordination of the factories was to become the sole preserve of management. This shift became necessary for a number of reasons. Once firms were again forced to compete for sales in the market, they found that the existing managerial strategy had two serious weaknesses. The first was that labour had adapted itself to the incentive payment system during the years of full employment and was exerting significant control over the pace of work while at the same time forcing British employers to pay wages closer to those found in British-based US firms. Second, changes in technology, which tended to integrate tasks into flow processes while at the same time raising capital–labour ratios, imposed greater penalties when production was lowered by low levels of labour effort or localized work stoppages (Friedman, 1977; Brown, 1971).

The initial change in machine methods in the 1950s in Britain did not lead to major changes in factory organization at first. British management appears to have continued to depend on the monetary incentive of piecework for both labour control and some of the basic co-ordination tasks within the factory. In Detroit the switch to automatic transfer machines led to a doubling of shopfloor supervisory staff over that found in the older Ford factories. But in Britain, where the change in technology was even more dramatic, the increase in shopfloor supervision did not come until years after the new machine methods were introduced. British management was slow to realize the need to control output levels directly with the higher capital investments (Turner, Clack, and Roberts, 1967, pp. 94–5; Expenditure Committee, 1975, no. 193).

There is evidence to suggest that the difficulties associated with the British move towards Fordism and direct control after 1950 had as much to do with the lack of professionalism within management as it did with the resistance by the unions (Expenditure Committee, 1975, no. 38). British firms had made little progress in integrating their sales and production organization, which Chandler has identified as a major feature of corporate capitalist firms. Sales and service directors were not appointed at BMC until the mid-1960s. Likewise, on the shopfloor, labour relations was not felt to be sufficiently important to warrant a director of industrial relations until Lowrey was appointed at BMC in the late 1960s. More worrying was the lack of managerial co-ordination skills. One example was the weakness of the accounting system in use, which prevented BMC determining the actual cost and profitability of individual product lines. It was not until well into the 1970s that a new accounting system allowed management to comprehensively assess areas of cost overrun. Management had also failed to develop work study departments, relying instead on relative bargaining strength to determine piecework prices.[19]

I would argue that the underdevelopment, as distinct from failure, of the managerial function in Britain can be directly linked with the decision in the 1920s not to follow the Fordist route, but to rely instead on incentive payment systems to provide the necessary degree of control and co-ordination within the factory. This decision helped to generate a series of institutional constraints which the industry found itself unable to overcome in the 1970s.

Young and Hood, in their analysis of the demise of a British firm which was taken over by a US firm in the 1960s, point a finger directly at the use of incentive payments as the ultimate problem:

Labour relations often have been handled by low-status ill-trained executives who have tended to place greater emphasis on financial incentives than on managerial–worker consultations. Moreover, top management has taken every opportunity to justify poor results in terms of labour problems. (Young and Hood, 1977, p. 225; see also Rhys, 1974.)

The above managerial strategy had generated acceptable profits until the late 1960s, but changes in technology and the associated rise in capital–labour ratios made more direct control over labour productivity necessary, bringing to an end the era of the British system of mass production.

The conversion to measured day work (MDW) in the industry began in the late 1960s, but BMC did not begin the transition until the early 1970s. There is little controversy regarding the direct implication of measured day work. It makes it necessary for management to fulfil the task of co-ordinating the factory as the direct link between wages and output is broken. A union representative from one of the BL factories summarized the difference between incentive systems and day work systems:

The only thing that has happened with the introduction of MDW is that where our people used to do their own chasing . . . at the present time, the management is responsible for supplying the material. Of course you do not get from individuals the same kind of approach to obtaining materials to keep the job rolling as you did previously. (Expenditure Committee, 1975, Vol. II, p. 43.)

Another union representative provided this picture of the transition to day work:

In the old days on piecework, because of the antiquated machinery, if anything happened to that machine, that affected their livelihood and the people who were brought up on piecework would put it right . . . they would keep the machine going with a piece of string. Now, because there is no incentive there, if the machine breaks down they do not bother to use their initiative now. (Expenditure Committee, 1975, Vol. II, p. 358.)

The switch to direct control did not take place without one last attempt to maintain the workforce's shopfloor control over the production process. BL had been promoting a form of labour-management participation through joint committees. In 1974 and 1975 the spread of industrial democracy was seen by Ryder and his government-appointed committee as one of the ways out of the industry's current problems. Ryder's strategy did not save the industry or reverse the decline. The report was criticized by both the Expenditure Committee and the Central Policy Review Staff. In 1977 Dobson was removed as the head of BL and replaced by Michael Edwardes. With the appointment of Edwardes, a radical change occurred in the strategy to save the industry. The industry had already been nationalized, and now Edwardes set out to rationalize production by closing down a number of the production units that BL had inherited from BMC. He also abandoned the industrial democracy route and moved towards a Fordist strategy of heavy capital investment and direct managerial control. New codes of discipline and the 1979 sacking of Derek Robinson, the head of the unofficial shop stewards' combine, were key events in the breaking down of the institutions that labour had erected to protect its interests (*The Economist*, 24 November and 1 December 1979).

Conclusions

This paper has traced the history of the British motor vehicle industry between 1896 and 1982. I have argued that the ultimate collapse of the industry in the 1970s can be explained as a result of decisions taken by firms trying to maximize profits, given initial constraints which were themselves the product of past history. My conclusion is that, in the process of maximizing profits, the industry contributed to the creation of new institutional constraints which limited long-run growth. In particular, the dependence on external financing, which was made possible by the well-developed British capital markets, and the tendency to distribute earned profits prevented successful firms from expanding as fast as they might have. These factors also tended to prevent capital–labour ratios from rising and increased the number of firms in the industry. In the period after World War I, management, responding in part to shopfloor demands for control, decided to limit capital investments and grant to labour some degree of control over the pace of work through the piece-work system. This strategy was successful in the short run, but eventually the underdevelopment of the managerial function, the rise of strong labour institutions, and the post-1945 change in technology produced a situation in which British firms were unable to compete.

The question remains as to whether the changes introduced since 1977 can succeed in rejuvenating the industry. This question takes on a broader importance in light of the problems North American producers are currently experiencing. The British industry appears to be moving towards Fordism at the very time that Fordism's appropriateness is being questioned in North America. The nationalization of the industry and the Edwardes plan, aided by abnormally high levels of unemployment in vehicle producing regions, have certainly resulted in short-run successes. Edwardes used government financing to introduce new models and was able to take advantage of high levels of unemployment to hold costs down and keep productivity up.

The more serious question is whether the new strategy will work when and if the economy returns to full employment. On the financial front, the nationalization of the industry has removed a major barrier to long-run growth, namely the treatment of the industry as a British 'cash cow'. The point is arguable, but it is unlikely that the government would appropriate profits should the industry recover. On the labour–management relations side, serious questions remain. There is little reason to believe that management has suddenly been able to acquire the skills that its experience with the British system left it lacking. Perhaps even more serious will be the inability to raise real wages given the new competition from low-wage offshore producers. This is likely to hamper any attempt to restructure social relations within the British factory, and eventually could lead to reduced levels of productivity. Britain's historical experience with the British system has placed it at a disadvantage today. The new mobility of capital in the world economy is likely to prevent it from overcoming its disadvantage.

Appendix

TABLE 1
Sources of capital, British motor vehicle industry

Company	Years	Change in net assets	Change in external financing	Percentage financed externally	Net profits earned
		(1)	(2)	(3)	(4)
Austin	1907–39	5,324,120	2,931,951	55.1	7,988,975
Belsize	1908–20	443,473	279,743	63.1	494,476
Crossley	1916–32	346,960	423,398	122.0	−147,983
Humber	1905–31	711,169	574,376	80.8	1,411,364
Riley	1900–29	201,363	101,443	50.4	117,618
Rolls Royce	1908–32	1,643,161	524,526	31.9	3,004,305
Rover	1900–31	438,205	85,946	19.6	558,605
Singer	1910–28	1,612,527	597,869	37.1	937,913
Standard	1914–32	507,102	251,075	49.5	848,207
Sunbeam	1906–19	1,050,183	165,587	15.8	930,557
Swift	1903–21	178,539	159,375	89.5	276,639
Totals		12,456,802	6,095,289	48.9	16,420,666

Sources: Company balance sheets.

TABLE 2

Sources of capital, US motor vehicle industry

Company	Years	Change in net worth	Change in internal financing	Percentage financed internally	Net profits earned	Percentage profits distributed
		(1)	(2)	(3)	(4)	(5)
Ford	1904–18	156,188,721	156,777,580	100.0	226,982,580	30.9
General Motors	1909–27	624,572,827	357,482,198	57.2	877,260,452	59.3
Studebaker	1910–26	77,602,233	69,755,322	87.3	144,652,851	48.3
Dodge	1914–26	109,978,610	100,230,070	91.1	152,700,196	48.4
Packard	1904–26	46,202,657	54,024,632	116.9	89,132,815	39.4
Nash	1917–26	31,097,216	37,227,499	119.7	83,600,348	55.8
Hudson	1910–26	42,415,440	42,452,680	100.0	65,270,534	35.0
Reo	1905–26	27,232,990	27,028,283	99.2	48,931,712	44.8
Totals		1,115,290,694	842,978,264	75.6	1,688,531,488	51.0

Sources: Seltzer (1928).

TABLE 3

UK and US nominal hourly wages, motor vehicle operatives

	UK (new pence)	US ($)	USA (new pence)*	Index of nominal wage, USA/UK
1948	16.96	1.69	41.93	247
1950	17.95	1.83	65.36	364
1952	20.63	2.13	75.80	367
1954	23.67	2.23	79.64	336
1956	27.04	2.44	87.14	322
1958	30.46	2.53	90.03	295
1960	37.92	2.87	102.50	270
1962	41.21	3.04	108.57	263
1964	46.75	3.12	111.82	239
1966	53.21	3.56	127.59	239
1968	60.25	3.96	165.69	275
1970	76.49	4.05	169.45	221
1972	98.42	5.18	215.83	219
1974	124.66	6.26	267.52	214
1976	170.10	7.13	396.11	232
1978	205.00	8.21	427.60	208
1980	272.80	9.80	422.40	155

*US wages were converted into sterling at the existing exchange rate.

Sources: British nominal wages obtained from *British Labour Statistics Historical Abstract* and the *Employment Gazette* for men over 21 employed in the vehicle industry. US nominal wage data from *Employment and Earnings in the US 1909—75* and continued in *Employment and Earnings*, Department of Labor, for production workers in the motor vehicle and equipment industry.

TABLE 4

Fixed capital per worker, various firms, 1905–1974

	Firm	Fixed capital per employee (£)
1905	Argyll	101
1906	Daimler	69
1907	Austin	112
1913	Humber	102
1914	Austin	76
1914	Sunbeam	116
1918	Austin	54
1918	Sunbeam	51
1920	Vulcan	220
1926	Austin	185
1930	Austin	183
1935	Austin	151
1938	Austin	176
1953	Standard	600
1960	Ford (UK)	1,427
1965	Ford (UK)	2,903
1969	British Leyland	882
1970	Ford (UK)	3,035
1973	Ford (UK)	2,957
1974	British Leyland	1,155

Sources: Church (1979), Melman (1958), Ryder (1975), Expenditure Committee (1975), and various balance sheets.

Notes

[1] For general works on the motor vehicle industry, see Turner *et al*. (1967), Maxcy and Silberston (1959), Dunnett (1980), IWC Motors Group (1978), Ryder (1975), Central Policy Review Staff (1975), and Expenditure Committee (1975).

[2] On the rise of corporate capitalism in the United States, see Chandler (1977) and Noble (1977).

[3] Kennedy (1976) has argued that the British capital markets failed to supply sufficient capital for the motor car industry (pp. 172–3). Lawson's exploits certainly scared some investors from investing in the new industry. On the whole, though, British firms appear to have been relatively successful when they called on the public markets, and they were certainly better served than the US motor car industry. Part of the reason for this, as Kennedy has pointed out, is that after 1878 the British banks were reluctant to supply long-term capital. This forced new firms to use public issues and led to an early development of equity markets (p. 162).

[4] Simms Papers, 16/33, Letter from Drake to Simms, 7 July 1896. 'The English Motor Industry: Description of Plant and Practice at the Daimler Company Works', (*The Cycle Referee*, 19 January 1899).

[5]EEF Archives, P(5)8, Meeting January 1904, Letter Humber to ASE 6 February 1904, and local conference, 17 March 1904.

[6]EEF Archives, A(2)3, T. C. Pullinger, 18 December 1906, E(1)12, United Kingdom Society of Coachmakers Monthly Reports. ASE(COV), 1 March 1906, 30 September–1 December 1908.

[7]Birmingham Daimler Collection, Chairman's Report Extraordinary Meeting 4 March 1897. Daimler Minute Books, 13 May, 1 July, and 7 July 1897, 20 October 1898. Simms Papers 9/58, Report of the Committee of Investigation, 10 December 1898.

[8]Holton has identified this period as one when 'A new configuration of attitudes and policies now emerged, which placed relatively less stress than hitherto on overt repression and somewhat greater emphasis on measures which acted as more subtle forms of social control' (Holton, 1976, p. 31).

[9]P. Martin, Works Organisation (*Proceedings of the Institute of Automobile Engineers*, 1906, p. 126). Daimler Minute Books, 13 February 1899, 24 July and 14 August 1902. For labour's reaction to the premium bonus system see UKS(COV), Quarterly Reports 1904, and ASE(COV), 14 December 1906 and 3 and 24 January 1907.

[10]See Maier (1970) for a study of Fordism in other European countries.

[11]For a detailed examination of this thesis, see Lewchuk (1983, pp. 99–104). For comments by labour in support of American management methods see, EEF, Special Conference 1 May 1925, p. 7, and Trades Union Congress, Comments on the Present Economic Position of the Engineering & Allied Industries, 1921, pp. 23–4.

[12]In 1914 Ford-UK was paying a minimum of £2.94 per week while the average piece-worker in the British factories was earning £1.89 (data from the Ford Motor Company and the Engineering Employers Federation).

[13]Pomeroy (1914–15, p. 21). EEF Archives, P(5)27, Local Conference CDEEA and CEJC, 6 March 1919, 13 March 1919.

[14]Ward Papers, MRG1, Organisation Section, w/8/29–34/13/476, pp. 2–14.

[15]EEF Archives, W(3)129, Piece Work in the Toolroom, 1 February 1934, pp. 26–8.

[16]Attempts to rationalize the structure of competition in the British industry include the STD combine which absorbed Sunbeam, and the Harper Bean-Vulcan merger. It is worth noting that both of these attempts failed to produce viable firms (see Maxcy, 1958, p. 393).

[17]Ford Archives, Acc 96, Box 8, Ford Motor Company Balance Sheets; Engelbach (1928).

[18]See Pollitt Notebooks (London), p2/2/5/9, Rover. Ford Archives, Acc. 125, Model T Cost Books. The above figure was obtained by making an adjustment for the different amounts of the vehicle that the two companies produced (see Lewchuk, 1982).

[19]See 'The Commercial Crunch' (*The Economist*, 26 November 1966, p. 949), 'The 67 Factory Question' (*The Economist*, 21 September 1968, p. 92), 'Options' (*The Economist*, 6 April 1977), Salmon (1975, pp. 59–61), Brown (1971).

Bibliography

Babcock, G. D. (1917). *The Taylor System and Franklin Management*. New York: Engineering Magazine.

Brown, W. (1971). 'Piecework Wage Determination in Coventry'. *Scottish Journal of Political Economy*, 18, 1–30.

Central Policy Review Staff (1975). *The Future of the British Car Industry*. London: HMSO.

Chandler, A. (1977). *The Visible Hand*. Cambridge, Mass.: Harvard University Press.

Church, R. (1979). *Herbert Austin: The British Motor Car Industry to 1941*. London: Europa.

Church, R. (1981). 'Marketing of Automobiles in Britain and the United States before 1939'. In *The Development of Mass Marketing*, ed. A. Okochi, and S. Koichi. University of Tokyo Press.

Church, R. A., and Miller, M. (1977). 'The Big Three: Competition, Management, and Marketing in the British Motor Industry, 1922–1939'. In *Essays in British Business History*, ed. B. Supple. Oxford: University Press.

Cycle Referee, The (1899). 'Repetition Bicycle Plant', 16 February supplement.

Dunnett, P. J. S. (1980). *The Decline of the British Motor Industry*. London: Croom Helm.

Edelstein, M. (1976). 'Realized Rates of Return on UK Home and Overseas Portfolio Investment'. *Explorations in Economic History*, 13, 283–329.

Elbaum, B., and Wilkinson, F. (1979). 'Industrial Relations and Uneven Development: A Comparative Study of the American and British Steel Industry'. *Cambridge Journal of Economics*, 3, 275–303.

Engelbach, C. R. F. (1928). 'Some Notes on Re-organisation'. *Proceedings of the Institute of Automobile Engineers*, 22, 496–544.

Engineer, The (1903). 'The Humber Works (Beeston)', 4 September.

Expenditure Committee (1975). *The Motor Vehicle Industry*, Fourteenth Report. London: HMSO, HC 617.

Friedenson, P. (1978). 'The Coming of the Assembly Line to Europe'. In *The Dynamics of Science and Technology*, Volume II, ed. W. Krohn *et al*. Dordrecht: D. Reidel.

Friedman, A. (1977). *Industry and Labour*. London: Macmillan.

Holton, B. (1976). *British Syndicalism, 1900 — 1914*. London: Pluto Press.

IWC Motors Group (1978). *A Workers' Enquiry into the Motor Industry*. London: Spider Webb.

Keene, P. (1928). 'Production; A Dream Come True'. *Proceedings of the Institute of Automobile Engineers*, 7, 27–35.

Kennedy, W. P. (1976). 'Institutional Response to Economic Growth: Capital Markets in Britain to 1914'. In *Management Strategy and Business Development*, ed. L. Hannah. London: Macmillan.

Lazonick, W. (1981). 'Production Relations, Labor Productivity, and Choice of Technique; British and US Cotton Spinning'. *Journal of Economic History*, 41, 491–516.

Lazonick, W. (1983). 'Industrial Organization and Technological Change: The Decline of the British Cotton Industry'. *Business History Review*, 57, 195–236.

Legros, L. A. (1911). 'Influence of Detail in the Development of the Automobile'. *Proceedings of the Institute of Automobile Engineers*.

Lerner, S. W., and J. Bescoby (1966). 'Shop Steward Combine Committee in the British Engineering Industry'. *British Journal of Industrial Relations*, 4, 154–64.

Lewchuk, W. (1982). 'The Economics of Technical Change: A Case Study of the British Motor Vehicle Industry, 1896–1932'. PhD thesis, University of Cambridge.

Lewchuk, W. (1983). 'Fordism and the British Motor Car Employers: 1896–1932'. In

Managerial Strategies and Industrial Relations, ed. H. Gospel, and C. Littler. London: Heinemann.

Lewchuk. W. (1985). 'The Return to Capital in the British Motor Vehicle Industry'. *Business History*, 27, 3–25.

Linley, O. (1914). 'Manufacturing on a Medium Scale'. *Motor Trader*, 8 July.

Lyddon, D. (1983). 'Workplace Organization in the British Car Industry'. *History Workshop*, 15, 131–40.

Maier, C. (1970). 'Between Taylorism and Technocracy: European Ideology and the Vision of Industrial Production in the 1920s'. *Journal of Contemporary History*, 5, 27–51.

Maxcy, G. (1958). 'The Motor Industry'. In *Effects of Mergers*, ed. P. L. Cook, and R. Cohen. London: George Allen and Unwin.

Maxcy, G., and A. Silberston (1959). *The Motor Industry*. London: George Allen and Unwin.

Melman, S. (1958). *Decision Making and Productivity*. Oxford: Basil Blackwell.

Merrett, A. J., and Sykes, A. (1973). *The Finance and Analysis of Capital Projects*, 2nd edn. London: Longman.

Michie, R. C. (1981). 'Options, Concessions, Syndicates, and the Provision of Venture Capital'. *Business History*, 23, 147–64.

Nevin, A., and F. Hill (1954). *Ford: The Times, the Man, the Company*. New York: Scribner.

Nixon, St John (1946). *Daimler, 1896—1946*. London: G. T. Foulis.

Noble, D. (1977). *America by Design*. Oxford University Press.

Overy, R. J. (1976). *William Morris*. London: Europa.

Pollard, S., and Robertson, P. (1979). *The British Shipbuilding Industry; 1870—1914*. Cambridge: University Press.

Pomeroy, L. H. (1914/15). 'Automobile Engineering and the War'. *Proceedings of the Institute of Automobile Engineers*.

Pratten, C., and A. Silberston (1967). 'International Comparison of Labour Productivity in the Automobile Industry, 1950–1965'. *Oxford Bulletin of Economics and Statistics*, 29, 373–94.

Rhys, D. G. (1974). 'Employment, Efficiency, and Labour Relations in the British Motor Industry'. *Industrial Relations Journal*, 5, 4–26.

Rostas, L. (1948). *Comparative Productivity in British and American Industry*. Cambridge University Press.

Ryder, D. (1975). *British Leyland: The Next Decade*. London: HMSO, HC 342.

Salmon, E. A. (1975). 'Inside BL'. *Management Today*, November, 59–61.

Saul, S. B. (1962). 'The Motor Industry in Britain to 1914'. *Business History*, 5, 22–44.

Seltzer, L. H. (1928). *A Financial History of the American Automobile Industry*. Boston: Houghton Mifflin.

Thomas, W. A. (1978). *The Finance of British Industry*. London: Methuen.

Tolliday, S. (1982). 'Government, Employers, and Shopfloor Organisation in the British Motor Industry, 1939–69'. Unpublished paper.

Turner, H. A., G. Clack, and G. Roberts (1967). *Labour Relations in the Motor Industry*. London: George Allen and Unwin.

Young, S., and N. Hood (1977). *Chrysler UK: A Corporation in Transition*. New York: Praeger.

Walker, J. (1981). 'Markets, Industrial Processes and Class Struggle: The Evolution of the Labour Process in the UK Engineering Industry'. *Review of Radical Political Economy*, 12, 46–69.

Willman, P. (1984). 'The Reform of Collective Bargaining and Strike Activity in BL Cars'. *Industrial Relations Journal*, 15, 6–17.

Zeitlin, J. (1983). 'Workplace Militancy: A Rejoinder'. *History Workshop*, 16, 131–6.

Technical Education and Industry in the Nineteenth Century

Julia Wrigley

University of California at Los Angeles

In 1868, William Henry Ripley, a Bradford dye manufacturer, remarked to a commission investigating science education that, knowing as he did the great want of scientific knowledge in Britain, it was perfectly astonishing to him that the country held the industrial position that it did (Ripley, 1868, p. 216). His opinion was echoed more bluntly by another observer of the dye industry, who told the commission that 'it is remarkable how well we do, considering how little we know' (Mundella, 1868, p. 277). Britain's industrial supremacy was not to last, however, and many later observers have traced her decline at least in part to her lagging scientific and technical education. The emergence of new science-based industries in the second half of the nineteenth century threw Britain's undersupply of scientifically educated managers or technically trained workers into sharp relief. While Britain's traditional production methods ultimately proved inadequate even in her staple industries such as textiles (Lazonick, 1980), it was in such new areas as the chemical and electrical industries that she first surrendered technological and industrial leadership to Germany and the United States (Roderick and Stephens, 1972, p. 7; Allen, 1976, p. 32).

The question of why Britain clung for so long to an outmoded educational system has attracted much attention. Many economists, historians, and others have argued that Britain failed to modernize her schools and universities because of a commitment to traditional values that predated her industrialization (Coleman, 1973; Allen, 1976; Landes, 1969, p. 347; Wiener, 1981). The British educational system was geared not to the production of industrial managers or scientists, but to the socialization of gentlemen into the cultural symbols of an elite (Ashby, 1959; Wiener, 1981). The schools reinforced the cultural leadership of an older aristocracy and helped to merge a rising group of manufacturers' sons into this circle; the merging occurred mainly on the cultural ground of the aristocracy (Erickson, 1959, p. 34; Allen, 1976, pp. 36–7).

This emphasis on traditional values does help explain some facets of Britain's educational development. The history of Oxford and Cambridge, or of the British public schools, reveals the strength of inherited notions about the proper curriculum and of disdain for trade (Wiener, 1981). Yet the emphasis on traditional values does not explain why Britain failed to change this educational system as her economic competitors gained ground in the latter part of the nineteenth century. Noted figures warned of Britain's impending economic decline if she did not invest in a more coherent, scientifically oriented educational system (see, for example, Playfair, 1870; Levinstein, 1886). Prominent commissions gathered evidence on Britain's lack of scientific and technical personnel and suggested reforms (Select Committee, 1868; Royal Commission, 1881). Little action resulted, however, and it is this lack of action in the face of what, in retrospect at least, were clear and prescient warnings, that demands explanation.

The problem of explaining this cultural continuity becomes all the greater when viewed in cross-cultural perspective. Germany had a more traditional social and political structure than Britain in the nineteenth century (Ben-David, 1971), yet her rulers built an educational system far more directed to national economic needs than Britain's. This, David Landes writes, is 'one of the strangest paradoxes in modern history', that Britain, with its liberal political system, should have retained schools that clung to the outmoded curriculum of an aristocratic elite, while Germany, a 'far more authoritarian society', should have built a more modern school system (1969, p. 348).

I will suggest that Britain's highly competitive form of capitalism contributed to the maintenance of a traditional educational system. British capitalism evolved in comparatively undirected fashion, without the state (or other institutions) playing a strong co-ordinating role. This meant that traditional values about classical subjects being suited for upper-class students and practical subjects being suited for working-class students (Ashby, 1959, p. 31), were not challenged by any powerful industrializing ideology backed up by state action. In Germany, the state was in the hands of a modernizing elite, and it created the polytechnics and the scientific facilities that aided Germany's emergence as a world leader in the chemical industries and other science-related fields. There is evidence that the German political leaders had to overcome some of the same kinds of cultural resistance that appeared in Britain. The German state had the concentrated political and social power to override traditional objections, and it had the industrializing ideology to motivate action, while in Britain there was no comparable mechanism for forcing change.

In what follows, I will first consider the technical and scientific education available for workers, and then that available for managers and the middle classes more generally. To make the section on the middle classes as historically specific as possible, I will focus on a particular case of British industrial failure, her inability to keep pace with Germany in the science-dependent dyestuffs industry.

Scientific and Technical Education for Workers

In Britain in the early nineteenth century members of all social classes considered artisans to be the appropriate bearers of technical skills (Ashby, 1959, pp. 50–1; Cotgrove, 1958, pp. 16–19). British artisans were noted for their mechanical abilities in the early stages of the Industrial Revolution (Musson and Robinson, 1969); it was illegal to enlist skilled workers for work abroad until 1825, an indication of the value placed upon their skills (Ashby, 1959, p. 60). Early industrial development depended very little on science. Most improvements were mechanical, and the prime skills needed were an inventive turn of mind and a practical ability to design and produce machinery (Bernal, 1953, p. 149).

British artisans owed little of their skill and knowledge to formal schooling (Ashby, 1959, p. 50). Historically, their skills had been transmitted through apprenticeships and practical experience. This stemmed in part from the weakness of the educational system. The British government did not establish the framework for a national system of elementary schools until 1870 (Wardle, 1970, p. 26). Even then, the schools established under the act were neither free nor compulsory (Curtis and Boultwood, 1964, p. 76). It was not until 1891 that most elementary schools became free (p. 78). Secondary education lagged still more, with almost no schools outside the private sector, an uneven distribution of schools in different areas of the country, and a frequent misuse of school endowments (p. 87). Although only a fraction of the students went on to universities, the secondary school curriculum was geared to these few; classics predominated in the curriculum to the virtual exclusion of science (Gowing, 1977, p. 74). Only at the dawn of the twentieth century, in 1902, did the British government begin to organize a coherent system of elementary and secondary education (Curtis and Boultwood, 1964, p. 168).

Britain stood out during the nineteenth century for the contrast between its national wealth and its educational penury. Britain was the richest country in Europe until almost the end of the century,

yet more parsimonious than any except perhaps France—even at a time of peace and great prosperity such as 1870 when revenue was buoyant, expenditure steady, income tax reduced ... and budget surpluses almost embarrassing. In 1870 government expenditure was a much lower percentage of gross national product than in 1850; and in 1890 it was lower still. (Gowing, 1977, p. 82.)

Scientific and technical education depended on artisan initiative and scanty sources of private support through the first half of the century. Artisan enthusiasm for science received impetus from the merger of scientific and mechanical skill (embodied by the collaboration of James Black and James Watt) that resulted in the development of the steam engine (Cardwell, 1957, p. 31). The popularization of science also stemmed from efforts by Benthamites and other middle-class leaders to rationalize a traditional educational system and orient it in a more scientific direction (p. 28). Skilled workers and mechanics believed a knowledge of science would reinforce the skills they had learned through apprenticeships and experience; in the intellectual climate of the early 1800s, science appealed both to middle-class Dissenters and to artisans as a means of challenging the conservative religious and political ideas of Britain's rulers (Simon, 1960).

During the 1820s and 1830s the science-oriented artisan educational movement led to the founding of hundreds of mechanics' institutes in the manufacturing centres of Britain (Hudson, 1851). These institutes provided the bulk of technical education. By the 1860s, there were records of 677 institutes in Britain with 116,076 members (p. vii). The institutes offered lectures and evening classes on such subjects as chemistry, natural philosophy, and the laws of motion. They also operated libraries; in 1850 these libraries recorded more than 2 million book issues to subscribers.

The mechanics' institutes differed from the state-financed technical institutes in the German states, Switzerland, or France. First, they received no government support. Artisan subscribers paid fees to the institutes (often about £1 a year—Hudson, 1851, p. 129), and, more importantly, capitalists contributed funds. In Manchester, for example, employers drawn mainly from machine making and cotton firms raised £7,000 to erect an institute building containing a large lecture hall, a chemical laboratory, classrooms, and a library (Heywood, 1843, p. 23).

Employers, like the artisans themselves, appear to have had mixed economic and political reasons for supporting the institutes. While some employers believed that educating artisans was politically dangerous (Cardwell, 1957, p. 30), others argued that the institutes might foster technical progress. Benjamin Heywood, a Manchester banker with ties to engineering firms, believed that educating artisans in science would improve Britain's competitive position *vis-à-vis* Germany (Heywood, 1843). Donors' attempts to control the institutes led to frequent conflicts with the artisan subscribers, weakening the institutes (Thompson, 1963, p. 744). The private funding also made the institutes vulnerable to fluctuations in enthusiasm on the part of their supporters.

Second, as the products of an artisan social and political movement, the early mechanics' institutes set themselves a strikingly ambitious goal. Rather than aiming at improving artisans' workplace skills, they proposed to teach artisans the sciences underlying their trades (Davies, 1831). This goal proved impossible because of the defective early educations of most artisans (Hole, 1853; Select Committee, 1868). Classes on chemistry and physics were over the heads of students who had generally received no secondary schooling and little primary schooling (Hole, 1853). (In 1841, 33 per cent of the men and 49 per cent of the women marrying in England and Wales signed the register with a mark because they could not write (Argles, 1964, p. 6).)

Artisans had believed they could learn science because they carried the nation's technical skills and because there were many links between early scientists and artisans (Wrigley, 1982). The mechanics' institutes, however, were founded in a period when science was becoming an intellectual enterprise further and further removed from workplace skills (Roderick, 1967). As the difficulties of learning science became apparent, the attendance of manual workers at the institutes began to decline. Increasingly, white-collar workers eager for general education, rather than craft workers seeking scientific education, began filling the institutes (Tylecote, 1957, p. 149).

By the mid-1800s, most observers acknowledged the decline of the mechanics' institutes (Hole, 1853; Hudson, 1851). Many employers argued before an 1868 select committee on technical instruction, chaired by Cleveland ironmaster Bernhard Samuelson, that there was little point in providing scientific education for workers. James Kitson, an ironmaster at Leeds, expressed this view bluntly. He told the commission that 'it would be useless to attempt to give scientific education to the general mass of our workpeople; it would be of no value to us in our works' (Kitson, 1868, p. 292). Henry Roscoe, a chemistry professor at Owens College in Manchester who had close ties to Manchester's business leaders, endorsed this view. He declared that it would be a mistake to try to teach science to the working class, although he thought there should be an opportunity for the most intelligent workers to rise (Roscoe, 1868, p. 328). Another witness went further in explaining why he believed scientific education for workers was irrelevant. Robert Rumney, a large chemical manufacturer in Manchester, said that the subdivision of industry meant most workers no longer had any need for scientific knowledge (Rumney, 1868, p. 349).

Two social developments of the nineteenth century—the progress of science as a body of knowledge and the increased specialization of tasks within industry—undermined the view that workers should learn science. This left working-class technical and scientific education in a curious limbo. After the 1850s the British government came under increasing pressure to improve scientific and technical training as a way of meeting the threat of foreign competition (Cardwell, 1957; Ashby, 1959; Select Committee, 1868). The lack of clarity about the usefulness of educating workers in science was perhaps one factor underlying a hesitant policy of providing science classes for workers—but doing so in a very cheap and limited form. When the mechanics' institutes had first arisen, the government had not tried to channel the early artisan enthusiasm for science into an economically productive direction. Its later venture into the field came when the contradictions in a policy of promoting science for workers but not for managers had become increasingly plain.

State Entry into Technical Education

Government-sponsored science classes for adult workers predated state provision of elementary schooling in Britain. The 1851 Exhibition, where British exhibits won most of the prizes but competitors displayed surprisingly sophisticated goods, fuelled calls for a more effective form of scientific and

technical education (Ashby, 1959, p. 53). This pressure resulted in the creation of the Department of Science and Art in 1853 (Argles, 1964, p. 18). The
Department's founding marked the first practical acknowledgement by the
government that technical education might improve Britain's industrial
future.

This recognition did not go very far, however. The Department tried to
encourage applied science by underwriting science classes, which, in the
traditional manner, were largely directed at skilled workers. Six years after
the Department's founding, it had spent a total of only £898 on the classes
(Argles, 1964, p. 19). The Department did undertake other activities, such as
aiding museums and exhibitions and, more importantly, operating educational institutions geared to producing scientifically trained managers and
industrial scientists. In particular, the Department operated the government
School of Mines (which, after 1853, amalgamated with the Royal College of
Chemistry) (Argles, 1964, p. 51). These activities remained on a small scale.
The School of Mines usually had fewer than fifteen full-time students and
only about fifty part-time students (p. 20).

In 1860 the Department of Science and Art began an expanded effort to
encourage science teaching. It did this in way that upheld conventional
British ideas about the role of the state, while very narrowly meeting increasing working-class pressure for schooling (Simon, 1960). The Department hit
upon the idea of creating a system of examinations; the Department would
help pay the salaries of science teachers and would provide extra money to
the teachers depending on how well their students did in the exams. This
'payment-by-results' method minimized the role of the state, as private citi-
zens had to be responsible for finding classroom space, gathering at least ten
students together, and finding a teacher (or, quite often it was the teacher
who assembled the class) (Roderick and Stephens, 1972, p. 13).

The chief official of the Department, Henry Cole, viewed the payment-by-
results plan not just as an adaptation to skimpy funding, but as a positive
expression of British philosophy towards education. Cole had earlier
remarked that the Department's efforts avoided the error of continental educational systems, where the state took the principal part (quoted in Argles,
1964, p. 20). An 1859 document outlining the payment-by-results plan
stated: 'It is hoped that a system of science instruction will grow up among
the industrial classes which shall entail the least possible cost and interference on the part of the State' (quoted in Roderick and Stephens, 1972, p. 13).
The state aid was to be 'simply auxiliary' to private effort (*Sixth Report*, 1859;
quoted in Argles, 1964, pp. 20–1).

The science classes secured large enrollments. By the end of the nineteenth
century, twenty-five subjects were recognized as appropriate for instruction,
and more than 170,000 students a year took the Department-sponsored classes (Roderick and Stephens, 1972, p. 14). The classes helped fill a gap caused
by the lack of state provision for secondary education. One author has com-

mented that the Department of Science and Art 'provided indirectly almost the entire secondary education for the masses for thirty years' (Hipwell; quoted in Roderick and Stephens, 1972, p. 14).

The classes were intended to be relevant to industrial production; the first subjects recognized were geometry, mechanical drawing, natural history, building construction, physics, and chemistry (Argles, 1964, p. 20). As Bernal has pointed out, in the nineteenth century aid was more forthcoming for physics and chemistry and related subjects than for the biological sciences, which involved more social controversy and had less application to industry (Bernal, 1939, p. 28). The actual relevance of these science classes to production is less clear, however. Critics charged that teaching in the Department-sponsored classes was usually dry and ineffective. Students often learned their subjects by rote, as this increased their chances of passing the Department exam and the teachers' chances of getting more money. Teachers concentrated on elementary material in the hope of getting more students through the exam (Playfair, 1868, p. 112).

Further, so little science instruction was available in universities or secondary schools that many of the teachers were self-taught. Almost none could earn a living from teaching the science classes (Kitson, 1868, p. 292). In 1871, out of 828 teachers, a majority earned less than £40 a year; only 26 earned more than £100 (Roderick and Stephens, 1972, p. 15). The payment of science teachers was so scanty, a parliamentary commission reported, that 'science teaching is scarcely ever followed as a profession, but only as an addition to some more profitable employment' (Select Committee, 1868, p. v). This in turn discouraged university and secondary students from taking science.

The classes organized by the Department of Science and Art faced a dilemma that bore some similarity to the problems earlier faced by the mechanics' institutes. The government-sponsored classes did not venture into trade training because they would have encountered immediate opposition from unions and from employers (Argles, 1964, pp. 21–2). This left the classes in the uneasy position of covering general science. As most students had deficient primary educations (Platt, 1868, p. 336; Rumney, 1868, pp. 345–6), the classes were usually on a quite elementary level, yet were also abstract in content. Employers seldom found students who had taken the classes to be more productive than other workers, or to have gained any particularly useful knowledge (Argles, 1964, pp. 37–8). This reinforced already existing doubts about the value of technical education. Although the British government entered upon the technical education of workers in a more serious way in the late 1800s, with an 1890 act subsidizing technical education with 'whisky money' raised through a new duty on beer and spirits (Gowing, 1977, p. 77), the commitment remained halfhearted.

The British government defined technical education so narrowly that the classes it sponsored for workers in fields such as engineering offered little competition to long-established methods of craft-oriented training (Saul, 1968, p. 230). In the United States, in contrast, the late nineteenth and early twentieth centuries witnessed a major overhaul of technical education for engineers, raising the occupation to the status of a profession rather than a craft speciality (Noble, 1979). US corporate leaders promoted university training for engineers and helped design courses of study that produced the type of trained men they wanted; state governments obliged by underwriting vast expansions of the university system. In Britain the universities moved only very hesitantly into engineering education (Sanderson, 1972, pp. 39–46). Even so, the supply of university-trained engineers outstripped the demand (p. 117), as manufacturers accepted the traditional view, endorsed by the government, that engineers should receive most of their education on the shopfloor. State funding for technical education in Britain often reinforced existing modes of training, and Britain continued to produce engineers and other skilled workers who relied more on craft skills than on scientific knowledge.

As early as 1868, many witnesses told the Samuelson Committee on technical instruction that it was more critical to educate managers and foremen in science than it was to educate workers. Lyon Playfair, a chemist and the head of the science section of the Department of Science and Art, maintained that 'the crying want of this country is a higher class of education for the foremen and managers of industry' (1868, p. 106). His opinions were echoed by other witnesses, who saw a value in the scientific education of workmen only to the extent that foremen were drawn from their ranks.

It proved immensely difficult, however, for the government and for businessmen to shift gears and start building science education programmes for prospective managers and middle-class students. The reasons for employers' continuing resistance to scientific education for managers, and, more generally, for their resistance to basing their production methods on science, will be explored in the next section, which will also consider the restrictions on the supply of scientists that stemmed from the comparatively unplanned evolution of British capitalism and its educational institutions. To make the discussion concrete, the section will focus on the coal-tar dye industry in Britain. The dye industry developed very differently in Britain than in Germany; because the contrast is so striking, it will be useful to consider how scientific and technical education affected the development of the industry in each country.

The Failure of the British Dye Industry

The dye industry had a special status, because it was one of the first great industries to be based on science (Perkin, 1869, p. 597). Chemistry emerged as the dominant science of the nineteenth century; more than physics, its findings could be turned to immediate profit (Bernal, 1953, p. 70). In few areas was the possibility of large profits as great as in the coal-tar dye industry.

In Germany this possibility became reality. Germany's success with the manufacture of artificial dyes led to the building of some of the world's largest firms (several of which ultimately combined into I.G. Farbenindustrie). The production of coal-tar dyes led to enormous advances in chemical knowledge for German scientists and to auxiliary gains for engineering, as a new breed of chemical engineers emerged who were able efficiently to design chemical plants (Levinstein, 1886, p. 354). The chemistry of coal-tar dyes was closely related to the chemistry of explosives and poison gases, making the industry a critical one in wartime. Success in making artificial dyes also led Germany to an early lead in making photographic film and drugs (Beer, 1959, p. 1). A British chemist and Fellow of the Royal Society, Raphael Meldola, wrote of the dye industry that it served as the world's best illustration of the marriage of science and industry (1908, p. 2225; see also Perkin, 1869, p. 365).

The dye industry never accounted for more than a tiny share of Britain's industrial output in the nineteenth century (Richardson, 1962, p. 111). Britain was more successful in other areas of the chemical industry, notably in the manufacture of heavy chemicals (Richardson, 1968, p. 297), but the early failure of Britain's dye production foreshadowed a longer, slower decline in her competitive posture in chemicals more generally. This decline became clearly evident after 1900 (p. 305). Earlier, however, the failure of the dye industry to take root in Britain had led to much debate about the role of scientifically trained personnel in industry.

Britain appeared to have all the initial advantages for a commanding position in the production of dyes. Her textile industry guaranteed a large home market for the dyes; she also had the raw materials for dye production, as tar distillates, one of the substances from which the dyes were made, was a by-product of coke recovery ovens. Germany had to import most of the raw materials for making dyes from Britain (Levinstein, 1886, p. 352). Britain also had a signal advantage in that a British chemist, William H. Perkin, discovered the process for making aniline dyes. During Easter vacation of 1856, Perkin, then 18, accidentally produced a mauve dye while working in a home laboratory trying artificially to prepare quinine (Perkin, 1869, p. 604). He recognized the significance of his discovery and immediately went into the dye business.

In spite of Britain's early start and basic advantages, by the mid-1870s she had decisively lost the industry to Germany. By 1890 Germany was producing six times as much dye as Britain, and by 1913 the German dye industry was twenty-five times the size of the British one (Richardson, 1962, p. 111). Germany at that point controlled 85 per cent of the world market; Britain imported German dye valued at roughly £1.8 million (pp. 110–11). When *The Times* reported in 1906 that a jubilee for W. H. Perkin was planned to mark the fiftieth year since the discovery of mauve, several manufacturers wrote cynical letters to the newspaper asking what Britain had to celebrate (*The Times*, 3 March 1906).

Germany's dye producers attributed their success to the employment of many well-trained chemists (Bayer; quoted in Levinstein, 1886, p. 351; see also comments by Heinrich Caro, quoted in Ehrhardt, 1924, p. 565). Carl Duisberg, the head of research at Bayer, one of Germany's largest chemical firms, said in 1896 that Bayer then employed about a hundred university-trained chemists; it also employed twenty-five engineers who had graduated from polytechnics (Duisberg, 1896, p. 427). German dyestuffs firms pioneered in the development of research laboratories (Beer, 1959). In Britain, by contrast, dye companies employed few chemists. One witness told the Samuelson Committee that he did not think there was a single dyer in the Nottingham area who was a good chemist (Mundella, 1868, p. 277). Similarly, William Henry Ripley, a Bradford dye manufacturer, reported that he did not 'know of a single foreman in the trade who possesses the scientific knowledge which is absolutely essential to produce the work at the cheapest rate' (Ripley, 1868, p. 219). Instead of trained chemists, the British dye industry relied heavily on practical dyers who had learned their skills through experience and who relied on trial and error methods (Miall, 1931, pp. 84–5; Thomas Henry, quoted in Clow and Clow, 1952, p. 198).

The contrast between Germany and Britain emerges on a broader level in figures on the total numbers of chemists in each country. In 1890 Germany had twice as many academic chemists as Britain (101 to 51). Germany also had far more students pursuing graduate work in chemistry; while 400 German chemists received doctorates or postgraduate diplomas in 1904–5, in Britain in 1908 only 300 students were pursuing advanced degrees in any branch of applied science (Sanderson, 1972, p. 23). Comparison of the number of published research articles on chemistry also reveals a strong German advantage. In 1872 the British *Journal of the Chemical Society* published 151 British abstracts compared with 809 German ones (Richardson, 1968, p. 303). The German superiority in organic chemistry was particularly striking, with 574 abstracts from Germany published in 1882 compared with 59 from Britain.

German industry was well supplied with chemists because of a strong development of scientific instruction and research, both in universities and in technical institutes (the Technische Hochschulen). Far from allowing an educational system to develop in a haphazard way, as the British educational system largely had, the rulers of the German states had consciously striven to develop educational systems that would bolster German strength and economic power. After Prussia's defeat by Napoleon, her rulers founded the University of Berlin (in 1809) to help rebuild and strengthen the state (Paulsen, 1912, pp. 183–5). Germany's late emergence as a nation helped foster a nationalistic spirit; this spirit underlay efforts to build a mass educational system.

The educational system was crowned by universities dedicated to research. In contrast to the British emphasis on exams, German universities emphasized the production of original research. They pioneered in the development of laboratory training for scientists (Beer, 1959). The state promoted and underwrote this research because it was intended to bolster national strength. German universities were so closely identified with the state that professors held ranks corresponding to those in the state administrative bureaucracy (Ringer, 1969). The German intellectual elite owed its privileges to the state. As Joseph Ben-David has written, 'The status and privileges of the universities were granted to them by the military-aristocratic ruling class, and were not achieved as part of the growth of free enterprise' (Ben-David, 1971, p. 135).

Even before Germany's unification, states such as Prussia, Saxony, and Bavaria had tried to stimulate economic growth by operating nationalized enterprises (such as railroads and coal mines) and by promoting technical progress (Henderson, 1975, pp. 78–9). Prussia sent representatives to Britain to study her newest technical discoveries, and the state set up model factories to demonstrate efficient production techniques (pp. 74–6). The German dye industry gained 'invaluable indirect help in the form of subsidies to the textile industry, enlightened, generous support of vocational and higher scientific education, and deliberately ineffective patent laws' (Beer, 1959, p. 103). At a later point the newly unified German state aided the dye industry further by promulgating the Imperial Patent Act of 1876 (p. 108). The early loose patent policy had benefited the German dye industry in its nascent stages, but once the industry was established, it wanted protection for expensive research investments in new processes. The 1876 Act was carefully designed to provide tight controls against patent infringements.

The German government saw patent, tariff, and educational policies as means for consciously promoting economic growth, a growth that took place so rapidly that by the last quarter of the nineteenth century Germany had become a leading industrial power (Henderson, 1975, pp. 173–5). Germany's efficient, science-oriented educational system aided this industrial growth. The greater readiness to train and use scientific personnel in German industry appears to have stemmed from factors related both to the supply of scientific personnel and to the demand for them.

On the supply side, the state intervened actively to promote technical education. In particular, the state was strong enough, and committed enough to industrialization, to override objections to technical education and applied science that stemmed from the same kinds of conservative, class-related values that were widespread in Britain. Though Germany's university professors were oriented towards aiding national goals, they were often deeply opposed to measures that appeared to threaten their prestige as guardians of scholarship. Members of a powerful conservative bloc in German universities fought the introduction of new subjects of an applied character (Ben-David, 1971, p. 35). They successfully resisted the introduction of engineering to the universities; they also opposed new fields such as bacteriology and fought efforts to broaden preparatory subjects in secondary schools. In these actions, the conservative German university professors were not far different from their counterparts at Oxford and Cambridge. The difference, however, lay in the response of the state. The German government did not accommodate to the conservatism of the universities, but instead founded a new set of institutions designed to help industry and the military. The rulers of the various German states had established polytechnics in the 1820s and 1830s for training engineers (Beer, 1959, p. 60). In the 1860s and 1870s, the polytechnics gained greatly in funds and academic standing. These technical institutes did not have to scrabble for funds the way the British civic universities did (Sanderson, 1972); the states usually provided lavish facilities for them, including well-equipped and even palatial laboratories.

To Germany's modernizing elite, the technical institutes played a critical role in training technical workers and managers for industry. British businessmen spoke with wonder of the reliance on polytechnic graduates in German industry. Anthony Mundella, a hosiery manufacturer and the Chairman of the Nottingham Chamber of Commerce, was familiar with German business practice because he owned a factory employing more than 700 people in Saxony. He reported that the manager of one of the largest machinery firms in Germany had told him that every man who wanted to become a foreman had to go through a course of instruction at the polytechnic. Those who showed promise then went through a course of scientific instruction that lasted for eighteen months or two years. The polytechnic graduate was then in a position to become a master workman (Mundella, 1868, p. 279). Scientific instruction was so widespread that it is estimated that by 1914 one in sixty German males had received some sort of chemical training (Richardson, 1962, p. 114).

The German states competed with each other to develop the polytechnics. The recency of Germany's national unification meant that each region had its own sense of identity and local culture (Tipton, 1976); this intensified state efforts to develop their own economies, and, correspondingly, their own polytechnics. As opposed to the universities, which were often in small towns, the technical institutes were usually located in the state capitals, reinforcing state identification with the institutes (Paulsen, 1912, pp. 196–7).

In 1899, over the objections of the university professors, the emperor Wilhelm II granted the technical institutes the right to confer PhDs (Ben-David, 1971, p. 130; Ringer, 1969, p. 28). The polytechnics had formally been raised to the status of the universities; their budgets and enrolments were stable enough that this was more than an empty gesture (Paulsen, 1912, pp. 196–7). By 1914 they had an enrolment of more than 11,000 students and could afford to disregard the continued hostility of the university professors (Ringer, 1969, p. 51). The German government had intervened directly to ensure that applied science had a strong place in the educational system.

On the demand side, Germany's industrial directors had greater incentive to hire scientists and technically trained managers than British capitalists did, in large part because Germany was entering into the game of industrialization as a later player. Her business leaders were both more aggressive about seeking manufacturing and commercial advantage and less hampered by ingrained opposition to modern approaches. While British capitalists remained committed to longstanding trial-and-error methods, German businessmen were often running industries that had only recently arisen in the country. As Jurgen Kocka has put it,

the industries most important in the German Industrial Revolution—railroads, the manufacture of machinery and chemicals, and some raw-materials production—had few if any predecessors, while textiles, the leading area in early British industrialization, had a well-developed tradition dating back to early modern times. (Kocka, 1980, pp. 107–8.)

British manufacturers were reluctant to abandon the practical, shopfloor training for workers and managers that had brought them success and large profits in the past (Beer, 1959, p. 44). A witness told the Samuelson Committee that 'our trade in the midland counties is three hundred years old. . . . We have gone on improving from generation to generation in the old track' (Mundella, 1868, p. 277). As the first industrial nation, Britain had enjoyed an early period without strong competition. The evolution of the economic system had appeared immensely successful; when success appeared more problematic later, the lack of planning or direction (or ideologies to support them) made it difficult to change either entrenched methods or institutions which had acquired their own rigidities.

Ivan Levinstein, a German chemist who moved to Britain in 1864 and ran one of the most successful dye firms in the country, argued that Britain's early success, and the attainment of large profits in her staple industries, handicapped her for developing industries based on science. He wrote that industrial enterprise in Britain had, for a generation preceding, been confined largely to cotton, wool, iron, and coal; the chemical industries had been left in the hands of men who sometimes succeeded, owing to luck and the natural wealth of the country, but failed to lay the groundwork for continued success. The general public remained in 'profound ignorance of industrial chemistry', which helped account for a 'total want of enterprise' on the part of manufacturers in chemical industries. The lack of connection between scientists and manufacturers increased the problem, but underlying the whole was 'the very great facility with which fortunes had been made in years gone by in what were then considered staple industries' (Levinstein, 1886, p. 353).

Levinstein, anticipating later theories by academics on the benefits of backwardness (Gerschenkron, 1962), believed Germany gained from her apparent disadvantages. In Germany,

There was no superabundance of accumulated wealth, nor the same easy opportunities for acquiring it, the great natural advantages did not exist, and a knowledge of chemistry was more diffused among the people; consequently new branches of chemical industry were eagerly sought for and energetically taken up by enterprising capitalists, supported by the people and the scientific man. (Levinstein, 1886, p. 353.)

Other observers agreed. A London *Times* correspondent wrote that 'The truth is, money was made here too easily in early days; lulled into a false sense of security, our manufacturers did not look ahead sufficiently and provide new strings for their bows emanating from a liberally supported scientific department in their own works' (*The Times*, 10 March 1906, p. 4). British financiers preferred enterprises in the traditional mould, rather than venturing into the relatively uncharted investment waters of science-based firms. Levinstein himself in 1877 was unable to secure money in Britain for a planned expansion of his firm. Although the financiers' reasons for turning him down are not known, his son, Dr Herbert Levinstein, many years later attributed his failure to a lack of 'educated' money in Britain. 'The application of knowledge', he said,

requires finance and capacity on the part of those who control finance to judge the value of a scientific discovery. The main cost of industrial research is not in the laboratory but in the application to the large scale. Who in England was going to find money for this? In Germany, the banks would and did find it. (Quoted in Reader, 1970, p. 261.)

Reliance on trial-and-error methods rather than knowledge of science had serious costs in the chemical industry. Many observers of the dye industry told the Samuelson Committee that these methods resulted in enormous waste (see, for example, Ripley, 1868, p. 260). Workers with experience and intuitive knowledge learned methods of mixing chemicals, but the lack of chemical understanding meant they could not reliably produce fast, bright dyes. The problem was particularly acute when manufacturers tried to dye fabrics that contained both animal fibres (wool) and plant fibres (cotton) (Ripley, 1868, p. 263). British dyers often worked by a process of trying to match colours already obtained, putting on a little more or a little less dye as seemed appropriate, rather than going directly to the result through a knowledge of chemical reactions (Birkin, 1868, p. 291).

A bleacher at Nottingham, testifying on waste arising from mistakes and ignorance, complained that the men doing the bleaching with solutions of soda did not even know the meaning of 'alkali' (Ashwell, 1868, p. 287). It was possible for firms relying on trial-and-error methods eventually to produce results, in the view of Bayer's technical director, Carl Duisberg, but progress would occur at a snail's pace (Duisberg, 1896, p. 427). Firms could remain competitive only if they quickly mastered and applied new chemical knowledge of dye-making, which most British manufacturers did not attempt to do.

British firms also found that it was difficult to rely partially on trial-and-error methods and partially on scientific ones. Firms faced risks in trying new production methods based on science unless their scientific advisers had an excellent knowledge of both chemistry and practical matters related to dyeing (Frankland, 1868, p. 452). The lack of a tradition of industrial science in Britain meant that few scientists had this combination of talents (Miall, 1931, p. 86). This in turn meant that any individual firm might be very ill-advised to abandon tested, if wasteful, methods of production in favour of untested ideas from scientists. (See Clow and Clow, 1952, for examples throughout of firms that could not make new, science-based methods of production work.) As Duisberg commented, 'technical chemists find even in simple chemical reactions most remarkable complications' (1896, p. 428), which meant that limited or half-hearted technical education would not necessarily help industry much.

British dye firms were substantially smaller than the German ones; even the two largest, Read, Holliday and Sons and Levinstein, Ltd, were small compared with the German giants (Richardson, 1962, p. 112). It is noteworthy, however, that to the German chemical companies the size of firms in the industry and their degree of competitiveness were not matters to be taken for granted as unchangeable features of the economic landscape. In its early stages, artificial dye production was enormously profitable for the German dye firms because they were competing primarily against the hapless producers of natural dyes and secondarily against the less efficient British and French firms. Once the producers of natural dyes had been driven out of business, a fierce, profit-destroying competitive struggle began among the German firms (Beer, 1959, pp. 117–21). Market dominance required research, which required long-run investment; the payoff to this investment seemed more and more in question, however, as artificial dye producers competed against each other. The German chemical firms responded to this situation by forming cartels; the first major one was formed in 1904, and by 1917 the industry was dominated by I. G. Farbenindustrie (Richardson, 1962, p. 113). The German managers were not content to be at the mercy of market forces and instead devised means of controlling the market, aided by German legal and public acceptance of cartels.

An example of German dye firms' long-range investment policies is their ultimately successful effort to destroy the market for Indian indigo by producing an artificial indigo. The lure of gaining the DM50 million or more that India received annually for its indigo crop (Beer, 1959, p. 69) led German dye firms to make enormous long-range investments in the search for an alternative. The BASF 'invested at least 18 million marks in the development of synthetic indigo, and did not sell a pound of it until 18 years after research was begun' (Hohenberg, 1967, p. 77). German chemical firms did not expect their chemists to produce immediately useful research; Duisberg reported, in fact, that the Bayer company did not care if a new chemist slated for the colour laboratory even knew what a colour was (Duisberg, 1896, p. 429). The great German dye chemist Heinrich Caro failed in his effort to synthesize indigo, but his company, the BASF, still greatly appreciated his early efforts because they gave the firm a scientific head start of at least four years over its competitors (Beer, 1959, p. 69). It should be added that German cartel arrangements helped make BASF's long-range investment in artificial indigo possible. In 1904, Bayer and the BASF agreed that Bayer would stay out of indigo research in return for the BASF not going into pharmaceuticals (Beer, 1959, p. 122).

The willingness to let scientists make their contribution, even at the cost of immediate profits, was far less evident in Britain where scientific research, if subsidized at all, was often the first item to be cut in a lean year. Joseph Lawrence, a machine manufacturer, expressed the common British view when he argued in 1906 that British firms could not afford scientific research because of the pressure of foreign competition. Such research might, he wrote, help the next generation, but the evil of foreign competition was at the British door, and firms had no choice but to cut their research staffs (*The Times*, 6 March 1906). When profits were high, scientific personnel were often deemed unnecessary; when they were low, the researchers were viewed as an expendable drain on the firm.

German dye firms also had a more long-range perspective on marketing strategies than did their British counterparts (*The Times*, 10 March 1906, p. 4; Miall, 1931, p. 85). The British dye manufacturers usually were content to send out circulars describing their products; the Germans sent technically trained salesmen who could answer consumers' questions about the use of the dyes (Richardson, 1962, p. 113). Aggressive marketing tied in with a German goal of planned industrial development, both within the nation and within the firm. The commitment to technical education also meant there was a ready supply of sales representatives with technical knowledge.

In sum, the competition between British firms, combined with the lack of a strong state role, meant that there was no ready mechanism for promoting technical education. When the German chemical firms combined, they greatly increased their research capacities and the demand for scientifically trained personnel. They also could rely on government-supported education to supply them. In Britain, manufacturers sometimes recognized the value of increased attention to science in an abstract sense, but saw little means within the established capitalist framework for making it come about. James Kitson, an ironmaster at Leeds, was asked why local manufacturers did not support science classes. 'Because', he replied, 'the question is so extensive that individual manufacturers are not able to grapple with it, and if they went to immense trouble to establish schools they would only be doing it in order that others might reap the benefit, and we do not do that in Yorkshire' (1868, p. 292). No one manufacturer wanted to pay for basic training in science, yet a reluctance to empower the state to do so remained strong even among advocates of increased technical education.

Lyon Playfair, probably more than any other person in nineteenth-century Britain, sounded the alarm over Britain's backwardness in science education (Argles, 1964, p. 16). Even he, however, attributed the disappointing development of the government-sponsored School of Mines to an overly aggressive state role. He was, he said, wary of state action to support science education too far in advance of popular sentiment (Playfair, 1868, p. 110). It was not until 1889 that Britain's civic universities, established with the goal of helping industry (Sanderson, 1972, p. 81), received their first state money; even then, they received only £15,000 between them (Argles, 1964, pp. 48–9).

The Role of Scientists in Germany and Britain

The successful early development of British industry led to the emergence of a prosperous middle class. This middle class fought against the aristocratic domination of the society, yet after winning some reforms, the middle-class movement, in the sphere of education at least, accepted many facets of the old order (Simon, 1960). British scientists conformed to this general pattern in a way that had considerable implications for applied science. As a group, they combined an emphasis on individualism with an adherence to older, more aristocratic values that conferred greater merit on disinterested, amateur research than on practically directed, applied work. In Germany, scientists more often saw themselves as playing a direct, bureaucratic role in building a powerful nation and an industrial economy. British scientists seldom had ambitions to run industry or to play a role in government (Bernal, 1939, p. 28). There was little in the way of an industrializing ideology to support a divorce from the more traditional values emphasizing amateur status.

William H. Perkin's history provides an example of the power exerted by the ideal of disinterested, pure scientific research. To an unusual degree, Perkin combined business acumen with scientific talent. He left the Royal College of Chemistry to start his own dye business after discovering how to produce the first artificial dye. Even though he had to overcome initial production difficulties (Perkin, 1869, p. 609), his business was markedly successful (Meldola, 1908, p. 2222). Perkin, however, had no desire to remain a manufacturer. Having made his fortune, he retired at thirty-six so that he could return to pure research. He later wrote of his pressing desire to return to research: 'I must confess that one of my great fears on entering into technical work was that it might prevent my continuing research work, but I determined that, as far as possible, this should not be the case' (Perkin, 1869, p. 605).

Perkin was not unusual in his desire to leave business and return to the study of theoretical science. Edward C. Nicholson, another noted English chemist, did the same, depriving the English dye industry of a second major figure (Beer, 1959, p. 46). Perkin and Nicholson formed part of a larger current in the history of British science, men who inherited or gained enough money to spend the best parts of their lives as independent, amateur scientists detached from bureaucratic institutions (Meldola, 1908, pp. 2233–4).

The English attachment to pure science was in keeping with a longstanding set of class values whereby abstract or classical subjects were a mark of status superiority for the upper classes. It was, in the words of one critic, 'fashionable to direct the intellect into useless channels' (Bailey, 1886, p. 358). In the universities, there was a general lack of support for science as compared with classical subjects—and scientists themselves sometimes disdained scientific enterprises that had any flavour of the practical. William Odling, who held the Oxford chemistry chair from 1872 to 1912, thought it was beneath the dignity of a professor to do laboratory work (Sanderson, 1972, p. 38). The holder of the physics chair at Oxford for fifty years until 1915, a Professor Clifton, was 'entirely opposed to research' (quoted in Sanderson, 1972, p. 38). Even at University College in London, which had been established as a counterweight to the conservatism of the ancient universities, many scientists disliked practical work or ties to industry. Plans to have a chair of engineering were dropped because other professors objected (Sanderson, 1972, pp. 2–3).

In Germany, in contrast, under the competitive pressure of the state-aided polytechnics, the universities in the early 1900s began offering chemists broad allied training in engineering and related applied fields (Beer, 1959, p. 61). The breakdown of the barriers between pure and applied science was accelerated by the introduction of state examinations and certification in chemistry during the same period. There was no such sustained institutional and state pressure on the universities in Britain, allowing aristocratic values of hostility to laboratory or applied science to reign far longer.

The differing emphases of the universities affected not only scientists, but also managers. The lure of prestige proved great enough to entice many manufacturers to send their sons to public schools, and, if further education was desired, to Oxford or Cambridge (Allen, 1976, pp. 36–7; Erickson, 1959, p. 34). Students acquired a disdain for business values in these institutions, in addition to a curriculum that had little or no practical relevance. The British gentry traditionally scorned the world of trade and manufacturing; it was the values of this gentry that the public schools and ancient universities presented to the sons of manufacturers. The failure of Britain's new generations of business leaders to learn scientific subjects probably made it hard for them to recognize the value of science more generally. It was much more common for German managers to have been educated in science (Ripley, 1868, p. 265).

In addition, Britain proved to be much slower than Germany and the United States in developing business administration programmes. Beginning in 1901, German institutions called 'Handelhochschulen' provided university-level business education (Allen, 1976, p. 46). These institutions enrolled nearly 5,000 students by the mid-1920s, and an additional 11,000 students studied economics and related subjects in other institutions of higher education. In Britain at the same time, there are estimated to have been fewer than 1,500 university students enrolled in economics or commerce programmes (p. 46). Britain's industrialists had accepted a form of education for their successors geared more to emphasizing class distinctions in cultural knowledge than to producing trained managers.

It is hard, in considering the role of scientists in British industry, to untangle supply from demand factors. Scientists may have preferred the study of pure science over industrial research, but it is also clear that nineteenth-century British industry offered few appealing posts to scientists. Those chemists who were produced by British educational institutions often faced uncertain futures (Frankland, 1868, p. 450). A considerable number of British scientists emigrated, presumably because of better opportunities abroad. Data on emigration rates are sketchy, but studies of the careers of nineteenth-century university graduates and members of professional associations report emigration rates of scientists ranging from 11 to 32 per cent (Roderick and Stephens, 1981, pp. 198–200). A London *Times* correspondent, entering into a debate on scientific education in Britain argued that there were British chemists available during the early years of the dye industry; they could not, however find adequate employment, and the lack of demand, in turn, discouraged the schools and universities from producing more (*The Times*, 10 March 1906).

Even where chemists were hired in industry, they were often confined to doing routine scientific analyses of materials rather than research (Beer, 1959, p. 47). In Germany, chemical firms brought scientists into top management; the career of Carl Duisberg at Bayer is the best-known example of this practice. In Britain, scientists chafed at subordinate roles that did not allow them exercise of their intellects or use of their training. One nineteenth-century observer described the situation, saying that he

could well remember the day when, in the majority of cases, the free, unshackled exercise of chemical science by the chemist was zealously excluded from the alkali and sulphuric acid works of this country, chiefly by those placed in authority as managers, to whom the authority of the chemist was as nothing, who practically trampled on his advice and subverted his doctrines, whose watchword as well as thunderbolt was— 'Give me my ounce of practice and you can keep your ton of theory'. (Bailey, 1886, p. 357.)

In Germany, too, old-line managers without scientific education often resisted the introduction of scientists and scientific methods into dye-making. Foremen and lower-level managers who had learned through experience how to mix dyes tried to sabotage the scientists. Valuing the skills of the experienced practical dyers, higher-level managers at companies like Bayer undertook long, patient, but determined campaigns to force them to accept the authority of the scientists in the production process (Beer, 1959, pp. 76–7). Because most British firms lacked this commitment to science at the top levels, little pressure was brought on intermediate employees to accept scientists and fully use their work.

The lack of adequate salaries, facilities, or research opportunities for top-flight chemists in Britain led some noted foreign-born chemists to return to their native countries in the 1860s (Miall, 1931, p. 86). Most importantly, August Hofmann, the leading figure at the Royal College of Chemistry (and Perkin's teacher), returned to Germany in 1865. His loss, along with those of Heinrich Caro, Carl Martius, and Otto Witt, greatly reduced the chemical talent available to the British dye industry. Each of these chemists went on to make important contributions to the German industry (Roscoe, 1868, p. 325).

At the same time, the failure of the educational institutions to produce scientists with industrially relevant training may have reinforced employers' reluctance to hire these graduates. British educational institutions produced few chemists who were familiar with manufacturing problems (Playfair, 1896, p. 576); this was particularly seen in the lack of chemical engineers (Levinstein, 1886, p. 353). Employers had little scientific aid in designing plants and appliances in chemical works, while in Germany engineering was a basic part of polytechnic training for chemists. Dye manufacturer Ivan Levinstein believed that in Britain employers might do better with rule-of-thumb methods, but only because technical education was so mismanaged that professors were 'placed at the head of our largest technical colleges who [had] never in their life done an hour's practical work in any manufactory or works' (1886, p. 354). The quite common British reliance on foreign chemists (Roscoe, 1868, p. 323; Kitson, 1868, p. 291; Sanderson, 1972, p. 18) suggests either that Britain produced insufficient numbers of chemists or that they were not appropriately trained.

In Germany, also, scientists appear to have been trained to accept bureaucratic roles much more readily than were British scientists (Beer, 1959, p. 47). German science education fostered specialization and division of labour. The great German chemist, Justus Liebig, had introduced the practice of intensive laboratory training for chemistry students (p. 58). His method encouraged students to work extremely hard, putting in long hours, partly under the stimulus of competition from fellow students. All of the students in the laboratory, however, viewed themselves as also working in a common endeavour under the direction of the laboratory's scientific head.

The autocratic role of German professors, in fact, early accustomed students to accept subordinate positions and to work hard on assigned problems that had meaning in the context of other scientific contributions. Only a few could expect eventually to direct laboratories themselves.

This training proved to be eminently suitable for students going into industry, where they could not freely follow their own inclinations about what topics to choose. Germany developed the idea of the industrial research team (Ben-David, 1971, pp. 126–7), an idea that had its birth primarily in the dye industry. The triumph of the German dye industry can be attributed in large part to the development of these research laboratories. The German dye industry 'won its ascendancy in the dye and chemical field by wrenching thousands of little facts from nature by massed assault. The whole colour-testing enterprise during the late 1890s came to be set up like a military operation' (Beer, 1959, p. 90). A high degree of specialization was enforced not only for efficiency, but in order to keep scientists from learning (and possibly selling) industrial secrets (p. 87). Science was far more organized and bureaucratized in Germany than in Britain; this was reflected in the early founding of scientific journals in Germany, which served to keep a body of scientists with common interests informed about research developments. In Britain, by the time the *Journal of the Society of Chemical Industry* appeared in 1881, Germany already had a half dozen scientific journals (Miall, 1931, pp. 85–6). The lone scientist working in an amateur fashion was much less the ideal in Germany than in Britain.

Conclusions

The growth of British competitive capitalism fostered the evolution of an educational system with poor articulation between its parts (Playfair, 1868, p. 102) and little connection to industrial needs. Reliance on short-run market considerations hindered efforts to develop the type of long-range educational investment and planning that helped Germany secure a strong position in the new electrical and chemical industries. Traditional class values about schooling governed the curriculum of secondary schools and universities. Pressures for reform resulted in some changes, such as Dissenters gaining the right to matriculate at Oxford in 1854 and at Cambridge in 1856 (Sanderson, 1972, p. 32). The founding of University College in 1828 itself represented a challenge to the dominance of the ancient, conservative universities. This challenge was never very far-reaching, partly because, once middle-class claimants and newly prosperous manufacturers gained entrance to established educational institutions, they tended to lose some of their reforming zeal (Simon, 1960). They, unlike the advocates of industrialization in Germany, also lacked the powerful aid of the state in restructuring the educational system.

In Britain only profound shocks overcame traditional objections to gov-

ernment planning and aid to scientific research. The British dyestuffs industry had never received the type of government support the German industry
had in terms of government provision of science education, tariff protection,
or patent policies. The patent problem was largely solved before the war, in
1907, when for the first time the holders of British patents were required to
work their patents in Britain (Reader, 1970, p. 259). It took the outbreak of
war in August 1914 to secure action in the other two areas.

The British dyestuffs firms had such a low output that at the start of the
war they had trouble supplying dyes for the khaki uniforms for the troops
(Reader, 1970, p. 266). As the war progressed, it became clear that dyestuffs
firms had a larger importance, as the experience in Germany showed they
could quite easily shift production from dyes to explosives and poison gases.
The Liberal, free-trade government of Asquith proposed the radical step of
helping to fund a reorganized dye industry (p. 270); the plan was to bring all
the British dyestuffs manufacturers into one company, which would receive
half its funds from the Treasury and half from the users (the textile companies). Parliament supported the scheme, and in March 1915 the government gave £1.7 million to aid the formation of British Dyes Ltd (Richardson,
1962, p. 115). This step marked a turning point in the relation of British
industry to government; the pressure of world war had spurred action where
an earlier industrial failure had not.

The government action remained limited, though. The government gave
British Dyes Ltd £100,000 for scientific research (Richardson, 1962, p. 115),
but critically, it acquiesced in traditional managerial distrust of scientists in
policy-making positions. The directors of the new firm included representatives of the users and of the government; there were no chemists among them.
The Parliamentary Secretary to the Board of Trade, M. M. Robertson, was
asked during parliamentary debate whether it might be best to follow the
German example of having chemists serve as directors of dye companies.
Robertson replied that in an ideal world it would certainly be desirable to
have chemists on the board. In reality, though, he observed, he was 'aware of
cases where concerns have been brought to ruin in the hands of most eminent
chemists'. And, besides, he went on,

the opinion of business men . . . is that if you have an expert or two experts on a board
of directors they practically command the situation . . . and a number of businessmen
prefer on that account to be able to take their counsel without having their counsellor
a co-director when he would be practically in a position to give orders. (Quoted in
Reader, 1970, pp. 270–1.)

Rather than forcing modernizing changes in industry, the British state
accepted managerial values that had their roots in Britain's early industrial
history.

In Britain education was so strongly linked to class identity that efforts to rationalize the educational system met entrenched opposition. The British working class had a heritage of technical expertise, but the state did little to foster this expertise. The British elite was not anxious to provide extensive schooling for members of the working class; the identification of technical subjects with the working class meant that the elite also had little interest in promoting technical education among other classes. Technical education for both workers and managers suffered from a lack of connection with industry; this arose, in the case of workers, from a fear of encroaching on employer secrets and union prerogatives, and, in the case of the middle class, from a fear of lowering the status value of education by contaminating abstract subjects with the practical.

This helps to account for a situation where Britain produced world-renowned scientists, yet had a poor record of industrial research (Playfair, 1896, p. 576). Ivan Levinstein pointed to the problem in the electrical industry. 'In the land where the dynamo and the arc lamp originated, the land which witnessed the birth of the electro-magnet, of the Swan lamp, and of the induction-coil, it is, indeed, pitiable to see—that electric pioneering has largely ceased' (*The Times*, 3 March 1906). Other countries, Levinstein predicted, would use industrial research teams to develop these inventions.

The failure to follow up on scientific discoveries and to employ scientists in significant numbers, or in responsible positions, stemmed from a mutually reinforcing set of supply and demand factors. Abstract education produced chemists who did not always have good training for entering industrial research; general scientific education, of a watered-down sort, seldom proved of industrial value for workers. Universities and other educational institutions played a role in maintaining the class system; this meant they had an institutional life of their own at least partially separate from economic conditions or demand factors. Their failure to turn out personnel who were useful to industry reinforced managerial distrust of technical education, which also had its own independent roots in the evolution of British capitalism.

Germany's history shows that a strong government committed to economic development could override traditional objections to the creation of a mass, science-oriented educational system. Her rulers did this in part by relying on conservative values, such as nationalism, to justify their economic and educational policies. This strategy had its own dangers; the state made no move to liberalize the universities except in the breadth of the scientific curriculum they offered. German university professors might have been forced to accept the rise of the polytechnics, but they opposed other perceived assaults on their social standing and as a group became increasingly reactionary (Ringer, 1969). Britain's more *laissez-faire* system did not give rise to Germany's form of political polarization, but her industrial and educational evolution hindered her ability to compete in the science-based industries of the twentieth century.

Bibliography

Aitken, W. C. (1868). 'Minutes of Evidence'. Pp. 359–63 in *Report*, by Select Committee on the Provisions for Giving Instruction in Theoretical and Applied Science to the Industrial Classes. Volume 1. Shannon: Irish University Press.

Allen, G. C. (1976). *The British Disease: A Short Essay on the Nature and Causes of the Nation's Lagging Wealth*. London: Institute of Economic Affairs.

Argles, M. (1964). *South Kensington to Robbins: An Account of English Technical and Scientific Education since 1851*. London: Longmans.

Ashby, E. (1959). *Technology and the Academics: An Essay on Universities and the Scientific Revolution*. London: Macmillan.

Ashwell, H. (1868). 'Minutes of Evidence'. Pp. 244–91 in *Report*, by Select Committee on the Provisions for Giving Instruction in Theoretical and Applied Science to the Industrial Classes. Volume 1. Shannon: Irish University Press.

Bailey, W. H. (1886). 'Discussion' [of Ivan Levinstein's 'Observations and Suggestions on the Present Position of the British Chemical Industries, With Special Reference to Coal-tar Derivatives']. *Journal of the Society of Chemical Industry*, 5, 357–9.

Beer, J. J. (1959). *The Emergence of the German Dye Industry*. Urbana: University of Illinois.

Ben-David, J. (1971). *The Scientist's Role in Society*. Englewood Cliffs, N.J.: Prentice-Hall.

Bernal, J. D. (1939). *The Social Functions of Science*. London: Routledge.

Bernal, J. D. (1953). *Science and Industry in the Nineteenth Century*. London: Routledge & Kegan Paul.

Birkin, T. I. (1868). 'Minutes of Evidence'. Pp. 287–91 in *Report*, by Select Committee on the Provisions for Giving Instruction in Theoretical and Applied Science to the Industrial Classes. Volume 1. Shannon: Irish University Press.

Cardwell, D. S. L. (1957). *The Organisation of Science in England*. London: Heinemann.

Chandler, A. D. Jr (1980). 'The Growth of the Transnational Industrial Firm in the United States and the United Kingdom: A Comparative Analysis'. *Economic History Review*, 2nd ser., 33, 396–410.

Clow, A., and N. Clow (1952). *The Chemical Revolution: A Contribution to Social Technology*. London: Batchworth.

Coleman, D. C. (1973). 'Gentlemen and Players'. *Economic History Review*, ser. 2., 26, 92–116.

Cotgrove, S. F. (1958). *Technical Education and Social Change*. London: Allen & Unwin.

Curtis, S. J., and M. E. A. Boultwood (1964). *An Introductory History of English Education Since 1800*. London: University Tutorial Press.

Davies, J. (1831). *An Appeal to the Public, on Behalf of the Manchester Mechanics' Institution, Cooper Street*. Manchester.

Duisberg, C. (1896). 'The Education of Chemists'. *Journal of the Society of Chemical Industry*, 15, 427–32.

Ehrhardt, E. G. (1924). 'Reminiscences of Dr Caro'. *Journal of the Society of Chemical Industry*, 43 (Part II), 561–5.

Erickson, C. (1959). *British Industrialists: Steel and Hosiery 1850–1950*. Cambridge University Press.

Frankland, E. (1868). 'Minutes of Evidence'. Pp. 447–54 in *Report*, by Select Committee on the Provisions for Giving Instruction in Theoretical and Applied Science to the Industrial Classes. Volume 1. Shannon: Irish University Press.

Gerschenkron, A. (1962). *Economic Backwardness in Historical Perspective*. Cambridge, Mass. Belknap Press of Harvard University Press.

Gowing, M. (1977). 'Science, Technology and Education: England in 1870'. The Wilkins Lecture. *Notes and Records of the Royal Society of London*, 32, 71–90.

Henderson, W. O. (1975). *The Rise of German Industrial Power, 1834–1914*. London: Maurice Temple Smith.

Heywood, B. (1843). *Addresses Delivered at the Manchester Mechanics' Institution*. London: Knight.

Hohenberg, P. M. (1967). *Chemicals in Western Europe: 1850–1914*. Chicago: Rand McNally.

Hole, J. (1853). *An Essay on the History and Management of Literary, Scientific and Mechanics' Institutions*. London: Longman, Brown, Green & Longmans.

Hudson, J. W. (1851). *The History of Adult Education*. London: Longman, Brown, Green & Longmans.

Kitson, J. (1868). 'Minutes of Evidence'. Pp. 291–5 in *Report*, by Select Committee on the Provisions for Giving Instruction in Theoretical and Applied Science to the Industrial Classes. Volume 1. Shannon: Irish University Press.

Kocka, J. (1980). 'The Rise of the Modern Industrial Enterprise in Germany'. In *Managerial Hierarchies: Comparative Perspectives on the Rise of the Modern Industrial Enterprise*, ed. Alfred Chandler Jr and Herman Daems. Cambridge, Mass.: Harvard University Press.

Landes, D. S. (1969). *The Unbound Promethus: Technological Change and Industrial Development in Western Europe from 1750 to the Present*. London: Cambridge University Press.

Lazonick, W. (1980). 'Industrial Organization and Technological Change: The Decline of the British Cotton Industry', Discussion Paper no. 794. Cambridge, Mass.: Harvard Institute of Economic Research.

Levinstein, I. (1886). 'Observations and Suggestions on the Present Position of the British Chemical Industries, with Special Reference to Coal-tar Derivatives'. *Journal of the Society of Chemical Industry*, 5, 351–9.

Meldola, R. (1908). 'Obituary Notices: William Henry Perkin'. *Journal of the Chemical Society*, 93, 2214–57.

Miall, S. (1931). *A History of the British Chemical Industry*. London: Ernest Benn.

Mundella, A. (1868). 'Minutes of Evidence'. Pp. 232–87 in *Report*, by Select Committee on the Provisions for Giving Instruction in Theoretical and Applied Science to the Industrial Classes. Volume 1. Shannon: Irish University Press.

Musson, A. E., and E. Robinson (1969). *Science and Technology in the Industrial Revolution*. Manchester University Press.

Noble, D. (1977). *America by Design: Science, Technology, and the Rise of Corporate Capitalism*. New York: Alfred Knopf.

Paulsen, F. (1912). *German Education Past and Present*. New York: Charles Scribner's Sons.

Perkin, W. H. (1869). 'The Origin of the Coal-tar Colour Industry, and the Contributions of Hofmann and his Pupils'. *Journal of the Chemical Society*, 69 (Part I), 596–637.

Platt, J. (1868). 'Minutes of Evidence'. Pp. 334–40 in *Report*, by Select Committee on the Provisions for Giving Instruction in Theoretical and Applied Science to the Industrial Classes. Volume 1. Shannon: Irish University Press.

Playfair, L. (1868). 'Minutes of Evidence'. Pp. 101–12 in *Report*, by Select Committee on the Provisions for Giving Instruction in Theoretical and Applied Science to the Industrial Classes. Volume 1. Shannon: Irish University Press.

Playfair, L. (1870). 'Address on Education'. London.

Playfair, L. (1896). 'Personal Reminiscences of Hofmann and of the Conditions which led to the Establishment of the Royal College of Chemistry and his Appointment as its Professor'. *Journal of the Chemical Society*, 69 (Part I), 575–9.

Reader, W. J. (1970). *Imperial Chemical Industries: A History*. Volume 1: *The Forerunners, 1870–1926*. London: Oxford University Press.

Richardson, H. W. (1962). 'The Development of the British Dyestuffs Industry Before 1939'. *Scottish Journal of Political Economy*, 9, 110–29.

Richardson, H. W. (1968). 'Chemicals'. In *The Development of British Industry and Foreign Competition, 1875–1914: Studies in Industrial Enterprise*, ed. Derek H. Aldcroft. London: Allen and Unwin.

Ringer, F. K. (1969). *The Decline of the German Mandarins: The German Academic Community, 1890—1933*. Cambridge, Mass.: Harvard University Press.

Ripley, H. W. (1868). 'Minutes of Evidence'. Pp. 254–66 in *Report*, by Select Committee on the Provisions for Giving Instruction in Theoretical and Applied Science to the Industrial Classes. Volume 1. Shannon: Irish University Press.

Roderick, G. W. (1967). *The Emergence of a Scientific Society*. London: Macmillan.

Roderick, G. W., and M. D. Stephens (1972). *Scientific and Technical Education in Nineteenth-Century England*. Newton Abbot, Devon: David and Charles.

Roderick, G. W., and M. D. Stephens (1981). 'The Universities'. In *Where did We Go Wrong? Industrial Performance, Education and the Economy in Victorian Britain*, ed. G. W. Roderick and M. D. Stephens. Barcombe, Sussex: Falmer Press.

Roscoe, H. (1868). 'Minutes of Evidence'. Pp. 320–34 in *Report*, by Select Committee on the Provisions for Giving Instruction in Theoretical and Applied Science to the Industrial Classes. Volume 1. Shannon: Irish University Press.

Royal Commission on Technical Instruction (1881). *First Report of the Royal Commissioners on Technical Instruction*. Shannon: Irish University Press.

Rumney, R. (1868). 'Minutes of Evidence'. Pp. 341–51 in *Report*, by Select Committee on the Provisions for Giving Instruction in Theoretical and Applied Science to the Industrial Classes. Volume 1. Shannon: Irish University Press.

Sanderson, M. (1972). *The Universities and British Industry, 1850–1970*. London: Routledge and Kegan Paul.

Saul, S. B. (1968). 'The Engineering Industry'. In *The Development of British Industry and Foreign Competition, 1875–1914: Studies in Industrial Enterprise*, ed. Derek H. Aldcroft. London: Allen and Unwin.

Select Committee on the Provisions for Giving Instruction in Theoretical and Applied Science to the Industrial Classes (1868). *Report*. Volume 1. Shannon: Irish University Press.

Simon, B. (1960). *The Two Nations and the Educational Structure, 1780–1870*. London: Lawrence & Wishart.

Thompson, E. P. (1963). *The Making of the English Working Class*. New York: Vintage.

Tipton, F. B. Jr (1976). *Regional Variations in the Economic Development of Germany During the Nineteenth Century*. Middleton, Conn.: Wesleyan University Press.

Tylecote, M. (1957). *The Mechanics' Institutes of Lancashire and Yorkshire before 1851*. Manchester University Press.

Wardle, D. (1970). *English Popular Education, 1780–1975*. Cambridge University Press.

Wiener, M. J. (1981). *English Culture and the Decline of the Industrial Spirit, 1850–1980*. Cambridge University Press.

Whitworth, J. (1868). 'Minutes of Evidence'. Pp. 129–37 in *Report*, by Select Committee on the Provisions for Giving Instruction in Theoretical and Applied Science to the Industrial Classes. Volume 1. Shannon: Irish University Press.

Wrigley, J. (1982). 'The Division between Mental and Manual Labor: Artisan Education in Science in Nineteenth-century Britain'. *American Journal of Sociology*, 88 (supplement), 31–51.

Industrial Research, 1900–1950

David C. Mowery*
Carnegie-Mellon University

A central factor in the economic decline of Britain during this century is the poor innovative record of British industry. A lack of innovation contributed to low levels of growth in manufacturing productivity and exports during much of the twentieth century.[1] The innovative performance of British firms was affected by low levels of industrial research, in which British firms invested fewer resources than did US enterprises. This paper analyses the development of British industrial research during 1900–50, focusing on the reasons for low levels of R & D investment in British manufacturing.

Recent empirical work provides a strong basis for the conclusion that R & D investment enhances national economic performance. Innovative activity at the firm and industry level (measured either in terms of inputs, e.g. expenditures or employment in research and development, or outputs, e.g. patents) has been shown in several studies to influence national productivity growth and export performance in both Western Europe and the United States[2] (Pavitt and Soete, 1980; Denison, 1968). While these studies are concerned only with the period since World War II, the linkages between technical and economic performance have been present for much of the twentieth century. Low levels of R & D activity thus appear to be important factors in understanding British export and productivity performance during 1900–50. During this period, British exports declined as a share of total world trade; even more dramatic was the decline in absolute terms of British exports during the 1920s. Reduced export growth reflected the continued dependence of British foreign trade on staple commodities, such as coal, iron, and textiles (Lewis, 1949).[3] The development of alternative export industries was impeded by low levels of R & D.

Productivity growth in the British economy during this period also lagged behind that of other European countries and the United States (Rostas, 1948; Phelps Brown, 1973). Clearly, influences other than R & D investment and innovative performance affected these trends. None the less, the weight of empirical evidence suggests that a more vigorous R & D effort might have offset this spiral of economic decline. The persistence of low levels of R & D

*Research for this paper has been supported by the National Science Foundation (PRA77-21852), the Division of Research of the Harvard Business School, the Andrew W. Mellon Foundation, and the Program in Technology and Society at Carnegie-Mellon University. The paper has benefited from comments by Louis Cain, Alfred D. Chandler, Jr, Bernard Elbaum, William Lazonick, Derek Morris, Richard Nelson, Nathan Rosenberg, the participants in the conference discussions, and the members of the Berkeley–Stanford Economic History Colloqium. I am grateful to Professor Chandler for the use of unpublished data.

investment in British industry is especially striking in view of the widespread acknowledgement in official and unofficial reports of the technological failings of British industry.

The structure of the British industrial research system during this period also undermined the effectiveness of the modest investment in R & D. British industry relied heavily on government-funded co-operative research organizations, engineers (as opposed to scientists) were scarce, and links between academic and industrial research were weak. Within firms, industrial research was often fragmented and poorly co-ordinated with other functions.

Three factors explain the low level and inefficient organization of British industrial research. The first is the structure of the British manufacturing firm. In the United States, the development of industrial research was closely associated with the reorganization of the US corporation described in Chandler (1977). Chandler's 'managerial revolution' in US business included the absorption into the firm of a range of activities formerly carried out, if at all, via the market. Among these functions was industrial research. In Britain such a transformation and reorganization of major firms occurred later than in the United States, and was less complete. Where research was carried out within the firm, the incomplete rationalization of internal firm structure often hampered its effectiveness. In short, the pattern of development of US industrial enterprises allowed for a more effective exploitation of the complementarities between research activity and production activity. These complementarities are exploited most effectively in a non-market (i.e., intrafirm) setting.

A second broad influence on the development of British R & D was the system of technical and managerial education at the secondary and university levels. A tradition of low levels of public financial support for such education did nothing to improve the number or professional training of engineers, who down to the present are much scarcer in Britain than in Germany or the United States (Peck, 1968; see also the paper by Wrigley in this volume). In addition, the informal linkages between higher and technical education and industry, which proved to be of great importance in the industrial research system within the United States and Germany during this period, failed to develop within Britain.

The third important influence, affecting both the development of the British firm and the organization of industrial research, was government economic policy. British *laissez-faire* policy influenced the growth of industrial research, particularly in older industries, by permitting anti-competitive price and market-sharing agreements among British firms. During the interwar period, government involvement in rationalization and protectionist policies cemented these agreements, undercutting the incentives for the pursuit of competitive advantage through innovative activity.[4] At the same time, however, the British government did attempt to take positive action by undertaking a novel programme of direct support of co-operative industrial research in the aftermath of World War I. An historical comparison of British and US government policies in industrial research is of particular interest in the context of recent policy debates over proposals to improve the innovative performance of US industry.[5]

These three explanatory factors interacted in a complex fashion. The structure of British firms enforced dependence on market, rather than intrafirm, co-ordination of numerous transactions, which in turn affected the demand of British industry for technical and managerial personnel. Government policy emphasized, above all, non-interference with the operations of the market. It is possible that a different set of goverment policies towards industrial structure and education could have substantially enhanced the level and effectiveness of British industrial research. None the less, even the more interventionist policies adopted by governments since 1945 have not brought about parity between British and US industrial research activity or technological performance.

The first section of this paper examines the available data on the level of research expenditures and/or employment in British and US manufacturing prior to 1950. Despite similarities in the inter-industry distribution of research activity, investment in research by US firms was well above that of British manufacturing firms. The next section considers the aspects of the structure and evolution of US and British firms that account for the apparently lower level of demand by British business enterprises for research expertise. The influence of the British educational system on the supply of technical manpower for industrial research is discussed in the subsequent section. Finally, the role of government policy is analysed.

Comparative levels of R & D in Britain and the United States prior to 1950

The existing data are consistent in suggesting that, during and after this period, the average research intensity of British manufacturing firms (measured either as the share of research employees in total firm employment, or the share of R & D expenditures in total firm sales) was substantially less than that of US manufacturing firms. Analyses of data on expenditures from the mid-1950s and employment data from the 1930s suggest that the level of research intensity in British firms was on average about one-third of its level in US manufacturing firms (Sanderson, 1972a; Freeman, 1962).[6] Lower levels of research activity in British manufacturing are not explained by transatlantic differences in the mix of industries in the manufacturing sectors of these two nations.[7] Other data on US and British industrial research from the 1930s and 1940s also suggest that R & D investment in British manufacturing was well below that of US manufacturing during this period.

Employment of research professionals in the laboratories of US manufacturing firms stood at 10,900 in 1933 (0.18 per cent of total manufacturing employment), rising to nearly 28,000 in 1940 (0.35 per cent) and 45,900 in 1946 (0.39 per cent) (National Research Council, 1933, 1946; Mowery, 1981). Surveys of research activity in British industry during the 1930s and 1940s provide a basis for estimates of research employment in manufacturing of 1,724 in 1933 (0.030 per cent of the total manufacturing workforce), 2,575 in 1935 (0.042 per cent) 4,505 in 1938 (0.066 per cent), and 5,200 in 1945–6 (0.080 per cent) (Federation of British Industries, 1951; da C. Andrade, 1946). Research intensity in US manufacturing overall thus was roughly four to five times as high as research intensity in British manufacturing during the 1930s and 1940s.[8]

These differences between the research intensity of British and US manufacturing partially reflect different levels of public funding of research in Britain and the United States, as well as differences in the institutional location of publicly funded research. British government research installations, such as the National Physical Laboratory and the quasi-public research associations, accounted for a substantially higher percentage of total British research expenditures than did US government facilities within US research activity. R & D expenditures by British industry were estimated to amount to £2.2 million in 1934 (prior to rearmament), while total research expenditures by the British government in the same year (including financial support of the research associations) were estimated to equal £2.95 million (Bernal, 1939). By way of contrast, total expenditures on research within US industry in 1937 were estimated to be $175 million (Perazich and Field, 1940). Total federal research expenditures in this year were $72 million, of which $38 million was spent within industry (US Senate Military Affairs Committee, 1945). It is possible that publicly funded research within Britain offset the impact on innovative performance of lower levels of in-house research employment within British manufacturing. However, very little British government-supported R & D was conducted within industrial firms during this period. The location of publicly funded R & D in the research associations (see below for further discussion) and national laboratories may have weakened the impact on industrial innovation of such funding.

While the available data suggest that research intensity in British manufacturing was well below its level in US manufacturing during much of the 1900–50 period, this comparison does not control for transnational differences in the size distribution of firms. A comparison of research activity among the 200 largest manufacturing enterprises in Britain and the United States during the 1930s and 1940s suggests that, if anything, the largest British firms were even further behind their US counterparts than was the rest of the British manufacturing sector.[9] In 1933, 116 of the firms in a sample of 160 US firms from the top 200 had research laboratories; in 1936 the number of firms among the largest 200 British firms with such in-house research facilities was 20. The postwar comparison is similarly dramatic. Of the 200 largest firms in US manufacturing as of 1948, 164 were listed by the National

Research Council as maintaining industrial laboratories. In Britain this proportion stood at 40 out of 200. Moreover, when US and British firms lying above an estimated threshold size necessary for the support of in-house research are compared for the 1930s, a much greater proportion of the US firms have research labortories. Of 33 US firms lying above this estimated threshold in 1933, 31 maintained research facilities; of 8 British firms lying above this threshold in the 1930s, only 1 reported an in-house research laboratory.[10]

How was the performance of individual British firms affected by the low levels of investment in research? Evidence on this point is very scarce, and does not cover all of the 1900–50 period. The available results are most abundant and convincing for the performance of firms within US manufacturing, but they also allow for weaker comparisons of the effects of research activity on the performance of British and US firms.

Research employment significantly enhanced the ability of US manufacturing firms to remain within the ranks of the top 200 during 1921–46, controlling for initial firm size (Mowery, 1983a). The growth of firms (measured as growth in the book value of assets) during 1933–46 also was higher among more research-intensive firms in the top 200, again controlling for initial firm size. The 1921–46 period is one during which scholars have argued that the level of turnover and instability within the ranks of the largest firms in the US economy declined significantly (see Edwards, 1975; Collins and Preston, 1961; or Kaplan, 1964). Industrial research in US manufacturing, the growth of which was very rapid during 1921–46, may have been partially responsible for this increasing stability in market structure. Many large US firms relied on industrial research to preserve positions of market power through aggressive and extensive patenting policies, and employed research to support product diversification and the acquisition of new technologies (see Reich, 1977, 1980; Mueller, 1955; Brock, 1981).

Within British industry, the aftermath of World War I does not constitute a similar point of transition from instability to stability in market structure. The survival rate among large British firms in the early twentieth century appears substantially lower than that observed among the largest US firms during the same period; only in the 1940s does a comparable increase in survival rates appear.[11] It is likely that the lower levels of in-house industrial research in Britain during the interwar period contributed to this later achievement of increased stability in market structure.

Other unpublished results, as well as the work of Terleckyj (1961), suggest that differences among US manufacturing industries in total factor productivity growth during 1921–46 are significantly and positively related to inter-industry differences in research intensity.[12] These results are of interest in view of the contrasts between British and US labour productivity growth in manufacturing during the early twentieth century. Rostas (1948) found that labour productivity growth during 1907–35 in US manufacturing substantially exceeded productivity growth in British manufacturing. This gap increased dramatically during the 1920s, the period of most rapid growth in the number and size of US industrial research laboratories.[13]

British manufacturing firms largely failed during 1900–50 to exploit an organizational innovation of considerable significance for economic growth and performance, and did so for reasons other than the size or structure of the British manufacturing sector. Below, the three suggested causes of this low level of research investment by British firms, relating to firm structure, the British system of higher and technical education, and government policy, are examined in greater detail.

The Structure of the British Firm: The Delayed Managerial Revolution and Its Consequences

The lower level of industrial research within British manufacturing, as well as the frequently dysfunctional organization of the research activity that was present within British industry, were closely connected with the structure of the British firm. A number of US firms underwent a transformation in internal structure and product lines, and an expansion in the range of functions incorporated within their boundaries, early in the 1900–50 period. In British industry this reorganization occurred later and, when it did occur, was somewhat less thorough.

The importance of this transformation for the development of industrial research stems from the characteristics of technical and scientific knowledge as commodities and industrial innovation as a process. For all but the most prosaic and routinized of activities, industrial research is most efficient and effective when conducted on an in-house basis. Commercially successful innovation requires the combination of skills and information from a wide range of functions within the firm, and often exploits firm-specific knowledge emerging from the production process (Mowery, 1983b; Cohen and Mowery, 1984). Contractual organization of such a complex process is fraught with uncertainties and moral hazard, and frequently does not allow for the effective utilization of firm-specific knowledge. Furthermore, the efficient organization of industrial research requires the development of a strong central staff within the firm, incorporating and co-ordinating such other functions as marketing or production engineering. Historically, the development of industrial research has required a range of complementary changes in the structure and organization of firms and markets. Where these changes have not occurred, industrial research has proceeded at a lower level of effort and efficiency.

The development of industrial research within the US firm was heavily affected by the reorganization of the US corporation during the late nineteenth and twentieth centuries. The growth of industrial research was encouraged by the presence of technically trained managers, a strong central office staff able to focus on strategic, rather than operating, decisions, and the integration within the firm of other functions, such as marketing. The in-house location of research activity allowed for a more efficient combination of the heterogeneous inputs necessary for commercially successful innovation. The research facility within the firm also was better situated to utilize and increase the stock of highly firm-specific knowledge gleaned from such sources as marketing or production personnel. In-house research was able to exploit the joint-product nature of manufacturing activity and certain forms of technical knowledge.[14]

Industrial research was not only an effect, but also a cause, of the development of the modern US manufacturing firm. The greater efficiency of in-house, as opposed to contract, research in US manufacturing is reflected in the declining share of total research employment accounted for by independent research organizations.[15] Research-intensive firms displayed superior performance and assumed an increasingly dominant role within the US and world economies. Industrial research also shaped firm and industry structure by supporting product diversification.

One of the clearest indications of the belated development of new managerial techniques and firm structure in Britain, by comparison with the United States, is in the industrial composition of the 200 largest firms in each nation. Organizational and structural changes in the US firm had the effect of substantially increasing firm size.[16] Industries utilizing continuous process or capital- and energy-intensive production technologies, such as chemicals or petroleum refining, are cited by Chandler (1977) as the leaders in the adoption of new management techniques and organizational structures. The US textile industry in particular lagged considerably in this structural transformation. As the changes in firm structure and management in Britain that occurred during the 1940s and 1950s initially affected continuous process industries, firms in these industries grew in size, and the British economic landscape gradually came to resemble that of the United States.

While the overall industrial composition of the manufacturing sector in the two nations near the close of the 1900–50 period was quite similar, the industrial composition of the dominant firms in the two economies differed greatly during the interwar period. In 1930 over 30 per cent of the top 200 British firms were engaged in food processing, while in the United States this proportion stood at 16 per cent. Textile concerns accounted for 12 per cent of the 200 largest British firms, versus 1.5 per cent of the largest US firms. In contrast, chemical firms accounted, respectively, for 4.5 and 9 per cent of the 200 largest manufacturing firms in Britain and the United States at this date. By 1948 the share of the largest British firms accounted for by the food and textiles industries had declined, while chemicals and primary metals firms as a proportion of the top 200 had expanded substantially.

The spread of new organizational and managerial structures within US manufacturing was aided by the merger wave of the late 1890s and early twentieth century. The firms emerging from the numerous horizontal mergers of that period were among the largest in the US economy, and gradually undertook policies of systematic internal reorganization and centralization, developing a strong central office staff to formulate policy for the numerous components of the firm. Such internal rationalization was of critical importance to the subsequent incorporation within the firm of major non-manufacturing activities, such as marketing and industrial research. In American Telephone and Telegraph, US Steel, and Du Pont, the development of a strong central office was closely associated with the establishment or significant expansion of a central research facility (Mowery, 1983a). Within the top 200, the largest firms pioneered in the establishment of in-house research facilities. During the early portion of 1921–46, in-house research employment was concentrated among the very largest firms (especially in chemicals), gradually spreading across industries and to smaller firms.[17]

Within Britain, the merger wave of the late nineteenth and early twentieth centuries was less significant:

in both numbers and value the US merger wave far outpaced that in this country [Britain]: in 1899 alone there were 979 firm disappearances by merger valued at $2,064 million (over £400 million), compared with 255 firm disappearances valued at only £22 million in the UK. A merger wave of such large proportions naturally caused an abrupt increase in over-all industrial concentration in the US: between 1896 and 1905 the largest 100 corporations increased their size on average by a factor of four, gaining control of 40 per cent of the nation's industrial capital. In Britain, by contrast, comparably high levels of industrial concentration were not to be achieved until the interwar years, and, of the firms which were extensively involved in merger activity in the decades covered by the present study, only a minority were destined to form the nuclei of important modern corporations. (Hannah, 1974a, p. 10.)

Moreover, this British merger wave was limited to a much narrower range of industries, primarily brewing and textiles. Many of the resulting firms did not undergo internal reorganization and rationalization. The failure to pursue such post-merger rationalization was partially responsible for the low success rate among such mergers, and contributed to the greater instability among the largest British firms, by comparison with the largest US firms, that was discussed above.

Both British and US manufacturing experienced another wave of mergers in the aftermath of World War I. In the United States this merger wave had a more modest impact on firm and market structure than its predecessor.[18] The British merger wave of the 1920s, however, led to the creation of such major modern British firms as ICI and Unilever (Hannah, 1974a). The development of the truly giant, centralized firm in Britain thus did not begin until well after the first US merger wave. This slower evolution of British firm structure almost certainly was a significant contributor to the observed differences between US and British industrial research activity during this period.

Where mergers did occur within British industry, the result in many cases was not a streamlined or efficient structure (Chandler, 1980; Payne, 1967; Hannah, 1974b). Frequently, the resulting firm remained an awkward collection of poorly co-ordinated, fiercely independent subsidiaries. Inefficient and excess capacity often persisted, owing to the resistance of some directors to the extinction of their firms or the closure of their factories. One of the most famous examples of incomplete rationalization was the Calico Printers' Association, formed in 1902 with a board of directors numbering no less than eighty-four. This merger was somewhat unusual, however, in that it survived. Interestingly, a committee appointed by the firm in 1907 to recommend ways of improving its poor performance strongly advocated the establishment of a central research department,

equipped with necessary appliances for research and experimental work, conducted by the ablest and best-trained chemists, specially qualified to pursue investigations, in which chemical processes and mechanical and electrical appliances are involved. This department would form a 'Clearing House' for difficulties experienced in any branch works in carrying out complicated processes, and in the introduction of new colours and methods of production. It would inquire into, and test if necessary, all new inventions, and obtain information from other countries of new developments in calico printing. It would be the brains of the business. . . . (Macrosty, 1907, p. 152.)

Despite this eloquent recommendation, no central research facility was established.

This pattern of incomplete rationalization was by no means confined to firms in the older staple industries. Wilson (1954) notes Lever's support of competition among subsidiaries[19] in his firm, a leader in the rapidly growing consumer goods market of twentieth-century Britain. Andrews and Brunner (1951) discuss the formation of the United Steel firm, one of the more progressive in the British steel industry, in the following terms:

United Steel was not intended to be a very centralized business. . . . There is no record of the founders of the business having as their object the achievement of increased productive efficiency horizontally, as between the businesses which were to become branches of the combine through what was later to be called 'rationalization', and an enforced specialization upon different parts of their joint market. That prospect was to come to the front later on. (Andrews and Brunner, 1951, p. 121.)

Only in the early 1930s, some seven years after the United Steel merger, was there established a central office and a more systematic policy of internal rationalization. Simultaneously, the Central Research Department was established.[20]

Major chemical, fabricated metal, and electrical machinery firms experienced difficulties in the central co-ordination of their newly merged subsidiaries. They frequently failed particularly in the strategic management and co-ordination of their research activities. Imperial Chemical Industries, for instance, consciously attempted to emulate many of the management techniques of Du Pont, and in fact spent a higher proportion of its revenue on research, yet did not achieve a unified organizational structure until the 1950s. One result of this failure was the fact that, 'By the time ICI had been in existence for a dozen years . . . then, the central research organization was still far from fully developed. Indeed, its fundamental principles had hardly been laid down, apart from the somewhat negative one of leaving the Groups alone as much as possible' (Reader, 1975, p. 93).[21]

Jones and Marriot (1970) described Associated Electrical Industries, formed in 1928 out of the merger of British Thomson Houston and Metropolitan Vickers, in the following terms: 'Before the merger of 1928 to create AEI, British Thomson-Houston and Metropolitan Vickers had been competitors in almost all their many products. After the merger that rivalry did not stop. Many said that it became more intense.' These authors attribute the slow development by British industry of a commercially practical jet engine in part to the inability of the two components of AEI to co-operate effectively.[22] The Marconi firm, absorbed in 1946 by English Electric after being controlled for many years by Cable and Wireless, operated with a similarly chaotic internal structure through the late 1940s (Baker, 1970).[23] Yet another large firm formed in the 1920s, Metal Box, was also characterized by a lack of internal cohesion.[24]

Even within large firms in technically progressive industries, then, powerful centrifugal forces worked against the development of the strong central staff that was associated with major industrial research performers in US manufacturing firms. The fact that such problems affected firms in both technically progressive and stagnant industries further suggests that these difficulties were not industry-specific, but were related to the overall structure and institutional environment of the British economy.

A striking contrast between the British and US institutional environment was the limited involvement of British financial institutions in corporate management and mergers. US financiers and banks played an important role in the finance and organization of such forerunners of the modern US corporation as the railroads, and in the subsequent development of industrial corporations. Outside financiers not only facilitated many large US mergers, but often oversaw the design of organizational and management structures in the new firms. The size of the firms resulting from these mergers, the mergers' financial requirements, and their organization by major financial houses all helped to weaken family control of major US firms long before managers replaced owners in British industry.

The reasons for the limited involvement of British financial institutions in the management of British firms are not clear.[25] Davis (1966) asserts that the early capital requirements of British industry were sufficiently modest that they could be met from private sources.[26] Davis also argued that the greater sophistication and level of development of the English capital market enabled firms to raise capital directly from the sale of stock. In contrast to Davis, Kennedy (1976) suggests that provincial banks *were* involved in industrial finance until the late nineteenth century, when a wave of bank failures induced a much more cautious approach.[27]

For whatever reason, through much of the early twentieth century. British industrial firms seeking long-term financing had little alternative to floating new issues on the stock market, or relying on nonbank sources for borrowing. Supervision of corporate development and organization by financial institutions was nowhere to be found in Britain. As the Committee on Finance and Industry noted in 1931.

British companies in the iron and steel, electrical, and other industries must meet in the gate their great American and German competitors who are generally powerful and closely supported by banking and financial groups with whom they have continuous relationships. British industry, without similar support, will undoubtedly be at a disadvantage. In the last few exceedingly difficult years it would have been of high value if the leaders, for instance of the steel or shipbuilding or other industries, had been working in the closest cooperation with powerful financial and banking institutions in the City with a view to their reconstitution on a profitable basis. The tasks still confronting us require great financial as well as industrial experience. (Committee on Finance and Industry, 1931, p. 165.)

British firms of all sizes remained far more dependent on the market for the organization and control of their activities than was true of the largest US firms. In industries such as textiles, the production process was carried on through a highly developed interfirm division of labour.[28] The non-electrical machinery and steel industries also were populated by relatively small firms that avoided any role in product marketing or distribution (Committee on Commercial and Industrial Policy After the War, 1918; Saul, 1968; Warren, 1979; Tolliday, 1979).

This reliance on market mechanisms for co-ordination was reflected in the importance of the consulting engineer, whose baleful influence on innovation and export performance was cited by a number of authors and official committees. The consulting engineer, whose job it was to design and supervise the production of complex capital goods for a given customer, worked against the development of more efficient corporate organization and in-house research in at least two ways. The persistence of custom design and production of machinery prevented sufficient standardization of product lines to support the development of larger firms capable of exploiting scale economies in design and production. In addition, the consulting engineers' mediating role in the R & D process supported the tendency of engineering firms to underinvest in research within their boundaries, preventing as well their exploitation of information from customers or suppliers. Saul's (1968) comment on the consulting engineer illustrates these difficulties:

the consulting engineer all too often was deprived of the opportunity of combining his theoretical knowledge with a deep practical understanding. The industrialist, for his part, called in the consulting engineer whenever calculations had to be made—fixing the proper thickness of wall for a hydraulic cylinder, or determining the strains in a simple lattice girder or workshop crane. Things had so fossilized that, if the poor consultant tried to give the manufacturer a free hand, there was a chorus of protest. . . . There is little point in arguing that German locomotive makers were more advanced in ideas of design than were the British, for by and large the use of consulting engineers meant that the British maker was concerned with organizing his works to the best of his ability, not with design. The consultant's aim tended to be to design a product of high technical quality which would do him credit in his profession. Executing the work in the most economical manner was not the prime object by any means. Not being in close contact with any one firm, he failed to design in a manner which fitted in with any particular manufacturing facilities. Standardization was extremely difficult to achieve and the method inhibited continued development work on plant when it was in operation. (Saul, 1968, p. 231.)[29]

The institution of the consulting engineer provides an excellent example of the effects on corporate organization of exclusive reliance on contractual arrangements in the innovation and design processes. Both directly, by off-setting the incentives faced by firms to invest in intrafirm research, and indirectly, by supporting an industry structure characterized by small firms and low levels of product standardization, the consulting engineer worked to prevent the emergence of modern, large corporations in the electrical and non-electrical machinery and shipbuilding industries. The persistence of the independent consulting engineer in such British industries as heavy electrical and non-electrical machinery contrasts with the decline in importance of the US independent research organization during this period.

In Britain during this period, the interaction between evolving firm structure and in-house research, which was of great importance to the development of the modern US industrial firm, was largely absent. The minor role played by industrial research reflected the lack of dramatic change in the structure of the British firm. As a result, within such industries as electrical and non-electrical machinery, the independent consulting engineer continued to play a major role. In other firms and industries, a large-scale, centralized research facility covering the full range of the firm's current and future activities often failed to develop, reflecting the weakness of the central office structure and the lack of technical expertise on the part of high-level managers. However, neither British nor US firms and research laboratories developed in a vacuum. In particular, the structure of the British firm, and its modest commitment to industrial research, were both responses to, and influences on, the broader institutional environment. Important elements of this environment were the higher educational system and government policy, which are examined below.

Scientific and Managerial Education in Britain and the United States[30]

A second key factor in the growth of industrial research in US manufacturing was the parallel growth of a large higher education network. It is hardly coincidental that the growth of US industrial research followed the development of research as a recognized professional activity within academia in the late nineteenth century. This parallel growth was supported by a complex web of linkages between academic and industrial research, including personnel, ideas, and financial as well as political support.[31]

Within Britain, comparable links between academic and industrial research failed to develop. This failure resulted in a relative shortage of professional engineers for industrial research, a lack of professionally trained managerial talent, and a dearth of the informal involvement by academic personnel in industrial research that developed during the 1920s and 1930s in the United States. The educational system clearly was not the sole factor behind these developments; the lack of professional training for managers reflected the family control of many British firms. Indeed, the educational system may be viewed more generally as the supply side of the mechanism resulting in research investment by firms. Low levels of demand for technical personnel on the part of industry, which in turn reflected low levels of R & D investment, meant that changes in the structure of the institutions supplying research and managerial personnel were unlikely.[32]

Compared with the college and university system of the United States, the British higher education system was tiny. The number of British university students stood at roughly 24,000 in the early 1920s, increasing to 50,000–60,000 by the late 1930s (Briggs, 1981). By contrast, the number of *degrees* awarded by US institutions of higher learning in 1914 amounted to over 48,000; by 1940, to more than 216,000 (US Bureau of the Census, 1975). With a total population equalling 35 per cent of the US population. Britain's higher educational system thus contained roughly 6 per cent as many students in the late 1930s.[33]

The small size of the higher education sector in Britain reflected the modest level of state support. This contrasted sharply with the US case, where substantial support for higher education was provided by state governments. Utilizing data from the University Grants Committee, Bernal (1939) estimated total government support of British university education in 1934–5 as equal to $9 million. Estimates from the Carnegie Foundation for the Advancement of Teaching (1976) place total government funding for US higher education in 1929–30 at $340 million. Whatever its problems with quality, the US system was in many cases better suited to provide technical education for the needs of industry. In particular, the US system placed much greater emphasis on the training of engineers.

Even in the 1950s and 1960s, Britain lagged far behind other industrialized nations in its output of engineers (Peck, 1968).[34] The experience of Nobels Industries, one of the key components of ICI, is suggestive of the problem in earlier decades. A history of the research laboratories at Nobels notes the complete absence of engineers, not only with the laboratory, but also (of equal or greater importance) within the management of the firm's manufacturing establishments:

this was to some extent the result of the decision made long before and hardened into a tradition at the end of the century, that the factory should be in the hands of chemists; but even if the attempt to employ qualified engineers had been made it must have failed, for engineers trained in the same way and to the same degree as chemists could not have been found in any number. Despite the fact that British industries were in the main engineering industries or conducted by engineers, the engineering profession had been very little concerned with full-time academic training, and indeed had a prejudice against any form of training other than that of the workshop and the evening school. (Miles, 1955, p. 58.)

It was only after World War II that Nobels established a research facility devoted primarily to engineering research on manufacturing processes.[35]

Compounding the problems of scarcity, the training of engineers in Britain tended to reinforce, rather than bridge, the barriers between science and industrial practice. As Miles's (1955) statement makes clear, the dominant form of British engineering education well into the twentieth century was a combination of night school and apprenticeship, both of which were conducted outside the major research universities. This system facilitated vertical mobility between the skilled trades and professional engineering, but at the cost of perpetuating the gap between the universities and the engineering profession:

The idea of 'vertical mobility' has always been dear to British engineers and industrialists, and the scheme of graded apprenticeship with supplementary evening classes in local technical schools is a ladder up which a large proportion of the ablest engineers have climbed to responsibility. The universities supply only a fraction, probably between one-tenth and one-fifth, of the higher technical personnel and are constantly pressed to keep their instruction on the highest scientific level. (Wickenden, 1929, p. 140.)[36]

Within the United States, engineers functioned as critical links between advanced scientific research and industrial practice. An additional important function of the US engineer was the integration of managerial and technical skills. US engineering education was far more heavily concerned with managerial instruction than was the case in Britain (or, indeed, in Europe).[37] The engineer–manager, examples of which include Kettering and Sloan of General Motors and Pierre Du Pont, played a major role in the integration of industrial research with the business practices of the US firm.[38]

A major factor in the close links between US higher education and industrial research was the state university, supported by local legislatures and founded with federal support (through the 1862 Morrill Act). In many cases, the university established departments to provide industry with applied engineering skills and expertise, as had been done previously with agricultural extension and research services. Examples include the Bureau of Industrial Research at the University of Washington, founded in 1916, and the Industrial Research Department at the University of Oklahoma, founded in 1916 (Thackray, 1982). These organizations functioned as well to train engineers and, increasingly, PhDs in chemistry or physics, for industrial research positions. Public funds for the support of higher education in the United States were supplemented by the grants of the large private foundations that grew rapidly in the early twentieth century. Much of the funding from such groups as the Rockefeller Foundation was intended to bolster the research links between university and industry. In Britain, co-operation between academia and industry was more informal, less widespread, and received much less public or private financial support.

The higher education complex in the United States also played a much more important role in training managers than did the British system. The US manager was more likely to have received a university degree than his or her British counterpart (Erickson, 1959; Chandler, 1977). Moreover, the level of technical training and expertise of US managers was in many cases well above that of British management personnel, who tended to be arts majors when they received any post-secondary education. Coleman (1973) suggests that the technical background of top-level British managers actually declined during 1900–50, a period during which the proportion of this group trained in either the public schools or the ancient universities increased sharply. In neither of these training grounds of the British business elite were future managers given a strong background in management techniques or the technological basis of modern manufacturing industry.

The lack of demand for professionally and technically trained British managers reflects not only the persistence of family or owner control of British manufacturing well into the 1940s, but also the absence of an extensive middle management hierarchy. It was the growth of middle management, in response to the increasing size and range of functions performed by the US manufacturing firm, as well as the shift of control to managers, that created a demand for professional management education in the United States. The failure of the British higher education system to develop a stronger technical and professional management training capacity, then, cannot be separated from the delayed and incomplete nature of the reorganization of British manufacturing firms.

The Role of Government

British government policy had indirect and direct impacts on research activity. Government policy reinforced the fragmented structure of the older industries, inhibiting the emergence of large firms that would have been better equipped to establish in-house research facilities. The government also attempted to compensate for the shortcomings of industrial research by promoting extramural research facilities. These facilities, however, proved to be largely ineffectual.

As international competitive pressure intensified during the late nineteenth century, small family firms, particularly those in the older industries, frequently sought refuge in restrictive agreements. Firms that sought to regulate industry output and pricing decisions faced minimal legal sanctions. This mode of market regulation represented a seemingly viable alternative to the development of unified corporate organizations.[39] Even for the pre-World War I period there are detailed accounts of price and output agreements among firms (Macrosty, 1907). These cartels and trade associations, however, had difficulty achieving stability during the era of free trade and British predominance in world markets. But in the 1920s and 1930s, trade association agreements came to cover much of the manufacturing sector (Lucas, 1937), aided in part by government policies of rationalization and protectionism which cemented anti-competitive organization. One result of this increasing cartelization was the discouragement of interfirm competition based on R & D.[40]

By contrast, in the United States such trade associations were of considerable importance only in the late nineteenth century, prior to the passage of the Sherman Antitrust Act (Galambos, 1966).[41] The increasingly stringent application of antitrust law reduced the feasibility and effectiveness of such agreements. Faced with the dubious legality of informal or formal price-fixing and market-sharing agreements, some firms resorted to mergers.[42] They created (with the aid of the rapidly expanding New York financial community) entirely new firms that effectively substituted intrafirm for interfirm means of control of prices, markets, and the organization of research.

There was no lack of awareness during the early twentieth century of the extent to which British industry lagged behind German and US practice in the exploitation of new technologies and in the development of new institutional mechanisms to promote innovation. Popular and official discussion of foreign (especially German) competition reached a local peak of sorts immediately prior to the outbreak of World War I. The extent of British dependence on foreign sources of supply for various critical chemical and optical products became excruciatingly clear in August of 1914:

The outbreak of war found us unable to produce at home many essential materials and articles. We were making less than a dozen kinds of optical glass out of over a hundred made by our enemies. We could hardly make a tithe of the various dyestuffs needed for our textile industries with an annual ouput of over £250,000,000. We were dependent on Germany for magnetos, countless drugs and pharmaceutical products, even for the tungsten used in our great steel works and for the zinc smelted from the ores which our own empire produced. (Advisory Council to the Committee for Scientific and Industrial Research, 1916, p. 8.)

The response of the British government to the supply crisis in technologically sophisticated materiel took several forms. A state-owned corporation, British Dyestuffs, was established to expand the production of synthetic dyestuffs and intermediates. This new corporation proved to be a mixed success. British Dyestuffs was forced by events (notably the 1915 shell crisis) to devote much of its effort to the production of explosives. It remained for two private firms. British Alizarine and Levinsteins Ltd, to produce most of the synthetic dyes for the war effort. British Dyestuffs did establish a research department; however, the in-house technical staff of the firm devoted the majority of its efforts to process engineering and improvement (concerned primarily with the manufacture of explosives), while

The research department was intended to work through 'colonies' in universities, where a number of professors of chemistry (W. H. Perkin at Oxford, A. G. Perkin at Leeds, Pope at Cambridge, Robinson at Liverpool) were each to have a few chemists 'at the rate of approximately £200 a year plus the university fees'. W. H. Perkin was to have a general oversight of this widespread exercise in devolution, but as late as October 1917 nothing much had come of it and apparently nothing ever did. (Reader, 1970, p. 275.)

Rather than encouraging research within the firm, government policy promoted a reliance by British Dyestuffs on external research organizations. British Dyestuffs failed to prosper after the war, despite the imposition of a prohibitive tariff on dye imports. In 1926 it was merged with Brunner Mond, Nobels, and United Alkali to form Imperial Chemical Industries (ICI).

The second major wartime policy initiative in industrial research was the establishment of the Department of Scientific and Industrial Research (DSIR). The Department assumed responsibility for the control of such major civilian governmental research establishments as the National Physical Laboratory, but a new policy associated with its establishment was the industrial research associations. Research associations (RAs) were and are co-operative research organizations that firms within a given industry are free to join. A central concern in the discussions leading to the RA scheme was the ability of co-operative research to function as a substitute for the in-house research facilities that were felt to be lacking within British industry at the time:

One of the principal impediments to the efficient organisation of industrial research was the small scale on which much of British industry operated. The investigation, for instance, of the fundamental properties of cotton fibres was outside the reach of all except the very large firms, and even in the latter management might only be prepared to spend a very small amount on it. . . . The implications were that, even apart from the traditional attitudes of British management to research, a certain minimum turnover was required before a firm could support a research department or even, at the lowest level of indivisibility, a research worker. (Johnson, 1973, p. 19.)

First established in 1916, the RAs were to be funded jointly by government and industry for a five-year period. At the end of this time, it was expected that industry support would be sufficient.[43]

The research association scheme initially appeared to be a considerable success. Over the first five years of the programme (1918–23), 24 RAs were established in industries ranging from woollen textiles to laundering. However, the groundswell of industry financial support failed to materialize. By 1923, when state aid was supposed to cease, only one RA, devoted to research on portland cement, was able to continue on the basis of industry support alone. For the remaining associations, the commitment of public funds was renewed for an additional five years. However, the size of this public grant was expected to shrink over the course of this period.

The 1920s were a difficult period for the RAs. A number of the associations failed as their income declined and business support dwindled. The total income of the RAs declined from roughly £224,000 in 1923 to £177,000 in 1928 (Johnson, 1973). By the end of the second five-year trial in 1928, it was clear that the RAs would collapse without additional public support. Financial aid was increased for a period ending in the early 1930s, when the budgetary crisis forced major reductions.[44] According to Hill (1947), 'In 1933 the average expenditure of the associations was only £14,500 a year and this average included a few very large associations so that the average for thirteen associations was less than £7,000 a year' (p. 45). The DSIR significantly increased its expenditures in support of the RAs through the rearmament years of the late 1930s. During and after World War II, state support of the co-operative research scheme expanded dramatically, and the future of the RAs was assured.

Despite the long history of the RAs, their impact on the innovative performance of British manufacturing was rather modest. In 1929 the Balfour Committee remarked on 'the admittedly inadequate extent to which the results [of the RAs' research work] have been utilized up to the present by British industries' (Committee on Industry and Trade, 1929, p. 54). The Committee argued that 'At present, it is too often the case that the information, compiled with great skill and labour, simply runs to waste for want of a properly equipped "receiving mechanism" within the works . . .' (p. 215). With this statement, the Committee accurately diagnosed one of the central difficulties of the RA scheme. The attempt to develop co-operative or extramural research institutions as substitutes for in-house research facilities foundered on the client firms' lack of enough in-house technical expertise to utilize the results effectively. Without such a 'receiving mechanism', the firm was less likely to benefit from the activities of the research associations.[45]

In particular, the RAs failed to do more to offset the effects of the structural legacy of small firms. Focusing on the supply of research and development rather than on the utilization of R & D results, the RAs have functioned largely as a complement to the established in-house research organizations of larger firms (Johnson, 1973).

The research associations, by far the most thorough and direct policy response by the British government to the perceived technical shortcomings of manufacturing, essentially became a more formalized version of the inter-firm co-operation that characterized the behaviour of British industrial firms in other areas. They were an extension of the organizational structure typified by the consulting engineer, rather than a significant change in the technological organization or foundations of British industry.

In general, the ineffectual or deleterious impact of British government policy on industrial research is remarkable, in view of the frequency and unanimity with which a specific set of factors was diagnosed as central to the lack of research activity. What was the basis for this reluctance on the part of the British government to move more forcefully in pursuit of the recommendations of any of the numerous studies that had been done on the technical and structural shortcomings of British industry? The preservation of the *laissez-faire* tradition and the weakness of rationalization policies may have been the result of the desire by a government dominated by Liberals or Conservatives to preserve the existing structure of industry ownership, rather than risk more fundamental upheavals through government intervention that might culminate in rationalization.[46]

Rather than addressing the underlying causes of lagging technical performance and underinvestment in R & D by British industry, the British government employed public funds to support industrial research directly, in the research associations. The RAs were an industrial policy that would disturb none of the institutions that hampered industrial research and innovation within British industry.[47] In view of the great obstacles to the development of a more progressive industrial and educational system, a far more inventive set of government policies would have been necessary to improve industrial research and innovative performance in British industry. During and after the period 1900–50, such policy initiatives were absent.

Conclusion

Industrial research is well-suited to historical analysis within an institutional framework for several reasons. The effects of research activity on industry and firm performance tend to be revealed in a dynamic context, e.g. in growth or productivity increases over time. Such issues of dynamic efficiency typically are not captured in analyses of static technical or allocative efficiency in British industry (McCloskey, 1973; Sandberg, 1974). The development and effectiveness of industrial research are sensitive to the institutional context. It is not simply the appropriability of the knowledge produced, but the way in which the research process is organized, that may critically affect the level and effectiveness of the research that is performed within a firm, industry, or nation. The in-house industrial research laboratory is in essence an organizational innovation, a component of firm structure that necessitates a wide range of complementary and supporting institutional innovations. Analysis of the development over time of industrial research requires a focus on institutional structure and development over time.

During the first half of the twentieth century, the British manufacturing sector failed to invest in industrial research as heavily as did US manufacturing. The gap between US and British levels of industrial research narrowed somewhat between the 1930s and 1950s, but remained substantial. The low level of industrial research within British manufacturing, as well as the large portion of such research that was not performed within manufacturing firms, both reflected the comparatively slow emergence of the modern, large corporate enterprise as a vehicle for co-ordinating economic activity. In the United States, on the other hand, many manufacturing firms actively pursued a substantial expansion in the range of products and functions included within their boundaries. The development of industrial research within the firm's boundaries was a central component of this reorganization of the US firm.

The failure of the British firm to undergo such a reorganization and expansion in its functions prior to 1950 is a critical element in explaining the substantially higher levels of research activity in US manufacturing. In industrial research, as in other activities, the British firm remained dependent on the market, rather than intrafirm organization, for the control and organization of transactions. The delayed managerial revolution within British industry was associated with a *laissez-faire* government policy environment, a lack of involvement of financial institutions in the management and reorganization of British firms, and the persistence of family control of British firms. As the structure of the British firm and manufacturing sector changed dramatically in the 1940–60 period, the level of industrial research activity within British industry grew, but the gap between US and British R & D investment remained large.

Firm structure was not the sole factor influencing the low level of industrial research within Britain. The educational system, particularly higher education, remained small, owing in part to low levels of financial support from the government for both higher and secondary education. The training of engineers in particular was deficient. The lack of engineers in research and management impaired the effectiveness of existing industrial research activity, and may have constrained its expansion, particularly that of applied research and development.[48] The small supply of engineers, and their predominantly non-academic training, perpetuated the divorce of British laboratory science from British technological practice. The former was of extremely high quality, while the latter often was severely deficient.

In addition to its lower level, the effectiveness of the industrial research that did exist within Britain was impaired by its frequent organization on a contractual, interfirm basis. The consulting engineer and the research associations were means of organizing research activity that did not allow for the exploitation of the advantages resulting from the combination of research and other activities within a single firm.

The structural development of the British firm, the lack of educational support for industrial research, and the growth of the research associations all were heavily influenced by government policy, which was conservative in design and modest in impact. Despite frequent and perceptive critical analyses of the technical performance of British industry, major policy shifts aimed at improving such performance were lacking. In the United States, by contrast, government policy-makers during this period paid little heed to the technological development of industry. However, the fundamental factors influencing the structure of industry and the supply of technical personnel were either considered to be beyond the direct control of the federal government, or were already established to such an extent that an activist policy to encourage the development of industrial research was not needed.

The failure of British industrial research to reach levels comparable with those of US manufacturing thus was influenced by the institutional legacy of an earlier era of industrial activity and organization, as well as by the failure of government policy to change this institutional environment. Within the United States, no direct government role in the control or funding of industrial research prior to World War II was necessary: private firms conducted these activities. Within Britain, the deficiencies of private-sector activity spurred a more directly interventionist government policy. Both during and after the period examined in this paper, however, the British government's role in funding and directing industrial research activity has been remarkably unsuccessful.

Notes

[1]Pavitt (1980) argues that 'British industrial inefficiency is reflected in low labour productivity and low efficiency of investment, both of which could be symptoms of lack of technical innovation in production processes. There are also disquieting but revealing features in the income and price elasticities of demand for British manufacturing exports and imports. The rest of the world's income elasticity of demand has been lower than the British income elasticity of demand for the rest of the world's manufacturing exports' (p. 2).

[2]See Mansfield (1968) and Terleckyj (1974) for empirical evidence on the links between industry and firm productivity growth and R & D activity. Keesing (1967)

concluded that 'There turns out to be a powerful correlation between the intensity of R & D activities in American industries and their export performance. . . . R & D "explain" competitive trading success in manufacturing industries considerably better than any other variables tested' (p. 45). Gruber, Mehta, and Vernon (1967) also support the existence of this linkage between export performance, and argue that it applies as well to Britain and West Germany during the postwar period.

[3]Concerning the structure of British export trade, Lewis (1949) noted that 'The largest category of British exports was in those commodities expanding least in world trade. The leader *par excellence* in world trade was the United States; only 17.1 per cent of her manufactures exports were in the lowest category [in terms of growth in world trade during 1913–29] compared with Britain's 42.1 per cent, and 28.6 per cent were in highest category, compared with Britain's 4.3 per cent. Germany also was well ahead' (p. 79). See also Matthews *et al*. (1982), where it is noted that 'The long-run fall in the proportion of British manufactures exported . . . was greater than the fall in the proportion of British GDP exported [during 1899–1973]. . . .' (p. 437).

[4]In Germany antitrust policy was also weak, while industrial research in many industries was substantial. However, other explanatory factors, notably the educational system and firm structure, contrasted sharply with conditions in Britain. Moreover, the organization of industrial research is as important as the level of R & D investment in affecting firm performance. German firms appear to have been more successful at organizing and managing industrial research within the firm, by comparison with British enterprises.

[5]For example, there have been a number of proposals in the past five years for the establishment within the United States of publicly funded co-operative industrial research enterprises. The Stevenson-Wydler Technology Innovation Act of 1980 authorized the establishment of 'centers of generic technology' (COGENTs), intended to conduct research on a co-operative basis in selected industries. The COGENT programme was not funded by the Reagan administration. Other recent efforts include the National Science Foundation's experiment in industry–university co-operation research centres. For a discussion of the theoretical basis and results of some of these programmes, see Mowery (1983c).

[6]Freeman (1962) stated that 'In terms of real expenditure per employee, research was about three times as big in the United States as in Britain in 1959. . . . In terms of qualified manpower, for every 1,000 workers employed in American manufacturing, there were 13 qualified scientists and engineers on research work, and for every 1,000 British workers there were five. . . .' (p. 24).

[7]Both Freeman and Sanderson found electrical machinery, chemicals, and petroleum products to be among the most research-intensive industries in both the United States and Britain during the 1930s and 1950s. Freeman concluded in addition that the most research-intensive industries in his analysis (including aircraft, chemicals, electrical and non-electrical machinery, and instruments) accounted for a larger percentage of net manufacturing output in Britain (32 per cent in 1935 and 45 per cent in 1958) than in the United States (28 and 40 per cent in 1935 and 1958, respectively). One implication of the data on industry mix in Britain is that the phenomenon of 'overcommitment' in the structure of British manufacturing, if it ever did exist, was not a significant factor by the mid-1930s in explaining either sluggish economic performance or the poor technical record of British manufacturing. Richardson (1962, 1965) presents the overcommitment argument, arguing that the

British economy was too heavily committed to the declining export staples, e.g. coal, steel, and textiles, during the interwar period. Richardson has been criticized in Dowie (1968), Alford (1972), and Buxton (1975).

[8]Fragmentary and qualitative evidence suggests that British firms may have been more research-intensive than manufacturing firms on the Continent. The evidence does not permit a serious evaluation of this argument. In industries such as chemicals and electrical machinery, German firms almost certainly invested more in research within the firm, relative to their size, than did British firms.

[9]Data on the identity of the 200 largest firms in British manufacturing were compiled from various sources by Alfred Chandler and associates, while data on the existence of in-house research facilities were taken from a 1936 survey (Association of Scientific Workers, 1936). Similar data for the 200 largest firms in US manufacturing in 1930 and 1948 were assembled by Chandler, and data on research employment among these firms were extracted from the National Research Council surveys of industrial research for 1933 and 1946.

[10]The tobit technique was employed in estimating the relationship between firm size (measured in assets) and research activity (measured as employment of research scientists and engineers). Tobit analysis was employed because of the presence within the sample of a significant number of firms without research laboratories (i.e., observations for which the dependent variable was zero). For a discussion of tobit analysis in this situation, see Goldberger (1964).

[11]'. . . only one half of the top fifty firms of 1919 are still in the group of the largest firms twelve years later in 1930' (Hannah, 1976, p. 117). This rate of turnover substantially exceeds turnover among large US manufacturing firms during this period. By the 1948–68 period, however, Hannah notes that the rate of turnover among large British firms had declined markedly (1976, p. 167).

[12]Regressing the percentage change in total factor productivity during 1921–46 for 15 two-digit SICs (taken from Kendrick, 1961) on research intensity (RI, defined as scientific research professionals per 1,000 wage earners in each SIC—from Mowery, 1981), the ratio of wages to value added less wages ($WVAW$, a proxy for the labor–capital ratio), and the average value added per establishment ($SIZE$), the following results were obtained:

C	RI	$WVAW$	$SIZE$	F	R^2
123.4	19.94	−0.299	0.118	12.1	0.77
(26.6)	(6.22)	(0.346)	(0.120)		

Ordinary least squares were used; standard errors are given in parentheses.

[13]Kendrick (1961, p. 136) concluded that total factor productivity in US manufacturing increased at an average annual rate of 5.3 per cent during 1919–29, and 1.9 per cent during 1929–37. Matthews *et al.* (1982, p. 229) estimate that total factor productivity in British manufacturing grew at an average annual rate of 1.9 per cent during 1924–37. While some tendency for British productivity growth to catch up with that of US manufacturing thus appears for the 1930s (possibly owing to the severe impact of the Great Depression on output growth in the United States), these estimates are broadly consistent with those of Rostas in pointing to a large gap in productivity performance during the 1920s.

[14]An example of the importance for technical change of the incorporation of several functions within the firm is Courtaulds' exploitation of the technology for rayon

production in the early 1900s. As Coleman (1969) points out, the fact that the firm was a textile, as well as an aspiring rayon yarn, producer was of 'considerable help in refining and exploiting the rayon production technology: 'Some part of Bocking's [the existing textile plant] contribution was essentially negative in nature: demonstrating what could not be done with viscose yarn, indicating either general limitations or present faults which called for improvement. Bocking's work helped the salesmen of Coventry's [the new rayon yarn plant] yarn; it thus contributed indirectly to the firm's total profits far more than its own sales of viscose-using fabric contributed directly to those profits. . . . That within a dozen years of its buying the viscose patent rights the company had emerged as the most successful of all viscose yarn producers undoubtedly owed a great deal to its existing textile business' (p. 66).

[15]As in-house research grew rapidly within US manufacturing during 1900–40, the proportion of total industrial research employment accounted for by independent contract research organizations declined from 15 per cent in 1921 to 7 per cent in 1946 (Mowery, 1983b). By 1940 over 60 per cent of the clients of such independent research organizations as the Mellon Institute had in-house research facilities, and contract research was operating primarily as a complement to, rather than as a substitute for, in-house research.

[16]Chandler (1977) noted that 'where the manufacturer became the coordinator, his firm grew to great size, and the decisions in his industry concerning current production and distribution and the allocation of resources for future production and distribution became concentrated in the hands of a small number of managers. This centralization of decision-making, and with it economic power, was of particular importance because it occurred in industries central to the growth and well-being of the economy' (p. 372).

[17]See Mowery (1983a). Note, however, that, while the largest firms were leaders in industrial research in the early years, they were no more research-intensive, relative to their size, during 1921–46 than during the later postwar period.

[18]Salter and Weinhold (1980) state that, 'While the merger wave of the 1920s was clearly as large or larger in absolute terms than the 1890–1904 wave, its relative impact was much less. In total, it apparently involved less than 10 per cent of the economy's assets rather than the former wave's over 15 per cent. Furthermore, in most industries, mergers embraced only a small proportion of the competing firms. Only in the food processing, metals, and chemicals sectors was industry structure substantially altered' (p. 4).

[19]'Within his own business he [Lever] salved his Victorian economic conscience by the application of competitive principles; all associated companies should compete strongly with Lever Brothers in every line . . .' (p. 273).

[20]Despite these reforms, Andrews and Brunner noted that, as of 1950, the entire central sales and administrative staff of the company amounted to 150 persons, out of a total employment of slightly more than 28,000.

[21]Reader (1975) goes on to argue that ICI, in sharp contrast to Du Pont, failed to master the integration of product diversification with its internal structure until the late 1950s:

The weakness of the organization, right through the period covered in this volume, was that no really satisfactory way was ever found of co-ordinating activities in the chemical industry unprovided for in the original structure of the business. That was designed in 1926 for the kind of work thought to be in prospect for the thirties. When that prediction turned out wrong no attempt seems to have been made to appraise the work of the second half of the century and to redesign the organization accordingly. Instead, the framework of 1926, patched and cobbled, was forced with increasing difficulty to serve purposes unimagined when it was set up. . . . The size of ICI and the weight of established interests in the larger Divisions, directly represented as they were on the Board, made rapid decision impossible on the creation of new Divisions, the amalgamation of old and proud ones, and the transfer away from some Divisions of activities over which they had presided from the start, in which they took some pride, and which they had run as profitable enterprises' (p.461).

[22]'. . . the sad case of the jet engine is also typical of the Metrovick–BTH relationship and of their individual characters. Starting in about 1935, they were the first two companies in the world to make the jet engine—quite independently of each other, of course. . . . AEI should have been able to build up a powerful aero-engine division, especially if Metrovick and BTH had co-operated, but they were too conservative to admit that, though risky, the jet engine had far more growth potential than their traditional products and therefore to divert resources towards jets and away from electricals' (Jones and Marriot, 1970, p. 155).

[23]'. . . the Company's Achilles Heel lay principally in the internal production organization, which consisted of a multifarious collection of small units, groups of which were engaged on kindred tasks but each independently of the other, with considerable wastage of research, development, and engineering efforts' (Baker, 1970, p. 332).

[24]Reader (1976) describes the firm as follows: 'the separate sales forces of the subsidiaries marched and counter-marched, calling on customers most of whom can have had no idea that these apparent competitors were under the same ownership. Within Metal Box and Printing Industries the duplication of effort was in theory deplored, but there was strong resistance to setting up a central sales organization. The various subsidiaries were supposed to offer each other business that they could not themselves take on, but whether much that was really worth having was offered in this way is doubtful. There was some exchange of technical information, some exchange of sales information, both rather grudging and probably less than fully frank' (pp. 40–1).

[25]The paper by Best and Humphries in this volume provides a more detailed review of this issue.

[26]'Other things being equal, therefore, the longer and more continuous industrial history of Britain should have made it easier for British firms to acquire finance without resorting to the capital markets. The evidence is sketchy, but what there is does suggest that this was in fact the case' (Davis, 1966, p. 259).

[27]

As industrial fixed capital requirements had grown steadily through the nineteenth century, banks had begun to play a major role in industrial affairs. By the middle decades of the nineteenth century, the banking system at a local level was playing a role strikingly similar to that played at the end of the nineteenth century by the German Great Banks on a national level. The unremitting increase in the size of plants demanded for efficient use of evolving technology in most links of production, however, began to outstrip the ability of most local banks to respond safely to these new requests for funds. The rash of mid-Victorian bank failures can be attributed directly to banks becoming too closely linked with local firms and over-lending as these firms attempted to expand. These failures reached a crescendo with the failure of the City of Glasgow Bank in 1878. This marked a final watershed for British banking before 1914. A point had been reached where the entire system had either to be re-organised to withstand the greater risks of steadily enlarging industrial requirements or the system had to withdraw from long-term industrial involvement. The system withdrew. After 1878, no longer would banks become willingly involved in the long-term financing of industry. (Kennedy, 1976, pp. 159–60.)

[28]The share of industry capacity accounted for by 'combined' firms, i.e. firms that carried out both weaving and spinning operations, declined substantially during 1884–1914, according to data in Tyson (1968).

[29]Byatt (1979) discusses the impact of the consulting engineer on the nascent electrical machinery and electrical supply industries late in the nineteenth century in the following terms:

It became accepted that consulting engineers should be independent of manufacturers and buyers and sellers dealt with each other at arms' length. Specifications became much more detailed. A system of guarantees and penalty clauses was introduced. Responsibility for design thus passed out of the hands of manufacturers and competition was concentrated on tender price. The position was very different in the United States and Germany, where manufacturers had much more say in the design of plant.

Although competitive tendering ensured low prices for a given plant, it reduced the extent to which small adaptations to new designs were made as a consequence of experience gained in actual working. There is a good deal of evidence to support the view that, where close contact between buyers and sellers took place, it resulted in a series of important minor improvements. This could be seen on the north-east coast, the only place in Britain where such a system was used. (Byatt, 1979, pp. 177–8.)

[30]A fuller review of this topic may be found in the paper by Wrigley in this volume.

[31]Graham (1983) provides a discussion of the relationship between academic and industrial research in the United States during and after the interwar period.

[32]Sanderson (1972a) argued that, 'If industry could be criticized for not contributing to the university as much as it ought to have done, was it also at fault in not absorbing its students? There was disturbing evidence that fault lay with the employers who were unwilling to take on more graduates. Sir William Ramsay lamented that, although the university could continue to turn out excellent chemists, yet "the demand for such men is not keeping up with the supply. Manufacturers are not as yet sufficiently alive to the necessity for employing chemists." The same was feared for engineers. The experience of the newly formed Appointments Board confirmed this, for they soon found themselves operating in the context of a vastly increased output of graduates creating an excessive supply for the rather restricted demand from industry, even in the thriving years up to the war. In 1909 "the supply of candidates with chemical and engineering qualifications exceeds the demand for persons holding such qualifications", and in 1910 chemists are still having "great difficulty" in getting into works . . .' (p. 117).

[33]The size of the higher educational system was an important 'supply-side' influence on the growth of industrial research; Beer (1959) cites the high rate of production of chemistry PhDs by German higher education in the late nineteenth century as an important influence on the growth of industrial research in the German chemicals industry. As the supply of professional chemists exceeded available academic employment opportunities, emigration or industrial research were the only alternatives open to the German graduate chemist.

[34]Peck (1968) contended that, 'As long as the major activity [within British manufacturing] was producing and selling established products, formal knowledge of

engineering was less critical than experience. However, when the introduction of new products from the laboratory becomes a major activity, the balance between formal education and experience shifts. Formal education now becomes necessary for plant managers to incorporate R & D output into production, for salesmen to communicate the values of new products, and for executives to evaluate research possibilities. . . . As the world changed to emphasize R & D, Britain's shortage of engineers became critical' (p. 453).

[35]'A more radical departure was the institution of a research engineering section. It had long been realised that explosives manufacture at Ardeer required more labour than modern practice, especially American practice, thought it necessary to employ. This conclusion had been emphasised in numerous visits made to the United States and Canada by members of both the research and manufacturing staffs. An increase of mechanisation could not be carried through without experimental construction and trial. Preliminary arrangements had therefore been made in 1939 for an engineering section to form part of the research organisation. At the end of the war a rapid enlargement of this section was undertaken' (Miles, 1955, pp. 155–6). It is significant, and consistent with Reader's portrayal of the internal structure of ICI, that, twenty years after the foundation of ICI, management of the Nobels research laboratory was still the province of the subsidiary, rather than being controlled by ICI headquarters.

[36]Floud (1978) focuses largely on the ability of this system of engineering education to respond to increasing industrial demand during the late nineteenth century, rather than considering the content and the implications for innovation of this form of engineering education, in arguing that British technical education during this period was not deficient.

[37]'From the days of Taylor on, US leadership in applying engineering methods to industrial organization and process has been unquestioned. In consequence our technical education reflects a wider spread of engineering activity than is common abroad, especially on the management side. The unity and freedom of our higher educational system have made it easier to introduce the economic sciences into education than in the compartmental systems abroad' (Wickenden, 1929, p. 258).

[38]Chandler (1962) noted the importance of the technically trained manager in US business in his discussion of the education of the managers who played a major role in the reorganization of such major corporations as General Motors and Du Pont:

Some correlation seems to exist between the education and training of the executives and their approach to organizational needs. Most of the men who showed the greatest interest in systematizing and explicit defining organizational relationships had engineering training. . . .

The significance of this correlation between education and organizational awareness is uncertain. Possibly the rigor required in working out scientific and engineering problems led these men to approach management needs in somewhat the same way. Also, in these years, engineers were beginning to consider the use of men in working the machines and not just the mechanics of the machines themselves.

In any case the connection between the engineering profession and the rationalizing and systematizing of industrial administration has always been close. (Chandler, 1962, p. 317.)

[39]Hannah (1980) states that 'In important respects—particularly in coordinating sales policies and securing monopolistic control over prices—cartels were an alternative to merger that was open to European entrepreneurs but closed to their counter-

parts in the United States. Firms that preferred to maintain a single-unit structure in Britain were therefore free to do so while, at the same time, reducing competition by joining a cartel; in the 1930s and during World War II, in fact, these arrangements were actively encouraged by the government. US industrialists like Gerald [*sic*] Swope, the dynamic president of the American General Electric Company, accustomed to the antitrust tradition, were advised by bankers in Britain that they need not create large, centralized corporations through mergers for their European operations; market competition could be regulated through agreement with other firms, and there was thus no need to acquire them' (p. 67).

[40]Reader (1979) notes that 'It was settled policy in ICI to avoid competition with customers or suppliers, which meant, in effect, avoiding competition with virtually every manufacturing company of any importance in the United Kingdom. For many years, accordingly, ICI kept clear of the range of chemical products associated with industrial alcohol, which were supplied by the Distillers' Company Ltd and which were of considerable importance in the fields of organic activity opening up in the late 1920s and early 1930s. Similarly, in order to avoid giving offense to Courtaulds, important customers for caustic soda, ICI, unlike Du Pont, kept well clear of rayon and cellophane' (p. 174).

[41]'This type of dinner-club association was rather common throughout US industry during the latter part of the nineteenth century. Although detailed information of other industries is lacking, this sort of association seems to have developed in the iron and steel, petroleum, and lumber industries—to mention only a few. Where high fixed costs or other characteristics of the industry intensified competition, the dinner-club associations quickly surrendered the economic function of stabilizing prices to tighter and more effective forms of combination; then the associations became merely adjuncts to the stability-oriented trusts or giant corporations' (Galambos, 1966, p. 35).

[42]This argument is stressed in Stigler (1950). The Supreme Court ruled in the Trans-Missouri Association case in 1898 and the Addyston Pipe Case in 1899 that the Sherman Act outlawed all agreements among firms on prices or market-sharing. According to Thorelli (1954), a total of 84 mergers occurred during 1890–7, followed by 24 in 1898, 105 in 1899, and a total of 83 during 1900–02. The evidence is circumstantial, but still strong, in support of the argument that the Supreme Court decisions had an impact on merger activity. See also Chandler (1977, pp. 331–6).

[43]'The government contribution will be made in the anticipation that when the new organisations are fairly launched on their career the need for direct state assistance will disappear, and British industry will be as self-sufficient in the field of industrial research as it has proved itself to be in other spheres of work' (DSIR, 1917, p. 49).

[44]Increased subventions for the research associations were urged by the Balfour Committee, which requested 'that there should be no relaxation or curtailment of the efforts of the Department of Scientific and Industrial Research, and no withdrawal of financial support on the part of the Government' (Committee Industry and Trade, 1929, p. 219).

[45]Albu's description (1980) of the research association in marine engineering is illustrative: 'By the time of the last war Parsons [marine engine and turbine] designs had become conservative. . . . The anxiety of the Admiralty led to the setting up of the Parsons and Marine Turbine Research and Development Association (PAMA-TRADA) in 1944; but although it had a well-staffed research department the marine

engine builders, most of whom were adjacent to the shipyards, were too small to be able to support it, and lacked the level of technical management to be interested in the results of research. The Association declined into a licensing organization for Parsons designs . . .' (p. 175).

[46]Tolliday has suggested that one reason for the character of British rationalization policies in the 1930s was the desire (especially on the part of the Bank of England) to forestall any move on the part of the government towards nationalization. See Tolliday (1979, p. 276).

[47]There are strong similarities between the interwar and postwar periods in the structure of British public policy towards R & D. During the postwar period, a high level of government spending on R & D has been overwhelmingly concentrated (or overcommitted—see Peck, 1968) in two sectors, nuclear energy and aircraft, that are both isolated from the rest of the British economy, and have important military applications. This policy has worked to reduce the resources (both financial and human) available for R & D elsewhere in the economy.

[48]Cf. the comment by Miles (1955) concerning the ICI research establishment.

Bibliography

Abramovitz, M. (1956). *Resource and Output Trends in the United States Since 1870*. New York: National Bureau of Economic Research.

Advisory Council to the Committee on Scientific and Industrial Research (1916). *Report*. London: HMSO.

Albu, A. (1980). 'Merchant Shipbuilding and Marine Engineering'. In *Technical Innovation and British Economic Performance*, ed. K. Pavitt. London: Macmillan.

Aldcroft, D. H. (1975). 'Investment in and Utilization of Manpower: Great Britain and Her Rivals, 1870–1914'. In *Great Britain and Her World*, ed. B. M. Ratcliffe. London: Longmans.

Alford, B. W. E. (1972). *Depression and Recovery? British Economic Growth 1918–1939*. London: Macmillan.

Allen, G. C. (1979). *British Industry and Economic Policy*. London: Macmillan.

da C. Andrade, E. N. (1946). *Industrial Research: 1946*. London: Todd.

Andrews, P. W. S., and E. Brunner (1951). *Capital Development in Iron and Steel*. Oxford: Basil Blackwell.

Association of Scientific Workers (1936). *Industrial Research Laboratories*. London: George Allen & Unwin.

Baker, W. J. (1970). *A History of the Marconi Company*. London: Methuen.

Beer, J. H. (1959). *The Emergence of the German Dye Industry*. Urbana: University of Illinois Press.

Bernal, J. D. (1939). *The Social Function of Science*. London: Routledge & Kegan Paul.

Briggs, A. (1981). 'Social History 1900–1945'. In *The Economic History of Britain Since 1700*, Volume 2, *1860 to the 1970s*, ed. R. Floud and D. McCloskey. Cambridge University Press.

Brock, G. W. (1981). *The Telecommunications Industry*. Cambridge, Mass.: Harvard University Press.

Buxton, N. K. (1975). 'The Role of the "New Industries" in Britain During the 1930s: A Reinterpretation'. *Business History Review*, 49, 312–36.

Byatt, I. C. R. (1979). *The British Electrical Industry 1875–1914*. Oxford University Press.

Carnegie Foundation for the Advancement of Teaching (1976). *The States and Higher Education*. San Francisco: Jossey-Bass.

Chandler, A. D. Jr (1962). *Strategy and Structure*. Cambridge, Mass.: Massachusetts Institute of Technology Press.

Chandler, A. D. Jr (1976). 'The Development of Modern Management Structures in the US and UK'. In *Management Strategy and Business Development*, ed. L. Hannah. London: Macmillan.

Chandler, A. D. Jr (1977). *The Visible Hand*. Cambridge, Mass.: Harvard University Press.

Chandler, A. D. Jr (1980). 'The Growth of the Transnational Industrial Firm in the United States and the United Kingdom: A Comparative Analysis'. *Economic History Review*, 33, 396–410.

Cohen, W. M., and Mowery, D. C. (1984). 'Firm Heterogeneity and R & D: An Agenda for Research'. In *Strategic Management of Industrial R & D*, ed. M. Crow, B. Bozeman, and A. Link. Lexington, Mass.: D. C. Heath.

Coleman, D. C. (1969). *Courtaulds: An Economic and Social History*, Volume 2, *Rayon*. Oxford University Press.

Coleman, D. C. (1973). 'Gentlemen and Players'. *Economic History Review*, 26, 92–116.

Collins, N. R., and L. E. Preston (1961). 'The Size Structure of the Largest Industrial Firms, 1909–1938'. *American Economic Review*, 51, 986–1011.

Committee on Commercial and Industrial Policy After the War (1918). *Final Report*. London: HMSO.

Committee on Finance and Industry (1931). *Report*. London: HMSO.

Committee on Industry and Trade (1927). *Factors in Industrial and Commercial Efficiency*. London: HMSO.

Committee on Industry and Trade (1928). *Factors in Industrial and Commercial Efficiency*. London: HMSO.

Committee on Industry and Trade (1929). *Final Report*. London: HMSO.

Condit, K. H. (1928). 'Economic Aspects of Standardization'. *Annals of the American Academy of Political and Social Science*, 137, 39–42.

Davis, L. E. (1966). 'The Capital Markets and Industrial Concentration: The US and the UK, A Comparative Study'. *Economic History Review*, 19, 255–72.

Davis, L. E., and D. J. Kevles (1974). 'The National Research Fund: A Case Study in the Industrial Support of Science'. *Minerva*, 12, 207–20.

Denison, E. F. (1967). *Why Growth Rates Differ: Postwar Experience in Nine Western Countries*. Washington, DC: Brookings Institution.

Denison, E. F. (1968). 'Economic Growth'. In *Britain's Economic Prospects*, ed. R. E. Caves. Washington, DC: Brookings Institution.

Denison, E. F. (1974). *Accounting for United States Economic Growth 1929–69*. Washington, DC: Brookings Institution.

Department of Scientific and Industrial Research (1917). *Report*. London: HMSO.

Dowie, J. A. (1968). 'Growth in the Inter-War Period: Some More Arithmetic'. *Economic History Review*, 21, 93–112.

Edwards, R. C. (1975). 'Stages in Corporate Stability and the Risks of Corporate Failure'. *Journal of Economic History*, 35, 428–57.

Eichengreen, B. J. (1981). *Sterling and the Tariff*, Princeton Studies in International Finance no. 48. Princeton University Press.

Erickson, C. (1959). *British Industrialists: Steel and Hosiery 1850–1950*. Cambridge University Press.

Federation of British Industries (1943). *Industry and Research*. London: Federation of British Industries.

Federation of British Industries (1951). *Industrial Research in Manufacturing Industry, 1950–51*. London: Federation of British Industries.

Floud, R. (1978). 'Technical Education Performance: Engineering in the Late Nineteenth Century'. Unpublished paper.

Freeman, C. (1962). 'Research and Development: A Comparison Between British and American Industry'. *National Institute Economic Review*, 20, 21–39.

Freeman, C. (1980). 'Government Policy'. In *Technical Innovation and British Economic Performance*, ed. K. Pavitt. London: Macmillan.

Galambos, L. (1966). *Competition and Cooperation*. Baltimore: Johns Hopkins University Press.

Goldberger, A. S. (1964). *Econometric Theory*. New York: John Wiley.

Graham, M. B. W. (1983). 'Industrial Research in the Age of Big Science'. Presented at the meetings of the Society for the History of Technology, Washington, DC, 22 October 1983.

Gruber, W., D. Mehta, and R. Vernon (1967). 'The R & D Factor in International Trade and International Investment of United States Industries'. *Journal of Political Economy*, 75, 20–37.

Hannah, L. (1974a). 'Mergers in British Manufacturing Industry, 1880–1918'. *Oxford Economic Papers*, 26, 1–20.

Hannah, L. (1974b). 'Managerial Innovation and the Rise of the Large-scale Company in Great Britain'. *Economic History Review*, 27, 252–71.

Hannah, L. (1976). *The Rise of the Corporate Economy*. London: Methuen.

Hannah, L. (1980). 'Visible and Invisible Hands in Great Britain'. In *Managerial Hierarchies*, ed. A. D. Chandler Jr and H. Daems. Cambridge, Mass.: Harvard University Press.

Hart, P. E., and S.J. Prais (1956). 'The Analysis of Business Concentration: A Statistical Note'. *Journal of the Royal Statistical Society*, ser. A, 119, 150–91.

Hill, D. W. (1947). *Co-operative Research in Industry*. London: Hutchinson.

Jenkins, R. W. (1975). *Images and Enterprise*. Baltimore: Johns Hopkins University Press.

Johnson, P. S. (1973). *Co-operative Research in Industry*. New York: John Wiley.

Jones, R., and O. Marriot (1970). *Anatomy of A Merger: A History of GEC, AEI, and English Electric*. London: Jonathan Cape.

Kaplan, A. D. H. (1964). *Big Business in a Competitive System*. Washington, DC: Brookings Institution.

Keesing, D. B. (1967). 'The Impact of Research and Development on United States Trade'. *Journal of Political Economy*, 75, 38–48.

Kendrick, J. W. (1961). *Productivity Trends in the United States*. Princeton University Press, for the National Bureau of Economic Research.

Kennedy, W. P. (1976). 'Institutional Response to Economic Growth: Capital Markets in Britain to 1914'. In *Management Strategy and Business Development*, ed. L. Hannah. London: Macmillan.

Kirby, M. W. (1973). 'The Control of Competition in the British Coal Mining Industry in the Thirties'. *Economic History Review*, 26, 273–84.

Lazonick, W. (1981). 'Factor Costs and the Diffusion of Ring Spinning in Britain Prior to World War I'. *Quarterly Journal of Economics*, 96, 89–109.

Lazonick, W. (1983). 'Industrial Organization and Technological Change: The Decline of the British Cotton Industry'. *Business History Review*, 57, 195–236.

Lewis. W. A. (1949). *Economic Survey, 1919–1939*. London: George Allen & Unwin.

Lucas, A. F. (1937). *Industrial Reconstruction and the Control of Competition*. London: Longmans.

Macrosty, H. W. (1907). *The Trust Movement in British Industry*. London: Longmans Green.

Mansfield, E. (1968). *The Economics of Technological Change*. New York: W. W. Norton.

Matthews, R. C. O., C. H. Feinstein, and J. C. Odling-Smee (1982). *British Economic Growth 1856–1973*. Stanford University Press.

McCloskey, D. N. (1973). *Economic Maturity and Entrepreneurial Decline: British Iron and Steel 1870–1913*. Cambridge, Mass.: Harvard University Press.

Miles, F. D. (1955). *A History of Research in the Nobel Division of ICI*. London: Imperial Chemical Industries.

Mowery, D. C. (1981). 'The Emergence and Growth of Industrial Research in American Manufacturing, 1899–1945'. Unpublished PhD dissertation, Stanford University.

Mowery, D. C. (1983a). 'Industrial Research and Firm Size, Survival, and Growth in American Manufacturing, 1921–46: An Assessment'. *Journal of Economic History*, 43, 953–80.

Mowery, D. C. (1983b). 'The Relationship Between the Contractual and Intrafirm Forms of Industrial Research in American Manufacturing, 1900–1940'. *Explorations in Economic History*, 20, 351–74.

Mowery, D. C. (1983c). 'Economic Theory and Government Technology Policy'. *Policy Sciences*, 16, 27–43.

Mowery, D. C. (1983d). 'British and American Industrial Research: A Comparison, 1900–1950'. Presented at the Anglo-American Conference on the Decline of the British Economy, Boston University, 1 October 1983.

Mueller, W. F. (1955). 'Du Pont: A Study in Firm Growth'. Unpublished PhD dissertation, Vanderbilt University.

National Research Council (1933). *Industrial Research Laboratories of the United States*, compiled by A. W. Flinn (Bulletin no. 91). Washington, DC: National Research Council.

National Research Council (1946). *Industrial Research Laboratories of the United States*, compiled by A. W. Flinn (Bulletin no. 113). Washington, DC: National Research Council.

National Research Council (1983). *International Competition in Advanced Technology: Decisions for America*. Washington DC: National Academy Press.

Nelson, R. R. (1981). 'Research on Productivity Growth and Productivity Differences: Dead Ends and New Departures'. *Journal of Economic Literature*, 19, 1029–64.

Noble, D. F. (1979). *America by Design*. New York: Alfred Knopf.

Pavitt, K. (1980). 'Introduction and Summary'. In *Technical Innovation and British Economic Performance*, ed. K. Pavitt. London: Macmillan.

Pavitt, K., and L. Soete (1980). 'Innovative Activities and Export Shares: Some Comparisons Between Industries and Countries'. In *Technical Innovation and British Economic Performance*, ed. K. Pavitt. London: Macmillan.

Payne, P. L. (1967). 'The Emergence of the Large-Scale Company in Great Britain, 1870–1914'. *Economic History Review*, 20, 519–42.

Peck, M. J. (1968). 'Science and Technology'. In *Britain's Economic Prospects*, ed. R. E. Caves. Washington, DC: Brookings Institution.

Perazich, G., and P. M. Field (1940). *Industrial Research and Changing Technology*, Works Progress Administration National Research Project Report no. M-4. Philadelphia: Works Progress Administration.

Phelps Brown, E. H. (1973). 'Levels and Movements of Industrial Productivity and Real Wages Internationally Compared, 1860–1970'. *Economic Journal*, 83, 58–71.

Prais, S. J. (1976). *The Growth of Giant Firms in Britain*. Cambridge University Press.

Reader, W. J. (1966). *Professional Men*. London: Weidenfeld & Nicolson.

Reader, W. J. (1970). *Imperial Chemical Industries: A History*, Volume 1, *The Forerunners, 1870–1926*. Oxford University Press.

Reader, W. J. (1975). *Imperial Chemical Industries: A History*, Volume 2, *The First Quarter-Century*. Oxford University Press.

Reader, W. J. (1976). *Metal Box: A History*. London: Heinemann.

Reader, W. J. (1979). 'The Chemicals Industry'. In *British Industry Between the Wars*, ed. N. K. Buxton and D. H. Aldcroft. London: Scolar Press.

Reich, L. S. (1977). 'Research, Patents, and the Struggle to Control Radio: A Study of Big Business and the Uses of Industrial Research'. *Business History Review*, 51, 208–35.

Reich, L. S. (1980). 'Industrial Research and the Pursuit of Corporate Security: The Early Years of Bell Labs'. *Business History Review*, 54, 504–29.

Reich, L. S. (1983). 'Irving Langmuir and the Pursuit of Science and Technology in the Corporate Environment'. *Technology and Culture*, 24, 199–221.

Richardson, H. W. (1962). 'The Basis of Economic Recovery in the Nineteenth-Thirties: A Review and a New Interpretation'. *Economic History Review*, 15, 344–63.

Richardson, H. W. (1965). 'Overcommitment in Britain Before 1930'. *Oxford Economic Papers*, 17, 237–62.

Rostas, L. (1948). *Comparative Productivity in British and American Industry*. Cambridge University Press.

Salter, M. S., and W. A. Weinhold (1980). *Merger Trends and Prospects*, report for the Office of Policy, US Department of Commerce. Washington, DC: Department of Commerce.

Sandberg, L. (1974). *Lancashire in Decline*. Columbus: Ohio State University Press.

Sanderson, M. (1972a). *The Universities and British Industry, 1850–1970*. London: Routledge & Kegan Paul.

Sanderson, M. (1972b). 'Research and the Firm in British Industry, 1919–39'. *Science Studies*, 2, 107–51.

Saul, S. B. (1968). 'The Engineering Industry'. In *The Development of British Industry and Foreign Competition*, ed. D. H. Aldcroft. London: George Allen & Unwin.

Scherer, F. M. (1965). 'Firm Size, Market Structure, Opportunity, and the Output of Patented Inventions'. *American Economic Review*, 55, 1097–1125.

Scherer, F. M. (1967). 'Market Structure and the Employment of Scientists and Engineers'. *American Economic Review*, 57, 524–31.

Servos, J. W. (1980). 'The Industrial Relations of Science: Chemistry at MIT'. *Isis*, 71, 531–49.

Soete, L. (1979). 'Firm Size and Inventive Activity: The Evidence Reconsidered'. *European Economic Review*, 12, 319–40.

Solow, R. M. (1957). 'Technical Change and the Aggregate Production Functions'. *Review of Economics and Statistics*, 39, 312–20.

Stigler, G. J. (1950). 'Monopoly and Oligopoly by Merger'. *American Economic Review*, 40, 23–34; reprinted in G. J. Stigler, *The Organization of Industry*. Homewood, Ill.: Irwin, 1968.

Terleckyj, N. (1961). 'Sources of Productivity Advance: A Pilot Study of Manufacturing Industries, 1899–1953'. Unpublished PhD dissertation, Columbia University.

Terleckyj, N. (1974). *Effects of R & D on the Productivity of Industries: An Exploratory Study*. Washington, DC: National Planning Association.

Thackray, A. (1982). 'University–Industry Connections and Chemical Research: An Historical Perspective'. In National Science Board, *The University–Industry Research Connection: A Collection of Papers*. Washington, DC: National Science Foundation.

Thorelli, H. B. (1954). *Federal Antitrust Policy*. Baltimore: Johns Hopkins University Press.

Tolliday, S. (1979). 'Industry, Finance, and the State: An Analysis of the British Steel Industry During the Inter-War Years'. Unpublished DPhil thesis, Cambridge University.

Tyson, R. E. (1968). 'The Cotton Industry'. In *The Development of British Industry and Foreign Competition*, ed. D. H. Aldcroft. London: George Allen & Unwin.

US Bureau of the Census (1975). *Historical Statistics of the United States: Colonial Times to 1970*. Washington, DC: US Government Printing Office.

US Department of Commerce Panel on Invention and Innovation (1967). *Technological Innovation: Its Environment and Management*. Washington, DC: US Government Printing Office.

US Senate Military Affairs Committee, Subcommittee on War Mobilization (1945). *The Government's Wartime Research and Development*. Washington, DC: US Government Printing Office.

Warren, K. (1979). 'Iron and Steel'. In *British Industry Between the Wars*, ed. N. K. Buxton and D. H. Aldcroft. London: Scolar Press.

Wickenden, W. E. (1929). *A Comparative Study of Engineering Education in the United States and in Europe*, Bulletin no. 16 of the Investigation of Engineering Education. New York: Society for the Promotion of Engineering Education.

Wilson, C. M. (1954). *The History of Unilever*, Volume 1. London: Cassell.

The City and Industrial Decline

Michael H. Best and Jane Humphries[*]
University of Massachusetts and Cambridge University

Industry and Finance

There is a tradition in British economic history of blaming financial markets and institutions for obstructing industrial development. Some allege that the massive flow of capital into overseas investment in the late Victorian era starved home industries of funds that could have been used to stave off relative retardation (Kennedy, 1976; Saville, 1961; Cairncross, 1953; Cole, 1935). Others claim that the return to gold at an overvalued parity in the interwar period favoured the interests of the City, but penalized the export trades (Stamp, 1931; Longstreth, 1979). Still others contend that the financial sector has neglected industry in the post-World War II period, preferring instead to invest abroad (Carrington and Edwards, 1979).

Yet there are also many who absolve the financial sector of blame (Sayers, 1960; Edelstein, 1976, 1981; Thomas, 1978; Committee of London Clearing Bankers, 1977; Vittas and Brown, 1982). Despite decades of research and debate, the role of finance in British industrial devolopment remains unresolved.

The main problem with previous debate is that it typically views the supply and demand for finance as independent phenomena, mediated by financial markets. To understand the role of finance in industrial development, we must distinguish between financial *intermediation* via capital markets and financial *integration* to accommodate long-run planning by capitalist firms. From the market-oriented perspective of neoclassical economic theory, the higher the degree of financial liquidity, the closer we are to social optimality. When we bring long-run investment planning into the picture, however, we must ask to what extent the operation of the capital market is compatible with the needs of industry.

We argue below that in Britain, from the late nineteenth century through the interwar period, suppliers of finance failed to become involved in the restructuring of industry so as to influence the profitability of enterprise and the demand for long-term industrial capital. The consequent lack of integration between finance and industry adversely affected the volume and allocation of British industrial investment and the long-term competitive performance of British industry compared with its international rivals.

[*]For comments we would like to thank William Lazonick, Michael Edelstein, Bernard Elbaum, Geoffrey Ingham, Steven Tolliday, and the participants of Leonard Rapping's Restructuring Seminar at the University of Massachusetts and Ajit Singh's Queens' College Political Economy Seminar as Cambridge University.

The next section of this paper briefly contrasts the roles played by financial integration in the early industrial development of Germany, the United States, and Britain. Subsequent sections describe the historical development of the British national banking system, its standard policy of providing capital to industrial enterprises only on a short-term basis, and its inadvertent post-World War I involvement with the long-term prospects of Britain's staple industries. Despite public and private demand for industrial reorganization during the depression of the later 1920s and 1930s, British banks were concerned principally with escaping from their financial overcommitment to industry with minimal losses, and refrained from backing new programmes for co-ordinated industrial modernization. By contrast, financial integration did provide a major impetus to Britain's interwar housing boom, as Britain's building societies proved able and willing to affect both demand and supply in the market for housing finance.

Long-term Finance

In nineteenth-century Britain, as in the United States, the principal sources of investment finance were family wealth and retained earnings—the most basic forms of financial integration (Cottrell, 1980; Mathias, 1983; Crouzet, 1972; Presnell, 1956; Cameron *et al.*, 1967). Through these means, capital was committed to specific firms, without the capital market playing a direct role.

By contrast, in Germany joint-stock investment banks were instrumental in founding large-scale industrial ventures. German banks operated within a context of state promotion of industrial development, protection of the home market, and relative capital scarcity. By the early twentieth century, industrial development had led German firms to depend more on retained earnings and less on external capital (Feldenkirchen, 1981). Nevertheless, the powerful German credit banks retained a close interest in industrial performance, as they continued to sit on the boards of large industrial concerns and underwrote financial issues, often holding a proportion on their own account and retaining the proxy rights of outside shareholders.

Moreover, in key sectors such as mining, machinery, steel, and electrical manufacturing, the credit banks, often acting in concert, led in the promotion of industrial combination and rationalization. The objects of sector reorganization were, as Riesser (1911, p. 369) put it, 'to get rid of troublesome competition, to combine the successive stages in the process of production, or to diminish the costs of production'.

In the United States, investment banks also played a prominent role in the reorganization of industry and the promotion of oligopoly. The US investment banks came of age during the railroad era. As Chandler puts it,

On those roads financed or refinanced by the investment bankers (and these include most of the major systems in the country), the relations between the boards and the operating managers came to be similar to those on the Vanderbilt roads. Morgan, trained in the Vanderbilt school, carefully picked experienced career managers as presidents of the roads he reorganized. . . . Members of the Morgan firm chaired the boards and sat on their executive and finance committees . . . Kuhn, Loeb; Lee, Higginson; Kidder, Peabody, Belmont and Speyer all acted in much the same manner. So too did such financiers as Harriman and Hill. (Chandler, 1977, p. 183.)

In the turn-of-the-century US merger movement, these same investment banks used their financial power to lead the restructuring of manufacturing industries where, despite the presence of some dominant firms, competition was still rife. In the process, they were able to pay off the owner–entrepreneurs of the merged firms, remove weak managers, and monetize the expected capitalized value of fixed assets.

Morgan, for example, went from railroads to steel, where he paid $420 million for Carnegie's holdings. In 1901 this sum represented a financial magnitude that approximated 40 per cent of British net investment, at home and abroad. Morgan was also active in securing 'harmony' and 'community of interests' (Winkler, 1930, p. 168) in mergers that created giant oligopolies such as American Telephone and Telegraph, General Electric Company, International Harvester Company, and Mercantile Marine Trust.

Market control enhanced the strategic planning capability of the managerial enterprises, which in turn made investment in these firms more attractive to the public. Aggressive investment banks reaped capital gains from sectoral restructuring and secured for themselves lucrative business as financial agents for the oligopolistic firms that they put together. By establishing dominant oligopolies, moreover, the investment banks were able to assure the US public that they too could share in the country's industrial prosperity. In effect, the merger movement of the 1890s and 1900s created a US market in industrial securities (Navin and Sears, 1955).

In contrast, markets in industrial securities that began to flourish in Britain in the last decades of the nineteenth century represented financial intermediation, not financial integration. Indeed, by providing easy access to funds for new capacity, British stock markets facilitated entry into industry and exacerbated competitive pressures. In turn, the uncertainty of survival that high levels of competition entailed forced British firms to adhere to high payout policies if they wanted to attract additional capital in the future (see paper by Lewchuk, this volume), thus limiting the ability of these firms to build up equity based upon retained earnings.

The provincial stock markets that sprang up after the passage of limited liability laws in the late 1850s and early 1860s exhibited high degrees of industrial specialization, reflecting the regional concentration of industry in various parts of the North and Midlands. In the new issues boom of the early 1860s and 1870s considerable long-term finance flowed into cotton spinning, iron and steel, and coal. Most of these industrial firms drew their finance from local sources familiar with the particular firms and products. As Edelstein argues,

the vast majority of provincial public limiteds were floated locally, without use of the full complement of professional issuing services available in London. A frequent procedure was to place securities privately among the former partners, the directors (if the firm was already a limited) and wealthy friends and contacts. At a minimum the services of a local solicitor, banker, professional stockbroker or London company promoter would be purchased to handle the legal formalities and the cash transactions. . . . the majority of new and old provincial limiteds would never have thought of offering securities to investors in distant regions of the country. Local investors were automatically involved in any thoughts on the subject, their superior knowledge, interest and loyalty simply assumed. (Edelstein, 1971, pp. 88, 92.)

As the scale of industrial needs continued to expand in the late nineteenth century, local resources became strained, and the larger limited liability companies had to look further afield, fostering the development of the London stock market (Cottrell, 1980, pp. 98–9, 183). Although the new issues boom beginning in 1895 focused primarily on domestic railways, municipal securities, colonial government securities, and domestic monopoly securities (such as water, tramway, and telegraph), there was also substantial demand for industrials such as breweries, cycles, motor vehicles, and chemicals. Edelstein (1971, p. 84) reports that long-term securities of domestic non-railway companies rose from 4 per cent of the stock of all securities in 1870 to 19 per cent by 1913.

Industrial issues were also associated with merger activity in tobacco, wallpaper, flour, soap, sewing cotton, and linoleum (Cottrell, 1980). But in general, even as national stock markets developed, the flotation of joint stock companies was not associated with the rationalization of industry as had been the case in the United States.

Short-term Finance

In Britain's industrial revolution bank credit was used chiefly for the short-term finance of sales transactions. The low fixed capital requirements of early industrialization (Feinstein, 1981; Mathias, 1983, p. 134ff.) meant that much of investment was in working capital. In normal conditions, stocks of goods turned over regularly, imparting liquidity to the operations of the firm.

The key credit instrument employed by local banks was the bill of exchange. In industrial or merchant sales transactions, the purchaser generally provided, in lieu of cash, a written acceptance of receipt of certain goods or materials. After expiration of a customary credit period, the purchaser was required to redeem the acceptance. In the interval, bank discount of acceptances provided firms with a means of raising funds in anticipation of their sales revenue. A legacy of Britain's commercial past was an extensive market that traded in discounted acceptances, or bills of exchange.

Through the bills market, the country banks of the late eighteenth and early nineteenth centuries were able to mobilize capital resources available in other regions. Banks in the industrial regions, having advanced credit to their customers on the security of bills of exchange, channelled the bills to the London market for rediscount there. Rediscounted bills were in turn bought by local country banks, which could tap short-term deposits of post-harvest agricultural savings.

This type of finance was preferred by the early industrial firms because it avoided the extension of ownership required by other methods of raising capital, such as the attraction of new partners or the issue of joint stocks. Belief was widespread that complete commitment to an enterprise was necessary for good management, and that spreading ownership would diffuse control and undermine responsibility: a high price to pay for the injection of new capital (Cottrell, 1980, p. 34ff.).

Early country banks were small in scale and developed in response to the credit and capital needs of specific industries. Banking grew in the Black Country in tandem with iron industry, and in Lancashire alongside cotton textile manufacturers (Crick and Wadsworth, 1936). The country bankers themselves were often industrialists who had been drawn into banking activities as a natural extension of their business (Cottrell, 1980, pp. 14ff.). Frequent coin shortages in the provinces, for example, caused firms to resort to note issues in order to meet their wage bills.

Personal relations between bankers and industrialists encouraged the greater sharing of information and reduced risk compared with anonymous market relations. Possessing intimate knowledge of industrial circumstance and personalities, mid-nineteenth-century local banks were willing to advance a certain amount of long-term as well as short-term capital to industry. At times, such long-term lending helped back major entrepreneurial ventures, such as in the 1872 loan of £26,000 by the Yorkshire Banking Company and the Yorkshire City and County Bank specifically to introduce the Bessemer process (Jeffreys, 1938, p. 77).

Stable relations between banks and firms also meant that short-term loans were often routinely 'rolled over', even in bad times (Cottrell, 1980; see also Mathias, 1983, pp. 156ff.). Mathias states: 'As the number of business histories accumulate, so it is being revealed that businesses not uncommonly got over the hump of a great decision to expand or survived a depression with bank capital' (1983, p. 136; see also pp. 156ff.), a viewpoint supported by Cottrell's (1980) study of the balance sheets of four banks in the period 1840–90 (pp. 212ff.).

As the local banks became more committed to the particular industries concentrated in their regions, the lack of industrial diversification in their asset portfolios left them vulnerable during cyclical downturns in business activity. By modern standards, the rate of bank failure was extremely high: 'between 1846–1857 about 100 banks, private and joint stock, failed with

assets totalling almost $50,000,000' (Jeffreys, 1938, p. 17). After the failure of
the Bank of Glasgow in 1878, British banks drew the lesson that they had
overextended credit to local industry, and refrained thereafter from explicitly
lending over the long term.

As the nineteenth century wore on, additional strains developed in the
customary relationship between finance and industry because of the gradual
growth in the scale of enterprise capital requirements. The high ratio of
advances to deposits, at times over 100 per cent, was, according to Crick and
Wadsworth (1936), 'a measure of the pressure upon local bank resources in
manufacturing districts'.

Growing capital requirements and local bank failures set the stage for the
rise of the national clearing banks. As early as 1826, the gradual liberaliza-
tion of company law pertaining to banks had promoted the establishment,
first in London but subsequently in the provinces, of joint stock banks that
had rapidly superceded hundreds of small private banks. Initially these joint
stock banks were indistinguishable in practice from their private predecessors, being, as Crick and Wadsworth (1936) emphasized, 'local in business
and without extensive branch systems' (p. 7). But in the decades prior to
World War I, there was a centralization of the banking system, characterized
by the rise of large national banks centred in London with branches in the
provinces. Truptil (1936) characterized the process of rationalization before
1914 as having been 'brought about almost entirely by the extension of joint
stock banks, which already possessing considerable ramifications, sought on
the one hand to increase their network of branches by absorbing local firms,
or on the other to acquire a London house in order to gain admission to the
clearing house of the City' (p. 63). The number of independent banks fell to
60 in 1901 and to 40 by 1917, by which time the five major clearing banks
controlled two-thirds of the system's resources (Cottrell, 1980).

The rationalization of the system of commercial banks and its centralization in the metropolis changed the scope of British commercial banking. Like
the older merchant banks, the London banks performed a variety of services
relating to international commerce and the financial needs of foreign governments (Bagehot, 1910; Balogh, 1947; Truptil, 1936; Crick and Wadsworth, 1936). The rise of national branch banking centralized in London
reduced the independence of the branches, permitted the banks to diversify
their portfolios across industries, and reaffirmed the principle of short-term
industrial finance (Cottrell, 1980; Mathias, 1983).

Clearing bank finance of industry generally took the form of bills of
exchange, loans for short definite periods, or overdrafts (Balogh, 1947, p. 74).
Loans 'were mostly granted for periods up to a year, although in meritorious
cases a bank may go up to three years' (Thomas, 1978, p. 57) and even the
latter, like overdrafts, came up for reconsideration every year.

In the 1930s, Truptil described the standard practice of the national clearing banks in the following terms:

The types of advance which the banks prefer are either those which are seasonal and which liquidate themselves automatically by the sale of the merchandise or products which the credits have financed, or those of 'average size'. . . . the average size for all advances is $1151. . . . It is much higher for industrial credits, being $10,900 for coal mines, and $12,000 for iron and steel and $12,000 for cotton. The branch managers have little or no latitude even in cases where the figures are not large. . . . Ordinarily, . . . all the requests for credits are forwarded to the head office where they are considered according to their size and importance by a superintendent of branches. . . . (Truptil, 1936, p. 108.)

(See also the testimony of Messers Beaumount-Pease and Hyde on this issue: Committee on Finance and Industry, 1931b, pp. 123 and 57–8, respectively.)

Recapitalization and Rationalization

Ironically, the extension of standard banking principles led the clearing banks to become heavily involved in industrial finance immediately after World War I. In the euphoria of 1918 and 1919, when 'everyone thought that the trade of the world was at our feet' (testimony of Mr Beaumount-Pease, Chairman of Lloyds Bank: Committee on Finance and Industry, 1931b, p. 132), banks advanced substantial overdraft facilities to firms in the traditional industries with little in the way of 'searching credit analysis' (testimony of O. M. W. Sprague: Committee on Finance and Industry, 1931b, p. 308). These funds were provided to firms as working capital in the belief that the staple industries would quickly regain and extend prewar markets. The funds were never intended to finance large-scale fixed investment or major restructuring (testimony of Mr Beaumount-Pease, Lloyds Bank: Committee on Finance and Industry, 1931b, pp. 122–36). Yet with strong postwar demand for cloth and steel products and the supply of plant and equipment relatively fixed, vast amounts of the 'short-term' overdrafts were actually used to buy up and recapitalize existing firms at what turned out to be tremendously over-inflated prices (Lazonick, this volume; Tolliday, this volume; Lucas, 1937).

The British staple industries did not regain their prewar markets. The extent of British industrial decline was abruptly revealed by the deep recession in 1920. The banks were forced to nurse along distressed firms to which they had inadvertantly become overcommitted. The financial crises facing firms in cotton and steel went unabated throughout the 1920s and in some cases were displaced on to their client banks (Lazonick, this volume; Tolliday, this volume; see also Lucas, 1937, ch. VII).

The actual magnitude of clearing bank advances to industry are not known for the 1920s. Even the Macmillan Committee was unable to obtain a consistent industrial classification of advances from the clearing banks for years before 1929, and it is not until 1936 that such figures are available on an annual basis. It is clear that banks were using this later period of increased industrial profitability not to reorganize, but rather to extricate themselves from industry with a minimum of loss. While total advances to industry of the ten largest London clearers dropped from £479.3 million in 1929 to £352.9 million in 1936, or 26 per cent, advances to heavy industry, including iron and steel, engineering, and shipbuilding, dropped by 35 per cent, textiles by 51 per cent and mining by 40 per cent (Grant, 1937).

At a time when substantial new long-term investment in British industry was necessary to match international competition, the clearing banks sought to sever any long-term commitment to industry. In 1936, W. F. Tukes, Chairman of Barclay's Bank, proclaimed the penchant of the national banking system for liquidity:

As our deposits are repayable on demand or at short notice, our advances must be arranged on the same conditions. This does not mean that in practice the repayment of advances is arbitrarily demanded but that, in making an advance, we must be reasonably confident that the transaction will be self-liquidating in a comparatively short period, or, alternatively, that the amount advanced will be forthcoming with reasonable promptitude in the event of a demand for repayment being made. (Barclays Bank Annual Meeting, 23 January 1936; cited in Grant, 1937, p. 185.)

(See also evidence of Messrs Hyde, Beaumount-Pease, Goodenough, and Rae before the Macmillan Committee: Committee Finance and Industry, 1931b).

The highly concentrated structure of the clearing banks in the interwar years could have produced credit policies that were in the interests of an industry *as a whole*. Instead, the clearing banks, like the firms, relied primarily upon market co-ordination and competition to shape industrial development. Keynes himself bluntly asked the Chairman of the Provincial Bank Ltd, Sir W. H. N. Goschen, 'Have you ever put pressure upon . . . a firm to conform to what you regard as being in the interest of the industry as a whole, as distinct from the interest of that particular firm?' He did not receive a positive answer (testimony before the Committee on Finance and Industry, 1931b, p. 114; see also evidence of Beaumont-Pease, pp. 122–36).

In both World War I and the interwar years, there were pressures to transform the structure of industry in order to create conditions for long-term planning and modernization. During the war government planners issued directives for administrative co-ordination, standardized parts, and integrated production, in the process exposing the limits of co-ordination by the market. The wartime organizational achievements were not forgotten, and they raised the spectre of nationalization and socialism as a means of modernization. In the interwar years, however, the potential of private-sector rationalization was demonstrated by leading industrialists of German origins, such as Sir Hugo Hirst of GEC and Lord Melchett of ICI, and successful US managerial influence, as in the American General Electric Company and General Motors' Vauxhall.

But these examples were exceptional. Much of the traditional British industry suffered from chronic excess capacity, and the new industries such as cars, rayon and silk, tobacco, leather and rubber, and paper and hardboard were developing only slowly in comparison with their foreign competitors. Long before the 1929 slump, the shipbuilding industry was operating at less than half its capacity; cotton was operating at three-quarters of capacity; and the coal industry was said to be capable of producing half as much again as it could sell (Lucas, 1937; British Association, 1935). Market prospects in the new industries were much more attractive. But their minor weight in total output meant that, despite impressive investment rates, they absorbed only 17 per cent of total fixed investment in manufacturing between 1920 and 1938 (Feinstein, 1965, p. 46). British industry was restructuring from the old to the rapidly growing, high-productivity sectors, but on a small scale and at a slow pace.

The backwardness of British industry was given wide publicity, particularly in the *Final Report* of the Balfour Committee on British industrial conditions. Influenced by the US and German models of big business development, as well as by the successful rationalization of the British chemical industry, the remedy was clear: '. . . the first step towards putting British industries in a position to compete successfully in overseas markets is to subject their organization and equipment to a thorough going process of reconditioning' (Committee on Industry and Trade, 1929, p. 297).

The Balfour Committee also recognized that competition might not be the optimal means for rationalizing industry:

The results of the prolonged competition of inefficient undertakings react on the more efficient, and tend to depress the whole industry; an operation of cutting out the dead wood may be essential for the speedy restoration of prosperity . . . There can be no doubt that the operation of free competition is a very slow and costly method for the purpose of securing such elimination. The tenacity of life shown by business working at a loss is sometimes extraordinary . . . it seems unquestionable that this operation can often be performed more steadily and rationally and with less suffering through the mechanism of consolidation or agreement than by the unaided play of competition. (Committee on Industry and Trade, 1929, p. 179.)

(See also Jevons, 1931.)

Unfortunately, the Balfour Committee was less explicit about the difficulties of achieving rationalization through concerted industrial consolidation. Had industrial concentration been synonymous with modernization, the British economy would have made rapid progress in the 1920s and 1930s, given the contemporary merger activity. But these mergers did not promote reorganization of business enterprise or productive capacity. Chandler, for example, dates the replacement of the personal and private enterprise by modern managerial structures in Britain as late as the 1960s and 1970s, a half-century behind the the managerial revolution in the United States (Chandler, 1976, p. 46). Big British firms were often no more than federations of family firms formed in pursuit of defensive strategies (Hannah, 1976, p. 199). Such amalgamations ensured continued family dominance of management positions, and offered growth through undigested acquisitions rather than internal expansion. Instead of promoting modernization, such organizations became another element in the structural logjam constraining rationalization.

Impressed by the need for a concerted approach to rationalization and by an attractive description of German practice, the Macmillan Committee proposed the banks as a suitable, directive 'outside agency' (Clay, 1957, p. 653). The Committee envisaged the evolution of a bank–industry relationship that would enable the former to negotiate planned restructuring and would oversee the elimination of excess capacity according to technological and organizational standards (Committee on Finance and Industry, 1931a, p. 165). Bankers' own testimonies are witness to their reluctance to assume this role; they sought support for a self-government approach which would place the responsibility for reorganization squarely back on industry (for example, see Beaumont-Pease, twelfth day of testimony, Committee on Finance and Industry, 1931b, pp. 122–36).

By the late 1920s, however, the British banking system had become a scapegoat for a whole gamut of problems characteristic of British industry. Keynes even blamed the banks for the General Strike. Organized industry, allied with labour, demanded that the government should assert control over the financial system in the determination of credit policy and, via the Macmillan Committee, examine the arcane workings of the gold standard (Middlemass, 1979). The 'individualism run riot' of the five major clearing banks led Sir Arthur Steel-Maitland, minister in the 1928 Conservative government to propose an industrial reorganization scheme backed by government loans (cited in Middlemass, 1979, p. 180).

Rationalization was presented as an alternative to wage-cutting as a means of reducing unemployment. For example, although the Samuel Commission's report on the coal industry of 1925 advocated reduced wages and longer hours, it also argues for a rationalization of industry involving increased investment and mechanization. The problem was the source of finance, the obvious alternatives being the banks or the government. As Sir Basil Blackett wrote in 1929,

Only rationalization can save us and get rid of unemployment. It means for us essentially getting rid of individualism in industry, cooperation, amalgamation, ruthless scrapping of out-of-date plant and out-of-date directors, and it can only be done if the banks come out boldly and fact it. . . . (Cited in Middlemass, 1979, p. 178.)

By the end of the 1920s, Montague Norman, the Governor of the Bank of England, was faced with a growing coalition of organized labour, industrial associations, and converted politicians, gathered together under the umbrella of rationalization. He also faced a desperate collection of smaller private banks whose own existence was threatened by the insolvency of firms in cotton, iron, steel, and heavy engineering. Norman responded by initiating active, though delimited, intervention in the affairs of industry.

In 1929 Norman established the Securities Management Trust (SMT), 'a temporary or industrial adjunct of the Bank of England' (Committee on Finance and Industry, 1931b, p. 295) and the Bankers' Industrial Development Company (BIDC), intended for 'taking these [industrial] questions out of the Governor's room' (Sayers, 1976, p. 326). The SMT was composed of a body of experts who were to advise on industrial reorganization and administer the funds that the Bank was channelling to such purposes. The BIDC shared the same experts but represented the Bank's decision at this juncture to try to involve the City in the rationalization efforts.

Norman sought to spread these new industrial commitments via the establishment of a financial consortium including private banks whose mandate would be to help with rationalization. In testimony before the Macmillan Committee, the Governor argued: 'the salvation of industry in this country lies first of all in the process of rationalization, and that is to be achieved by the unity or unification or marriage of finance and industry.' Norman presented the BIDC optimistically as 'another company which will unite the City as a whole in willingness . . . to assist industry towards the goal of rationalization' (Committee on Finance and Industry, 1931b, p. 212). To this end, the board of BIDC included the heads of the most powerful merchant banks in the City, Baron Schroder of Schroders, Mr Peacock of Barings, Mr Wagg of Helbert Wagg, plus Sir Charles Bruce-Gardner, Sir Guy Granet, and Norman of the Bank (Committee on Finance and Industry, 1931b, p. 288). Subscriptions were shared between the Bank of England, which put up £1.5 million, and the private banking community, which offered £4.5 million.

Despite these appearances, in practice, the BIDC was not well supported by the banking community. Its first public issues were for shipbuilding and cotton schemes, and neither went well (Sayers, 1976, p. 547). By April 1931, only two years after BIDC's creation, the Bank had abandoned public issues and limited rationalization schemes to those that could be met from its own resources. BIDC clearly failed to 'unite the City as a whole' in the 'salvation of industry', as Norman had envisioned it would. Similarly, the staff of high-powered experts assembled by the Bank to analyse rationalization projects were underutilized. Most of their time was absorbed by the problems of two Bank investments, one in steel (Armstrongs) and the other in heavy engineering (Beardmores). By 1933–4 most of the original members of the

SMT–BIDC cadres were gone, and little industrial expertise remained within the Bank (Sayers, 1976, p. 548).

Obviously, the failure to effect a 'marriage of finance and industry' cannot be ascribed to BIDC alone. The enormity of the rationalization task was compounded by the slow growth and the fragmented structure of British industry. Nevertheless, the Bank's strategy was inherently flawed. In theory, it suggested a rationalization effort overseen and directed by the central bank but without any long-term financial ties or accountability to the government. In practice, the problem for BIDC was that rationalization involves picking winners and backing them with long-term finance even at the cost of under-cutting competitors and the competitors' banks. Norman baulked at this role because it violated the traditional neutrality of the central bank.

Norman briefly tried to shift responsibility for the definition of the interests of the industry *collectively* away from the Bank and on to the trade associations (Lucas, 1937). But in the UK the trade associations were singularly unsuited to such a task: they were primarily defensive unions determined to preserve the status quo rather than supervise the dissolution of weaker members (Middlemass, 1979; Daniels and Campion, 1935). Aid to one industrial firm could, and did, escalate the demands for aid from competitors. Pursuing this strategy risked intervention by the government as the democratically accountable institution to formulate investment criteria for choosing winners and losers. Since the Bank could not autonomously develop these criteria, Norman and the BIDC faced a difficult choice: either to retreat from rationalization, leaving it to the market, or to accept the politicization of bank activities.

Building Societies: A Case of Institutional Innovation

In contrast to its low level of domestic industrial investment, interwar Britain experienced a remarkable housing boom. The conventional explanation of the housing boom runs in terms of rising real incomes, falling house prices, and low interest rates. But these were only permissive conditions, and cannot explain either the timing or the extent of the boom (Nevin, 1944, p. 275; Feinstein, 1965, p. 42). The interwar period presented favourable oppor-tunities for the building market, but it was the building societies that organ-ized the market by operating on both the supply of and demand for mortgage loans.

Although British real income had been rising steadily in the decades pre-ceding 1920, the surge in housing activity occurred only subsequently, dur-ing the interwar period of comparatively uneven growth and industrial depression. Falling house prices and interest rates helped sustain the boom, but were less important in making home ownership a feasible option than changes in the terms of mortgage agreements, which reduced the duration of loans and the size of required down payments.

An extension in the duration of a mortgage loan from, say, 16–20 years to 20–25 years had a crucial impact on the size of monthly repayments (Bellman, 1949, p. 152; MacIntosh, 1951). Evidence from individual building societies indicates that they began to extend the duration of mortgages in the 1920s as an effective way of bringing new demand into the housing market (*Building Societies Yearbook*, selected years; Bellman, 1949, p. 152; Humphries, 1984).

For the same reasons, building societies began, at roughly the same time, to pursue means for reducing the proportion of house prices required as down payment. The most important development on this front involved the use of collateral security to cover the building societies for losses on loans advanced in excess of the customary 75 per cent mortgage. The availability of collateral security was controversial in the 1920s as it appeared to be excluded by the Building Societies Acts. By authorizing local authorities to guarantee building society advances, however, the Housing Act of 1923 seemed to institutionalize collateral security and was used by the movement to legitimate and justify the practice more generally (see Harvey, 1928).

The next important development involved the institutionalization of collateral security in the system known as 'the builder's pool'. As usual, the building societies advanced up to 75 per cent of the value of the house against the personal security of the purchaser and the security of the house itself. In addition, by having builders deposit sums with them, the building societies made a further advance which might bring the total up to 95 per cent. The purchaser repaid the whole amount, including the builder's loans with interest (Bowley, 1945).

These arrangements between the financier and the producer of the product had certain drawbacks. Nevertheless, the pool was a powerful instrument in facilitating home-ownership among those in income and occupational groups who would otherwise have found the initial down payment a prohibitive hurdle (Bellman, 1949). The proportion of building society business that resulted from pool arrangements cannot be known with certainty, but an informed guess for the larger societies puts it at 50 per cent of their total (*The Economist*, 18 February 1939).

On the supply side, the building societies capitalized on favourable tax arrangements to increase the flow of funds available to them in deposits and shares. During the latter nineteenth century, with a prevailing tax threshold of £160, ascertaining the tax liabilities of building society investors would have been very expensive, and feasible only with building society co-operation. The resolute refusal of the societies 'to give any assistance to the revenue authorities' (Nevitt, 1966, p. 51) provided them with leverage in their struggle with the Inland Revenue. An 1894 agreement provided that only 50 per cent of each society's income was to be subject to tax, to be paid by the society and not the individual investor or depositor. The Inland Revenue believed it obtained the same amount of tax as if each investor had been individually assessed while saving the expense involved in collecting small amounts of tax from large numbers of people.

The building societies allocated the tax burden uniformly over all interest and dividends paid out. Investors with incomes below the taxable level had to pay a small amount of tax, while better-off investors, who would otherwise have incurred taxes on 100 per cent of their building society income at possibly higher rates, were able to reap substantial savings from the uniform tax rule.

Despite the tax levy, low-income investors and depositors received a higher return from the building societies than from short-term post office and savings bank deposits. Particularly in the 1920s, however, low-income investors may well have been better advised to put their money in Consols or long-term savings certificates (Grant, 1937, 243). Even then, the attraction of the building societies was often not simply the return on capital, but also on possibility of obtaining a future mortgage loan.

Although the arrangements were modified in 1932, 1935, and 1940, the basic idea of a single 'composite' rate of tax lower than the standard rate remained unchanged and was given statutory backing in 1952. As tax thresholds were reduced and real incomes rose, the benefits implicit in these arrangements for middle-income investors became more and more significant (Cleary, 1965). These benefits were a major factor in the increasing use of building societies as investment outlets by the middle class and in the increased average size of building society shares and deposits (Bellman, 1930, 1949). Despite the inferences of some commentators (Nevitt, 1966), these tax advantages were no mere accident. They had been actively pursued by the societies, and were even more stalwartly defended (Mansbridge, 1934, p. 91; Price, 1958, p. 389).

In sum, the interwar building boom was to a significant extent the product of the vigorous institutional response of building societies to their market and regulatory environment. Unlike the mainstream of British finance, which kept its distance from industry, the building societies actively promoted demand for house building by developing innovative means to attract and lend capital.

Conclusion

Our argument is not that the financial sector failed British industry *at the margin* because of risk aversion, lack of information, uncertainty, or inherent bias, but that the contribution that finance could have made—indeed, did make in other countries and even in certain sectors of the British economy—to the *restructuring* of British industry was not forthcoming. Attempts to locate responsibility for Britain's economic decline either with the financial intermediaries, for not supplying capital to industry, or with industry, for not being profitable enough to demand funds effectively, miss this critical point: the contribution of financial intermediaries to industrial development can go, and often has gone, beyond the provision of liquidity to firms to the participation in, and even initiation of, the reorganization of those firms. In terms of the analyses developed in this volume, it was in its inability to become a dynamic force in the reorganization of basic industry that, in comparative and relative terms, the British financial system 'failed'.

Bibliography

Bagehot, W. (1910). *Lombard Street*. London: John Murray.

Balogh, T. (1947). *Studies in Financial Organization*. Cambridge University Press.

Bellman, H. (1930). 'Building Societies as Financial Institutions'. *Building Societies Yearbook*.

Bellman, H. (1949). *Bricks and Mortals*. London: Hutchinson.

Bowley, M. (1945). *Housing and the State*. London: George Allen and Unwin.

British Association (1935). *Britain in Depression*. London: Pitman and Sons.

Cairncross, A. K. (1935). *Home and Foreign Investment, 1870–1913*. Cambridge University Press.

Cameron, R. E. *et al.* (1967). *Banking in the Early Stages of Industrialization*. New York: Oxford University Press.

Carrington, J. C., and G. T. Edwards (1979). *Financing Industrial Development*. London: Macmillan.

Chandler, A. D. Jr (1977). *The Visible Hand: The Managerial Revolution in American Business*. Cambridge, Mass.: Harvard University Press.

Clay, H. (1957). *Lord Norman*. London: Macmillan.

Cleary, E. J. (1965). *The Building Society Movement*. London: Elek.

Cole, G. D. H. (ed.) (1935). *Studies in Capital and Investment*. London: New Fabian Research Bureau.

Committee on Industry and Trade (Balfour Committee) (1929). *Final Report*, Cmd. 3282. London: HMSO.

Committee on Finance and Industry (Macmillan Committee) (1931a). *Final Report*, Cmd. 3897. London: HMSO.

Committee on Finance and Industry (Macmillan Committee) (1931b). *Minutes of Evidence taken before the Committee* (2 volumes). London: HMSO.

Committee of London Clearing Bankers (1977). *Evidence by the Committee of London Clearing Bankers to the Committee to Review the Functioning of Financial Institutions*. London: Longman Group.

Cottrell, P. L. (1980). *Industrial Finance 1830–1914*. London: Methuen.

Crick, W. F., and J. E. Wadsworth (1936). *A Hundred Years of Joint Stock Banking*. London: Hodder and Stoughton.

Crouzet, F. (1972). *Capital Formation in the Industrial Revolution*. London: Methuen.

Daniels, G. W., and H. Campion (1935). 'The Cotton Industry'. In *Britain in Depression*, prepared by the British Association. London: Pitman.

Edelstein, M. (1971). 'Rigidity and Bias in the British Capital Market, 1870–1913'. In *Essays on a Mature Economy: Britain after 1940*, ed. D. McCloskey. London: Methuen.

Edelstein, M. (1976). 'Realized Rates of Return on UK Home and Overseas Portfolio

Investment in the Age of High Imperialism'. *Explorations in Economic History*, 13, 283–329.

Edelstein, M. (1981). 'Foreign Investment and Empire, 1860–1914'. In *The Economic History of Britain Since 1700*, ed. R. Floud and D. McCloskey. Cambridge University Press.

Feinstein, C. H. (1965). *Domestic Capital Formation in the United Kingdom, 1920–1938: Studies in the National Income and Expenditure of the UK*. Cambridge University Press.

Feinstein, C. H. (1981). 'Capital Accumulation and the Industrial Revolution'. In *The Economic History of Britain since 1700*, ed. R. Floud and D. McCloskey. Cambridge University Press.

Feldenkirchen, W. (1981). 'The Banks and the Steel Industry in the Ruhr', *German Yearbook on Business History*. Berlin: Springer-Verlag.

Grant, A. T. K. (1937). *A Study of the Capital Market in Post-War Britain*. London: Macmillan.

Hannah, L. (ed.) (1976). *Management Strategy and Business Development*. London: Macmillan.

Harvey, W. (1928). 'The 90 per cent Mortgage and Collateral Security'. *Building Societies Yearbook*.

Humphries, J. (1984). 'Interwar Housebuilding, Cheap Money and the Building Societies: The Housing Boom Revisited'. Unpublished paper.

Jeffreys, J. B. (1938). 'Trends in Business Organisation in Great Britain since 1856'. PhD thesis, University of London.

Jevons, J. S. (1931). 'The Second Industrial Revolution'. *Economic Journal*, 41, 1–18.

Kennedy, W. P. (1976). 'Capital Markets in Britain to 1914'. In *Management Strategy and Business Development*, ed. L. Hannah. London: Macmillan.

Longstreth, F. (1979). 'The City, Industry and the State'. In *State and Economy in Contemporary Capitalism*, ed. C. Crouch. London: Croom Helm.

Lucas, A. F. (1937). *Industrial Reconstruction and the Control of Competition*. London: Longman.

MacIntosh, R. M. (1951). 'A Note on Cheap Money and the British Housing Boom, 1932–1937'. *Economic Journal*, 61, 167–73.

Mansbridge, A. (1934). *Brick on Brick: A History of the Cooperative Building Society*. London: J. M. Dent.

Mathias, P. (1983). *The First Industrial Revolution*. London: Methuen.

Middlemass, K. (1979). *Politics in Industrial Society*. London: André Deutsch.

Navin, T. R., and M. V. Sears (1955). 'The Rise of a Market for Industrial Securities, 1887–1902'. *Business History Review*, 29, 105–38.

Nevin, E. (1944). *The Mechanisms of Cheap Money: a Study of British Monetary Policy*. Cardiff: University of Wales Press.

Pressnell, L. S. (1956). *Country Banking in the Industrial Revolution*. Oxford University Press.

Price, S. J. (1958). *Building Societies: Their Origin and History*. London: Franey.

Riesser, J. (1911). *The German Great Banks and their Concentration in Connection with the Economic Development of Germany*. Washington, DC: US Government Printing Office.

Saville, J. (1961). 'Some Retarding Factors in the British Economy before 1914'. *Yorkshire Bulletin of Economic and Social Research*, 13(1), 51–60.

Sayers, R. S. (1960). 'The Return to Gold, 1925'. In *Studies in the Industrial Revolution*, ed. L. S. Pressnell. London: Athlone Press.

Sayers, R. S. (1976). *The Bank of England, 1891–1944*, Volumes I and II. Cambridge University Press.

Stamp, Sir J. (1931). 'The Report of the Macmillan Committee'. *Economic Journal*, 41, 424–35.

Thomas, W. A. (1978). *The Finance of British Industry, 1918–1976*. London: Methuen.

Truptil, R. J. (1936). *British Banks and the London Money Market*. London: Jonathan Cape.

Vittas, D., and R. Brown (1982). *Bank Lending and Industrial Investment: A Response to Recent Criticisms*. London: Banking Information Service.

Winkler, J. K. (1930). *Morgan the Magnificent*. New York: Vanguard.

Interwar Responses to Regional Decline

Carol E. Heim*

University of Massachusetts, Amherst

The decline of the British economy frequently is discussed in terms of a failure to move sufficiently rapidly from declining nineteenth-century industries into twentieth-century growth industries: motor cars and other new engineering industries, electrical goods, rubber, rayon, certain branches of chemicals, and others. But the problem for a national economy is not only the overall shares of old versus new industries; the geographical distribution of each is crucial. New industries can expand rapidly in new areas without relieving the problems of depressed areas, particularly in times of general depression.[1]

The nineteenth-century pattern of economic growth, present in an extreme form in Britain, was based on highly specialized regional economies. British coal, iron and steel, shipbuilding, and textile production were geographically concentrated in a small number of locations heavily dependent upon their dominant industries. Severe distress resulted when the staple trades collapsed after World War I. Other industries expanded, but primarily in the South and the Midlands rather than in the depressed industrial areas of the North and West. Awareness of serious economic problems was widespread, unlike the pre-World War I era when relative decline had begun but confidence remained high. By the end of the 1920s, the difficulties were widely recognized to be more than cyclical and temporary. Yet the response was minimal and ineffective. High unemployment persisted in the depressed areas, and very little diversification occurred before World War II. Regional differentials have narrowed since, but the depressed areas remain a problem for national policy.

An examination of the interwar regional problem can shed light on the flexibility of British institutions and their role in aiding or hindering needed structural changes. To what extent was the lack of diversification in the depressed regions due to a set of institutions well adapted to a nineteenth-century regime of 'competitive capitalism' but not to the requirements of successful twentieth-century growth? On the other hand, how much was British adjustment hampered by other factors: the extreme degree of regional

*Financial assistance was provided by the Concilium on International and Area Studies and the Department of Economics, both of Yale University, and by the Economic History Association. Permission from the Governor and Company of the Bank of England and from Deloitte Haskins & Sells (for the Nuffield Trust Papers) to quote relevant material is gratefully acknowledged. I would like to thank Michael Best, Ray Boddy, Sir Alec Cairncross, Barry Eichengreen, Bernard Elbaum, Joel Krieger, and William Lazonick for helpful discussion and comments on points raised in this paper.

specialization, and depressed macroeconomic conditions influencing both private decisions and public policy?

The first section below examines the legacy of regional industrial specialization. It is argued that there are specifically regional dynamics of decline (which would not, for example, be so extreme if declining industries were distributed uniformly across a national economy rather than being regionally concentrated). But reliable mechanisms for endogenous regional revival, in the sense of the generation of a new regional industrial base, do not seem to exist within nineteenth-century industrial regions. Moreover, the consequences of regional specialization meant that institutions more conducive to the growth of new industries within Britain generally might not greatly benefit the depressed regions or result in re-employment of displaced workers. The second section considers the formation of regional policy to respond to the problems of the depressed regions. It traces the impact of both institutional factors and macroeconomic conditions in limiting the scope and effectiveness of regional policy. Attitudes and priorities of the financial community are shown to be particularly important. The concluding section summarizes the findings on the role of institutions and other factors in Britain's lack of response to the regional problem in the interwar period.

Consequences of Regional Industrial Specialization

Throughout Europe and the United States, industrialization in the nineteenth century created specialized regions. Close economic, social, and political linkages existed among local producers, and strong working-class organizations emerged in many cases. The regional economies generally were based upon extractive industries or upon manufacturing industries characterized by special resource needs (such as ports for shipbuilding) or concentrations of specialized fixed capital.

To a considerable degree, 'industry' and 'region' are inherently nineteenth-century concepts, in the sense that they are most useful in understanding nineteenth-century development patterns. Nineteenth-century industries had locational determinants *as industries* for several reasons. Some were rooted by raw material resources (first-stage processing activities) or tied to final markets (local service industries). These continue to locate for much the same reasons to the present. For potentially more footloose manufacturing, however, the crucial factors were (1) lack of development of transport and communication, or of alternative energy sources, which meant that they too were tied to the raw materials; and (2) lack of development of the firm. Firms tended to be relatively small, to operate within a single industry, and to have important linkages with cognate producers. Individual firms often were not large enough to operate distant branch plants or to locate outside existing linked complexes of firms sharing external economies

(Florence, 1948, pp. 52–4). Such factors help to explain the clustering of textile firms in Lancashire.

The emergence of large firms, a defining feature of twentieth-century capitalist development, tends to dissolve the earlier entities of industry and especially of region. Large firms in some cases separate out parts of the production process that individually have quite different locational determinants than would the 'industry' as a whole if located together. Assembly is sent to areas of low-wage labour, skilled tasks to old industrial centres with the necessary skilled labour, and management and research functions to metropolitan centres (Massey, 1979, pp. 237–8). When such firms locate production in older industrial regions (as they did in Britain's depressed areas after World War II), it is often in search of elements not integrated into previous productive structures: new labour for low-wage assembly, for example, rather than displaced workers from the older industries (Firn, 1975, p. 411; Massey, 1983; North Tyneside Community Development Project, 1978). Incorporation of such new elements neither transforms the region as a whole nor provides a new integrated regional economy, though it is a form of restructuring. Nineteenth-century industrial regions, in other words, decline *as regions*, but they do not necessarily revive or restructure *as regions*. This dynamic helps to explain why even the strong growth of new industries nationally may transform but not solve the regional problem, if the new activity that declining regions acquire consists primarily of externally controlled branch plants with unskilled assembly jobs (Massey, 1979, pp. 239–43).

Britain's prosperity at the time of World War I was based upon a very narrow range of export trades. In 1907 coal, iron and steel (including non-electrical machinery and railway equipment), shipbuilding, and textiles made up roughly 50 per cent of total net domestic industrial production and 70 per cent of British exports. In 1921 they accounted for approximately 51 per cent of industrial employment and 20–25 per cent of the total gainfully employed population (Kahn, 1946, pp. 65–7). These industries were geographically concentrated in highly specialized regions (see Tables 1 and 2).

When Britain's export industries declined after the war, regional specialization intensified the resulting problems. Any initial employment decline within a national economy will have adverse multiplier effects. But if the decline is spatially concentrated rather than dispersed, it is more likely to set off cumulative processes of regional decline. Such dynamic effects have a long-run impact above and beyond losses arising from unemployment in the short run. Results may include decay of local infrastructure owing in part to a weakening of the local tax base (especially important in the period before centralized financing of social capital expenditure); selective migration of the best of the workforce; and a reduction in the level of local activity below that necessary to sustain external economies such as specialist suppliers and business services (Brown, 1972, p. 333; Dennison, 1939, pp. 129–30, 190–3; Lee,

TABLE 1

Regional distribution of industries in Britain, 1924

Industry	Lancs., etc. (%)	Northumb., etc. (%)	S. Wales and Mon. (%)	All of Wales (%)	W. Central Scotland (%)	All of Scotland (%)
Cotton spinning	83.9	–	–	–	–	–
Cotton weaving	88.0	–	–	–	–	–
Coal mines	12.6	18.1	19.9	(21.5)	4.9	(12.5)
Iron smelting and rolling	8.3	11.1	n.a.	(24.1)	n.a.	(12.6)
Iron and steel foundries	10.1	8.1	–	–	8.9	(23.5)
Tinplate	–	–	86.0	n.a.	–	–
Mechanical engineering	23.2	6.9	0.7	(0.8)	13.4	(16.5)
Shipbuilding	11.7	26.3	5.3	(5.7)	26.7	(31.3)

Note: Figures indicate the net value of the output of each industry in each region as a percentage of the net value of total production in the industry. Regions indicated are the Census of Production regions: Lancashire, Cheshire, and the Glossop and New Mills District of Derbyshire; Northumberland, Durham, and the North Riding of Yorkshire; South Wales and Monmouthshire; and West Central Scotland.
Source: Political and Economic Planning (1939, pp. 278–81).

TABLE 2
Regional specialization in Britain

Region	Year	% of insured persons in dominant industries	Dominant industries
North East Coast	1924	64	Coal; Iron and steel; Engineering; Shipbuilding; Chemicals; Shipping
South Wales	1923	62	Coal mining; Iron and steel smelting, rolling, puddling, etc.; Tinplate manufacture
West Cumberland	1923	60	Pig-iron making, steel smelting, etc.; Coal mining; Iron ore mining; Coke-ovens; Shipbuilding; Engineering
Lancashire*	1929	56	Cotton; Engineering; Coal mining
West of Scotland*	1924	35	Coal mining; Pig-iron, steel, etc.; Tinplates; Iron and steel tubes; General engineering; Marine engineering; Shipbuilding and repairing

*Figures are for percentages of employed insured persons.
Sources: Great Britain, Board of Trade (1932c, p. 436); Great Britain, Board of Trade (1932a, p. 10); Jewkes and Winterbottom (1933, p. 3); Great Britain, Board of Trade (1932b, p. 28); Great Britain, Board of Trade (1932d, pp. 193–7).

1971, pp. 204–5; Political and Economic Planning, 1939, pp. 140–4). The area becomes less attractive to mobile industry from outside, and existing local employment is jeopardized.

In interwar Britain such processes were matters of public discussion, particularly with the agitation for depressed areas legislation in the 1930s and the investigations of the Barlow Commission (Royal Commission on the Distribution of the Industrial Population, 1937–9, 1940). A related line of argument stressed the social costs arising from 'wasteful' duplication of social infrastructure in prosperous areas while utilization of existing infrastructure dropped in depressed areas. One estimate indicated that approximately £300 per person might be required for the development of new areas (Royal Commission, 1940, pp. 95–6; Dennison, 1939, p. 117).

Depressed local markets, in turn, work against the generation of new industries—particularly the home market industries that were expanding rapidly in interwar Britain—within a region to replace those declining. Limited information on regional purchasing power in 1936 shows a sharp differential in favour of the more prosperous areas in the South and the Midlands (see Table 3). The legacy of regional specialization appears in qualitative characteristics as well as in the absolute size of local markets. The North and West did not have the large middle-class market for new consumer goods industries and services that existed in the South. The problem was not only that the staple trades were depressed, but also that such a middle-class market depended upon an occupational and class structure not present in the older industrial regions even in more prosperous times (Rubinstein, 1977).

The industrial and occupational structure of the nineteenth-century staples, particularly those characterized by large manufacturing plants, may also have tended to diminish the number of local persons who could serve as entrepreneurs in new activities (Chinitz, 1961, pp. 284–5; Fothergill and Gudgin, 1982, pp. 113–33). Britain's depressed areas have not been strong in generating new entrepreneurs. Some argue that the problem has intensified with post-World War II branch plant development in the depressed areas, which reduces local managerial expertise and increases the proportion of unskilled labour-intensive activities (Cross, 1981, pp. 268, 282; Firn, 1975, p. 410; Northern Region Strategy Team, 1977, pp. 53–5, 127–9).

The decline of industries in which regions have specialized thus gives rise to regional dynamics of decline that subsequently affect other economic and social activities within the region. There do not appear to be forces endogenous to such nineteenth-century industrial regions, on the side of either labour or capital, that can be relied upon to generate revival as a region. One apparently plausible mechanism is wage decline: it has been suggested that, if there are no barriers to the downward mobility of wages, new industries will be generated or attracted to replace the old and employ displaced workers. But low wages, because of their role as a demand as well as a cost factor, do not necessarily stimulate new industries. They also may not be sufficient to attract industry to regions that are unattractive on other grounds, especially during a period when labour is available in more prosperous areas near major markets.

In interwar Britain, moreover, relatively footloose expanding industries tended to fall broadly into two groups: male-employing new industries, many of which were relatively high-wage; and low-wage industries, including many diverse light industries, employing high proportions of females and juveniles. Except in Lancashire, the unemployed in declining regions were mostly men. But the male-employing new industries often paid higher wages than even the predominantly male-employing staple industries. If an existing wage differential had not already attracted new industries to the declining regions, a greater differential brought by a drop in male wages there might not do so

TABLE 3
Regional markets in Britain, 1936

Market	Purchasing power index, 1936
Great Britain	108
South and Midlands	
Greater London	115
Bedford	131
Birmingham	128
Coventry	126
Luton	129
Oxford	131
Slough	110
Watford	129
North and West	
Barrow-in-Furness	102
Blackburn	89
Burnley	96
Darlington	106
Gateshead	77
Liverpool	90
Manchester	120
Newcastle-on-Tyne	100
Salford	98
South Shields	79
Wigan	89
Cardiff	96
Merthyr Tydfil	62
Rhondda	60
Swansea	86
Coatbridge	82
Edinburgh	109
Glasgow	94
Paisley	99

Note: The index is constructed from six factors, weighted as follows: employed insured, 38; unemployed insured, 2; families earning £500 a year or over, 25; families earning £250–£499 a year, 21; owners of private cars, 7; telephone subscribers, 7.
Source: Chisholm (1937, pp. 48–9). Indices are provided for a total of 127 markets.

either. Data on male earnings in declining and expanding industries in 1935 are presented in Table 4. Unfortunately, the available figures for average weekly hours cover all workers rather than males only, and some of the expanding industries had lower proportions of adult males than the heavily male-employing industries listed. Since females worked fewer hours per week, industries in which they were more important (electric cable and lamp

TABLE 4

Male earnings in Great Britain and Northern Ireland in the week ended 12 October 1935

Industry	Average weekly earnings, men 21 and over (s. & d.) (1)	Average weekly hours, all workpeople (2)	Average hourly earnings (d.) (1)/(2)
Declining industries			
Pig iron manufacture	65 11	52.1	15.2
Coal mining*	51 0	39.4†	15.5
General engineering (firms with less than 10 workers)	61 7	47.6	15.5
General iron and steel founding	63 3	48.2	15.7
General engineering (firms with 10 or more workers)	66 0	49.1	16.1
Shipbuilding and repairing	62 0	45.9	16.2
Marine engineering	65 4	47.8	16.4
Iron and steel smelting, rolling, etc.	71 2	46.9	18.2
Tinplate and galvanized sheets	69 8	41.8	20.0
Expanding industries			
Motor engineering (firms with less than 10 workers)	55 9	49.0	13.7
Electric cable making	61 10	49.1	15.1
Cycle and motor accessories	63 7	47.3	16.1
Electrical engineering	66 11	49.0	16.4
Heating and ventilating engineering	68 1	49.0	16.7
Rubber goods	67 10	48.6	16.7
Silk throwing, spinning and weaving (including artificial silk weaving)	66 10	46.9	17.1
Electrical and scientific instrument making	70 7	49.0	17.3
Typewriters, calculating machines, etc.	69 9	48.5	17.3
Artificial silk spinning	67 3	46.0	17.5
Aircraft manufacture	74 10	50.2	17.9
Electric lamp manufacture	71 9	48.0	17.9
Electrical contracting	73 6	48.7	18.1
Motor engineering (firms with 10 or more workers)	78 5	48.0	19.6

Figures are for average weekly hours and earnings during the fourth quarter of 1935, and include cash earnings and allowances in kind.

Based on 5¼ shifts (of 7½ hours) per week.

Source: Ministry of Labour Gazette (1937, pp. 46–8, 133–5, 174–6, 257).

making, rubber, artificial silk) will show higher average hourly earnings than they should for males alone.

Expanding industries in Table 4 do tend to show higher average hourly earnings. Of course, these are industry-wide averages, so one cannot conclude directly that earnings in depressed areas were lower. But the degree of locational concentration of industries suggests that the data may also indicate regional differences. In the one industry for which detailed regional earnings data are available—engineering—men in declining regions did have lower earnings than those in prosperous regions where the motor car, aircraft, and other new engineering activities were found (Knowles and Robertson, 1951, pp. 190–2). To the extent that this is the case, it suggests that male-employing new industries had not previously been locating on the basis of the cheapest source of male labour, and would not necessarily be attracted by lower wages.[2]

The industries primarily seeking cheap and adaptable labour often hired females and juveniles instead. Their earnings tended to be one-third to one-half those of adult males (*Ministry of Labour Gazette*, 1937, pp. 46–8, 88–9, 133–5, 174–6, 257–8), and they were less organized in trade unions. This type of labour was sought both in certain new industries and in traditional light industries that were modernizing and moving into mass production. During the interwar period such labour could be found easily in prosperous areas, a situation that persisted until sustained high levels of demand during and after World War II tightened labour markets in prosperous areas.

Thus a simple dynamic of wage decline will not necessarily lead to endogenous regional revival. A more complex argument points to the role of decline of the old, largely male-employing industries in driving women and young people into greater participation in the wage-labour force (Massey, 1983; Harrison, 1982, pp. 42–4). But as these authors point out, while decline can serve in this way as a prelude to the utilization of new labour, the ensuing process does not create a new regional industrial base analogous to the old one. Unemployed male workers may never be re-integrated into the new structures on a large scale. The firms involved often are large, headquartered outside the region, and utilizing labour throughout the world. The process depends heavily on developments exterior to the region: on improvements in transport and communication, the evolution of the large-scale firm, and political factors. The political factors include not only macroeconomic, tariff, and regional policies, but also the shifting political climates that other countries offer to manufacturers seeking inexpensive fresh labour.

From the side of existing local capitalists as well as labour, there do not appear to be reliable mechanisms for regional revival. In part, this is due to institutional features predisposing firms to place available funds in financial investments rather than entering new manufacturing industries within the region. Organizational limitations and managerial inadequacy often characterized the single-industry family firms found in nineteenth-century industrial regions. These firms had no special advantages in terms of organizational, technical, or marketing expertise for producing in the twentieth-century growth industries. A number of firms that did attempt to diversify shortly after World War I ran into serious problems, as Hannah and others have discussed (Hannah, 1976, pp. 184–202). When such firms experienced difficulties, banks sometimes pressured them to strip away recently acquired activities and return to the original line of business (Armstrong Papers, 1926; Sayers, 1976, 1:315–18, 321–2; Hume and Moss, 1979, pp. 5–10).

But even had the firms been more successful, it is worth noting that many of their diversification activities were not located within the depressed regions. Armstrongs, for example, purchased an existing motor car company in the Midlands, as well as embarking on a huge pulp and newsprint operation in Newfoundland. Present-day merger and acquisition activity by large firms in the United States suggests that firms with the funds and managerial capacity to diversify do not necessarily do so within declining regions, or by investing directly in production facilities for new manufacturing activities.

Many British firms in older industries, especially shipbuilding and armaments, came out of World War I or even the 1920s with considerable financial resources. But while some did attempt to diversify into new manufacturing activities, domestic and foreign securities were an attractive alternative. Earnings from financial assets then helped to sustain them during the lean 1930s. Lyle Shipping had a healthy balance sheet at the end of World War I. The directors decided in 1919 to restructure, liquidating management and single-ship companies, paying off loans, and transferring unencumbered assets and reserves to a new firm. The company's survival after 1919 despite the collapse of the shipping market was attributed in part to its capital position and accounting policy. Income from financial investments and management fees provided important protection. In the 1930s investments were sold to pay for needed new tonnage, reducing reserves from £123,037 to £30,000 in 1936–7. The reserves were rebuilt when substantial profits were recorded at the end of the 1930s. Investments by 1938–9 included government securities and shares of ICI, Shell Transport and Trading Co., Phoenix Assurance Co., Commercial Union Assurance Co., Scottish Iron and Steel Co., Stewarts and Lloyds, and J. and P. Coats (Orbell, 1978, pp. 68–9, 77, 85–6).

R. & W. Hawthorn Leslie & Co., a Tyneside shipbuilding firm, made an abortive attempt to diversify into locomotive building in 1920–1, then concentrated on placing available funds into financial investments:

The substantial trading profits of 1919–21, almost £½ million, were largely converted into gilt-edged securities; such holdings rose from £230,646 in 1921 to £679,766 a year later. This policy, begun in 1917, created a basis of regular income at a time when expansion in shipbuilding or engineering was a doubtful prospect. (Clarke, 1979, p. 93)

Dividend distribution depended upon investment income. During 1923–37 £375,836 was distributed, while investment income was £439,522. In only one of those years did the three productive departments together contribute more to profits than did investment income. The company history concludes that

holdings in investments continually exceeded the value of fixed assets. Sadly one must conclude that in this period these entrepreneurs decide [sic] that the return on Government securities was a more profitable prospect than the expansion of their technological productive capacity. (Clarke, 1979, p. 94)

Hawthorn Leslie did survive; it maintained a certain amount of employment, and satisfied shareholders. Its primary aim, as for many firms, seems to have been holding the company together to pursue its 'proper' lines of activity in better times, rather than using the organization to move into new industrial sectors.

Swan Hunter and Wigham Richardson, another Tyneside shipbuilding and marine engineering firm, followed a similar path. Its directors made clear in 1924 that 'the satisfactory character of the results is not due to additional work . . . but is the result of the very conservative policy adopted as regards investments and management of assets' (Clarke, 1979, p. 93). The firm did become involved in the late 1930s in one of the 'new' industries assisted by a special finance organization (the Nuffield Trust) to set up on Tyneside. But the undertaking was a plywood factory, for which the shipbuilding industry was to be a major source of demand (Nuffield Trust Papers, 1937).

Evidence on the tendency of capital in old industry sectors to move, if at all, into financial investments rather than direct investments in new industries is provided by two recent studies on what might be termed regional capital and regional capitalists. *The Anatomy of Scottish Capital* (Scott and Hughes, 1980) describes the movement of capital as early as the 1870s from old industries (at that time, the Dundee jute industry) into investment trusts and mortgage companies, at least one of which channelled surplus funds to American undertakings. Between 1873 and 1900, nineteen trusts and a number of mortgage companies were established in Scotland; they attracted English as well as Scottish capital (Scott and Hughes, 1980, pp. 25–6). In the interwar period,

the decline and restructuring of the old industrial base was matched by a massive expansion of the financial sector, particularly the investment sector. Scottish capital flowed into investment trusts, old and new, which invested in stable companies, and government and foreign stock. (Scott and Hughes, 1980, p. 107)

Wealthy old-industry families began to diversify their holdings rather than having all their interests tied up in one concern. But these were portfolio decisions carried through in the financial markets, not investment strategies for the family businesses. In the years after the post-World War I boom, many Scottish companies

were brought under foreign control, were amalgamated with English companies, or were absorbed into larger Scottish concerns. As a consequence, considerable funds must have been available to the former shareholders of these companies. This wealth, however, was not put back into industry but was put into the formation and extension of investment trusts. (Scott and Hughes, 1980, p. 70)

More recently, nationalization and the take-over of Scottish companies by outside interests have made large sums of money available to former owners. Again, these have largely found their way into the financial sector rather than being directly reinvested in industry (though Scottish finance apparently has played an important role in North Sea oil development) (Scott and Hughes, 1980, pp. 261–3).

A similar argument, coupled with the idea of a regional capitalist class becoming progressively integrated into wider national and international networks, has been made for the North East Coast (Benwell Community Project, 1978). Diversification took the form not of reinvestment within existing companies, but rather of the movement of funds and personnel into the finance capital sector by later generations of the small number of families who had established the old heavy industries. Investment trusts and holding companies emerged. Some of the trusts had been set up in the early years of the century to develop new techniques for electricity generation. But they had much wider interests as well. One, the Tyneside Electrical Development Co., became reconstituted as the Tyneside Investment Trust in 1929 with a public share issue; in 1930 only 23 per cent of its investment portfolio was in North East Coast industry (Benwell Community Project, 1978, p. 59).

In a few instances family members moved into new consumer goods industries, although not necessarily within the same region. Sir P. W. Richardson (of Swan Hunter and Wigham Richardson) and his son G. W. Richardson were involved in the development of Airspeed (1934) Ltd, an aircraft manufacturer with a factory at Portsmouth.[3] The Straker (coal) family opened a motor vehicle distribution company selling Ford cars in Newcastle. Some individuals served as directors of new-industry firms such as Brush Electrical Engineering. There was considerable involvement in public utilities, especially electric companies (on the part of coal families). But the most noticeable shift was into banking, insurance, investment holding companies, building societies, and money-management-oriented professions such as law and stockbroking. Again, the movement was even more pronounced after World War II when nationalization transformed the coal owners' capital from fixed assets to liquid government bonds (Benwell Community Project, 1978, pp. 54, 58).

Characteristics of firms adapted to nineteenth-century growth thus do play a role in the failure of old regions to diversify from within, and in the tendency of capital to move from industrial to financial activities rather than across industries within the firm or region. But the lack of endogenous transformation in old regions is also a function of the local inducement to invest, the question of whether there is a sufficient market best served by local production, or cheap elements of production attractive in comparison with their equivalents elsewhere. These factors do not depend solely on features of the existing institutional structure.

Concerning the ability to attract industry from outside the depressed areas, I have argued elsewhere that, given the relatively slow evolution of the large-scale firm in Britain, expansion of aggregate demand would have had much less of an effect in the short or medium run in stimulating branch-plant development in the depressed areas than it did after World War II (Heim, 1983). In any event, strong expansion of demand was lacking in the interwar period, as was strong application of regional policy—two respects in which the post-World War II experience differs significantly. The weakness of aggregate demand was due partly to attitudes towards state intervention that may be arued to be part of a complex of institutions associated with nineteenth-century competitive capitalism. But Britain faced the adjustment problem at a time when international economic conditions were extremely unfavourable. Government intervention might not have been able fully to counteract their effects. Moreover, if industry were attracted from outside in the same manner as after World War II, this would have ameliorated conditions in the depressed areas but not fully solved the regional problem.

Although its precise effects have been debated, there is wide agreement that, when regional policy was applied strongly (e.g., in the 1960s as opposed to the 1950s), it did affect the distribution of industry. Particularly, it attracted mobile industry to the depressed areas and prohibited expansion in prosperous areas (Brown, 1972, pp. 281–318; Fothergill and Gudgin, 1982, pp. 134–52; McCallum, 1979; McCrone, 1969, pp. 149–66; Moore and Rhodes, 1973). The weakness of the earlier interwar regional policy, examined in greater detail below, reflects the influence of institutional factors as well as macroeconomic conditions.

The Formation of Interwar Regional Policy

The governmental response to Britain's regional problem was limited and *ad hoc*. In the 1920s the focus was on labour transference—moving workers to jobs. In the 1930s both the content of regional policies and the degree of intervention changed, but the desire to minimize direct state involvement and to work through markets never disappeared (Daly, 1978, pp. 367–9).

During the later 1930s, when the main efforts focused on providing rental factories on trading estates and improving the operation of the capital market in depressed areas, the priorities and attitudes of financial institutions played a clear constraining role. But depressed macroeconomic conditions influenced both early labour transference programmes and the special finance programmes. Finally, the strength of regional interest groups, a consequence of regional specialization, may also have weakened the special finance programmes by sharply skewing the distribution of assistance.

Labour transference schemes, first established for coal miners in the late 1920s, assisted individual workers or households to move to more prosperous areas. The schemes were handicapped by being attempted during the worst of the economic downturn. Total individuals transferred through the employment exchanges reached 43,698 in 1929, the second year of the programme, but dropped to 33,031 in 1930 and continued to decline to a low of 13,443 in 1933 before increasing again. Household and family removals showed a similar pattern to the mid-1930s (Pitfield, 1973, Table XXI).

Transference generated opposition on both the sending and receiving ends, especially in the case of juveniles. The Trades Union Congress conceded a qualified support mainly, it seems, in recognition of the lack of alternatives. A statement issued in 1937, after the programme had been in operation many years, argued that juveniles should be in school to the age of sixteen and that 'the Labour Movement does not believe that the problem of the distressed areas can be solved by a system of transferring young workers to other relatively more prosperous districts' (Trades Union Congress, 1937, p. 118). But other solutions would take time, and it was felt that under certain conditions transference 'may be regarded as better than nothing' and 'cannot be opposed on principle' (Trades Union Congress, 1937, pp. 118–19). The Miners Federation of Great Britain and the Labour and Liberal Parties also supported the programme (Pitfield, 1973, pp. 174–5). Other bodies were less tolerant: the London Trades Council was implacably opposed to the influx, claiming in 1935 that

the whole scheme is reminiscent of the days of child slavery of last century. . . . It is perhaps unnecessary to inform the Minister of Labour that many of the employers in the new industries on the outer belt of London are carrying the exploitation of juvenile labour to an extent verging on a public scandal. . . . the whole question should be tackled by bold schemes of reconstruction calculated to provide employment for the people near their own homes. (London Trades Council, 1935, p. 3)

Juveniles were not the only persons transferred, but their transference aroused the most controversy. The question of their 'after-care' in their new environments came up repeatedly in Parliament.

Particularly during the worst of the depression, there was conflict in London over the employment of men from the depressed areas. The Building

Trades Unions protested loudly, and ultimately eliminated an Office of Works policy of preference for men from the depressed areas in its new building and maintenance work (PRO LAB 2/493, 1931). Objections were raised in other towns as well. In an earlier case in Birmingham, the Ministry of Labour was decidedly unsympathetic. Its secret report to the Cabinet in 1928 pointed out that, over a period during which 156 persons had been placed in employment in Birmingham under the transference scheme, there were probably as many as 15,000 labour engagements in an insured population of 347,950. Miners thus took one engagement out of every 100 (PRO CAB 24/198, 1928a). Unemployment in Birmingham at the time was 10.9 per cent—higher than in London or Oxford but low in comparison with Bishop Auckland (42.9 per cent), Merthyr Tydfil (75.9 per cent), or other depressed areas.

Despite various problems with the programme, including high rates of 'wastage' or return of transferred workers, transference reached its peak in 1936 and thus, as Pitfield argues, was promoted for a time even while policies to stimulate industry and otherwise improve conditions in the depressed areas were being formulated (Pitfield, 1978). The Special Areas (Development and Improvement) Act 1934 defined severely depressed Special Areas in South Wales, Durham and Tyneside, West Cumberland, and Scotland, and appointed two Commissioners for the Special Areas, one for England and Wales, one for Scotland. The Commissioners were given limited powers and funds for the 'economic development and social improvement' of the Special Areas. But the Minister of Labour, Betterton, could still write to the Prime Minister in 1934 that transfer (between industries as well as areas) was the essential policy, adding that he had considered a new 'drive' for transference but felt the time was not right (PRO LAB 18/28, 1934).

By early 1937 the emphasis had shifted to moving industry rather than workers. The Commissioners were empowered to assist businesses in the Special Areas by constructing trading estates with rental factories and by contributing to firms' rent, rates, and income taxes. A letter from Skinner (Assistant to the Governor of the Bank of England) to Weir (a director of SARA, a special finance organization set up to fund small businesses in the depressed areas) in December 1936 explained that

whether we like it or not, the Chancellor has already promised further measures of help to the Special Areas, and a 'sister for S.A.R.A.' would not be surprising. At any rate some form of encouragement to business in South Wales, etc., seems a settled policy and the wholesale removal of population is not at the moment practical politics. (BOE SMT 2/19, 1936.)

He added that the latter would in any case be more expensive than assisting industrial development, as only the pick would transfer, leaving a very expensive relief problem. The shift to the policy of taking jobs to the workers was partly due to the fairly rapid depletion of suitable or easy candidates for transfer (younger single men), and to the recognition that a serious problem of older long-term unemployed remained. Even in 1928 there had been awareness of the programme's potential limitations:

One of the most serious obstacles in the way of the successful carrying out of the transfer policy is the difficulty of finding employment for married men with families outside the depressed areas. These constitute a substantial proportion of the unemployed in the depressed areas. (PRO CAB 24/198, 1928b.)

Arguments supporting the 'move-industry' policy were formulated explicitly in the *Reports* of the Commissioner for the Special Areas in England and Wales and the Royal Commission on the Distribution of the Industrial Population. The desirability of avoiding further concentration of industry and population in the more prosperous areas was stressed.

Efforts to redirect industry rather than transfer workers have remained the focus of British regional policy. Some argue that transference policy has never been given a fair trial in Britain, claiming it was introduced at a time of such unfavourable macroeconomic conditions that unwarranted evaluations were made (Beaumont, 1979, pp. 67–8; Pitfield, 1973, pp. 218, 257, 399). In addition to the depression limiting its effectiveness, however, one must take account of the relatively low mobility of the workforce. Both assisted and unassisted migration did occur, but interregional mobility of workers was impeded by factors related to patterns of nineteenth-century formation of working-class organization, culture, and community (Dennison, 1939, pp. 186–90). Even workers who had relocated often returned when conditions improved in the depressed areas (as with rearmament in the late 1930s). This rootedness was intensified by the degree of regional specialization in Britain, as well as by factors such as housing policy (which, however, reflects the greater state intervention associated with twentieth-century rather than nineteenth-century institutions). Beyond the question of mobility of the labour force, however, remained the problem of structural mismatch between the types of workers being displaced and those sought in many of the expanding industries.

The strategy that evolved—assisting businesses in the depressed areas through the provision of finance and rental factories—was designed to avoid direct government involvement with business as much as possible. It was sparked by immediate political pressures, particularly adverse press in *The Times* and elsewhere and opinion in Parliament (Daly, 1978, pp. 168, 364–7). The primary focus, reflecting the policy's origins, was employment rather than growth. There was no clear conception of industrial policy in the sense of developing new growth sectors in the depressed regions or elsewhere in Britain. The major policy concern was rationalization in the older industries. Encouragement to new industries throughout Britain was limited primarily to industries considered important for national defence and those such as coal-oil schemes which also might improve conditions in the depressed staple trades.

Assistance in the depressed areas was not restricted to new industries. The Nuffield Trust, in particular, helped a number of firms in declining industries to preserve employment. All the funding organizations assisted a large share of diverse light industries rather than new industries proper (Heim, 1982, Table V-32; PRO T187/61, n.d.). Employment in light industries was thought necessary to balance that in the traditional heavy trades; it also was commonly assumed that light consumer goods industries were less cyclically sensitive than the export trades (Political and Economic Planning, 1939, pp. 136–7). Outside of Lancashire, development of light industries employing high proportions of females and juveniles would not jeopardize the labour supply to established industries that employed men. In response to the inquiry of the Royal Commission on the Distribution of the Industrial Population, the Newcastle and Gateshead Chamber of Commerce suggested in 1938

that Tyneside should be enabled to retain its available labour by the attraction of new industries, care being taken that the heavier industries, which have been and must still be the backbone of the industrial activity of the district, are not faced with an ultimate labour shortage. (Council of the City and County of Newcastle upon Tyne, 1938, p. 584)

In some areas, particularly Scotland, there were complaints by existing industrialists and public figures about the lack of local entrepreneurship, and local development efforts focused on encouraging 'new men' (entrepreneurs). But again there was no clear sense of direction in terms of developing new growth industries and no clear distinction between new men in new versus light industries. The emphasis generally on employment persisted even after World War II (Cairncross, 1979, pp. ix–xiv). Only recently have industrial policies focusing on the encouragement of new industries been designed (Silberston, 1981).

The interwar focus on special finance resulted largely from the combination of short-term, pragmatic policy formulation and a climate of criticism of Britain's financial machinery dating to the Macmillan *Report* of 1931 and earlier. The impetus came from political pressures to do something about the depressed areas, pressures that had particularly targeted the problem of finance (PRO T175/90, n.d. (but 1935)). The three special finance programmes were all very small in relation to the size of the adjustment problem: the Special Areas Reconstruction Association, Ltd (SARA), set up in 1936 under the auspices of the Bank of England with a nominal capital of £1 million; the private Nuffield Trust, established the same year by a gift of £2 million from Lord Nuffield; and the Treasury Fund, a £2 million government fund created in 1938 partly in response to criticism of SARA.

Initial leadership of the programmes by the financial community allowed the government to avoid more direct involvement; state participation in SARA was limited to the provision of administrative expenses and certain guarantees against losses on loans. This leadership also meant that the priorities of the financial institutions would significantly affect implementation. Apparently few in London financial circles thought the programmes necessary, or believed that finance was the main problem of the depressed areas. The aim of the financial community was to do enough to allay criticism and forestall more extensive government intervention, yet not itself create large-scale programmes of assistance.

The Bank of England, in its involvement with SARA, thus endeavoured to keep the programme small and as close as possible to ordinary banking practices concerning interest rates, outside capital requirements, and evaluation of applicants (for details see Heim, 1984). SARA could not make loans above £10,000 without special permission from the Treasury. One result of the limitation to small firms was the concentration of assistance in diverse light industries rather than new industries proper, which often had larger capital requirements for production or distribution organizations.

The Nuffield Trust and the Treasury Fund did not share this particular restriction, and the Treasury Fund did assist a higher proportion of enterprises in the new industries proper. It was, however, criticized (as was SARA) for behaving too much like an ordinary banking house, especially in terms of the security required for loans. In addition to meeting the outside capital requirement of 50 per cent, applicants had to demonstrate that they had already been refused by ordinary financial sources. The Treasury programme came into operation only a short time before the war and assisted a total of only 24 firms, paying out £1,160,500 of its total £2,000,000 funding.

The Nuffield Trust, considered by contemporaries to be the most successful of the programmes, was not bound by ordinary banking (or government) priorities and concerns. It provided share as well as loan capital and in several cases worked in co-operation with the other funds to enable enterprises to meet their outside capital requirements. Its loss rate was actually somewhat lower than that of the Treasury Fund, although it was considered able to take greater risks. The relative success of the Nuffield Trust and its role in extending the usefulness of the other programmes point up the institutional constraints limiting the bank and government programmes. Although special finance could not provide a complete solution to the problems of the depressed areas, in part for reasons discussed in the first section above, the experience of the Nuffield Trust suggests that more of this type of assistance would have had beneficial effects.

SARA's focus upon small firms was due in part to the desire to avoid the political complications the Bank had faced when involved with large firms in rationalization schemes. But it also reflected the fact that SARA's capital had been contributed partly by large companies in Britain. Those connected with raising the finance stated explicitly that companies did not want the funds used to set up competitors. Sensitivity to the charge of selective subsidization generally was another force hampering the extension of interwar regional policy and especially the efforts of the Treasury Fund, the organization most closely identified with the government. The depressed macroeconomic conditions probably heightened fears of existing firms.[4]

Careful enquiries were conducted before funding enterprises, in order to assess the reaction of major producers and associations. Concern about subsidized competition existed not only in the new industries proper but in diverse light industries where barriers to entry were lower and some existing producers had been slow to move into mass-production methods (Scottish Economic Committee, 1938). In at least one industry the Treasury Fund capitulated to association pressure and agreed to make no further loans. The Nuffield Trust was similarly circumspect, as the case of W. H. Pease & Co. demonstrates. The firm was an English business recently established under German auspices to make special process machines for various industries, principally under German patents. A Nuffield Trust minute for 24 January 1938 reports that 'the Applicants [Pease & Co.] have submitted their correspondence with Messrs. Walmsleys Ltd. of Bury in order to demonstrate the friendly relations existing with that Company and to show that there is no intention to embark in business in any way competitive with that Company' (Nuffield Trust Papers, 1938a). The proposal ultimately was not funded, however, because the Trustees did not want to take too large a part of the new undertaking's financial burden, and Walmsleys, though it had considered taking an interest in the company and putting a director on the Board, declined to participate (Nuffield Trust Papers, 1938a, 1938b).

The funding agencies did not always yield to pressure, even from powerful firms. ICI, which held a patent for a particular process, requested at one point that additional firms producing zip fasteners not be funded. The request was denied, and Flex Fasteners, a firm founded by European immigrants, became one of the more successful operations funded in South Wales (BOE SMT 2/28, 1938). Much earlier, a spokesman for the Treasury had explained its general policy regarding the entry of foreign firms into British industries which might have excess capacity:

This is not to say, however, that on occasion, where we had reason to suspect that the home manufacturer was behind the foreigner in methods of production, organisation and so forth, we should mind putting some particularly agile foreign cat among the more slow moving of our domestic pigeons. (PRO BT 56/40, 1931.)

But in general there was a growing acceptance, especially during the 1930s, of restrictions on market competition, and this was reflected in the behaviour of the funding agencies. In a sense, the worst of both worlds prevailed, and the problem thus was not simply one of excessive reliance on the market mechanism. Entry by new producers who might contribute to diversification in older regions became increasingly difficult as cartels and restrictive practices multiplied in the depression, supplanting the market mechanism in defensive rather than constructive ways. Yet prevailing attitudes and existing institutions resisted thoroughgoing intervention in the economy, or the creation of new institutional forms.

Pressure shaping the implementation of regional policy also came from the regions themselves. One consequence of regional specialization had been the creation of strong regional working and capitalist classes, able in some cases to mount vocal and politically embarrassing demands for assistance. Although one should not overstate the effectiveness of such demands in the 1930s, their impact was enhanced by the lack of a coherent national pro-gramme. The clearest case is Jarrow, which had one of the highest unem-ployment rates in the nation owing to the decline of the local shipbuilding industry. The closing of the Palmer's Shipyard as part of the rationalization plans of National Shipbuilders' Security, and the blocking by Teesside steel interests of a new integrated Bessemer mill at Jarrow, had fuelled a sense of injustice. The Jarrow march of 1936 was one result.

Jarrow received a disproportionate share of total funds for regional assis-tance. From the Treasury Fund it obtained £330,000 for its iron and steel schemes, or 28 per cent of the total lent. The Nuffield Trust provided £360,000 in share capital, or 16 per cent of its total loans and investments in shares (PRO T187/6–7, 1942–8; Nuffield Trust Papers, 1962). In this case the strength of regional interest groups helped produce not only the concentration of assistance in Jarrow, but a focus on existing heavy indus-tries there, rather than new or diverse light industries. The schemes involved highly modern and expensive plant which provided little employment in relation to the huge sums expended. The Secretary to the Nuffield Trust recalled that his organization, which favoured the establishment of light industries, was

pressed into the scheme not by any wish expressed by Lord Nuffield (who incidentally also looks somewhat askance upon the case) but to serve the political necessity of the time to 'do something' for Jarrow which had succeeded in making itself a nuisance to the Government of the day. This was also the reason why the Bank of England joined in. (Nuffield Trust Papers, 1944.)

Conclusion

An effective response to Britain's interwar regional problem required diver-sification into industries with significant growth and employment potential in an advanced economy, as well as rationalization in the older industries. To what extent did British institutions adapted to nineteenth-century capitalism impede diversification, especially in the depressed regions?

The most obvious case is the impact of financial institutions upon regional policy. Their concerns—many of which were shared at the Treasury—kept the special finace programmes small and relatively ineffective. Although special finance and trading estates were regarded as less objectionable forms of intervention than direct government involvement, the programmes consistently were described as 'experimental', 'extraordinary', and a response to special conditions that had generated public criticism.

The government, bound by its *laissez-faire* traditions, was unwilling to intervene strongly in regional policy or macroeconomic demand management, although the degree of intervention did increase somewhat over the course of the interwar period. The stronger hand of government in regional policy since World War II, however, has raised the question of possible conflicts between regional policy and industrial policy: measures addressing the regional problem are not necessarily the best means of developing internationally competitive industries. Given the emergence of this conflict in the post-World War II period, it is not entirely clear what directions stronger intervention should have taken in the interwar period, beyond simply the maintenance of aggregate demand.

Nineteenth-century institutions also were relevant at the level of the firm, although the argument here is complex. The failure of older regions to diversify from within is partly due to the predominance of single-industry family firms lacking managerial capacity to diversify or special advantages in producing in the expanding industries. The movement discussed above into financial capital can be viewed as reflecting an awareness of this incapacity. The ability to attract more industry from outside the depressed regions also would have been constrained in the short or medium run by the stage of development of the firm even if macroeconomic policy had been stronger. Yet in both cases the issue is not only the character of existing institutions, but conditions in the depressed areas relative to those outside. There was no particular reason in the 1930s for most firms in expanding industries to be interested in investing in the depressed areas.

British institutions, both public and private, thus were ill-suited in many respects for coping with the regional problem. But the scale of the problem challenging those institutions was immense. Both the degree of regional specialization and the world depression were extreme. The consequences of regional specialization, and the availability of fresh labour and other resources elsewhere in interwar Britain, meant that even stronger growth of new industries nationally would not necessarily have solved the problems of the depressed regions. New growth within advanced economies is often grounded in the creation of new, rather than the transformation of old, regions and productive structures. Even when limited diversification in the depressed regions did occur after World War II, under much more favourable regional policy and aggregate demand conditions, this restructuring was based heavily upon the incorporation of new elements rather than the transformation of integrated regional economies and the re-employment of workers from the older industries in new industries. Compounding the difficulties of the interwar years, macroeconomic depression—only partly a consequence of government inaction—kept labour markets from becoming tight in prosperous areas, restricted competitive conditions, and affected the administration of both transference policy and efforts to stimulate industrial development in the depressed areas.

Notes

[1]Some authors criticize the idea that there was a significant, identifiable block of new industries in the interwar British economy (see, for example, Dowie, 1969; von Tunzelmann, 1982). The view adopted in this paper is that rationalization in the major declining export trades, while making an important contribution to overall British economic performance, at its best would not have solved the regional unemployment problem. Expanding industries (including diverse light industries and services as well as new industries proper characterized by scientific and organizational innovation) did exist in interwar Britain, but were not strongly represented in the depressed areas whose continuing decline was an important aspect of national economic decline.

[2]Two qualifications to this argument should be noted. The differentials in Table 4 are not extreme, and one could argue that a drastic fall in male wages in the declining regions might overcome other locational factors. Employers also might have been · concerned that wages were only temporarily low, and would rise if conditions improved in the depressed areas. Support for this view is provided by 1938 earnings data, which, while not strictly comparable, do suggest increases in male earnings in several of the declining industries listed in Table 4 (Ainsworth, 1949, pp. 45–8).

[3]This case provides an interesting illustration of the difficulties to be overcome in moving from old to new industries:

One of the Swan Hunter directors, a trifle disillusioned by the methods of the aircraft industry, so different to the solid Victorian approach of shipbuilders, introduced Tiltman and Norway to this remarkable Dutchman [Anthony Fokker], no doubt thinking that he would be a most valuable ally in offering an independent view of these strange goings-on at Portsmouth. Swan Hunter could not understand the mentality of these apparently frivolous aeronautical engineers. Hessell Tiltman told the story of a conversation with one of their directors who said, 'Tiltman, I cannot understand why you need thirty five draughtsmen to design these tiny aeroplanes, we designed the Mauretania with far less!' (Middleton, n.d., ch. 4, pp. 11–12)

[4]Apparently such attitudes did not disappear: according to Checkland, a similar concern was voiced by the heads of two Glasgow-based banks when the Industrial and Commercial Finance Corporation was proposed by others in Scotland as a means of attracting newer industries to diversify the post-World War II Scottish economy. 'They were concerned that new firms backed by the proposed body might be competitive with existing Scottish companies' (Checkland, 1975, pp. 598–9).

Bibliography

Ainsworth, R. B. (1949). 'Earnings and Working Hours of Manual Wage-Earners in the United Kingdom in October, 1938'. *Journal of the Royal Statistical Society*, ser. A, 112, part I.

Armstrong Papers (1926). Schedule C 9, 'Report to the Directors' (by Mr J. Frater Taylor and Sir Gilbert Garnsey, FCA), 30 March 1926, and 'Report' (Supplementary and Final to Report dated 30 March 1926), 27 November 1926; and Schedule C 29, Minutes 1896–1929, Meeting of 18 November 1926. Tyne and Wear Record Office, Newcastle upon Tyne.

Beaumont, P. B. (1979). 'An Examination of Assisted Labour Mobility Policy'. In *Regional Policy: Past Experience and New Directions*, ed. Duncan Maclennan and John B. Parr. Oxford: Martin Robertson.

Benwell Community Project (1978). *The Making of a Ruling Class: Two Centuries of Capital Development on Tyneside*. Newcastle: Benwell Community Project.

BOE SMT 2/19 (1936). Skinner to Weir, 10 December. Bank of England Archives, London.

BOE SMT 2/28 (1938). S.A.R.A., Cases to be put before the Board on Thursday, 19 May. Bank of England Archives, London.

Brown, A. J. (1972). *The Framework of Regional Economics in the United Kingdom*. Cambridge University Press.

Cairncross, Sir Alec (1979). 'Foreword'. In *Regional Policy: Past Experiences and New Directions*, ed. Duncan Maclennan and John B. Parr. Oxford: Martin Robertson.

Checkland, S. G. (1975). *Scottish Banking: A History 1695–1973*. Glasgow: Collins.

Chinitz, Benjamin (1961). 'Contrasts in Agglomeration: New York and Pittsburgh'. *American Economic Review*, 51(2).

Chisholm, Cecil (1937). *Marketing Survey of the United Kingdom* (2d edn). London: Business Publications.

Clarke, J. F. (1979). *Power on Land and Sea: 160 Years of Industrial Enterprise on Tyneside, A History of R. & W. Hawthorn Leslie & Co., Ltd, Engineers and Shipbuilders*. Wallsend: Clark Hawthorn.

Council of the City and County of Newcastle upon Tyne (1938). *Proceedings of the Council of the City and County of Newcastle Upon Tyne for 1937–1938*. Newcastle: Co-operative Printing Society.

Cross, Michael (1981). *New Firm Formation and Regional Development*. Farnborough, Hants: Gower Press.

Daly, Mary E. (1978). 'Government Policy and the Depressed Areas in the Inter-War Years'. DPhil thesis, Oxford University.

Dennison, S. R. (1939). *The Location of Industry and the Depressed Areas*. London: Humphrey Milford.

Dowie, J. A. (1969). 'Growth in the Inter-War Period: Some More Arithmetic'. In *Economic Growth in Twentieth-century Britain*, ed. Derek H. Aldcroft and Peter Fearon. London: Macmillan.

Firn, J. R. (1975). 'External Control and Regional Development: The Case of Scotland'. *Environment and Planning* A, 7, June.

Florence, P. Sargant (1948). *Investment, Location, and Size of Plant: A Realistic Inquiry into the Structure of British and American Industries*. Cambridge University Press.

Fothergill, Stephen and Graham Gudgin (1982). *Unequal Growth: Urban and Regional Employment Change in the UK*. London: Heinemann.

Great Britain, Board of Trade (1932a). *An Industrial Survey of South Wales*. London: HMSO.

Great Britain, Board of Trade (1932b). *An Industrial Survey of the Lancashire Area (Excluding Merseyside)*. London: HMSO.

Great Britain, Board of Trade (1932c). *An Industrial Survey of the North East Coast Area*. London: HMSO.

Great Britain, Board of Trade (1932d). *An Industrial Survey of the South West of Scotland*. London: HMSO.

Hannah, Leslie (1976). 'Strategy and Structure in the Manufacturing Sector'. In *Management Stategy and Business Development*, ed. Leslie Hannah. London: Macmillan.

Harrison, Bennett (1982). 'Rationalization, Restructuring, and Industrial Reorganization in Older Regions: The Economic Transformation of New England since World War II'. Working Paper no. 72, Joint Center for Urban Studies of MIT and Harvard University, Cambridge, Mass.

Heim, Carol E. (1982). 'Uneven Regional Development in Interwar Britain'. PhD thesis, Yale University.

Heim, Carol E. (1983). 'Industrial Organization and Regional Development in Interwar Britain'. *Journal of Economic History*, 43(4).

Heim, Carol E. (1984). 'Limits to Intervention: The Bank of England and Industrial Diversification in the Depressed Areas'. *Economic History Review*, 37(4).

Hume, John R., and Michael S. Moss (1979). *Beardmore: The History of a Scottish Industrial Giant*. London: Heinemann.

Jewkes, John, and Allan Winterbottom (1933). *An Industrial Survey of Cumberland and Furness*. Manchester University Press.

Kahn, Alfred E. (1946). *Great Britain in the World Economy*. New York: Columbia University Press.

Knowles, K. G. J. C., and D. J. Robertson (1951). 'Earnings in Engineering, 1926–1948'. *Bulletin of the Oxford University Institute of Statistics*, 13(6).

Lee, C. H. (1971). *Regional Economic Growth in the United Kingdom since the 1880s*. Maidenhead, Berks: McGraw-Hill.

London Trades Council (1935). *Transfer of Juveniles from Depressed Areas*, London Trades Council Memorandum, 31 October. London: Twentieth Century Press (1912).

Massey, Doreen (1979). 'In What Sense a Regional Problem?' *Regional Studies*, 13(2).

Massey, Doreen (1983). 'Industrial Restructuring as Class Restructuring: Production Decentralization and Local Uniqueness'. *Regional Studies*, 17(2).

McCallum, J. D. (1979). 'The Development of British Regional Policy'. In *Regional Policy: Past Experience and New Directions*, ed. Duncan Maclennan and John B. Parr. Oxford: Martin Robertson.

McCrone, Gavin (1969). *Regional Policy in Britain*. London: Allen & Unwin.

Middleton, D. H. (n.d.) 'Years Ahead of their Time: The Story of Airspeed Ltd'. Unpublished manuscript, Glasgow University Archives.

Ministry of Labour Gazette (1937). 'Average Earnings and Hours of Labour in October, 1935'. February, March, April, May, and July issues.

Moore, B. and J. Rhodes (1973). 'Evaluating the Effects of British Regional Policy'. *Economic Journal*, 83(329).

Northern Region Strategy Team (1977). *Strategic Plan for the Northern Region*, Volume 2: *Economic Development Policies*. London: Northern Region Strategy Team.

North Tyneside Community Development Project (1978). *North Shields: Women's Work*. North Shields: North Tyneside Community Development Project.

Nuffield Trust Papers (1937). Minute Books, Meeting of 18 October 1937. Nuffield Library, Oxford.

Nuffield Trust Papers (1938a). Minute Books, Meeting of 24 January 1938. Nuffield Library, Oxford.

Nuffield Trust Papers (1938b). Minute Books, Meeting of 31 January 1938. Nuffield Library, Oxford.

Nuffield Trust Papers (1944). Box 12, Mr B. Seebowm Rowntree, Miscellaneous Correspondence 13 January 1937–30 August 1946. Roney (Secretary to the Nuffield Trust) to Rowntree (a Nuffield Trustee), 21 April 1944. Nuffield Library, Oxford.

Nuffield Trust Papers (1962). Box 1, Forty-first Report of the Trustees to the Rt. Hon. Viscount Nuffield, GBE, CH. Final Report and Accounts, 31 July 1962. Nuffield Library, Oxford.

Orbell, John, with Edwin Green and Michael Moss (1978). *From Cape to Cape: The History of Lyle Shipping Company*. Edinburgh: Paul Harris.

Pitfield, D. E. (1973). 'Labour Migration and the Regional Problem in Britain, 1920–1939'. PhD thesis, University of Stirling.

Pitfield, D. E. (1978). 'The Quest for an Effective Regional Policy, 1934–37'. *Regional Studies*, 12(4).

Political and Economic Planning (1939). *Report on the Location of Industry*. London: Political and Economic Planning.

PRO BT 56/40 (1931). Browett (Chief Industrial Adviser's Department, Treasury) to Gomme (Ministry of Labour), 9 November 1931. Public Record Office, London.

PRO CAB 24/198 (1928a). 'Industrial Transference Scheme'. Memorandum by the Minister of Labour, 1 November 1928. Public Record Office, London.

PRO CAB 24/198 (1928b). Interdepartmental Committee on Unemployment, Interim Report, 2 November 1928. Public Record Office, London.

PRO LAB 2/493 (1931). Bondfield to Lansbury, 10 July 1931. Public Record Office, London.

PRO LAB 18/28 (1934). Draft letter from Betterton to the Prime Minister, 17 March 1934. Public Record Office, London.

PRO T175/90 (n.d. but 1935). 'Financing Small Businesses'. Memorandum (by E. Skinner, Assistant to the Governor of the Bank of England). Public Record Office, London.

PRO T187/61 (n.d.). 'Provisional List of Firms Established in the Special Areas of (1) England and Wales and (2) Scotland between January 1937 and 30th September, 1939, including a few firms established previously but given financial assistance to expand during that period'. Public Record Office, London.

PRO T187/6–7 (1942–8). Special, etc. Areas Loans Advisory Committee, Notes for Meetings, Minutes of Meetings and Correspondence Relative thereto, 23 January 1942–27 December 1945, and 1 January 1946–12 August 1948. Public Record Office, London.

Royal Commission on the Distribution of the Industrial Population (1937–9). *Minutes of Evidence taken before the Royal Commission on the Geographical Distribution of the Industrial Population*. London: HMSO.

Royal Commission on the Distribution of the Industrial Population (1940). *Report of the Royal Commission on the Distribution of the Industrial Population*, Cmd. 6153. London: HMSO.

Rubinstein, W. D. (1977). 'The Victorian Middle Classes: Wealth, Occupation, and Geography'. *Economic History Review*, 2nd ser., 30(4).

Sayers, R. S. (1976). *The Bank of England 1891–1944*, 3 vols. Cambridge University Press.

Scott, John P., and Michael Hughes (1980). *The Anatomy of Scottish Capital: Scottish Companies and Scottish Capital 1900–1979*. London: Croom Helm.

Scottish Economic Committee (1938). *Light Industries in Scotland: A Case for Development*. Glasgow: Scottish Economic Committee.

Silberston, Aubrey (1981). 'Industrial Policies in Britain'. In *Industrial Policy and Innovation*, ed. Charles Carter. London: Heinemann.

Trades Union Congress (1937). *Report of Proceedings at the 69th Annual Trades Union Congress*. London: Trades Union Congress.

von Tunzelmann, G. N. (1982). 'Structural Change and Leading Sectors in British Manufacturing, 1907–68'. In *Economics in the Long View: Essays in Honour of W. W. Rostow*, Volume 3, *Applications and Cases, Part II*, ed. Charles P. Kindleberger and Guido di Tella. New York University Press.

The State and Economic Decline

Peter A. Hall*

Harvard University

Just as the rise of the British economy was one of the miracles of the nineteenth century, so its decline has been one of the enigmas of the twentieth. Although her absolute rate of growth improved during world-wide expansion after World War II, Britain's performance relative to other industrial competitors, in both efficiency and output terms, has been one of continuous deterioration since the 1880s (Matthews, Feinstein, and Odling-Smee, 1982, p. 498; Boltho, 1982; Maddison, 1977). As a result, the British share of world exports of manufactures fell from 31 per cent in 1913 to 8 per cent in 1983, and GNP per capita is barely half that in Germany, France, Scandinavia, or the United States. (NIER, 1984). Overall productivity per worker in British manufacturing is the second lowest among the ten largest economies of the West (Pollard, 1982, p. 11).

Britain's economic problems have been structural rather than conjunctural. Whatever the contribution of international fluctuations or relative factor endowments to growth, the British economy does not employ its resources as effectively as do overseas competitors (cf. Denison, 1967). In particular, its industries have been characterized by low levels of investment (OECD, 1970, p. 46), a reluctance to innovate or expand, (Harley, 1974; Lewis, 1967; Buxton, 1975), and outmoded forms of work organization at both the managerial and shopfloor levels (Hannah, 1974; Supple, 1977; Kilpatrick and Lawson, 1980; Central Policy Review Staff, 1975). Such factors are the proximate causes of economic decline (Kirby, 1981). However, the presence of these conditions in Britain must still be explained.

This paper is concerned with the contribution of public policy to those conditions. What was the role of the state in Britain's economic decline? To answer that question, we examine three aspects of the state's activities that might have alleviated or contributed to Britain's economic problems: the growth of the public sector, macroeconomic management, and industrial policy. The following sections begin with a review of policy in each area to see if there are distinctive patterns to British policy that might be associated with economic performance. They go on to assess the relative impact of each kind of policy on the economy. Finally, they attempt to explain why these

*The author is grateful to Samuel Beer, Barry Eichengreen, Charles Feinstein, Carol Heim, Henry Jacek, Peter Lange, Harvey Rishikof, Rosemary Taylor, and the editors of this volume for their comments on an earlier version of this chapter, and, for various forms of research assistance, to Susan Pedersen, Anne Stewart-Hill, Philip Oxhorn, Christopher Jackson, Beverly Peterson, and Robert Perlmutter.

particular patterns of policy were pursued and why the state did not correct the market conditions that lay behind economic decline. The explanation itself enables us to revise several longstanding notions about intervention and the theory of the state.

The Size of the State

There are three variations to the view that the expansion of the British state itself is the principal source of Britain's economic problems. The first suggests that the growth of the public sector diverted critical resources from more productive pursuits in the private sector (Bacon and Eltis, 1976; Eltis, 1979). The second variant argues that the growth in public spending, especially in the transfer payments of the welfare state and correlative increases in taxation, impaired growth by reducing the incentives of private sector actors to put more work effort and investment into the economy (Jones, 1978; Joseph, 1976). A third view maintains that the rising public sector borrowing requirement associated with increased levels of public expenditure began to 'crowd out' private investment over the last two decades (Chrystal, 1979, ch. 9; Congdon, 1978; Carlson and Spencer, 1975).

All of these positions begin from the incontrovertible fact that the share of national resources being channelled through the public sector has increased dramatically in the period since World War II. In Britain, public expenditure as a share of GNP rose from 32 per cent in 1950 to 45 per cent in 1980. The public sector borrowing requirement (PSBR), which hovered around 4 per cent in the 1950s, reached 8 per cent of GNP in the 1970s before falling in the recent period. The critical issue, however, is one of causation. Did the expansion of public activity actually limit the growth of the private sector in Britain?

Despite the jeremiads of recent years, there is little evidence to support the existence of a causal connection between public sector growth and economic decline. First, the timing of the two occurrences is not coincident. The performance of the British economy relative to that of her trading partners began to decline at least fifty years before the public sector began to grow appreciably. In absolute terms, British growth rates actually improved during the period when most public sector expansion took place. This implies that the growth of the welfare state may have enhanced economic performance.

Comparative analysis also suggests that the growth of the public sector had little to do with Britain's relatively poor economic performance. In many European nations whose rates of growth exceeded that of Britain over the postwar period, including Germany, France, Sweden, Norway, the Netherlands, and Austria, government spending as a portion of GNP was equal to or higher than the British level. Recent studies have found a significant positive correlation between the expansion of the public sector and rates of growth over the postwar period (Kohl, 1981; Smith, 1975).

Careful attempts to analyse the causal relation between public sector expansion and economic performance in Britain itself have also produced negative results. Hadjimatheou and Skouras (1979) call into question both the premises and empirical data of Bacon and Eltis (1976). The rather physiocratic contention that public sector activity is 'unproductive' neglects the contribution that health policy, education, and infrastructure make to national production; and the argument that public sector growth in the 1970s squeezed the manpower resources available to the private sector seems implausible given the high levels of unemployment that prevailed during much of the period.

Similar considerations cast doubt on the view that the costs of the welfare state impaired British economic performance. In all of the faster-growing nations cited above, taxes consumed a substantially greater portion of GNP than in Britain, and in many, marginal rates of tax were also higher for most income levels (Ward and Neild, 1978, p. 102). Empirical studies have found that the impact of personal taxation on work effort is negligible (Stern, 1976; Fiegehen, 1980), and that the incidence of corporate taxation in Britain actually fell over the postwar period (King, 1975; Moore and Rhodes, 1976).

Finally, while the large portion of institutional funds currently being invested in government gilt rather than industrial capital may be a cause for concern, no satisfactory evidence has been found to link a high PSBR with lower levels of private investment. Most studies suggest that government borrowing has not squeezed the funds available to industry (HM Treasury, 1977), and that investment in Britain responds much more strongly to expectations of demand and profitability than to changes in the interest rate induced by the PSBR (Savage, 1978). Public sector deficits still seem more likely to expand investment through their impact on demand than to restrict it via monetary effects.

In general, no search for the causes of British economic decline should turn too quickly to the state. The essays in this volume suggest that relative decline must be seen, in the first instance, as one of the central consequences of the market itself. After all, Britain has had one of the most unconstrained market economies in the world. She was the first European nation to develop a self-regulating market system, and her markets have been free from state intervention to a degree that has no continental parallel (Kurth, 1979; Tawney, 1943; Gerschenkron, 1962). From the repeal of the Corn Laws in 1846 to the tariff measures of the 1930s, Britain remained the principal defender of free trade in the international system (Kenwood and Lougheed, 1983). Her governments stayed with this policy throughout the Great Depression of 1876–90 when most other nations enacted substantial trade barriers; and during the 1930s, when many countries employed public works programmes to secure reflation, Britain relied on the market system to revive the economy

(Gourevitch, 1977, 1984). Even the Keynesian system of demand management pursued after World War II was welcomed by both political parties
because it seemed to free them from the need to intervene directly in industrial markets (Skidelsky, 1979). Government interference into industry was
so rare and restrained in this period that Shonfield (1969) could conclude
that Britain had an 'arm's-length state'.

In such a context, we can ask why the government did not do more to
transform the market conditions associated with slow growth? Many theories
of the state suggest that it could have been expected to provide the necessary
correctives, whether as the custodian of the public interest or as the 'ideal
collective capitalist' (Jessop, 1977; Krasner, 1980). A central problem is to
explain why it did not. Two broad areas of policy are relevant: those of
macroeconomic management and microeconomic intervention.

The Role of Macroeconomic Policy

Macroeconomic policy in Britain, from 1918 to the floating of the pound in
1972, was dominated by a concern to maintain the value of sterling on the
foreign exchanges. From 1918 to 1925 this took the form of a determination
to return to the gold standard at the prewar parity ($4.86 to the pound). As a
result, the Bank rate was raised to 7 per cent and monetary policy remained
tight throughout the 1920s, despite a rate of unemployment which never fell
below 10 per cent. The single relaxation of 1922 coincided with a strengthening of sterling across the foreign exchanges. Public spending was also
slashed, in line with the recommendations of the Geddes Committee, so that
Winston Churchill could announce a return to the gold standard, in April
1925, which overvalued the pound by about 10 per cent (Keynes, 1925;
Kirby, 1981, p. 39). Thus, the return to parity dictated a constellation of
policies, and the subsequent need to reduce British wage rates in order to
maintain international competitiveness led directly to the wage cuts and
General Strike of 1926.

Despite the urging of Keynes, the Liberals, and many trade unionists, the
Labour government of 1929 refused to abandon the deflationary policies
recommended by the Treasury and City (Gourevitch, 1984; Skidelsky, 1967).
Once Britain was forced off gold in 1931, the new coalition lowered the Bank
rate to 2 per cent; but it did so specifically to lower the carrying costs of the
public debt rather than to inspire industrial expansion, and fiscal policy
remained tight until rearmament in the late 1930s. It was the recommendations of the May Committee, rather than those of the Macmillan Committee,
that guided policy through the 1930s (Youngson, 1960, pp. 83–92; Richardson, 1967).

By the end of World War II a profound transformation had taken place in
the economic philosophy guiding British policy-makers. They embraced a
variant of Keynesianism which suggested that variations in fiscal and

monetary policy could be used to attain their new goal of full employment (HM Government, 1944; Dow, 1964). Despite this development, however, the maintenance of a high exchange rate remained an overriding priority for successive governments. When aggregate demand was expanded, rising levels of imports produced a deficit in the balance of payments; and rather than devalue the exchange rate to correct this imbalance, British governments chose to deflate the domestic economy. Hence, expansion gave way to a famous series of 'stop–go' cycles. The timing of the 'stops' indicates they were not the result of Keynesian moves to moderate the fluctuations of the business cycle but a direct consequence of attempts to protect the value of sterling (Hansen, 1969; Mosley, 1976).

How much impact did this pattern of macroeconomic policy have on the performance of the British economy? Many commentators attribute the poor performance of British industry directly to macroeconomic policy. Although the effect of alternative policies is ultimately a hypothetical issue, we can gain considerable insight by examining recent experience with alternative policies and comparing Britain's stance with that of other nations.

Essentially, there are four respects in which macroeconomic policy may have impaired the performance of the British economy. First, the timing or intensity of demand management in the postwar period may have been destabilizing for the economy (Dow, 1964; Hansen, 1969; Caves, 1968). Second, the particular monetary instruments on which the government relied for demand management in the postwar decades and the frequency with which they were applied may have been especially disruptive to investment (Aldcroft, 1982, p. 43; Channon, 1973, p. 47). Third, it can be argued that failure to devalue often impaired the competitiveness of British products on world markets (Beckerman 1972; Posner and Steer, 1979). Finally, British policy over the entire period may have been more deflationary than necessary, thus needlessly inhibiting the growth of investment, output, and productivity (Hansen, 1969; Pollard, 1982).

The notion that demand management was destabilizing has been the subject of considerable debate (Worswick, 1977). Although British policy remained the least stabilizing of the seven nations usually studied, recent evidence (Boltho, 1982; OECD, 1973) suggests that postwar policy was positively destabilizing only if the investment of public enterprise is considered a component of policy. Policy was also more correctly timed in the years after 1965. In comparative terms, overall variations around the trend of output and investment, including the impact of demand management, have still not been as great in Britain as in many nations with faster growth; and one finds plenty of instances of destabilizing policy in such nations (Bispham and Boltho, 1982; Whiting, 1976; Surrey, 1982; Price, 1978).

Similarly, the contention that British reliance on monetary instruments for demand management had an adverse effect on industry is contradicted by recent studies that have failed to find any convincing relationship between interest rates and the level of investment in Britain (Savage, 1978). Many industrialists have testified that short-run changes in such instruments had no effect on their long-term investment plans; and it now seems likely that postwar controls on bank lending did not effectively restrict the money supply (Radcliffe Report, 1959; Goodhart, 1975; Smethurst, 1979). Although nominal interest rates have been slightly higher in the UK over the postwar period, the real rate of interest on long-term loans has been lower than in most other industrialized nations. In these terms, British monetary policy has not been unduly restrictive.

The consequences of Britain's high exchange rate policies have also been widely debated. Moggridge (1972) and Pressnell (1978) argue that, if Britain had adopted a lower parity for the pound in the 1920s, her share of world exports would not have declined so dramatically in that decade. However, the temporary advantages gained from the 1931 devaluation were soon offset when other nations followed suit; and Britain's real wage costs were so high relative to those of other nations, and the price elasticity of demand for British exports so low in the 1920s, that a moderate devaluation would probably have had only a small effect on exports and economic growth (Mowatt, 1955, p. 268; Kirby, 1981, p. 53; Lewis, 1949, p. 82).

Devaluation might also have been considered between 1949 and 1967 when Britain's competitiveness fell steadily, but the post-1968 experience must render one less sanguine about its advantages (Cambridge Economic Policy Group, 1978; Stout, 1977). The case for devaluation rests on an optimistic reading of four parameters: (1) and (2) the price elasticities for British exports and foreign imports in Britain, (3) the propensity of British exporters to utilize price advantages for profit-taking versus reorganization and higher volume production, and (4) the rapidity with which real wages adjust to the domestic price inflation that devaluation entails (Posner and Steer, 1979). Recent experience suggests that there are few grounds to assume that developments on any of these fronts would make devaluation work. In particular, the apparent absence of 'money illusion' among British unions means that wage costs rise rapidly in the wake of a devaluation (Tarling and Wilkinson, 1977; Ball *et al.*, 1977; Henry *et al.*, 1976); and the price advantages of the 1967 devaluation had disappeared by 1971 (Tew, 1978). If the export price advantages last only until lagging real wages adjust, a series of devaluations would have been required to maintain competitiveness over the postwar period. When this policy was pursued in 1972–9, Britain's share of world exports did increase after falling by 7 per cent in the preceding thirteen years, but the increase was marginal, and by no means did it eliminate balance of payments problems or render deflation unnecessary.

Moreover, one should question any strategy that depends on depressing real wages, because the more recent problem is not real wage rates, which have increased far less in Britain than in most European nations: it is lower levels of productivity growth that render British goods less competitive on world markets. Devaluation simply limits the impact of low productivity on exports—it does not remedy the causes of the problem. The long-term effect of the strategy would have been to render Britain even more dependent on low-wage industries and low productivity for its national income at a time when most industrialized nations prospered by concentrating on high-wage and high-value-added industries in the face of increased competition from the developing world. Indeed, as quality considerations came to play an increasing role in export competitiveness, it would have been particularly short-sighted for Britain to focus on price competitiveness (Kravis and Lipsey, 1971; Stout, 1977; Panic, 1975). In short, while devaluation in the early 1920s or 1960s might have made a contribution to the competitiveness of British industry, it was unlikely to be a panacea for the underlying problems of the economy.

To deal with the contention that British policy has been overly deflationary, we must distinguish between the interwar and post-World War II periods. During the interwar years Britain pursued policies that seem to have unnecessarily restricted growth and adjustment, especially during the 1920s, when both fiscal and monetary policy were highly contractionary. Howson (1975, p. 63) argues that 'technical progress and structural factors are not independent of aggregate demand and with one million unemployed there could have been more expansion . . . if aggregate demand had been growing sufficiently to create profit expectations favorable to investment in the new industries' (cf. Aldcroft, 1967). Although monetary policy was loosened in the 1930s, Britain's growth rates remained low by international standards, perhaps because she failed to adopt the expansionary fiscal policies that accompanied more rapid growth in Sweden, Germany, and the United States (Richardson, 1967; Middleton, 1981).

It is more difficult to assess the effects of British policy in the postwar period. The gap between actual GDP and potential GDP (assuming full factor use) between 1955 and 1973 was only slightly higher in Britain than the European average or the gap in nations, such as Germany, Austria, Belgium, and the Netherlands, which achieved much higher rates of growth (Bispham and Boltho, 1982, p. 305). Similarly, the aggregate impact of British budgetary policy on demand was low by European standards but only slightly less than that in France, Sweden, and Belgium over the 1955–77 period (Hansen, 1969; OECD, 1978). The British stance was not greatly out of line with those of many high-growth nations, and given the underlying buoyancy of consumption, there may have been little room for more expansionary policy (Paish, 1970; Matthews, 1968).

A highly reflationary policy would have been possible only if, as a by-product, it altered the relatively high income elasticity for imports and low trend rate of productivity growth in Britain which rapidly imposed balance of payments constraints on expansion (Thirlwall, 1978; Panic, 1975).[1] Even those who argue that expansion should be used for this purpose, however, admit that it would have to be accompanied by stringent controls on imports and incomes (Cambridge Economic Policy Group, 1978; Singh, 1979). Such a strategy runs serious risks, beyond the possibility of foreign retaliation. Protection could fuel domestic inflation and shift resources into the least efficient sectors of the economy without forcing them to rationalize, as the tariff of 1932 seems to have done (Corden *et al.*, 1978).

In short, these results suggest that more frequent devaluation or further expansion would have had a marginal impact at best on British rates of growth. To blame Britain's problems primarily on her macroeconomic policies is to mistake the source of the problem; and to look to better macroeconomic management alone for the solution is to overestimate the impact that alternative policies could have had on a stagnant economic base (Brown and Stout, 1979).

The Pattern of Industrial Policy

The analysis in this volume indicates that our attention must be focused more directly on policies that transform the nature of industrial activity. Only in conjunction with an activist industrial policy could more expansionary macroeconomic policies have begun to address the underlying problems of the economy. Yet industrial policy remains a neglected feature of most analyses. All too often it is viewed as no more than a set of funding programmes for industry. Every industrial policy, however, contains three components: the volume of funds it channels to industry; the set of criteria that governs the choice of sectors, firms, and projects to be supported; and the degree of government pressure that is brought to bear on the reorganization and reallocation of resources within industry. Since 1918, British policy has followed a pattern that is distinctive in each of these respects.

The amount of money that British governments were willing to spend on industry was negligible until the 1960s. Despite some advances under the Trade Facilities Act of 1921, the Treasury kept a tight hold on the public purse strings during the interwar period. Instead, tariffs were used to augment the public coffers and protect the private sector (Grove, 1962, p. 245). By contrast, Sweden, Japan, Germany, and even the United States spent considerable sums on guaranteed loans, industrial subsidies, and public works in this period (Lewis, 1949). As late as 1961, the British state spent over £270 million on aid to agriculture and less than £50 million on industry and employment (Grove, 1962, p. 265). Modest tax allowances were the principal investment incentive. In the 1960s, however, subsidies replaced tax allowances, and they increased during the 1970s as successive governments began to rescue firms hit by the post-1974 recession. Between 1971 and 1979, the government spent £9,290 million in subsidies to the private sector as well as large sums on the nationalized industries (*British Business*, 8 February

1980). By the 1970s, therefore, Britain was spending almost the same percentage of GDP on industrial grants as France or Germany (Dechery, 1980).

The set of criteria that guided British industrial support remained more distinctive. A substantial portion of British aid has been devoted to regional development programmes whose object is not to promote specific firms or sectors but to transfer resources to the depressed regions of the country. Britain was a pioneer of such policies, implementing the Special Areas Act in 1934, the Town and Country Planning Act in 1947, the Regional Employment Premium of 1968, and the Industry Acts of 1972 and 1975 (McCrone, 1969; MacLennan, and Parr, 1979). Although regional policy was not notably successful until the 1960s, even then its effect was more to shift the location of investment than to stimulate new investment or rationalization (Moore and Rhodes, 1973; Ashcroft, 1979). Many British legislators favoured this form of policy precisely because it was voluntary, non-selective among firms, and likely to have little impact on the structure of industry (Grant, 1982). In 1979 the portion of public expenditure devoted to regional aid was twice as great in Britain as in most other European nations (Nicol and Yuill, 1982, p. 435).

British policy has also emphasized research and development, which consumed almost 50 per cent of public spending on industry since 1970. Although the programme is seemingly analogous to continental efforts, British funds were put to far more restricted uses. Since the 1960s, well over 70 per cent of state spending on R & D has gone to the defence, aerospace, and nuclear sectors (Grove, 1962, p. 268). By contrast Germany, France, and Japan spent equivalent sums on a broader spectrum of promising industries, including chemicals, electrical goods, transportation, and machine tools (Freeman and Young, 1965; Grant, 1982, p. 76; Channon, 1973, p. 33).

Finally, the British criteria have tended to channel the remaining selective aid to unprofitable firms and declining sectors (Young and Lowe, 1974). For instance, over £500 million of the £600 million allocated to the National Enterprise Board, which the Labour government established in 1975 to rejuvenate British industry, was spent to rescue a few large firms such as British Leyland, Rolls Royce, Ferranti, and Alfred Herbert (Fleming, 1980, p. 149). At first glance this seems eminently reasonable: unprofitable firms most need support. In a few cases, the policy enabled a sound firm to survive; in most cases it sent vast resources to firms or sectors where Britain's prospects could never have been too promising. While most nations began some rescue operations after the 1974 recession, France, Japan, and Germany have been more inclined to focus aid on profitable firms in sectors targeted for long-term growth (Vernon, 1974).

The third component of industrial policy, after the volume of funding and the criteria for support, involves the degree of public pressure used to inspire rationalization within manufacturing sectors. The object is generally to consolidate existing firms into units of the most efficient size, to improve the level of investment or technology, to alter work practices or product specialization, and to reallocate resources within and between industrial sectors. State intervention of this sort can take many different forms, however, and it is important to distinguish those in which the government enforces reform on particular firms and industries from those in which state-supported schemes are essentially directed by the private sector. The striking feature of British intervention has been its reliance on the latter. With the exception of an occasional nationalization, compulsory schemes have been avoided in favour of an approach that has been highly consensual, or 'quasi-corporatist', to use Samuel Beer's (1969, p. 297) term.

Since 1918, industries in Britain have essentially been asked to rationalize themselves. The government initially encouraged sectors to form trade associations so as to have a partner with whom to bargain (Blank, 1973). When a sector seemed in need of reorganization, the government then authorized these associations to negotiate common pricing policies, mergers, production quotas, and investment or marketing schemes with their members; in order to facilitate such schemes, it made public resources available, either in the form of tariff protection during the 1930s or in the form of subsidies, tax concessions, or import quotas during the postwar period. While these resources were often presented as inducements, they were rarely used as sanctions, and the government's role in reorganization remained limited. Such a consensual approach to industrial policy stands in striking contrast to the more *dirigiste* policies of France or Japan, where sectoral plans were drawn up by the state rather than industry, where individual firms were the direct object of much policy, and where a host of public sanctions was employed to enforce implementation (Shonfield, 1969; Warnecke and Suleiman, 1975; Zysman, 1983; Magaziner, 1979; Johnson, 1982).

The case of the coal industry was representative of British policy during the interwar period. After nationalization was rejected in 1919, the Mining Industry Act of 1926 authorized the Railways and Canal Commission to amalgamate neighbouring collieries, but the initiative was left with industry and few results followed (Kirby, 1973). The 1930 Coal Mines Act created a cartel in the sector, mandated improvements in wages and working conditions, and established a Coal Mines Reorganization Commission to undertake amalgamation; however, amendments that might have given the Commission power to enforce rationalization were defeated by industry opposition in the House of Lords in 1930 and again in 1936 (Youngson, 1960, p. 66). As a consequence little changed, and the British watched coal output per man-shift rise by barely 10 per cent in 1913–36 versus 117 per cent in Holland, 81 per cent in Germany, 50 per cent in Belgium, and 25 per cent in France (Pollard, 1969, p. 111). This pattern was repeated in one sector after another, including steel, shipbuilding, and cotton (Pollard, 1969; papers by Tolliday, Lazonick, and Lorenz and Wilkinson, this volume; Allen, 1951). *The Economist* (15 June 1940, cited in Harris, 1972) described interwar industrial policy as:

a set of notions that sees its ideal of an economic system in an orderly organization of industries, each ruled feudally from above by the business firms already established in it, linked in associations and confederations and, at the top, meeting on terms of sovereign equality with such other Estates of the Realm as the Bank of England and the Government. Each British industry, faithful to the prescription, has spent the past decade in delimiting its fief, in organising its baronial courts, in securing and entrenching its holdings and administering the legal powers of self-government conferred on it by a tolerant State.

By 1956, over 2,550 restrictive agreements had been made public, and many others undoubtedly remained underground (Channon, 1973, p. 26).

Collusive practices were viewed less benevolently in the 1950s, but the general thrust of policy did not change. The Industrial Development and Organization Act of 1947, which might have begun a process of active economic planning in Britain, left the initiative to form development councils up to private sector actors, with the result that only four were ever established (Blank, 1973; p. 85; Grove, 1962, p. 291). Apart from belated action on restrictive practices and the introduction of investment allowances, whose impact was marginal at best, the government's principal effort was on regional development (Caves, 1969, p. 61). In 1962 the Conservatives established a National Economic Development Council ('Neddy') to discuss economic policy with the Trades Union Congress and Federation of British Industries. Although some policy-makers hoped the Council would become a vehicle for economic planning on the French model, it never assembled the sanctions that put teeth into the French plans. Neddy remained a body for tripartite consultation between government and industry (Budd, 1978; Leruez, 1975; Opie, 1972).

The Labour government of 1964–70 tried to introduce a more *dirigiste* industrial policy by establishing a Department of Economic Affairs to formulate national plans, a Ministry of Technology to foster research and development, the Industrial Reconstruction Corporation to facilitate mergers and modernization in the private sector, and a National Prices and Incomes Board to encourage productivity agreements between industry and labour (Beckerman, 1972; Shanks, 1977; Hague and Wilkinson, 1983; Young and Lowe, 1974). However, the DEA failed in the face of Treasury resistance; and the other institutions did not begin to move beyond consensualism until the last eighteen months of their existence (Graham, 1972; Brown, 1970). Although these programmes represented a brief attempt to go beyond the existing patterns of policy, they supplied too little too late.

Under the Conservatives in 1970–4 and Labour in 1974–9, industrial policy reverted to its normal course, marked only by larger sums of aid for declining sectors. After an abortive switch to investment allowances, the Industry Act of 1972 restored a system of subsidies, but almost all went to regional development grants or the industrial bail-outs of British Leyland, Rolls Royce, and Cammel Laird (Young and Lowe, 1974). The industrial policies of the Labour government were very similar. Only one of the 'planning agreements' that the 1973 programme advertised as a scheme for imposing investment plans on industry was ever negotiated; and the National Enterprise Board became little more than a source of capital for ailing firms whose redundancies the government was unwilling to tolerate (Wilks, 1981; Grant, 1982). The 'new industrial strategy' of November 1975 created thirty-nine sectoral working parties (SWPs) operating by consensus at the sectoral level, much like the state-sponsored cartels of the 1930s.

What were the effects of this pattern of industrial policy? In political terms the answer is clear. Despite the growth of the state apparatus and the nominal extension of intervention, British policy tended to reinforce the power of private sector actors *vis à vis* the government. The result was 'less the domination of public over private powers than their interpenetration leading to the creation of a broad area of shared authority' (Beer, in Blank, 1973, p. xi). The principal effect of the SWPs, for instance, was to enhance the capacity of industrial actors to lobby the government for various forms of protection (Grant, 1980). This suggests that we must be careful to distinguish between different forms of 'state intervention'. The form of state involvement in the economy that emerged in Britain was fundamentally different from that in France, and it had different consequences. In particular, it was characterized more by the growth of bargaining between the government and the two sides of industry than by the growth of unilateral state control (cf. Winkler, 1976).

Similarly, analyses that treat the British case as the diametrical opposite of a corporatist system may have to be corrected (cf. Schmitter and Lehmbruch, 1979). We should distinguish between the two dimensions of policy-making that 'corporatism' often conflates. When the term refers to a process whereby policy is formulated in a highly centralized fashion by peak associations that can impose agreements on their constituencies, it applies very rarely to the British case (Cox, 1982; Marsh and Grant, 1977). However, to the extent that the term denotes a form of policy-making in which a great deal of policy is the product of bargaining between the state and producers' groups, it clearly applies to Britain more than many other nations. The process is simply less centralized in Britain.

The economic effects of industrial policies are harder to assess. On balance, British policy seems to have reinforced the ability of existing firms to resist market pressure for reorganization. By providing subsidies, authorization for price fixing, production quotas, or import protection to these sectors, without at the same time bringing sufficient pressure in favour of rationalization to bear on the individual firms in an industry, British policy tended to enhance rather than reduce the structural rigidities of many markets. That is reflected in the middling results that have followed from these schemes. For instance, the tariffs and state-sponsored cartelization of the 1930s kept prices high in many sectors, but did little to tackle the underlying inefficiency of the firms (see papers by Tolliday, Lazonick, this volume; Singh, 1979, p. 96). By contrast, the more activist policies of Germany contributed to the dramatic improvement of its manufacturing base from an even worse situation (Lewis, 1949).

Similarly, most studies of postwar policy conclude that insufficient resources were devoted to the problem (Clarke, 1973), that policy was not sustained enough to produce results (Hague and Williamson, 1983; Broadway, 1969), or that it had very little impact on the investment and allocation decisions of private sector actors (Imberg and Northcott, 1981; Mottershead, 1978). Although British policy cushioned the impact of contraction in declining sectors, it seems to have had little effect on the most serious problem underlying poor economic performance, namely, productivity (Caves and Krause, 1980, p. 185). Only in the one period when industrial policy veered towards *dirigisme*, under the Labour government of 1964–70, did the growth of the capital–labour ratio and output per person begin to approach continental levels. The experience of other nations, such as France and Japan, suggest that in order to tackle underlying productivity problems Britain would have needed an industrial policy based less on voluntarism and more on rationalization enforced directly by the state.

The Roots of Policy

These patterns in British policy present us with a double problem. On the one hand, the very presence of such consistent patterns of policy in a world of flux should be explained. On the other hand, most contemporary theories of the state would lead us to expect the British government to adopt policies that remedy the nation's economic problems, whether it acts as an instrument of popular will (Dahl, 1970), as the relatively autonomous agent of a dominant class (Poulantzas, 1976), or as an independent guardian of the public interest (Krasner, 1980); yet the British state did not pursue effective policies for restoring the profitability, productivity, and growth of the British economy. This, too, must be explained.

To arrive at an answer we must abandon the idea that the actions of all states, even within industrialized societies, are driven by the same set of functional exigencies. Most governments, especially of a democratic character, may respond to a similar set of imperatives associated with the maintenance of power (cf. Levy, 1980; Block; 1977; Jessop, 1977; Tufte, 1979). However, the nature of their response is subject to wide variation, and the precise form it takes is strongly influenced by the institutional setting within which the state finds itself. In other words, the state is an endogenous variable within a particular social, economic, and international system. The constraints on its action are not specified simply by a given mode of production or form of government: within both of these broader frameworks there is a great deal of relevant institutional variation. British policy was different from the policies of other capitalist democracies in large part because of the institutional peculiarities of the British environment.

There are four aspects of the structural setting of the British state that had an important influence over policy: the position of Britain within the international system, the organizational configuration of British society, the institutional structure of the state itself, and the nature of the wider political system, understood as the network of political parties and interest intermediaries that seek to influence policy. Each of these variables affected the likelihood that the government would be *willing* to formulate a particular policy or the chances that it would be *able* to implement such a policy. Together, they pushed policy-makers in a particular direction by altering the balance of perceived costs and benefits that accrued to any one policy. Sometimes the variables acted on policy-makers' perceptions; as often, they exacted real costs.

Like British markets, the British political setting was shaped by two of the formative experiences in British history: early industrialization and empire. Britain's experiences as the 'first industrializer' and as an imperial power left her with a peculiar set of international relations, financial institutions, producers' organizations, and governmental structures that were revised in the ensuing two centuries but never entirely replaced (Hobsbawm, 1969; Kurth, 1979).

Britain's International Position

Although Britain's macroeconomic stance had only a limited impact on her relative economic performance, the government's persistent defence of the pound drew attention and resources away from the problems of the domestic economy. This approach to policy was rooted in the experience of empire. During the interwar period, a clear-cut set of international concerns and obligations pressed policy-makers into the return to gold (Moggridge, 1972; Best and Humphries, this volume). Even after British hegemony had declined, however, the imperial legacy continued to influence policy.

One aspect of this legacy was an overhang of foreign sterling balances. The net holdings in sterling and short-term sterling assets of foreigners grew to a considerable size because a major portion of world trade was once conducted in sterling. These balances continued to average £3.5 billion for most of the postwar period, rising at times to as much as £6 billion (Caves, 1969; Tew, 1978). They intensified the possibility that any weakening in the exchange rate, or balance of payments deficit, could lead to massive sales of sterling and a precipitous drop in the value of the currency. This heightened the pressure on policy-makers to respond with deflation to any balance of payments crisis; and the latter became a kind of hair-trigger inducing the periodic 'stop–go' cycles of macroeconomic management (Blank, 1978; Brittan, 1970).

Along with this financial legacy came a diplomatic one. Most of the overseas balances were held in the official reserves of nations who once belonged to the old sterling area. Any fall in the British exchange rate would reduce the value of these reserves and have serious diplomatic repercussions. As a result, British policy-makers were inclined to see devaluation as a form of default on Britain's international obligations. The impact of this consideration influenced civil servants and politicians alike. Although the Bank of England is often portrayed as the only agency resisting devaluation, the Bank itself suggested a floating exchange rate in 1952. The scheme, known as 'Operation Robot', might have left Britain with a more advantageous parity at a critical time in her postwar recovery. However, it was vetoed by the Cabinet on the grounds that any drop in the exchange rate would mean abdication of Britain's duty to the overseas holders of sterling (Butler, 1971, p. 159; Brittan, 1970; Roseveare, 1969).

Similarly, overseas spending to meet Britain's extensive military and diplomatic obligations intensified pressure on the balance of payments. For most of the postwar period, private sector transactions across the external account were in surplus, but the public sector ran a sufficient deficit to throw the entire balance of payments off and trigger periodic 'stop–go' cycles (Pollard, 1982; Manser, 1971).

Because Britain had been one of the principal suppliers of capital to the rest of the world, her governments also became accustomed to relying on a surplus in the invisible account, derived primarily from repatriated profits and shipping fees, to make up for a growing deficit in traded goods (Manser, 1971). When exports began to decline during the interwar period, this cushion reduced the pressure on the state for action to revive manufacturing. Moreover, when Britain was deprived of the surplus by World War II (in which she lost overseas assets worth £100 million a year to the balance of payments and acquired significant external liabilities), the nation was bound to face recurring balance of payments problems (Caves, 1969, p. 153). A series of postwar governments had to face the consequences of relying for too long on the financial advantages of imperial power.

Finally, the experience of empire left Britain with a set of financial institutions that were heavily oriented towards overseas lending (Clarke, 1967). Therefore, the City became a powerful lobby against devaluation, which was widely expected to weaken international confidence in British financial markets, and a proponent of deflation in the face of balance of payments crises (Thomas, 1968; Blank, 1978; Cairncross and McRae, 1974). A pertinent contrast is Germany, where the banks' equity position in domestic industry and the country's less developed international role gave them a stronger interest in policies that would expand German industry and exports. The German financial sector agitated successfully to keep the Deutschmark undervalued on the world exchanges (Kreile, 1978; Joint Economic Committee, 1981; Hall, 1983b).

Societal Structure

There are those who discount the effect that society can have on public policy because they point, quite properly, to the ability of the state to resist societal pressure (Nordlinger, 1981). However, this view neglects the fact that, in the era of the managed economy (Beer, 1969), public policy is implemented to a great extent through societal rather than state organizations. Therefore, differences in the organization of society may, on the one hand, affect the problems with which states are forced to deal, and on the other hand, may affect their capacity to implement policies that tackle these problems. In these respects, two features of British society had profound consequences for economic policy.

The nature of British financial institutions and their relationship to industrial capital was one such feature. Partly because the nation industrialized during the textile era, when start-up costs were low, British manufacturers came to depend primarily on internally generated funds and public issues of equity for finance (Kurth, 1979; Cottrell, 1980). Therefore, Britain did not develop the large investment banks common to the Continent. Because the latter held long-term debt or equity in most sectors, they became interested in industrial modernization, capable of financing it, and influential enough to enforce it on recalcitrant firms (Hall, 1983b; Zysman, 1983). Since Britain acquired no such co-ordinating agents, the tasks facing the British state were greater than those in many other nations.

In addition, the organization of British financial markets limited the state's ability to control the flows of funds in the banking system in order to finance or induce compliance with a more aggressive industrial policy. Industry was relatively independent from the banks because it borrowed only over the short term and relatively sparingly from them; and, in any event, the banks were insulated from government control by the powerful Bank of England. Even after nationalization in 1949, the Bank used its quasi-autonomous status to resist any reforms that might adversely affect the City (Sayers, 1976; House of Commons, 1970). Its sponsorships of the Bankers Industrial Development Co. in 1930, the Industrial and Commercial Finance Corporation in 1945, and the Finance Corporation for Industry in 1946 were all undertaken to forestall the more radical attempts of a Labour government to establish public investment banks (Grove, 1962, pp. 247, 449).

The relevant counter-case is that of France, where the long-term lending practices of the banks gave them considerable leverage over industry, and the detailed control that the Ministry of Finance exercised over the flows of funds in the financial sector through the subordinate Bank of France allowed it to orchestrate the investment strategies of entire industrial sectors long before President Mitterrand came to office (Joint Economic Committee, 1981; Hall, 1982a). These institutions, rather than those of the Planning Commission, were the real key to the *économie concertée*.

The form of organization of British labour and employers placed another set of constraints on state economic policy. Britain had developed a strong labour movement by 1918, when over four million people were affiliated to a trade union, and by 1975 union membership covered 50 per cent of the work force. Since large portions of labour were organized along craft lines, however, the Trades Union Congress remained a loose federation without much central control over its members (Martin, 1980). Employers' associations took a similar form: organization was extensive, but most national associations were merely loose confederations of smaller units.

The organizational strength of the unions forced the government into negotiating with them to secure industrial peace, initially during World War I and then in the interwar period. The Ministry of Labour expanded more than any other agency in this era; and these early attempts to bargain with the representatives of labour and capital set a pattern for most subsequent policies in the industrial arena. The British state passed up unilateral action in favour of negotiating the path of subsequent arrangements with organized labour and capital (Middlemas, 1979).

If the strength of the unions *vis-à-vis* the government initially pressed the state into a particular pattern of policy *formulation* based on bargaining, however, the internal weakness of union and employer organizations, *vis-à-vis* their members, limited the options facing the government for policy *implementation*. In particular, it prevented the state from using these associations to impose industrial reorganization on their members, as nations with more corporatist arrangements were able to do (Schmitter and Lehmbruch, 1979, 1981). Thus the Mond–Turner talks of 1928, several agreements with the CBI, and a series of incomes policies broke down in the face of rank-and-file defections. The organizational features of Britain's unions and employers' associations rendered them more effective as veto groups than as positive contributors to an active industrial policy (cf. Olson, 1982).

State Structure

Finally, Britain was governed throughout this period by a state that had a particular institutional structure, imparting a consistent bias to policy. Just as the shape of a market influences the behaviour of individuals in it, so the structure of the state affects the set of incentives, balance of power, and flow of information facing individuals at different positions within it. This, in turn, influences the kind of policies they are likely to implement. Because policy is the product of a collective process, the particular form of aggregation that each state uses influences the outcome.

The British state contained a particularly powerful central bank, which was a private corporation until 1949 and even afterwards retained the right to hire its own staff, deal directly with the prime minister, and take public positions at variance with government policy (Sayers, 1976; Keegan and Pennant-Rae, 1979). As the only public repository of expertise on monetary matters, the Bank of England was able to dominate decision-making in this area. It 'deliberately cultivated a mystique that at best befuddled discussion and at worst intimidated those who had to take political responsibility' (Sayers, 1976, vol. II, p. 387). The Chief Economic Advisor to the Treasury, for instance, did not learn about the 1957 increase in Bank rate until after it had been accomplished; and even when political leaders suspected there might be viable alternatives to the Bank's advice, they usually followed the Bank for fear that no one else could assess the options (Hall, 1982b, ch. 7; Chapman, 1968).

Because Bank officials saw themselves as spokesmen for an internationally oriented financial community, custodians of the exchange rate, and financiers for the public debt, they tended to oppose devaluation, alterations to the financial system, and expansionary measures that might lead to higher borrowing or balance of payments difficulties (Grove, 1962, p. 449; Moggridge, 1972; Wilson, 1971; Brittan, 1970). Therefore, they acted as a powerful force for fiscal conservatism in both the interwar and postwar periods.

The other institution at the heart of British policy apparatus has been HM Treasury. For most of the period, it supervised all departmental promotions and every spending proposal going to the Cabinet (Roseveare, 1969). As a result, the 'Treasury view' exercised a pervasive influence throughout the civil service. One Minister of Labour, for instance, complained that his departmental staff lacked 'the necessary audacity of imagining schemes which they felt would certainly be frowned on by the Treasury' (Lowe, 1978, p. 283).

The Treasury emerged from the nineteenth century as an institution dedicated to the control of public expenditure. Until a few changes were made in 1975, its officials had virtually no familiarity with, or direct concern for, the progress of British industry. Therefore, they were far more likely to suggest reductions, rather than expansion, in the funds being spent on industry (Beer, 1959, p. 77). Just as the Treasury opposed granting spending powers to the industrial commissions of the 1930s, so it opposed the National Enterprise Board in 1975 (Middlemas, 1979, p. 229; Marsh and Locksley, 1983, p. 53). Moreover, Gladstone existed uneasily beside Keynes. The Treasury rejected fiscal expansion in the 1920s and 1930s in order to protect the exchange rate and public debt; and many postwar officials, with one eye on rising expenditure totals, were relieved to be able to use balance of payments problems as an excuse for reducing public spending (Winch, 1969; Roseveare, 1969; Heclo and Wildavsky, 1974). As late as 1962 there were still no more than a dozen economists in the Treasury: its principal focus remained the control of expenditure, yet it has continued to dominate economic policy-making (Grove, 1962, p. 113; Heclo and Wildavsky, 1979). The British case stands in contrast to that of France or Germany, where one of the principal preoccupations of the Ministry of Finance and Economics is the economic conditions facing industry, or that of Japan, where the Ministry of International Trade and Industry is far more powerful in such matters than the Ministry of Finance (Katzenstein, 1978; Johnson, 1982).

The organization of the British civil service also reduces the state's capacity to pursue innovative economic policies (Hall, 1983a). Its upper echelons are staffed almost exclusively with personnel who spent their life in the service; information and advice is channelled to political leaders through a few individuals at the top of the hierarchy; and promotion is dependent on the approval of these civil servants rather than that of elected officials. Most economic decisions are made in great secrecy, and few official documents are ever exposed to public scrutiny. As a result, the access of political leaders to alternative sources of advice is limited; power is concentrated in the hands of those with the greatest interest in longstanding approaches to policy (Roseveare, 1969, p. 271; Benn, 1980; Thomas, 1968). The character of the civil service system and the politics–administration nexus in Britain may thus contribute to the extraordinary continuity that has characterized her economic and industrial policies.

The Political System

Does this mean there was no room for change in the British system? In many nations, a coalition of social groups, forged by political elites around a new set of policies, has been the agency for a major change in direction (Gourevitch, 1984; Ferguson, 1984). Why did we not see the emergence of such a coalition dedicated to a more activist industrial policy in Britain? To answer this question we must consider the institutional features of the wider political system, including both the political parties and interest intermediaries in Britain who would have had to organize such a coalition.

In the first place, the nature of the constituent groups who would form the building-blocks of such coalitions was different in Britain from that in many other nations. Early commercialization of agriculture, marked by widespread enclosures and the rapid spread of industrialization, reduced the independent farmers to very small numbers by 1918 (Moore, 1966; Kemp, 1969). Unlike the Social Democrats in Sweden and the Democrats in the United States, therefore, the Labour Party in Britain lacked the option of forming a workers–farmers' alliance around farm supports and reflationary policies (Gourevitch, 1984). Similarly, the more pronounced divisions between industrial entrepreneurs and the financial sector in Britain meant that business pressure on both parties was more heavily weighted towards the concerns of international finance than in many other nations.

If a new social coalition were to take power in Britain, it would also have to do so through the party system. However, party organizations develop deeply rooted doctrines which become central to their existence and resistant to change because they link leaders to followers and the parties' present actions to their past ones. In Britain, these doctrines contained longstanding lines of thought that tended to militate against more coercive state intervention. In addition, the close ties that British parties developed with particular interest groups also limited their range of action.

Within the Conservative Party, two strains of thought existed uneasily side by side. One segment, associated with the Tory democracy of Disraeli, was prepared to condone a measure of intervention, in the form of regulations or transfer programmes to limit the effects of the market on the populace (Gilmore, 1977). In the 1930s, for instance, a small group of MPs associated with Harold Macmillan agitated for industrial reorganization, but they sought statutory authority only for schemes that had the support of a substantial majority of the firms in an industry (Macmillan, 1934). During the postwar period, these ideas were pressed most strongly by a group of MPs around R. A. B. Butler, who persuaded the party to accept the basic programmes of the welfare state (Beer, 1969, ch. 11). However, in the industrial sphere, the most they were willing to advocate were consultative mechanisms such as those mentioned in the Industrial Charter of 1947 (Harris, 1972).

Even these proposals encountered opposition from the other strain of thought that ran through party doctrine. Its proponents defended the unimpeded operation of market mechanisms and opposed most forms of state intervention altogether (Joseph, 1976; Greenleaf, 1984). Their influence within the party can be traced to the *laissez-faire* sentiments that many businessmen defecting from the Liberals brought to the party at the turn of the century; but they became particularly powerful in the mid-1950s and again after Mrs Thatcher assumed the leadership in 1975 (Harris, 1972; Behrens, 1980). Neither stream of Conservative thought condoned state intervention of the sort that right-wing governments in France frequently practised. Moreover, the proposals of Tory democrats were always susceptible to defeat within the party by a coalition of free market ideologists and the business leaders who were respected advisors to the party on such issues. Macmillan's schemes for industrial reorganization in the 1930s lost to just such a coalition.

In some respects, the Labour Party seems a more appropriate vehicle for an activist industrial policy. Its postwar programme of nationalization certainly reflected a clear-cut willingness to intervene. However, the longstanding ideology of the party centred on precisely this—nationalization—and not on how the state might be used to revive private industry. Labour MPs were reluctant to use public funds for schemes that raised profits; they were more interested in reducing unemployment in declining sectors. For instance, Labour members attacked the British Sugar (Subsidies) Bill of 1924 on the grounds that it was inappropriate for the government to subsidize any private industry (Hansard, 18 December 1924, p. 1300). In a mixed economy, however, an efficient industrial policy must often direct funds away from declining sectors to more promising, and perhaps already profitable, sectors and firms. The highly effective and interventionist industrial policies of France and Japan were conducted during long periods of *conservative* rule. In Sweden and Austria, socialist governments were careful to adapt their policies to a mixed economy (Müller, 1983; Martin, 1979).

The close ties between British political parties and particular interest intermediaries also constrained their action. It is often observed that Britain has a 'strong' state, or one relatively impervious to direct pressure from organized interest groups; and it is true that the British executive dominates the legislature, employs a highly insulated bureaucracy, and concentrates power in the hands of the Cabinet (Katzenstein, 1978). However, British political parties have enjoyed no such insulation. The trade unions pay most of the Labour Party's expenses and dominate its annual conference (Minkin, 1978; Allen, 1960); many Conservative MPs not only depend on business interests for their electoral funds but continue to devote a substantial portion of their time to employment in the City or industry while in office (Mellors, 1978; Ramsden, 1979). Therefore, while both parties have a degree of independence that derives from their need to appeal to a broad cross-section of society, their policies have been heavily influenced by the groups on whom they depend for finance, advice, and personnel. These groups were also inclined to oppose state intervention in the industrial area.

In contrast to many socialist parties in Europe, which embraced Marxism and interventionist doctrine before they formed an alliance with the trade unions, the Labour Party was created to defend the independence of the labour movement (Drucker, 1979; Miliband, 1961). The formative experiences of the British trade unions, which pitted them against a state attempting to break their power, left them staunch opponents of any policies that seemed to limit their autonomy to determine wages and working conditions through collective bargaining (Pelling, 1976; Fenley, 1980). The lessons of Taff Vale and the Osborne decision remained alive in the memories of many trade unionists. So the Labour governments that came to power in the inter-war period strove not so much to revive British manufacturing as to protect the industrial power of the unions. This goal lent their economic policies a non-interventionist cast.

In the postwar era, Labour's approach to industry was again primarily consultative. Representatives who urged more activist policies at the annual conference often met stiff opposition from a coalition of party leaders (influenced by the structural constraints of Government and electoral appeal) and trade unionists who saw such policies as a threat to their autonomy in the workplace (cf. Minkin, 1978; Hatfield, 1976; Coates, 1975).

Within the Conservative Party, the influence of City interests, concerned about international confidence rather than industrial modernization, has been particularly strong. Even the employers' associations remained defenders of the status quo structure of industry. They did not become the agents for a rationalizing alliance between the most dynamic sections of capital and the state that the French CNPF became in the 1970s (Blank, 1978; Hall, 1982a). Although a few businessmen, such as Sir Alfred Mond, were willing to consider such an alliance, the British employers' associations were never ready to endorse an interventionist policy. Because they were trying to assemble a broad membership, ever ready to desert to competing associations, they usually refrained from any action that might disturb the vested interests of their members (Grant and Marsh, 1977). Therefore, just as the unions waged bitter battles against industrial relations legislation in 1968 and 1971, the employers fought to remove selective inducements from the Coal Mines (Reorganization) Act of 1930, the Industrial Organization and Development Bill of 1954, and the Industry Act of 1972 (Jenkins, 1970; Crouch, 1977; Harris, 1972; Mowatt, 1955).

The Two Postwar Conjunctures

The inertia of the political system became most important during the critical conjunctures that followed the two world wars. Many European nations seized these moments to change direction. Although Britain did not suffer the trauma that accompanied defeat, these were periods of widespread disillusionment with the old order and rising aspirations for the future. The extension of intervention during the war also provided a precedent on which the state might have built a new industrial policy. Why did the political system not respond?

The prospects for change after World War I depended heavily on the possibility that an interventionist coalition might emerge around Lloyd George. As Minister of Munitions and Prime Minister during the war, Lloyd George masterminded Britain's first serious steps toward state direction of industrial resources. He drew to his side Winston Churchill and the most interventionist of the Conservatives, such as Austen Chamberlain, Lord Birkenhead, Arthur Balfour, and Stanley Salvadge; and it was widely believed that they might form a Fusion Party (Middlemas, 1979, p. 169; Cook, 1976). Drawing on the intellectual legacy of Joseph Chamberlain and Randolph Churchill, such a party might have built a programme around the extension of tariffs, the welfare state, and the enforced rationalization of industry.

However, Lloyd George was viewed as a dangerous maverick, and the chances for fusion faded when Bonar Law's followers threw their support to the Conservatives rather than trust his machinations (Mowatt, 1955, pp. 135ff.). Adroit manoeuvring by Stanley Baldwin, which committed the Conservative Party to protection before Lloyd George could draw support on that issue, sealed the fate of the Fusionists. Britain's future would lie with the Conservatives or Labour.

At a second critical conjuncture, after World War II, Labour secured a majority in Parliament and inherited a system of physical controls that might have been adapted, as in France, to industrial planning (cf. Cohen, 1977). After implementing the nationalization proposals of its 1945 manifesto, however, the government did little else to influence the direction of industry. Precisely the sort of factors outlined above inhibited further action. The trade unions opposed any extension of manpower planning, and opposition from business associations scuttled Stafford Cripps's attempt to establish tripartite development councils in most industries. The desperate state of the balance of payments preoccupied economic policy-makers, and inhibited any attempts to reorganize the financial sector. With one eye on the export earnings of insurance, for instance, the Treasury opposed Aneurin Bevan's plans to nationalize the industrial assurance companies; and the nationalization of the Bank of England remained a technical exercise. It retained control of the Bank rate, and the rest of the financial sector remained untouched (Morgan, 1984; Eatwell, 1979; Rogow, 1955). Despite the reforms in other areas, the postwar Labour government missed its opportunity to take control over the domestic flows of capital within the financial sector. The French case suggests that such a move would have been necessary if a more active industrial policy or effective system of planning were to have been implemented (cf. Zysman, 1983).

Instead, the remaining energies of the Labour government went into the creation of the social programmes, such as unemployment insurance, superannuation, and the National Health Service, that we now associate with the welfare state. They were a remarkable achievement, and one around which support could be rallied much more readily within both the party and the electorate, who were more interested in social reform than in socialism. On the economic side of its platform, the party needed most of all a plank that seemed to make full employment possible. Its leaders were gradually won over to the view that a version of Keynesianism, based on the management of aggregate demand, could accomplish this task (cf. Crosland, 1956). This was an important step. Since Keynesianism seemed to provide a technique for achieving full employment without the need for more detailed intervention into the decisions of industrial sectors, it was instrumental in persuading both parties that they could abandon economic planning without sacrificing economic performance (Skidelsky, 1979; Schott, 1982). As such, Keynesianism played a major role in the victory of the 'revisionists' within the Labour Party, and contributed to the convergence in party politics known as 'Butskellism' (cf. Crosland, 1956; Butler, 1971). The nation that most avidly embraced Keynesianism also adopted the most arm's-length industrial policy in Europe. In that respect, while Keynes's doctrine solved many of the parties' political problems, it by no means solved Britain's economic problems.

Conclusion

This analysis suggests that the state is not primarily responsible for Britain's economic decline. But it is not an innocent bystander. If the principal causes of economic decline lie elsewhere, successive British governments did little to address them. There were alternatives. The French experience in the post-war period suggests that a state can transform the operation of its economic system, but first it must transform itself (cf. Hoffmann, 1978). The British have found that difficult because institutional rigidities affected the actions of the British state, just as such rigidities influenced the operation of the British economy (cf. Shepsle and Weingast, 1984). The structure of Britain's inter-national position, state, and society pushed policy-makers in a particular direction by influencing the perceived costs and benefits that accrued to any one policy.[3]

This observation has important implications for contemporary theories of the state. None of the main theoretical alternatives quite fits the British case. Those who explain state action as a response to the dictates of capital or the functional imperatives of capitalism cannot explain the inadequacies of Brit-ish policy from the point of view of capital or the great variation in policies across capitalist nations (cf. Jessop, 1977; Poulantzas, 1976). Pluralists who view the state as a respondent to the concerns of competing social groups miss the fact that policy-makers had interests and inclinations of their own and that the biases inherent in their institutional setting precluded an equal response to all groups (cf. Truman, 1971). And the more recent group of state-centric theorists who view the state as a free-floating actor, generating its preferences in relative autonomy from the rest of society, cannot explain how the preferences of the state are generated (cf. Nordlinger, 1981). They imply that the policy preferences of the state are relatively unaffected by the configuration of society; yet if there is one lesson to be learned from the course of British economic policy, it is that policy is not made from a *tabula rasa*; policy-makers are profoundly influenced by societal factors.

In short, this case suggests that we need a theory of the state that recog-nizes that policy-makers' actions are deeply conditioned by the institutional structures within which they operate. We already know that the structure of the state and its position in the international system can affect the prefer-ences of policy-makers and their capacity to act (Skocpol and Finegold, 1983; Katzenstein, 1978). Here we see that these preferences and capacities can also be affected by the configuration of societal institutions such as trade unions and banking systems, as well as the institutional memory embedded in the organizations of the wider political system. Nowhere is this more true than in Britain.

The very stability of the British political system, so long a valued asset, has become something of a liability in an era of rapid economic change. The consequences have been grave because economic failure in the modern age is also political failure. After several decades in which politicians claimed credit for every economic success, electorates have begun to hold them responsible for every economic failure. Consequently, Britain's economic crises engendered a crisis of political authority. One of the results has been a profound disruption in the party system, marked by increasing electoral volatility, partisan dealignment, and the rise of a new party (Harrop, 1981). Another has been the election of a government that rejected the Keynesianism on which postwar consensus was built.

Margaret Thatcher was elected in 1979 because many sections of the electorate were dissatisfied not only with the performance of the economy but also with the rising level of conflict between trade unions and the state (Penniman, 1981). Such conflict invariably appeared during the penultimate stage of tripartite bargains about incomes policy, which had become an indispensable supplement to the Keynesian techniques of successive postwar governments. It was often disruptive enough to defeat the government at the next election. In that sense, an 'industrial relations cycle' has been as important as the political business cycle in Britain (cf. Alt, 1980). In short, the Thatcher government came to power as much because of a backlash against the system of functional representation which had become central to economic policy-making in Britain as because that system produced poor economic results (Jessop, 1982).

Under Thatcher, the Conservatives mounted an electoral appeal that spoke directly to dissatisfaction with the tripartite bargaining of the past. Drawing on the *laissez-faire* strain of Conservative thought, Thatcher repudiated the consensualist Keynesianism which had dominated the economic thinking of both parties for forty years. Her advisors adapted monetarist economic theory into a highly political creed that promised economic prosperity without the need for either corporatist bargaining or state intervention in much the same way that Labourites had adapted Keynesianism for another purpose thirty years before (Keegan, 1984; Stephenson, 1980; Behrens, 1980).

Perhaps because this version of monetarism has such an affinity with the neoclassical economics of the 1920s, the course of policy under the Thatcher government has closely resembled policy in that decade. The pursuit of a lower borrowing requirement, spending reductions, lower taxes on the upper incomes, a tight monetary policy, and initially a high exchange rate have all been rationalized in very similar terms; and once again these policies reflect a greater sensitivity to the concerns of the City than to those of British industry (Winch, 1969; Longstreth, 1983; Barker, 1980). In these respects, there has been a real continuity between Mrs Thatcher's macroeconomic policies and those of the interwar period. Some would argue there has also been a continuity of result (Kaldor, 1984).

The object of the Thatcher government has been to reinforce the operation of market mechanisms in the hope that they will rejuvenate the economy with a minimum of state intervention. Its goal has been to begin a new period of *laissez-faire*. Paradoxically, however, that task has required a great deal of state intervention in order to alter many longstanding practices and institutions in the economy. The Thatcher regime has been characterized by what Andrew Gamble termed 'the strong state in a weak economy' (Gamble, 1979; Amott and Krieger, 1981). The government has attacked the power of the trade unions by limiting their rights to strike, enforcing lay-offs in the nationalized industries, and limiting wage settlements in the public sector. To enforce public spending reductions, far-reaching changes have been made in relationships with the local authorities and the programmes of the welfare state. Several firms have been denationalized; and the movement of capital has been decontrolled (Hall and Jacques, 1983; Drucker *et al.*, 1983).

These measures have altered many aspects of the British economy. As a result of government pressure and rising levels of unemployment, the unions have been forced to accept lay-offs, de-skilling, and the reorganization of work. An austere economic climate drove many small firms out of business and compelled the large enterprises to contract. The British economy has been put on a diet, and some of its operations are undoubtedly slimmer (Pratten, 1982). In this light the government's policies can be seen as a break with the recent past. They represent one, classically conservative, strategy for tackling Britain's problems.

However, the essays in this volume suggest that there are many defects in such a strategy. Policies aimed primarily at the unions tackle rigidities on only one side of the economic system. The Thatcher government has done little to correct the defects in management, supply of investment, organization of production, and distribution that are more significant obstacles to the effective performance of British capitalism. Moreover, the trade unions are not going to disappear, and the Thatcher policies provide no basis for constructive dealings with them over the long term.

Second, these policies are based on the premise that self-regulating markets can be relied upon to restore British industry to a healthy international status. However, the analysis in this volume suggests that attempts to secure industrial adjustment exclusively through market mechanisms are likely to fail. Even with unions at their weakest, British industries do not move naturally towards international competitiveness. The monetarist vision depends on a neoclassical image of self-equilibrating markets that simply does not conform to reality.

Finally, Thatcher's economic policy relies on the sanctions of economic austerity to enforce changes in behaviour. As such, it exacts costs that threaten to destroy much of Britain's industrial base before they can render it more efficient. Although output per person rose by 5 per cent between 1979 and 1983, overall industrial production fell by 6 per cent. It is unclear whether the efficiencies that are attained through austerity can be maintained if prosperity ever returns. The kind of efficiencies secured under Thatcher derive from losses of labour rather than from a more fundamental reorganization of the productive apparatus. As such, they may impose tremendous human hardship yet provide few long-term benefits (Barker, 1980). Similarly, most of the government's economies have been secured by cuts in spending on capital programmes rather than in current expenditure, and so threaten to run down the social infrastructure on which further growth may depend.

The Thatcher experiment does not augur well. However, it indicates that political parties remain vehicles for innovation in economic policy. Institutional analysis of the polity, as of the economy, underlines the magnitude of the obstacles that stand in the way of reform; but it also reminds us that economic performance is not entirely a matter of fate or the product of iron laws in economics. The institutions that affect the performance of the economy are ultimately shaped by political action, and from time to time we may recast them.

Notes

[1]Simulations conducted on the NIESR model found that, when policy was fine-tuned in retrospect, sterling was devalued by 15 per cent in 1964, and a successful incomes policy was imposed, the maximum economic growth that could be secured between 1964 and 1969 was still virtually identical to that actually achieved, unless the structural parameters were changed (Surrey and Ormerod, 1978).

[2]The issue is correctly posed in terms of probabilities, because none of these structural features absolutely determines the direction policy will take. There is always a possibility that policy may follow an alternative path, not least because policy-makers have a human will and more resources than many political actors (see Sabel, 1981). Even if they are not ultimately determinative, however, the biases that such institutional structures impart to policy are far from insignificant. At the very least they raise obstacles to a change in direction; and in many instances their direct impact on policy can be demonstrated. In this respect, it is significant that policy is made not by an individual actor, but by a collective intelligence whose thinking is mediated by political and bureaucratic organizations and whose ability to act is dependent on a complex set of institutional ties (Wilensky, 1967; Steinbrunner, 1974).

[3]It is important to avoid blaming the direction of policy on any one culprit. As we have seen, even the Bank of England and the City were not responsible for all of the bias against devaluation: politicians vetoed the move in 1952. And one of our most striking findings is that the leaders of industrial capital in Britain contributed as much as the City to the defects of economic policy, by opposing state-led attempts to enforce industrial adjustment. Nevertheless, it is likely that these structural factors affected those in government more than those out of it because the political parties so often did a *volte face* when they entered office.

Bibliography

Aldcroft, Derek (1967). 'Economic Growth in Britain in the Inter-War Years: A Reassessment'. *Economic History Review*, 2nd ser., 20(20), 311–26.

Aldcroft, Derek (1982). 'Britain's Economic Decline 1870–1980'. In *The British Malaise*, ed. Gordon Roderick and M. Stephens. London: Falmer Press.

Aldcroft, Derek and H. W. Richardson (1970). *The British Economy 1870–1939*. London: Macmillan.

Allen, G. C. (1951). *British Industries and their Organization*. London: Macmillan.

Allen, U. L. (1960). *Trade Unions and the Government*. London: Longman.

Alt, James (1980). 'Political Business Cycles in Britain'. In *Models of Political Economy*, ed. P. Whiteley. London: Sage.

Amott, Thersa and Joel Krieger (1981). 'Thatcher and Reagan: State Theory and the "Hyper-Capitalist" Regime'. *New Political Science*, 8, 9–37.

Ashcroft, Brian (1979). 'The Evaluation of Regional Economic Policy: The Case of the United Kingdom'. Studies in Economic Policy no. 12. Glasgow: Centre for the Study of Public Policy, University of Strathcycle.

Bacon, Robert and Walter Eltis (1976). *Britain's Economic Problem: Too Few Producers*. London: Macmillan.

Ball, R. J., and T. Burns (1976). 'The Inflationary Mechanism in the UK Economy'. *American Economic Review*, 66, 467–84.

Ball, R. J. *et al*. (1977). 'The Role of Exchange Rate Changes in Balance of Payments Adjustment—the United Kingdom Case'. *Economic Journal*, 87, 1–29.

Barker, Terry (1980). 'The Economic Consequences of Monetarism: A Keynesian View of the British Economy 1980–90'. *Cambridge Journal of Economics*, 4, 319–36.

Bealey, Frank (1970). *The Social and Political Thought of the British Labour Party*. London: Weidenfeld and Nicolson.

Beckerman, Wilfred (1972). *The Labour Government's Economic Record 1964–70*. London: Duckworth.

Beer, Samuel (1959). *Treasury Control*. London: Oxford University Press.

Beer, Samuel H. (1969). *Modern British Politics*. London: Faber.

Beer, Samuel H. (1982). *Britain Against Itself*. New York: W. W. Norton.

Behrens, Robert (1980). *The Conservative Party from Heath to Thatcher*. Farnborough, Hants: Saxon House.

Benn, Tony (1980). 'Manifestos and Mandarins'. In *Policy and Practice: The Experience of Government*. London: Royal Institute of Public Administration.

Bispham, John and Andrea Boltho (1982). 'Demand Management'. In *The European Economy: Growth and Crisis*, ed. A. Boltho. London: Oxford University Press, pp. 289–328.

Blank Stephen (1973). *Government and Industry in Britain*. Farnborough, Hants: Saxon House.

Blank Stephen (1978). 'Britain: The Politics of Foreign Economic Policy, the Domestic Economy and the Problem of Pluralistic Stagnation'. In *Between Power and Plenty*, ed. P. Katzenstein. Madison: University of Wisconsin Press.

Block, Fred (1977). 'The Ruling Class Does not Rule: Notes on the Marxist Theory of the State'. *Socialist Review*, 33, 6–28.

Boltho, Andrea (1982). 'Growth'. In *The European Economy: Growth and Crisis*. London: Oxford.

Brittan, Sam (1970). *Steering the Economy*. Harmondsworth: Penguin.

Broadway, Frank (1969). *State Intervention in British Industry 1964–68*. London: Kaye and Ward.

Brown, C. J. F., and T. D. Stout (1979). 'Deindustrialization: A Background Paper'. In *Deindustrialization*, ed. F. Blackaby. London: Heinemann, pp. 233–62.

Brown, George (1970). *In My Way*. London: Macmillan.

Bruce-Gardyne, Jock (1974). *Whatever Happened to the Quiet Revolution*. London: Charles Knight.

Bruce-Gardyne, Jock and Nigel Lawson (1976). *The Power-Game: An Examination of Decision-making in Government*. London: Macmillan.

Budd, Alan (1978). *The Politics of Economic Planning*. London: Fontana.

Buiter, W. H., and Marcus Miller (1981). 'The Thatcher Experiment: The First Two Years'. *Brookings Papers on Economic Activity*, 2, 315–79.

Butler, R. A. B. (1971). *The Art of the Possible*. London: Hamish Hamilton.

Buxton, Neil K. (1975). 'The Role of the "New" Industries in Britain during the 1930s: A Reinterpretation'. *Business History Review*, 49, 205–22.

Cairncross, F., and H. McRae (1974). *Capital City*. London: Methuen.

Cambridge Economic Policy Group (1978). *Economic Policy Review*, 4, Cambridge: Department of Applied Economics.

Capie, Forrest (1984). *Protection and Depression*. London: Allen and Unwin.

Carlson, K. M., and R. W. Spencer (1975). 'Crowding Out and its Critics'. *Bulletin of the Federal Reserve Bank of St Louis*, December, 2–22.

Caves, Richard (1969). 'Market Organization, Performance and Public Policy'. In *Britain's Economic Prospects*, ed. R. Caves *et al*. Washington: Brookings Institution, pp. 279–323.

Caves, Richard and Lawrence Krause (1980). *Britain's Economic Performance*. Washington: Brookings Institution.

Caves, Richard *et al*. (1969). *Britain's Economic Prospects*. Washington: Brookings Institution.

Central Policy Review Staff (1975). *The Future of the British Car Industry*. London: HMSO.

Channon, Derek (1973). *The Strategy and Structure of British Enterprise*. Boston: Harvard Business School.

Chapman, Richard (1968). *Decision Making*. London: Routledge and Kegan Paul.

Chrystal, K. A. (1979). *Controversies in British Macroeconomics*. Oxford: Philip Allan.

Clarke, Sir Richard (1973). 'Mintech in Retrospect'. *Omega*, 1, 25–38; 137–63.

Clarke, William (1967). *The City in the World Economy*, Harmondsworth: Penguin.

Coates, David (1975). *The Labour Party and the Struggle for Socialism*. Cambridge University Press.

Coates, David (1980). *Labour in Power*. London: Longman.

Cohen, Stephen (1977). *Modern Capitalist Planning*. Berkeley: University of California Press.

Congdon, Tim (1978). *Monetarism: An Essay in Definition*. London: Centre for Policy Studies.

Cook, Chris (1976). *A Short History of the Liberal Party*. New York: St Martins Press.

Corden, W. M., I. M. D. Little, and M. F. G. Scott (1978). 'Import Controls versus Devaluation and Britain's Economic Prospects', Guest Paper no. 2. London: Trade Policy Research Centre.

Cottrell, P. (1980). *Industrial France 1830–1914*. London: Methuen.

Cox, Andrew (1982). 'Corporatism as Reductionism'. *Government and Opposition*, 81, 78–90.

Crosland, Anthony (1956). *The Future of Socialism*. London: Strauss Farrar.

Crouch, Colin (1977). *Class Conflict and the Industrial Relations Crisis*. London: Heinemann.

Dahl, Robert (1970). *A Preface to Democratic Theory*. University of Chicago Press.

Dechery, B. (1980). 'Quelques Commentaires sur les Politiques Industrielles de la France et de la RFA'. Paris: Commissariat General au Plan.

Denison, E. F. (1967). *Why Growth Rates Differ*. Washington: Brookings Institution.

Dow, J. C. R. (1970). *The Management of the British Economy 1945–60*. London: Cambridge University Press.

Drucker, H. M. (1979). *Doctrine and Ethos in the Labour Party*. London: Allen and Unwin.

Drucker, Henry *et al*. (1983). *Developments in British Politics*. London: Macmillan.

Eatwell, Roger (1979). *The 1945–51 Labour Governments*. London: Batsford.

Eltis, Walter (1979). 'How Rapid Public Sector Growth can Undermine the Growth of the National Product'. In *Slow Growth in Britain*, ed, Wilfred Beckerman. London: Oxford University Press.

Feinstein, Charles (ed.) (1983). *The Managed Economy*. London: Oxford University Press.

Fenley, Anthony (1980). 'Labour and the Trade Unions'. In *The Labour Party*, ed. Chris Cook and Ian Taylor. London: Longman, pp. 50–83.

Ferguson, Thomas (1984). 'From Normalcy to New Deal'. *International Organization*, 38, 41–94.

Fiegehen, G. C. (1980). *Companies, Incentives and Senior Managers*. Oxford University Press.

Fleming, Michael (1980). 'Industrial Policy'. In *The British Economy in the 1970s*, ed. Peter Maunder. London: Heinemann, pp. 141–69.

Freeman, C., and A. Young (1965). *The Research and Development Effort in Western Europe, North America and the Soviet Union*. Paris: OECD.

Gamble, Andrew (1979). 'The Strong State in the Weak Economy'. In *The Socialist Register 1979*, ed. R. Miliband and J. Saville. London: Merlin Press.

Ganz, Gabrielle (1977). *Government and Industry*. London: Professional.

Gerschenkron, Alexander (1962). *Economic Backwardness in Historical Perspective*. Cambridge, Mass.: Harvard University Press.

Gilmour, Ian (1977). *Inside Right*. London: Hutchinson.

Glyn, Andrew and Bob Sutcliffe (1972). *British Capitalism, Workers, and the Profits Squeeze*. Harmondsworth: Penguin.

Goodhart, C. A. E. (1975). *Money, Information, and Uncertainty*. London: Macmillan.

Gough, Ian (1978). *The Political Economy of the Welfare State*. London: Macmillan.

Gourevitch, Peter Alexis (1977). 'International Politics, Domestic Coalitions and Liberty'. *Journal of Interdisciplinary History*, 8, 281–313.

Gourevitch, Peter Alexis (1984). 'Breaking with Orthodoxy: The Politics of Economic Policy Responses to the Depression of the 1930s'. *International Organization* 38(1), 95–130.

Graham, Andrew (1972). 'Industrial Policy'. In *The Labour Government's Economic Record 1964–70*, ed. Wilfred Beckerman. London: Duckworth, pp. 178–217.

Grant, Wyn (1980). 'The Last Labour Government's Industrial Strategy'. Paper presented to the Public Administration Conference, York University, September.

Grant, Wyn (1982). *The Political Economy of Industrial Policy*. London: Butterworths.

Grant, W., and D. Marsh (1977). *The CBI*. London: Hodder and Stoughton.

Greenleaf, W. H. (1984). *The British Political Tradition*. London: Methuen.

Grove, J. W. (1962). *Government and Industry in Britain*. London: Longmans.

Hadjimatheou, G., and A. Skouras (1979). 'Britain's Economic Problem: The Growth of the Non-Market Sector'. *Economic Journal*, 89, 392–401.

Hague, Douglas and Geoffrey Wilkinson (1983). *The IRC: An Experiment in Industrial Intervention*. London: Allen and Unwin.

Hall, Peter A. (1982a). 'Economic Planning and the State: The Evolution of Economic Challenge and Political Response in France'. In *Political Power and Social Theory*, Volume III, ed. G. Esping-Andersen, R. Friedland, and M. Zeitlin. Greenwich, Conn.: JAI Press.

Hall, Peter A. (1982b). *The Political Dimensions of Economic Management*. Ann Arbor, Mich.: University Microfilms International.

Hall, Peter A. (1983a). 'Innovation and the Structure of the State: The Politics-Administration Nexus in Britain and France'. *The Annals*, 466, 43–60.

Hall, Peter A. (1983b). 'Patterns of Economic Policy among the European States: An Organizational Approach'. In *The State in Capitalist Europe*, ed. S. Bornstein, D. Held, and J. Kreiger. London: Allen and Unwin.

Hall, Stuart and Martin Jacques (1983). *The Politics of Thatcherism*. London: Lawrence and Wishart.

Hannah, Leslie (1974). 'Managerial Innovation and the Rise of the Large-scale Company in Interwar Britain'. *Economic History Review*, 2nd ser., 27, 252–70.

Hansen, B. (1969). *Fiscal Policy in Seven Countries 1955–1965*. Paris: OECD.

Harley, C. K. (1974). 'Skilled Labour and the Choice of Technique in Edwardian Industry'. *Explorations in Economic History*, 11, 391–414.

Harris, Nigel (1972). *Competition and the Corporate Society*. London: Methuen.

Harrod, Roy (1967). *Towards a New Economic Policy*. London: Methuen.

Harrop, Martin (1981). 'The Changing British Electorate'. *Political Quarterly*, 53, 385–402.

Hatfield, Michael (1976). *The House the Left Built*. London: Gollanz.

Heclo, Hugh and Aaron Wildavsky (1979). *The Private Government of Public Money*. London: Macmillan.

Henry, S. G. B., *et al.* (1976). 'Models of Inflation in the United Kingdom—An Evaluation'. *National Institute Economic Review*, 77, 60–71.

Hobsbawm, Eric (1968). *Industry and Empire*. New York: Pantheon.

Hodgman, Donald (ed.) (1983). *The Political Economy of Monetary Policy*. Boston: Federal Reserve Bank.

Hoffmann, Stanley (1978). *France: Decline or Renewal?* New York: Harper and Row.

House of Commons (1970). *First Report from Select Committee on the Nationalized Industries: Bank of England*, Session 1969–70. London: HMSO.

Howson, Susan (1975). *Domestic Monetary Management in Britain 1919–38*. London: Cambridge University Press.

HM Government (1944). *Employment Policy After the War*, Cmnd. 6527. London: HMSO.

HM Treasury (1977). *Evidence on the Financing of Trade and Industry to the Committee to Review the Functioning of Financial Institutions*. London: HMSO.

Imberg, D., and J. Northcott (1981). *Industrial Policy and Investment Decisions*. London: Policy Studies Institute.

Jenkins, Peter (1970). *The Battle of Downing Street*. London: Charles Knight.

Jessop, Bob (1977). 'Recent Theories of the Capitalist State'. *Cambridge Journal of Economics*, 1, 353–73.

Jessop, Bob (1982). 'The Dual Crisis of the State in Postwar Britain: Recent Developments'. Paper presented to the 'Conference on Representation and the State', Stanford University.

Johnson, Chalmers (1982). *MITI*. Berkeley: University of California Press.

Joint Economic Committee, US Congress (1981). *Monetary Policy, Economic Growth and Industry in France, Germany, Sweden and the United Kingdom*. Washington: US Goverment Printing Office.

Jones, F. E. (1978). 'Our Manufacturing Industry—the missing £100,000 million'. *National Westminster Bank Quarterly Review*, May, 8–17.

Joseph, Sir Keith (1976). *Monetarism is Not Enough*. London: Centre for Policy Studies.

Kaldor, Lord Nicholas (1984). *The Economic Consequences of Mrs Thatcher*. London: Duckworth.

Katzenstein, Peter (1978). *Between Power and Plenty*. Madison: University of Wisconsin Press.

Kay, J. A., and M. A. King (1980). *The British Tax System* (2nd edn). London: Oxford.

Keegan, William (1984). *Mrs Thatcher's Economic Experiment*. London: Allen Lane.

Keegan, William and R. Pennant-Rae (1979). *Who Runs the Economy?* London: Maurice Temple Smith.

Kemp, Tom (1969). *Industrialization in Nineteenth Century Europe*. London: Longmans.

Kenwood, A. G., and A. L. Lougheed (1983). *The Growth of the International Economy 1820–1960*. London: Allen and Unwin.

Keynes, J. M. (1925). *The Economic Consequences of Mr Churchill*. London: Macmillan.

Kilpatrick, A., and T. Lawson (1980). 'On the Nature of Industrial Decline in the UK'. *Cambridge Journal of Economics*, 4(1), 85–100.

Kindleberger, C. (1963). 'The French Economy'. In *In Search of France*, ed. S. Hoffmann *et al*. New York: Harper and Row.

King, M. A. (1975). 'The UK Profits Crisis: Myth or Reality'. *Economic Journal*, 85, 33–47.

Kirby, M. W. (1973). 'Government Intervention in Industrial Organization: Coal Mining in the Nineteen Thirties'. *Business History*, 15(2), 160–73.

Kirby, M. W. (1981). *The Decline of British Economic Power since 1870*. London: Allen and Unwin.

Kohl, Jurgen (1981). 'Trends and Problems in Public Expenditure Development in Western Europe and North America'. In *The Development of Welfare States in Europe and America*, ed. P. Flora and A. Heidenheimer. London: Transaction, pp. 307–46.

Krasner, Stephen (1980). *Defending the National Interest*. Princeton University Press.

Kravis, I., and R. Lipsey (1971). *Price Competitiveness in World Trade*. New York: Columbia University Press.

Kreile, M. (1978). 'West Germany: The Dynamics of Expansion'. In *Between Power and Plenty*, ed. P. Katzenstein. Madison: University of Wisconsin Press.

Kurth, James (1979). 'The Political Consequences of the Product Cycle: Industrial History and Political Outcomes'. *International Organization*, 33(1), 1–36.

Leruez, Jacques (1975). *Economic Planning and Politics in Britain*. London: Martin Robertson.

Levy, Margaret (1980). 'A Predatory Theory of Rule'. *Politics and Society*, 10, 431–65.

Lewis, W. Arthur (1949). *Economic Survey 1919–1939*. London: Allen and Unwin.

Lewis, W. Arthur (1967). 'The Deceleration of British Growth 1873–1913'. Unpublished paper, Princeton, NJ.

Longstreth, Frank (1979). 'The City, Industry, and the State'. In *State and Economy in Contemporary Capitalism*, ed. C. Crouch. London: Croom Helm, pp. 157–90.

Longstreth, Frank (1983). 'The Dynamics of Disintegration of a Keynesian Political Economy'. Paper presented at the Centre for European Studies, Harvard University.

Lowe, Rodney (1978). 'The Erosion of State Intervention in Britain 1917–24'. *Economic History Review*, 2nd ser., 31(2), 270–86.

Lucas, A. F. (1937). *Industrial Reconstruction and the Control of Competition*. London: Longman.

MacLennan, D., and J. B. Parr (1979). *Regional Policy: Past Experience and New Directions*. Oxford: Martin Robertson.

Macmillan, Harold (1934). *Reconstruction: A Plea for a National Policy*. London: Macmillan.

Maddison, Angus (1977). 'Phases of Capitalist Development'. *Banca Nazionale del Laboro Quarterly Review*, 00, 000–00.

Magaziner, Ira (1979). *Japanese Industrial Policy*. London: Policy Studies Institute.

Magaziner, Ira and Robert Reich (1982). *Minding America's Business*. New York: Harcourt, Brace Jovanovitch.

Manser, W. A. P. (1971). *Britain in Balance*. London: Longman.

Marsh, D., and W. Grant (1977). 'Tripartism: Reality or Myth'. *Government and Opposition*, 12, 194–211.

Marsh, David and Gareth Locksley (1983). 'Capital in Britain: Its Structural Power and Influence over Policy'. *West European Politics*, 6(2), 36–60.

Martin, Andrew (1979). 'The Dynamics of Change in a Keynesian Political Economy: The Swedish Case and Its Implications'. In *State and Economy in Contemporary Capitalism*. London: Croom Helm.

Martin, Roderick (1980). *TUC: History of a Pressure Group*. London: Oxford University Press.

Mason, Sandra (1976). *The Flow of Funds in Britain*. London: Paul Elek.

Matthews, R. C. O. (1968). 'Why Has Britain Had Full Employment Since the War?' *Economic Journal*, 77, 555–69.

Matthews, R. C. O., C. H. Feinstein, and J. C. Odling-Smee (1982). *British Economic Growth 1856–1973*. Stanford University Press.

McCrone, G. (1969). *Regional Policy in Britain*. London: Allen and Unwin.

McRae, H., and F. Cairncross (1973). *Capital City*. London: Methuen.

Mellors, C. (1978). *The British MP*. Farnborough, Hants: Saxon House.

Middlemas, Keith (1979). *Politics in Industrial Society*. London: Andrè Deutsch.

Middleton, Roger (1981). 'The Constant Employment Budget Balance and British Budgetary Policy 1929–39'. *Economic History Review*, 34(2), 266–87.

Miliband, Ralph (1961). *Parliamentary Socialism*. London: Merlin Press.

Minkin, Lewis (1978). *The Labour Party Conference*. London: Allen Lane.

Moggridge, D. E. (1972). *British Monetary Policy 1924–31*. London: Cambridge University Press.

Moore, Barrington (1966). *The Social Origins of Dictatorship and Democracy*. Boston: Beacon Press.

Moore, B., and J. Rhodes (1976). 'The Relative Decline of the UK Manufacturing Sector', *Economic Policy Review*, 2, 36–41.

Moore, B., and J. Rhodes (1973). 'Evaluating the Effects of British Regional Economic Policy'. *Economic Journal*, 83, 87–110.

Morgan, Kenneth, O. (1984). *Labour in Power, 1945–1951*. New York: Oxford University Press.

Mosley, Paul (1976). 'Towards a "Satisficing" Theory of Economic Policy'. *Economic Journal*, 86, 59–72.

Mottershead, P. (1978). 'Industrial Policy'. In *British Economic Policy 1960–74*, ed. Frank Blackaby. London: Cambridge University Press.

Mowatt, Charles L. (1955). *Britain Between the Wars*. University of Chicago Press.

Müller, Wolfgang (1983). 'Economic Success Without an Industrial Strategy: Austria in the 1970s'. *Journal of Public Policy*, 3(1), 119–30.

NIER (1984). *National Institute Economic Review*, 108, 70–84.

Nicol, William and Douglas Youill (1982). 'Regional Problems and Policy'. In *The European Economy: Growth and Crisis*, ed. A. Boltho. London: Oxford University Press.

Nordlinger, Eric (1981). *On the Autonomy of the Democratic State*. Cambridge, Mass.: Harvard University Press.

OECD (1970). *The Growth of Output 1960–1980*. Paris: OECD.

OECD (1973). 'The Measurement of Domestic Cyclical Fluctuations'. *OECD Economic Outlook — Occasional Studies*, July. Paris: OECD.

OECD (1978). 'Budgetary Indications'. *OECD Economic Outlook — Occasional Studies*, July. Paris: OECD.

Olson, Mancur (1982). *The Rise and Decline of Nations*. New Haven, Conn.: Yale University Press.

Opie, Roger (1972). 'Economic Planning and Growth'. In *The Labour Governments Economic Record 1964–70*, ed. W. Beckerman. London: Duckworth, pp. 157–77.

Paish, F. W. (1970). *How the Economy Works*. London: Macmillan.

Panic, M. (1975). 'Why the UK Propensity to Import is so High'. *Lloyds Bank Review*, 115, 1–12.

Pelling, Henry (1976). *A Short History of British Trade Unionism*. Harmondsworth: Penguin.

Penniman, Howard, R. (1981). *Britain at the Polls, 1979*. Washington: American Enterprise Institute.

PEP (1960). *Growth in the British Economy*. London: Allen and Unwin.

Phelps Brown, Henry (1977). 'What is the British Predicament?' *Three Banks Review*, 116, 3–29.

Pollard, Sidney (1969) *The Development of the British Economy 1914–1967* (2nd edn). New York: St Martins Press.

Pollard, Sidney (1982) *The Wasting of the British Economy*. London: Croom Helm.

Posner, Michael (ed.) (1978). *Demand Management*. London: Heinemann.

Posner, Michael and Andrew Steer (1979). 'Price Competitiveness and the Performance of Manufacturing Industry'. In *Deindustrialization*, ed. F. Blackaby. London: Heinemann, pp. 141–65.

Poulantzas, Nicos (1976). *Political Power and Social Classes*. London: Verso.

Pratten, C. F. (1982). 'Mrs Thatcher's Economic Experiment'. *Lloyds Bank Review*, 143, 36–51.

Pressnell, L. S. (1978). '1925; The Burden of Sterling'. *Economic History Review*, 2nd ser., 31, 67–88.

Price, R. W. R. (1978). 'Budgetary Policy'. In *British Economic Policy 1960–74*, ed. Frank Blackaby. London: Cambridge University Press, pp. 135–217.

Radcliffe Report (1959). *The Committee on the Working of the Monetary System, Report*, Cmnd. 827. London: HMSO.

Ramsden, J. (1979). 'The Changing Base of British Conservatism'. In *New Trends in British Politics since 1945*, ed. C. Cook and J. Ramsden. London: Macmillan.

Richardson, H. W. (1967). *Economic Recovery in Britain 1929–39*. London: Weidenfeld and Nicolson.

Rogow, A. A. (1955). *The Labour Government and British Industry, 1945–1951*. London: Macmillan.

Roseveare, Henry (1969). *The Treasury*. New York: Columbia University Press.

Sabel, Charles (1981). *Work and Politics*. Cambridge University Press.

Sandberg, Lars (1969). 'American Rings and English Mules: The Role of Economic Rationality'. *Quarterly Journal of Economics*, 83, 25–43.

Savage, David (1978). 'The Channels of Monetary Influence'. *National Institute Economic Review*, 84, 73–89.

Sayers, R. S. (1976). *The Bank of England 1891–1944*. London: Oxford University Press.

Schmitter, P., and G. Lehmbruch (1979). *Trends in Corporatist Intermediation*. Beverly Hills: Sage.

Schmitter, P., and G. Lehmbruch (1981). *Patterns of Corporatist Policy-making*. Beverly Hills: Sage.

Schott, Kerry (1982). 'The Rise of Keynesian Economics in Britain 1940–64'. *Economy and Society*, 11(3), 292–316.

Seldon, Arthur (1980). *Corrigible Capitalism, Incorrigible Socialism*. London: Institute for Economic Affairs.

Shanks, Michael (1977). *Planning and Politics*. London: Allen and Unwin.

Shepsle, Kenneth and Barry Weingast (1984). 'Political Solution to Market Problems'. *American Political Science Review*, 78, 417–34.

Shonfield, Andrew (1958). *British Economic Policy Since the War*. Harmondsworth: Penguin.

Shonfield, Andrew (1969). *Modern Capitalism*. Oxford University Press.

Singh, Ajit (1977). 'U.K. Industry and the World Economy: A Case of De-Industrialisation?' *Cambridge Journal of Economics*, 1, 113–36.

Singh, A. (1979). 'North Sea Oil and the Reconstruction of UK Industry'. In *Deindustrialization*, ed. F. Blackaby. London: Heinemann.

Skidelsky, Robert (1967). *Politicians and the Slump*. London: Macmillan.

Skidelsky, Robert (1979). 'The Collapse of the Keynesian Consensus'. In *State and Economy in Contemporary Capitalism*, ed. Colin Crouch. London: Croom Helm.

Skocpol, Theda and Ken Finegold (1983). 'State Capacity and Economic Intervention in the Early New Deal'. *Political Science Quarterly*, 97, 256–78.

Smethurst, R. G. (1979). 'Monetary Policy'. In *The Economic System in the UK*, ed. D. Morris. London: Oxford University Press, pp. 339–69.

Smith, David (1975). 'Public Consumption and Economic Performance'. *National Westminster Bank Quarterly Review*, November, 17–30.

Steinbrunner, John (1974). *Cybernetic Theory of Decision*. Princeton University Press.

Stephenson, Hugh (1980). *Mrs Thatcher's First Year*. London: Jill Norman.

Stern, H. N. (1976). 'Taxation and Labour Supply—A Partial Survey'. Paper presented at the Institute of Fiscal Studies, London.

Stewart, Michael (1977). *Politics and Economic Policy Since 1964*. Oxford: Pergamon Press.

Stout, D. K. (1977). *International Price Competitiveness: Non-price Factors and Export Performance*. London: National Economic Development Office.

Stout, D. K. (1979). 'Deindustrialization and Industrial Policy'. In *Deindustrialization*, ed. Frank Blackaby. London: Heinemann.

Strange, Susan (1971). *Sterling and British Policy*. Oxford University Press.

Supple, Barry (1977). *Essays in British Business History*. Oxford University Press.

Surrey, Michael (1982). 'United Kingdom'. In *The European Economy: Growth and Crisis*, ed. A. Boltho. London: Oxford University Press, pp. 528–53.

Surrey, M. J. C., and Paul Ormerod (1978). 'Demand Management in Britain 1964–81'. In *Demand Management*, ed. M. Posner. London: Heinemann, pp. 101–26.

Tarling, R. J., and F. Wilkinson, (1977). 'The Social Contract: Postwar Incomes Policies and Their Inflationary Impact'. *Cambridge Journal of Economics*, 1, 395–414.

Tawney, R. H. (1943). 'The Abolition of Economic Controls 1918–1921'. *Economic History Review*, 12, 1–30.

Tew, J. H. B. (1978). 'Policies Aimed at Improving the Balance of Payments'. In *British Economic Policy 1960–74*, ed. Frank Blackaby. London: Cambridge University Press, pp. 304–59.

Thirlwall, A. P. (1978). 'The UK's Economic Problem: A Balance of Payments Constraint?' *National Westminster Bank Quarterly Review*, February, 24–32.

Thomas, Hugh (1968). *Crisis in the Civil Service*. London: Anthony Blond.

Truman, David (1951). *The Governmental Process*. New York: Alfred Knopf.

Tufte, Edward (1979). *Political Control of the Economy*. Princeton University Press.

Vernon, Raymond (ed.) (1974). *Big Business and the State*. Cambridge, Mass.: Harvard University Press.

Ward, T. S., and R. R. Nield (1978). *The Measurement and Reform of Budgetary Policy*. London: Heinemann.

Warnecke, Steven and E. Suleiman (1975). *Industrial Policies in Western Europe*. New York: Praeger.

Whiteley, Paul (1983). 'The Political Economy of Economic Growth'. *European Journal of Political Research*, 11, 197–213.

Whiting, A. (1976). 'Is Britain's Poor Growth Performance Due to Government Stop–Go-Induced Fluctuations?' *Three Banks Review*, 109, 26–46.

Wiener, Martin (1981). *English Culture and the Decline of the Industrial Spirit*. Cambridge University Press.

Wilensky, Harold (1967). *Organizational Intelligence*. New York: Basic Books.

Wilks, S. (1981). 'Planning Agreements: The Making of a Paper Tiger'. *Public Administration*, 59, 399–419.

Williams, K. *et al*. (1983). *Why are the British Bad at Manufacturing?* Boston: Routledge & Kegan Paul.

Wilson, Harold (1971). *The Labour Government 1964–1970*. London: Weidenfeld and Nicolson.

Wilson, Trevor (1966). *The Downfall of the Liberal Party 1914–1935*. Ithaca, NY: Cornell University Press.

Winch, Donald (1969). *Economics and Policy*. London: Hodder and Stoughton.

Winkler, J. (1976). 'Corporatism'. *European Journal of Sociology*, 17(1), 100–36.

Worswick, G. D. N. (1977). 'The End of Demand Management'. *Lloyds Bank Review*, 123, 1–18.

Young, Stephen and A. V. Lowe (1974). *Intervention in the Mixed Economy*. London: Croom Helm.

Youngson, A. J. (1960). *The British Economy 1920–1957*. Cambridge, Mass.: Harvard University Press.

Zeitlin, Jonathon (1980). 'The Emergence of Shop Steward Organization and Job Control in the British Car Industry'. *History Workshop Journal*, 10, 119–37.

Zysman, John (1983). *Politics, Governments and Growth*. Ithaca, NY: Cornell University Press.

Index